The Dying Sahara

The Dying Sahara

US Imperialism and Terror in Africa

JEREMY KEENAN

PlutoPress
www.plutobooks.com

First published 2013 by Pluto Press
345 Archway Road, London N6 5AA

www.plutobooks.com

Distributed in the United States of America exclusively by
Palgrave Macmillan, a division of St. Martin's Press LLC,
175 Fifth Avenue, New York, NY 10010

British Library Cataloguing in Publication Data
A catalogue record for this book is available from the British Library

ISBN   978 0 7453 2962 8   Hardback
ISBN   978 0 7453 2961 1   Paperback
ISBN   978 1 8496 4826 4   PDF eBook
ISBN   978 1 8496 4828 8   Kindle eBook
ISBN   978 1 8496 4827 1   EPUB eBook

Library of Congress Cataloging in Publication Data applied for

This book is printed on paper suitable for recycling and made from fully
managed and sustained forest sources. Logging, pulping and manufacturing
processes are expected to conform to the environmental standards of the
country of origin.

10   9   8   7   6   5   4   3   2   1

Typeset from disk by Stanford DTP Services, Northampton, England
Simultaneously printed digitally by CPI Antony Rowe, Chippenham, UK and
Edwards Bros in the United States of America

CONTENTS

To Jan Burgess
whose courage and professionalism as an editor
did much to lay bare the truths of American imperialism
and its GWOT in Africa.

And in memory
of
Claude Meillassoux.

PREFACE AND ACKNOWLEDGEMENTS

This is the second of my two volumes on the so-called Global War on Terror (GWOT). The first, *The Dark Sahara* (Pluto Press, 2009), was completed shortly before the death of Aleksandr Solzhenitsyn, whom I quoted in saying that writers and artists, amongst whom I include academics, had greater responsibilities than to not merely 'participate in lies'. To paraphrase his words, we have to do much more: we have to 'defeat the lie'. Much that has been written about the GWOT has merely reiterated and reinforced what Solzhenitsyn would call 'the lie'. This volume, by taking *The Dark Sahara* much further, both chronologically and in terms of evidence, defeats the lie, at least as far as it pertains to much of North Africa, the Sahara and Sahel.

Since the publication of *The Dark Sahara*, Western governments have made no attempt either to engage in argument over its central message – that the US, since 9/11, has fabricated terrorism to justify the GWOT – or even to try and rebut what I said. Rather, their response has been either to try and ignore it, even to the extent of striking from the record works that have cited *The Dark Sahara* (and my other writings) as a source reference, or, when pressed, to try and disparage it as a 'conspiracy theory'. That, too, is not surprising, as a 'conspiracy' no longer means an event explained by a conspiracy but is simply any explanation or 'fact' that is out of step with government explanation. This volume, at least in the language of governments and their compliant media, is even more of a 'conspiracy' than *The Dark Sahara* in that it provides 'evidence-based' explanations – 'truths' – that are wholly out of step with what Western governments would want us to believe.

As with *The Dark Sahara*, I am unable to thank any funding agencies or research councils for support, as I have been able to do so often in the past. There are, however, at least two positive aspects to this. First, it helps other academics, young researchers in particular, to understand that research that threatens government 'conspiracies' (what Solzhenitsyn would call 'lies') is unlikely to be funded. Indeed, the scandal which Britain's Economic and Social Research Council (ESRC) brought upon itself in 2006 is described in Chapter 11. Second, these two volumes, which are the outcome of twelve years' continuous research, show that significant and important research can be done without funding. It involves sacrifice and at times can be extremely difficult, but it is by no means impossible. Indeed, the 'alternative university' is not far way.

Nevertheless, in spite of these background difficulties, I am especially grateful to a number of people and institutions. In particular, I would like to thank the Department of Social Anthropology and Sociology and colleagues at SOAS (the School of Oriental and African Studies), London University, for providing me with an academic home since 2008. Amongst many Algerian friends and colleagues, I would like to give special thanks to Mohamed Larbi Zitout, former Algerian Deputy Ambassador to Libya and co-founder in 2007 of the Rachad Movement. He defected from his post in 1995 after learning that the atrocities being committed by alleged Islamists were in many cases being committed by groups under the control of the Algerian regime.

I am, as always, grateful to my publisher, Roger van Zwanenberg, and all those at Pluto Press. Dr Penny Nicholls did much appreciated work in editing an initial draft, helping me to reduce its length by some 30,000 words. I am also indebted to Martha Farley who has been exceptionally generous in sharing her expertise on much of this region of Africa.

In *The Dark Sahara*, I expressed my appreciation to a number of academic journal editors for inviting me to write for them. Since then, I would like to thank especially Penny Green of the International State Crime Initiative (ISCI) and the *State Crime Journal*, Robert Weiss of *Social Justice*, Fatiha Talahite of *Revue Tiers Monde* and Gustaf Houtman of *Anthropology Today*. I would also like to thank Jude McCulloch, Sharon Pickering, Kenneth Omeje, Scott Poynting and David Whyte for inviting me to contribute chapters to books they have edited. In 2009, I singled out *ROAPE* (*Review of African Political Economy*), for whom I had written 14 articles in the previous five years. Sadly, that has come to a stop. Following the editorial board's shameful removal of Jan Burgess as managing editor, to whom this book is dedicated, I, along with a number of other scholars, am no longer prepared to write for *ROAPE*.

There are also many journalists and media editors with whom I have worked in one way or another on Saharan and North African matters. I am very grateful to them for helping to tell the appalling story of the Sahara and its peoples over the last few years. Above all, however, I would like to thank the editorial staff at *Al Jazeera*, for whom I have written some 15 articles over the last two years, in addition to broadcast contributions. Sadly, *Al Jazeera* appears to have succumbed recently to the pressures of Qatar's ruling family to keep the spotlight off Algeria.

This is the sixth book I have written on the Sahara and its peoples. In my preface to *The Dark Sahara*, I explained how they have all been written for the peoples of the Sahara, especially the Tuareg whom I first visited in 1964, in order to document their history and explain the circumstances of their lives. While that remains true for both *The Dark Sahara* and *The Dying Sahara*, there has been another and equally important purpose in writing them. This is to document how US foreign policy since 9/11, through its GWOT, has led to the worst and most prolonged human catastrophe that this part of Africa has yet experienced. And it is likely to get much worse.

Those who read this book will at least be able to understand the complexities of what is happening in the Sahara: why tens of thousands of people have lost their livelihoods; why almost 500,000 Malians have had to flee their homes and why hundreds, if not thousands, more local people may die – and for reasons they are unlikely to understand. Those who read this depressing story will be shocked at both the nature and consequences of the lies and deceptions that have been perpetrated by the West – notably the US, the EU, the UK and France – and its main proxy power in the region, Algeria, in the name of the ubiquitous GWOT or, as President Obama now prefers to call it, the 'Long War'. This volume raises serious questions about the extent to which government counterterrorism policies are invariably nothing more than a cover for state terrorism, while al-Qaeda is revealed as something very different from what is portrayed to the public by Western governments and their intelligence services.

On 10 July 2012, too late for inclusion in this book, *The National Interest* published an article by John R. Schindler entitled 'The Ugly Truth about Algeria', which blew the whistle on Algeria's creation of terrorists and their use in 'state terrorism'.[1] Schindler is a former high-ranking US intelligence officer and member of the National Security Council (NSC). He is currently Professor of National Security Affairs at the US Naval War College at Newport, Rhode Island. His exposé of Algeria's secret intelligence service, the Département du Renseignement et de la Sécurité (DRS), and his expressed concerns over the relationship between Washington and Algeria's DRS lend much weight to the fundamental thesis of this book, namely that most of the terrorism, both real and imagined, in North Africa, the Sahara and Sahel has been fabricated by Algeria's DRS in collusion with US and other Western military intelligence agencies.

While that is shocking, perhaps even more disturbing is the evidence now emerging that the US Department of Defense and US AFRICOM (Africa Command) have together been acquiring even greater funding for the implementation of their counter-terrorism policies in North Africa and across the Sahara-Sahel on the basis of extensive help from Algeria's DRS in the form of intelligence which they have known to be false. The word that comes to mind is 'fraud'. Indeed, as this book reveals, AFRICOM was created in a web of duplicity. Chapters 2 and 5 reveal how its first commander, General William 'Kip' Ward, was economical with the truth. In September 2012, a 99-page report, based on a 17-month investigation by the Pentagon's Office of the Inspector-General, revealed that he had taken AFRICOM's ethos of disingenuousness a step further by his involvement in extensive embezzlement. There are political forces in Washington who have been critical of AFRICOM since its inception. This volume will give them further reason to reflect on whether it really serves the US's best interests.

Since I began exposing the operations of Algeria's DRS and its collusion with the US and other Western powers in the GWOT, I have, not surprisingly, received considerable 'hate mail' and personal abuse from a number of self-appointed 'security experts' and 'right-wing' bloggers. I would now merely refer them, along with those others who have dismissed my work on the GWOT in the Sahara, notably Daniel Volman, whose review of *The Dark Sahara* was so appreciated in Washington, and *Le Monde Diplomatique*'s editor who refused to publish my commissioned article on 'What is Happening in the Sahel' because of concern for Algeria's DRS, to John Schindler's publication(s).

Much of the information in this book could not have been collected and verified without extensive help from a host of people in the media, intelligence and security services, other government agencies and, above all, 'on the ground' in Algeria, the Sahara and Sahel. Many of these people are Tuareg and Algerians whom I regard as friends. It is the nature of the world in which they live that for their own safety, their identities cannot be revealed. I thank them all. Without their invaluable and often courageous help, I could not have compiled or verified much that is documented in this book.

Postscript: January 2013

Now, media commentators are talking about developments in Mali as a new phase in the GWOT. However, what they are addressing is the outcome of the US's launch of the GWOT in the Sahara-Sahel in 2003. What we are now seeing, precisely ten years later, is the 'blow-back', the region-wide conflagration that I have long predicted.

After ponderous deliberations, on 20 December the UNSC finally authorised the deployment of the African-led International Support Mission in Mali (AFISMA) to oust the Islamists. But, with experts claiming that it would take months to train ECOWAS forces, an intervention was not foreseen before September 2013.

The unanimity of the UNSC resolution masked major disagreements between France and the US. While France had long been pushing for military intervention, the US, mindful of its alliance with Algeria, harboured major reservations. On 18 December, US Ambassador to the UN Susan Rice had called the military intervention plan 'crap'.

Three weeks later, on 10 January, the Islamists broke out suddenly from their de facto border with southern Mali and occupied the town of Konna on the main road to Bamako. With Mopti and the strategic Sévaré military air base within the Islamists' sights, only 50 kilometres away, the Malian government turned desperately to France for help.

Why the Islamists made their sudden advance is not yet clear. Although they claimed it was to provoke Mali and the West and to draw France into a trap, my own view is that Iyad ag Ghaly saw it as a means of preventing the further fragmentation of the three main Islamist groupings into a number of smaller, more ethnically and locally based groups. Mokhtar ben Mokhtar (MBM) had already broken away from AQIM on 3 December, while Iyad's own Ansar al-Din was to fracture decisively within two weeks. Whatever the Islamists' thinking, it appears to have been a grave miscalculation. France immediately launched heavy air strikes on Konna and Islamist bases across northern Mali: at Gao, Ansongo, Timbuktu, Kidal and elsewhere.

Although the Islamists counterattacked and temporarily occupied the town of Diabali, the advance of French ground troops, supported by the accelerated deployment of ECOWAS and Chadian forces and continuous French air strikes, led to the Islamists being driven out of their front-line positions and also out of both Gao and Timbuktu.

By 27 January, observers were describing their flight as a stampede. In Gao, residents danced in the streets as thousands cheered the liberating troops with shouts of 'Mali, Mali, France, France'. At Kidal, French bombs reportedly reduced Iyad's house to rubble. Back in Washington, General Carter Ham was busy apologising for the inept failure of the AFRICOM mission.

On 16 January, 'terrorists' attacked the In Amenas gas plant in Algeria. At least 49 foreign nationals and 31 terrorists died. Reportedly undertaken by MBM as revenge for Algeria granting France overfly rights to attack the Islamists in Mali, many experts believe that the attack may have been a DRS false-flag operation that went wrong.

This is not the end of the story. The Islamists have been neither totally eliminated nor yet driven entirely out of northern Mali. The possibility of 'spillover' into neighbouring states and human catastrophe is still high. So too is the likelihood of the perpetration of revenge atrocities by Mali's humiliated army and others. The International Criminal Court (ICC) has confirmed that it will investigate the atrocities committed in northern Mali. In so doing, it will also examine the role of Algeria's DRS.

ABBREVIATIONS

4WD	four-wheel drive
ACSRT	African Centre for the Study and Research on Terrorism
AFP	Agence France-Presse
AFISMA	African-led International Support Mission in Mali
AFRICOM	US Africa Command
ANAC	Agence National de l'Aviation Civil (Mali)
ANI	Nouakchott News Agency
AQIM	al-Qaeda in the Islamic Maghreb
AQIS	al-Qaeda in the Sahel
APW	Assemblée Populaire de Wilaya
ASL	Algerian Students League
ATT	Amadou Toumani Touré
AU	African Union
AUPSC	AU Peace and Security Council
BBC	British Broadcasting Corporation
BRC	Brown & Root Condor
CEMOC	Comité d'état-major opérationnel conjoint
CFA	Central African franc
CIA	Central Intelligence Agency
CJTF-HOA	Combined Joint Task Force – Horn of Africa
CNPC	Chinese National Petroleum Company
COGEMA	Companie Générale des Matières Nucléaires
COS	Commandement des Opérations Spéciales
CRIDEM	Carrefour de la République Islamique de Mauritanie
DCRI	Direction Centrale du Renseignement Intérieur
DCSA	Direction Centrale de la Sécurité de l'Armée
DDSE	Direction de la Documentation et de la Sécurité Extérieure
DEA	Drug Enforcement Administration (US)
DFID	Department for International Development
DGSE	Direction Générale de la Sécurité Extérieure
DGSN	Direction Générale de la Sûreté Nationale
DoD	Department of Defense (US)
DPA	Department of Political Affairs (UN)
DRS	Département du Renseignement et de la Sécurité
DSB	Defense Science Board
DST	Direction de la Surveillance du Territoire
EACTI	East African Counter-Terrorism Initiative

ECOWAS	Economic Community of West African States
ENTV	Entreprise Nationale de Télévision (Algeria)
ESRC	Economic and Social Research Council
ESISC	European Strategic Intelligence and Security Centre
EU	European Union
EUCOM	US European Command
FAN	Forces Armées Nigériennes
FARC	Fuerzas Armadas Revolucionarias de Colombia
FBI	Federal Bureau of Investigation
FCO	Foreign and Commonwealth Office
FFR	Front des Forces de Redressement
FIS	Front Islamique de Salut
FLAA	Front de Libération de l'Azawak et de l'Aïr
FLN	Front de Libération Nationale
FNIS	Force National d'Intervention et de la Sécurité (Niger)
FOREX	Foreign Exchange
GEF	Global Environmental Facility
GIA	Groupes Islamiques Armées
GMT	Greenwich Mean Time
GSI	Groupes Speciaux d'Intervention
GSPC	Groupe Salafiste pour le Prédication et le Combat
GWOT	Global War on Terror
HQ	headquarters
HUMINT	human intelligence
ICC	International Criminal Court
ICG	International Crisis Group
IRA	Initiative de résurgence du mouvement pour l'abolition de l'ésclavage
IRIN	Integrated Regional Information Networks
ISI	Inter-Services Intelligence (Pakistan)
JTAC	Joint Terrorism Analysis Centre
LDC	less-developed country
LIFG	Libyan Islamic Fighting Group
LNG	liquified natural gas
LRA	Lord's Resistance Army
MAOL	Mouvement Algérien des Officiers Libres
MBM	Mokhtar ben Mokhtar
MENA	Middle East and North Africa
MERLN	Military Education Research Library Network
MiPAL	Military Policy Awareness Links
MNJ	Mouvement des Nigériens pour la Justice
MNLA	Mouvement National de Libération de l'Azawad
MNSD	Mouvement National pour la Société du Développement

MPA	Mouvement Populaire de l'Azawad
MPLA	Mouvement Populaire pour la Libération de l'Azawad
MRRA	Mouvement républicain pour la restauration de l'Azawad
MTNM	Mouvement Touareg du Nord Mali
MUJAO	Mouvement pour l'Unicité du Jihad en Afrique de l'Ouest
NATO	North Atlantic Treaty Organisation
NEPD	National Energy Policy Development (Group)
NGO	non-governmental organisation
NTC	National Transitional Council
OCHA	Office for the Coordination of Humanitarian Affairs
OFAC	Office of Foreign Assets Control
P2OG	Proactive, Preemptive Operations Group
PNAC	Project for the New American Century
PSI	Pan-Sahel Initiative
RFI	Radio France Internationale
ROAPE	*Review of African Political Economy*
RPG	rocket-propelled grenade
SACEUR	Supreme Allied Commander, Europe
SAS	Special Air Service
SIS	Special Intelligence Service
SITE	Search for International Terrorist Entities
SM	Sécurité Militaire
TRIAL	Track Impunity Always
TS	top secret
TSCTI	Trans-Sahara Counterterrorism Initiative
UN	United Nations
UNDP	UN Development Programme
UNESCO	UN Educational, Scientific and Cultural Organisation
UNHCR	UN High Commission for Refugees
UNODC	UN Office on Drugs and Crime
UNSC	UN Security Council
UNWGIP	UN Working Group for Indigenous people
UPI	United Press International
US/USA	United States/United States of America
USAID	US Agency for International Development
VOA	*Voice of America*
WTO	World Tourism Organisation

TIMELINE

1960s

17 April 1961	'Bay of Pigs'. US-backed Cuban exiles fail in bid to overthrow government of Fidel Castro.
13 March 1962	Northwoods Operation plan presented to US Defense Secretary Robert McNamara.

1990s

3 June 1997	Project for the New American Century (PNAC): publication of Statement of Principles.
15 April 1999	Abdelaziz Bouteflika becomes President of Algeria after a disputed (rigged) election.

2001

20 January	George W. Bush inaugurated as President of the USA.
April	Public disclosure of the Northwoods Operation.
May	Publication of 'Cheney Report'.
11 September	('9/11') Terrorist attack on New York's World Trade Center, the Pentagon and Flight UA93.

2002

16 August	Proactive, Preemptive Operations Group (P2OG) programme 'leaked'.
18 October	Failed false-flag terrorist abduction of Swiss tourists in Algerian Sahara.

2003

February–March	32 European tourists taken hostage in Algerian Sahara.
10 March	Announcement in Djanet (Algeria) of $20 million World Bank–United Nations Development Programme (UNDP) funding for Algeria's Ahaggar and Tassili-n-Ajjer National Parks.
20 March	US invades Iraq.
17 May	17 hostages released in Algerian Sahara.
18 August	14 remaining hostages (one died) released in Mali.

2004

January–March	El Para's 'terrorists' allegedly chased from Mali to Chad.
10 January	US launches Pan-Sahel Initiative (PSI).
12 February	Rhissa ag Boula dismissed as Nigerien government minister. Detained three days later.

| September | Niger sends troops into Aïr in response to Tuareg militancy. |
| October | El Para allegedly returned to Algeria. |

2005

8 February	Gaddafi secures release of Nigerien soldiers from Tuareg militants.
4 March	Rhissa ag Boula released after 13 months' detention without charge.
20 April	Gaddafi speech to Tuareg at Oubari about a Tuareg 'state'.
3 June	'Terrorist' attack on Lemgheity garrison in northern Mauritania.
6 June	US launches Trans-Sahara Counterterrorism Initiative (TSCTI).
10 July	Tamanrasset riots.
3 August	Mauritania's President Maaouya Ould Sid'Ahmed Taya overthrown in coup d'état.

2006

15–16 February	Three US transporters airlift US Special Forces from Stuttgart to Tamanrasset.
10 April	Gaddafi speech in Timbuktu advocates 'Great Saharan state'.
23 May	Tuareg rebellion in Kidal, Mali.
11 September	Groups Salafiste pour le Prédication et le Combat (GSPC) changes name to al-Qaeda of the Islamic Maghreb (AQIM).
19 September	Tuareg attack alleged terrorist traffickers in northern Mali.
23 October	Tuareg attack alleged 'terrorists' near Araouane.
December	Defense Secretary Donald Rumsfeld recommends President Bush to authorise establishment of US Africa Command (AFRICOM).

2007

January	Formal announcement of GSPC name change to AQIM.
6 February	Defense Secretary Robert Gates formally announces President Bush's authorisation of AFRICOM.
8 February	Nigerien Tuareg rebellion begins with attack on Iferouane army post.
11 May	Tuareg rebellion spreads to Mali following Ibrahim ag Bahanga's killing of two policemen near Tin Zaouatene.
24 August	Nigerien government declares state of alert.

11–12 September	Tuareg fire on US C-130 bringing 'relief' supplies to Tin Zaouatene.
8 November	Algeria reports attack on Djanet airport by Tuareg youths as an AQIM 'terrorist' action.
21 November	Iyad ag Ghaly appointed as Mali's Consul General to Saudi Arabia.
11 December	Suicide car bomb destroys UN offices in Algiers; 17 killed.
2008	
14 February	US Special Forces ransack Tin Zaouatene in northern Mali.
18 February	In London, US Deputy Assistant Secretary of Defense for African Affairs, Theresa Whelan, denies presence of US forces in northern Mali.
22 February	Two Austrians, Wolfgang Ebner and Andrea Kloiber, taken hostage in Tunisia.
29 March	UN notified of genocide by Nigerien army against Tuareg.
1 October	Official establishment of US AFRICOM.
30 October	Two Austrian hostages released.
14 December	Two Canadian diplomats, Robert Fowler and Louis Guay, taken hostage near Niamey, Niger.
2009	
20 January	Barack Obama inaugurated as President of the USA.
22 January	Four European tourists (Mariane Petzgold (German), Werner and Gabriela Greiner (Swiss) and Edwin Dyer (British)) taken hostage near the Nigerien-Malian border.
22 April	Fowler, Guay, Petzgold and Greiner released.
31 May	Edwin Dyer executed.
10 June	Lieutenant Colonel Lemana Ould Bou assassinated in Timbuktu.
5 August	Mohamed Ould Abdel Aziz inaugurated as President of Mauritania after winning election. (He had deposed democratically elected President Abdallahi on 6 August 2008 in a military coup d'état.)
27 October	European Union's (EU's) External Relations Council expresses concern over Sahel security situation.
2 November	Boeing 727 cocaine flight found incinerated at Tarkint, Mali.
25 November	Pierre Camatte (French) taken hostage in Ménaka, Mali.

27 November	AFRICOM Commander General 'Kip' Ward visits Bamako.
29 November	Three Spanish aid workers (Albert Vilalta, Roque Pascual and Alicia Gámez) taken hostage in Mauritania.
18 December	Two Italians (Sergio Cicala and Philomène Kabouré) kidnapped near Kobenne, Mauritania.

2010

19 February	Niger's President Mamadou Tandja deposed in coup d'état.
20 April	Michel Germaneau (French) taken hostage in northern Niger.
21 April	Establishment by Comité d'état-major opérationnel conjoint (CEMOC) of joint command headquarters (HQ) at Tamanrasset.
23 April	Pierre Camatte released.
22 July	Franco-Mauritanian raids into Mali.
6–7 August	Security conference in Bamako. Algeria absent.
16 September	Seven AREVA employees (five French, one Togolese, one Malagasy) taken hostage at Arlit, northern Niger.
14–15 October	Second security conference in Bamako. Algeria absent.
9 December	Département du Renseignement et de la Sécurité (DRS) General Rachid Laalali flies from Berlin to Bamako following arrest of Sultan Ould Badi for drug smuggling.
18 December	European Commission receives its commissioned Study on *Political Islam in the Sahel and Neighbouring Countries*. (Report is subsequently redacted.)

2011

3–10 January	Widespread rioting throughout much of Algeria.
8 January	Two young Frenchmen, Antoine de Leocour and Vincent Delory, killed in failed rescue bid after abduction from Niamey.
14 January	Tunisia's President Zine Abidine Ben Ali flees country.
2 February	An Italian tourist (Maria Sandra Mariani) taken hostage in Tadrart region of south-eastern Algeria.
11 February	Egypt's Hosni Mubarak resigns.
15 February	Beginning of Libya's rebellion against Gaddafi regime.
24 February	Three of AREVA hostages released. Four French retained.

7 April	Mahamadou Issoufou inaugurated as Niger's President following presidential election on 31 January and 12 March.
1 June 1	General Carter Ham, Commander of AFRICOM, gives speech in Algiers saying he can 'see no evidence' of Algerian support for the Gaddafi regime.
16 October	Mouvement National de Libération de l'Azawad (MNLA) established.
20 October	Gaddafi killed at Sirte, Libya.
20 October	General Khaled Nezzar arrested by Swiss authorities in Geneva.
22–23 October	Three European aid workers kidnapped from Rabuni refugee camp near Tindouf, Algeria.
24 November	Two Frenchmen abducted from hotel in Hombori, Mali.
24 November	Four tourists seized in Timbuktu (one German killed; a South African, a Swede and a Dutchman taken hostage).
10 December	Mouvement pour l'Unicité du Jihad en Afrique de l'Ouest (MUJAO) announces its existence and claims responsibility for Tindouf hostage-takings.
15 December	Ansar al-Din announces its existence.
20 December	Algerian armed forces enter northern Mali.
26 December	General Athman Tartag replaces General Ahmed Kherfi as head of DRS's internal security service.
2012	
17 January	First shots fired at Ménaka in MNLA rebellion.
24 January	Massacre of Malian soldiers at Aguelhok.
22 March	Coup d'état in Bamako, Mali, led by Captain Sanogo.
29 March	Rebels take over Gao.
1 April	Rebels take over Timbuktu.
5 April	Seven Algerian diplomats allegedly taken hostage in Gao.
6 April	MNLA proclaims Independence of Azawad.
25–26 June	Fighting between MNLA and Islamists results in MNLA being ousted from Gao. Mokhtar ben Mokhtar (MBM) is reported killed. Timbuktu, Gao and Kidal now under control of Ansar al-Din, MUJAO and AQIM.
June–July	Islamists desecrate holy shrines in Timbuktu. Harsh shari'a law meets with growing popular anger and resistance. Some 400,000 have fled Azawad.

29 July	Couple stoned to death in Aguelhok for alleged adulterous relationship.
August–December	Ongoing deliberations between AU, ECOWAS, UN Security Council (UNSC) on possible military intervention in Mali.
16 November	MNLA suffer heavy losses in Gao. Islamists' intensify shari'a crackdown.
18 December	Susan Rice, US Ambassador to UN, calls plan for military intervention in Mali 'crap'.
20 December	UNSC resolution authorises military action to oust Islamists from northern Mali.

2013

10 January	Islamists launch unexpected 'break-out' from northern Mali. Seize control of Konna and threaten whole of southern Mali.
11 January	France responds to Mali request for help with air strikes against Islamists' advance and rear bases.
16 January	Over 80 killed in 'terrorist' attack on Algerian gas plant at In Amenas. Attributed to MBM, but analysts suspect DRS collusion.
28 January	French air and ground forces, supported by ECOWAS troops, recapture Gao and advance on Timbuktu. Islamists reported to be in flight. Iyad ag Ghaly's house in Kidal destroyed by French air strike.

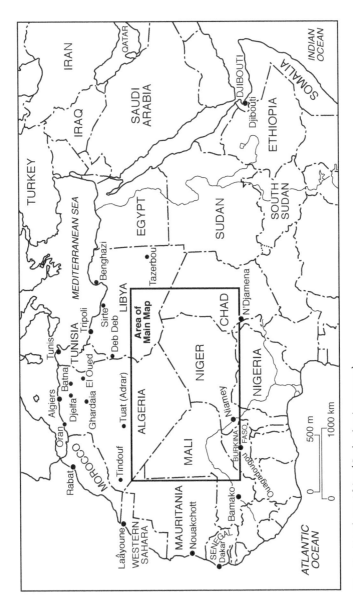

Map 1 Northern Africa (Catherine Lawrence)

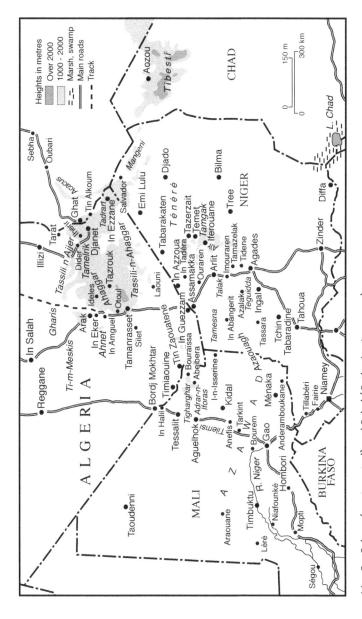

Map 2 Sahara (west-central) and Sahel (Catherine Lawrence)

xxv

1

P2OG: A LONG HISTORY OF
FALSE-FLAG TERRORISM

El Para's Kidnapping of 32 European Tourists

At 5.34 a.m. Baghdad time on 20 March 2003, the US commenced its military invasion of Iraq. In the preceding few weeks, 32 European tourists, in seven separate parties, had disappeared in one of the most remote corners of Algeria's Saharan desert. The two events were not entirely unrelated.

The region where the tourists disappeared, known as the Piste des Tombeaux (Graveyard Piste) because of the numerous prehistoric tombs scattered along its way, became the Sahara's Bermuda Triangle: the tourists had disappeared into thin air. For weeks, there were no clear leads on what had happened to them. Rumours and theories abounded. Gradually, however, the evidence, such as it was, pointed towards their having been taken hostage by Islamic extremists belonging to Algeria's Groupe Salafiste pour le Prédication et le Combat (GSPC), renamed al-Qaeda in the Islamic Maghreb (AQIM) in 2007. The leader of the kidnappers was Abderrazak Lamari. Sometimes known as Amari Saifi, or a dozen other aliases, he was usually referred to by his *nom de guerre*, El Para, a name derived from his time as a parachutist in the Algerian army.

The hostages were held in two groups. One group of 17 was released on 13 May after an Algerian army assault on the kidnappers' hideout in Gharis, an isolated range in southern Algeria's mountainous region of Ahaggar. The 15 members of the other group had been held captive in Tamelrik, part of another range on the northern edge of Ahaggar some 300 kilometres to the east of Gharis. After the release of the first group, those who had been held in Tamelrik were taken on a tortuous, weaving journey by their captors, estimated at some 3,000 kilometres, to the remote desert regions of northern Mali where they were finally released on 18 August after the alleged payment of a €5 million ransom.

Even before this second group of hostages had been released, the Bush administration had branded El Para as Osama bin Laden's 'man in the Sahara' and identified the Sahara as a new front in its 'Global War on Terror' (GWOT). After four months in Mali, El Para and his 60 or so terrorists, who had recruited about 15 helpers while in Mali, were driven out of their desert retreats somewhere in the region to the north of Timbuktu and around the Adrar-n-Iforas mountains of north-eastern Mali and reportedly chased by a combination of Malian, Nigerien and Algerian forces, assisted by US Special Forces and aerial reconnaissance, across the desert tracts of north-eastern Mali, the Aïr mountains and Ténéré desert of northern Niger and on into the Tibesti mountains of northern Chad. There, in the first week of March 2004, forces of the Chadian regular army, supported by US aerial reconnaissance, were said to have surrounded them. Forty-three of El Para's men were reportedly killed in the ensuing battle, with El Para and a handful of followers escaping the carnage, only to fall into the hands of Chadian rebels.

With El Para holed up in Chad, Washington was not short of hyperbole, imagination or downright lies in portraying this new terrorist threat as having spread right across the wastelands of the Sahel, as the southern 'shore' of the Sahara is known in Arabic, from Mauritania in the west, through the little known desert lands of Mali, Niger and southern Algeria, to the Tibesti mountains of Chad, with, beyond them, the Sudan, Somalia and, across the waters, the 'Talibanised' lands of Afghanistan and the debacle that was Iraq.

Whether the 'El Para story' was real or fabricated, the Generals of the US's European Command (EUCOM), based in Stuttgart but charged with responsibility for most of Africa, were quick to seize the opportunities presented by this new threat. Marine Corps General James (Jim) Jones, Supreme Allied Commander, Europe (SACEUR), the Commander of EUCOM and from

January 2009 until November 2010 President Obama's National Security Advisor (NSA), talked enthusiastically about constructing a 'family of bases' across Africa. His Deputy Commander, with responsibility for Africa, the gung-ho Air Force General Charles Wald, described the Sahara as a 'swamp of terror', a 'terrorist infestation' which 'we need to drain'.[1] Back at the White House, press officers described the Sahara as 'a magnet for terrorists'. Within proverbial minutes of El Para's flight across the Sahel becoming public knowledge, Western intelligence and diplomatic sources were claiming to be finding the fingerprints of this new terrorist threat everywhere. For instance, it took only a few days after the Madrid train bombings for that atrocity to be linked to al-Qaeda groups lurking deep in the Sahara.[2] Western intelligence-security services warned that al-Qaeda bases hidden deep in the world's largest desert could launch terrorist attacks on Europe.

The US's military commanders went out of their way to alert Europe to the threat of terrorist activity from North Africa. They pointed explicitly to the bombing of a synagogue in Tunisia in 2002, suicide bombings in Casablanca that had killed 33 innocent civilians and wounded more than 100 in May 2003, the arrest of al-Qaeda suspects in Morocco and the abduction of the 32 tourists in Algeria. They warned of terrorists from Afghanistan and Pakistan swarming across the vast ungoverned and desolate regions of the Sahara desert, as they described them, and turning the region, Europe's back door, into another Afghanistan. The GSPC, so the US warned, had already emerged in Europe as an al-Qaeda recruiting organisation and in North Africa it sought nothing less than the overthrow of the Algerian and Mauritanian governments.

*   *   *

The Dark Sahara

I was in the Ahaggar region of the Algerian Sahara when the 32 tourists were abducted, as well as for much of the time that they were held in captivity. I was also in the region when El Para and

his men were reportedly being chased across the Sahel. Neither I
nor many of the local Tuareg peoples, with whom I was living at
the time, recognised the literally terrifying image of the Sahara
that the Bush administration and its military commanders were
portraying to the world.

I was able to record and document almost all that happened
in these regions of the Sahara and Sahel at that time. *The Dark
Sahara*,[3] the prequel to this volume, recounts in detail what
happened to the 32 hostages and how both I and my Tuareg
companions became increasingly suspicious and aware of the
role played in the kidnapping by Algeria's *mukhabarat* (police
state), especially the 'dirty tricks' department of its intelligence
and security service, the Département du Renseignement et de la
Sécurité (DRS). As the evidence documented in *The Dark Sahara*
makes abundantly clear, the operation simply could not have been
undertaken without the facilitation of the DRS.

Indeed, as François Gèze and Salima Mellah of Algeria-Watch,
Algeria's respected human rights organisation, concluded:

> We have undertaken an in depth enquiry into the affair of the European
> hostages in the Sahara. A close study of the facts shows that there is no
> other explanation for this operation than the directing of the hostage-taking
> by the DRS, the Algerian army's secret service.[4]

As this volume reveals, with the passage of time, further evidence
of the DRS's fabrication and orchestration of terrorism in the
Sahara and Sahel regions has come to light.

The evidence my Tuareg companions and I gathered at that
time, which is documented in *The Dark Sahara*, indicated that El
Para was not merely a DRS agent, but perhaps also a US Green
Beret trained at Fort Bragg in the 1990s. Indeed, *The Dark Sahara*
pointed overwhelmingly to collusion between the US and Algeria's
DRS in the 2003 abduction of the 32 tourists, thus providing
the Bush administration with its justification for its launch of a
Sahara-Sahelian front, or what became known as a 'second front'
in the GWOT in Africa.

However, although the evidence of US-Algerian collusion in
the fabrication of terrorism presented in *The Dark Sahara* was

strong, it lacked, as some critics pointed out, the 'smoking gun'. It is difficult, indeed, sometime almost impossible, to 'prove a negative'. In the case of the alleged chase of El Para's group of 'terrorists' into Chad in March 2004 and the battle at Wour in which 43 were allegedly killed, the only evidence that the battle took place is that the US military said it happened. No evidence has ever been provided by the US to actually confirm that the battle took place and that 43 GSPC terrorists were killed. Given Washington's long and extensively documented record of support for state terrorism on almost every continent, along with the US government's brazen record of dissembling and downright lying, Washington's word that something happened is certainly not 'proof'. Nor is it likely that Donald Rumsfeld's Department would have left a written confession of its activities in the region. Indeed, as this volume spells out, the US has continued to collaborate with Algeria's DRS in the fabrication and orchestration of terrorist activities in the region.

Proactive, Preemptive Operations Group (P2OG)

What I should have documented in *The Dark Sahara*, but did not, simply because I was unaware of it until after the book had gone to press, was how the El Para operation fitted into the US's long history of supporting state terrorists (and dictators) and creating false-flag incidents to justify military intervention. There is, in fact, a direct link between El Para's operation in the Sahara and the US Secretary of Defense, Donald Rumsfeld, in the form of a plan which was put into operation under Rumsfeld's direction in the third quarter of 2002. That is not to credit Rumsfeld with any great novelty for the plan. The precursor of the plan that was put into operation with El Para in 2003 had actually been conceived by the Joint Chiefs of Staff precisely 40 years earlier. Its origin stemmed directly from the US's 'Bay of Pigs' disaster in 1961, when a Central Intelligence Agency (CIA)-trained force of Cuban exiles, with the support of US government armed forces, attempted unsuccessfully to invade Cuba and overthrow the government of Fidel Castro. The invading force, which landed at the Bay of Pigs, was all but wiped out by Castro's forces within three days.

In the wake of the Bay of Pigs disaster, the Department of Defense and the Joint Chiefs of Staff, under the Chairmanship of General Lyman Lemnitzer, drew up plans, codenamed 'Operation Northwoods', to justify a US military invasion of Cuba. The plan, described as 'the most corrupt plan ever created by the US government',[5] was written with the approval of the Chairman and every member of the Joint Chiefs of Staff and presented to President John Kennedy's Defense Secretary, Robert McNamara, on 13 March 1962. Entitled 'Justification for US Military Intervention in Cuba (TS [top secret])',[6] Operation Northwoods proposed launching a secret and bloody war of terrorism against their own country in order to trick the American public into supporting an ill-conceived war that the Joint Chiefs of Staff intended to launch against Cuba. It called on the CIA and other operatives to undertake a range of atrocities:

> Innocent civilians were to be shot on American streets; boats carrying refugees fleeing Cuba were to be sunk on the high seas; a wave of violent terrorism was to be launched in Washington, D.C., Miami, and elsewhere. People would be framed for bombings they did not commit; planes would be hijacked. Using phony evidence, all of it would be blamed on Castro, thus giving Lemnitzer and his cabal the excuse, as well as the public and international backing, they needed to launch their war against Fidel Castro's Cuba.[7]

The plan was ultimately rejected by President Kennedy. Operation Northwoods remained 'classified' and unknown to the American public until declassified and disclosed by the National Security Archive and the investigative journalist James Bamford in April 2001.[8] In 2002, 40 years after the Northwoods plan was presented to Robert McNamara, a not dissimilar plan was presented to Donald Rumsfeld by his Defense Science Board (DSB).[9] Excerpts of the DSB's 'Summer Study on Special Operations and Joint Forces in Support of Countering Terrorism' were revealed on 16 August 2002,[10] with Pamela Hess,[11] William Arkin[12] and David Isenberg,[13] amongst others, publishing further details and analysis of the plan.

The DSB recommended the creation of a 'Proactive, Preemptive Operations Group', a covert organisation which would carry out secret missions to 'stimulate reactions' among terrorist groups by provoking them into undertaking violent acts that would expose them to 'counterattack' by US forces, along with other operations which, through the US military penetration of terrorist groups and the recruitment of local peoples, would dupe them into conducting 'combat operations, or even terrorist activities'.[14]

The existence of the Proactive, Preemptive Operations Group, or P2OG as it became known, raises huge questions about all terrorist actions since 2002. In short, how many terrorist incidents, such as the Madrid and London bombings in March 2004 and July 2005 respectively, as well as the GWOT's Sahara-Sahel front, were perhaps linked either directly or indirectly to this programme? We do not know, although Andrew Cockburn's[15] and Nafeez Mosaddeq Ahmed's[16] investigations, in 2008 and 2009 respectively, indicate that the GWOT may not be as straightforward as the US and other Western countries would like their publics to believe. For example, in May 2008, George Bush was reported to have signed a secret finding authorising and requesting some $400 million funding for terrorist groups across much of the Middle East–Afghanistan region in a covert offensive directed ultimately against the Iranian regime. An initial outlay of $300 million was approved by Congress with bipartisan support.[17]

One of the most detailed investigations into contemporary terrorism is that undertaken by Nafeez Ahmed, the author of such in-depth investigations as *The War on Freedom*,[18] *Behind the War on Terror*,[19] *The War on Truth*[20] and the *The London Bombings*.[21] In Nafeez Ahmed's recent investigation of false-flag operations,[22] he states that the US investigative journalist Seymour Hersh[23] was told by a Pentagon advisor that the Algerian (El Para) operation was a pilot for the new Pentagon covert P2OG programme.

The timing of the developments between Washington and the Algerian Sahara are significant. The P2OG programme 'leak' came on 16 August 2002, 16 days after Marion E. (Spike) Bowman,[24] Deputy General Counsel for the Federal Bureau of Investigation (FBI), presented crucial evidence to the Senate Select Committee on Intelligence in regard to proposed amendments concerning the Foreign Intelligence Surveillance Act. Until Bowman's evidence, the US intelligence community was anxious about working too closely with their Algerian counterparts for fear that they would pass sensitive information to Palestinian organisations. However, Bowman's statement, in which he presented the background and nature of what the FBI called the 'International Jihad Movement', dispelled many of the anxieties in Washington about collaborating with the Algerians by showing how close Algeria was to the US in its fight against al-Qaeda and terrorism.

During the course of the next two months, false-flag terrorism incidents were planned for the Algerian Sahara. The first attempt to fabricate terrorism in the region was not El Para's operation in February–March 2003, but an attempt to hijack and abduct four Swiss tourists on 18 October 2002 near Arak in southern Algeria. However, the operation, which I described in *The Dark Sahara*, was botched and the tourists escaped.[25]

There is no 'smoking gun' to show the US Department of Defense was involved in the Arak operation. I was in the area at the time and came across no evidence of any direct US participation. However, by that time Algeria's DRS was already hand in glove with US intelligence services and it is inconceivable, in the light of the very close 'post-Bowman' relationship between the US and Algerian intelligence services, that the US would have been unaware of the Arak operation. Indeed, the question which the US has never been able to answer is why, if there had been no terrorism in the region at the time of the Arak operation, did the State Department's Counterterrorism Office at that very moment send two officials, AF DAS Robert Perry and S/CT Deputy Coordinator Stephanie Kinney,[26] to brief the governments of Mali, Niger, Chad and Mauritania on the Bush administration's planned counterterrorism Pan-Sahel Initiative (PSI)? The answer, surely, can only be that the US administration either had foreknowledge of future terrorism in the region or, as we now know, that it was already planning, with the help of the DRS, to turn the region, as the following chapters demonstrate, into a 'Terror Zone'.

Bush's PSI, what local people called the 'US invasion', did not officially roll into action until January 2004. Even so, either CIA operatives or US Special Forces or, more likely, a combination of both, were operating covertly in the region as early as the autumn of 2002 in what now appears to have been the pilot for Rumsfeld's new P2OG programme.

US and Algerian Motives for False-Flag Operations

Why both Algeria and the US, which was preoccupied at that time with its invasion of Iraq, should have involved themselves in such a heinous and duplicitous crime is explained in *The Dark Sahara*. Since then, and as this volume reveals, the motives of both countries for their continuous involvement in the fabrication of terrorism in the Sahara-Sahel region over the subsequent nine to ten years – up to the time of going to press in May 2012 – have morphed. But before exploring how the GWOT has developed and impacted on these regions over these last nine years, let me briefly remind readers of the reasons why both countries, Algeria and the US, decided to fabricate terrorism in the Sahara-Sahel.

Algeria's motives at that time were quite simple. The country's 'dirty war' of the 1990s,[27] ostensibly between its security forces and Islamic militants, had left an estimated 200,000 dead, many killed in horrific civilian massacres for which Algeria's security services must bear as much blame as the Islamic militants, if not more. The struggle, however, reduced Algeria to the status of an international pariah, with consequent arms embargoes leaving its armed forces severely under-equipped in terms of modern surveillance, communications and weapon systems. The attacks on New York's World Trade Center and Washington's Pentagon building, now known as '9/11', provided the Algerian regime with a heaven-sent opportunity to rectify both these situations. By befriending and allying itself to the Bush administration in its GWOT, Algeria hoped to procure new high-specification technical equipment for its military and, by attaching itself to Washington's coat-tails, to come in from the cold and attain a place of significance at the high table of international relations.

The US's motives, by contrast, were far more global. While Washington's globalisation of the war on terror during and immediately after its invasion of Iraq had much to do with its deceptive strategy of trying to link its invasion of Iraq with its war against al-Qaeda, the expansion of the GWOT into Africa had much more to do with Africa's newfound strategic importance to the US than justifying the Iraqi invasion.

Africa's strategic importance to the US over the last decade has undergone several significant shifts and reappraisals. However, at the time of the abduction of the 32 hostages, the US's primary interest in Africa was as a solution to its own domestic energy crisis. In 1998, US dependency on foreign oil supplies surpassed the psychologically critical 50 per cent level and in 2000 became an election issue as George W. Bush pledged to make energy security a top priority of his presidency. True to his word, he established a National Energy Policy Development (NEPD) Group within two weeks of taking office. The Group, under the Chairmanship of Vice-President Dick Cheney, published its strategically critical report in May 2001, four months before 9/11.[28] Although the intended impact of the report was subsumed by the overwhelming events of 9/11, the Cheney Report, as it became known, set the direction of subsequent US policy towards Africa by identifying the continent, especially West Africa, as a major new source of US oil imports. The report had estimated that Africa would provide 25 per cent of US oil imports by 2015. Since 2001, US oil imports from Africa have nearly doubled, with more recent estimates putting Africa's contribution by 2015 as high as 35 per cent.[29] It is not surprising that the Bush administration, shortly after coming to power, defined African oil as a 'strategic national interest' and thus a resource that the US might choose military force to control.[30]

The Opportunity of '9/11'

The opportunity afforded by 9/11 enabled Bush to choose a military structure, the GWOT, to secure access to Africa's oil. However, launching a new front in the GWOT in a continent largely devoid of terrorism was a little trickier. The continent's few terrorist incidents, apart from those perpetrated by many of the continent's more repressive regimes against their own peoples, had been confined predominantly to its periphery: the Mediterranean littoral of the Maghreb, East Africa and debatably Somalia – places that were a long way from the oil resources coveted by Washington. How does one wage a war against something, in this case terrorism, which isn't there? The answer was to fabricate it.

The terrorism which the Bush administration and its regional allies, notably Algeria, fabricated in order to justify the launch of a Sahara-Sahelian front in the GWOT centred on El Para's abduction of the 32 European tourists and his subsequent alleged escapades across the Sahel, the geographical location of which led me to talk of what I dubbed Washington's 'banana theory' of terrorism.[31] This 'theory' explained how the Bush administration envisaged ('imagined' would be a better word) how the terrorists assumed to have been dislodged from Afghanistan by American forces in 2001 fled to the Horn of Africa and then 'swarmed', to use the US military term for it, across the Sahel, in what US military maps have subsequently depicted as a banana-shaped curve, to link up with terrorist movements in North Africa's Maghreb, notably Algeria's GSPC (now AQIM). From this banana-shaped swathe across the map of Africa, this imaginary threat stood poised to spread terror into both Europe to the north and the rest of Africa, especially the strategic oil areas of West Africa, to the south. The terrorism threat to Africa, so Washington's 'banana theory' had it, came from these vast, ungoverned 'empty spaces' of the Sahara-Sahel region. As the *The Dark Sahara* has revealed, the theory was grand, persuasive and terrifying, but untrue. It was a fiction, based on scarcely a thread of evidence, and yet regurgitated and embellished upon, in thousands of articles, analyses and reports in the world's media, burgeoning security industry and, most shamefully of all, academe.

In looking back on the El Para saga, we might now conceivably regard it as a farcical comedy, except to the hostages themselves, for in many ways that is what it was. Except for three things, which have all been extremely serious:

- First, in spite of the Pentagon's denials, the extraordinary narrative of *The Dark Sahara* – a monstrous conspiracy between the US and Algerian intelligence services – underpinned the launch of Washington's GWOT into Africa and the subsequent creation, on October 1, 2008, of a new, independent, fully autonomous and operational US military command for Africa (US AFRICOM).
- Second, the launch of the GWOT into the Sahara-Sahel region exacerbated the region's political and economic instability and was a major cause of the Tuareg rebellions that broke out in Niger and Mali in 2007. These rebellions, characterised by President Tandja's genocidal policy, or what the local Tuareg called an 'ethnocide', in Niger and the considerable loss of life in Mali, and which have still not been resolved in terms of satisfactory long-term peace agreements, were the direct outcomes of Washington's reckless policy.
- Third, in October 2010, the region was placed at the top of the EU's security agenda. The Pentagon's 2003–04 maps and Washington's accompanying hyperbole, which had branded El Para's operational area – the vast expanse of the western half of the Sahara-Sahel region from Mauritania, through Mali, southern Algeria, Niger and Chad – as a 'Terrorist Corridor', a 'Terrorist Area' and a 'Terror Zone', had finally become – as I predicted at that time – a self-fulfilling prophecy. The region, at least for Westerners, is now a 'No-Go' area.

Over the course of these nine years, hundreds of thousands of people, perhaps as many as 2 million, mostly the indigenous Tuareg population, have suffered in varying ways and varying degrees from this thoroughly evil policy. Far too many of them have died, some grotesquely, as in Niger's 'genocide' of 2007–09. Many others, especially Tuareg, have been obliged to turn to 'banditry' as a form of survival and have thus been criminalised, while many young army soldiers have died in fighting something which they never really understood. Some Tuareg even say that the Sahara itself is now dying.

This volume explains how this vast tract of Africa has finally become, after ten years of imagined, exaggerated and fabricated state terrorism, the alleged domain of AQIM, or simply al-Qaeda as many writers now abbreviate it. It also explains the background to and creation of AFRICOM and the key role of this latest of US combatant commands in achieving US imperial designs in Africa. Primarily, however, this book details over the course of these ten years the impact of US foreign policy, namely the GWOT – although President Obama no longer refers to this policy by this name – on the Tuareg: the indigenous peoples of this part of Africa.

While the primary responsibility for this appalling debacle rests with Washington, the story does not end there. It is too easy to ascribe all the blame to Washington. Other actors have played their part. Not only has Algeria been much more than a submissive partner, but Western European countries, notably the UK and France, have increasingly shown their willingness to play supportive roles, with their policies towards the region, as this volume explains, and as the UK's Foreign and Commonwealth Office (FCO) has admitted, being based knowingly and in a calculated manner on myth. That myth was based on El Para's operation and it justified the subsequent Saharan-Sahelian front in the GWOT. The ideological obsession of Western governments and their intelligence services with terrorists and Islamists – their 'bogeymen' for the last ten years – was such that they chose to live a lie. Only now, as the Arab revolt sweeps across the region, is the West beginning to realise and admit that the terrorists and Islamists in whom they have been so obsessed may only be a very small part of the scene.

2

THE US INVASION OF
THE SAHARA-SAHEL

The Pan-Sahel Initiative

On 10 January 2004, President Bush's Pan-Sahel Initiative (PSI), or the 'American invasion' as many local people referred to it, rolled into action with the disembarkation in Nouakchott, Mauritania's Atlantic seaboard capital, of an 'anti-terror team' of 500 US troops. A further 400 US Rangers were deployed into the Chadian-Nigerien border region the following week. US Deputy Undersecretary of State Pamela Bridgewater, addressing the attendant corps of journalists in Nouakchott the next day, confirmed that the corporate sector – in keeping with the Bush administration's policy of privatising the military – would get a large slice of the financial action. Although US troops, so Bridgewater told the journalists, would do the work in Mauritania and Mali, Pacific Architects & Engineers, the Los Angeles-based defence contractors, would pick up the work in Chad and Niger.[1]

With the world's gaze fixed on the unfolding debacle of Iraq, what went on in some of the least known and most remote corners of Africa went largely unnoticed. The PSI was no exception.

The PSI first came to public attention in November 2002 when the US State Department issued a press release announcing that two officials from the Office of Counterterrorism, AF DAS Robert Perry and S/CT Deputy Coordinator Stephanie Kinney, were traversing Mali, Niger, Chad and Mauritania to discuss with officials in those countries a scheme aimed at fighting terrorism, controlling illicit trade and enhancing regional security.[2] General Kohler, head of planning at the US European Command (EUCOM), along with other senior US commanders, State Department and Pentagon officials, continually emphasised the region as being an 'ungoverned area'. 'We're helping to teach them [the Malian military] how to control this area themselves so they can keep it from being used by terrorists', said the US Ambassador to Mali.[3]

The PSI was the most overt part of the Bush administration's strategy of creating the ideological conditions for the militarisation of Africa. Its justification had been provided by the kidnap of the 32 European hostages the previous year. Without El Para there could have been no PSI. As Rafi Khatchadourian, one of the more eloquent journalists to cover the El Para operation, explained: 'For the Defense Department, Saifi's [El Para's] activities became the central and most vivid justification for expanding the U.S. military presence in the Sahel ... The hostage-taking, according to General Wald, was a "blessing in disguise". It provided European Command with not only an important test case, but also the strongest argument for its newfound mission in Africa.'[4]

The Bush administration started making use of El Para's actions in the Sahara long before the hostages were even released. By July 2003, the US was already asking Algeria for military basing rights, saying that it wanted to 'employ Algerian military bases for counter-insurgency missions and the protection of oil interests'.[5]

As far as North and West Africa were concerned, the US State and Defense Departments had spent much of the two years following the invasion of Afghanistan discussing and planning for a US military presence, or at least greater military access rights, in the countries stretching from the Horn of Africa to the Atlantic. In 2002, US Central Command moved many of its facilities from Saudi Arabia to the former French base of Camp Lemonier in Djibouti, which was to become the base for the US's Combined Joint Task Force in the Horn of Africa (CJTF-HOA) and its East African Counter-Terrorism Initiative (EACTI).

With its forces established in Djibouti, the US then sought enhanced military facilities across North Africa, including port facilities, closer military ties with countries like Morocco and Tunisia and long-term access to bases in countries like Algeria and Mali, in the belief that North Africa, the southern Mediterranean and the Horn of Africa would become a major source of tension in the next decade.[6] In May 2003, General Jones spelt out US strategic thinking. He said: 'We might wish to have more presence in the southern rim of the Mediterranean, where there are a certain number of countries that can be destabilised in the near future, large ungoverned areas across Africa that are clearly the new routes of narco trafficking, terrorist training and hotbeds of instability.' Two months later, with the hostages still held captive, General Jones was even more specific: 'As we pursue the global war on terrorism, we're going to have to go where the terrorists are. And we're seeing some evidence, at least preliminary, that more and more of these large uncontrolled, ungoverned areas [vast swaths of the Sahara, from Mauritania ... to Sudan] are going to be potential havens for that kind of activity.'[7]

In early January 2004, at the same time as El Para's group was being chased out of Mali, US government officials confirmed that a key goal of the Bush administration was to establish basing rights in Algeria and Morocco and that the issue had been raised by Secretary of State Colin Powell as well as a range of US military leaders during their visits to North African states during 2003.[8] Although the likelihood of the US acquiring basing rights in Algeria was never likely, what General Jones actually envisaged for Algeria was not akin to the Cold War era bases, but a more flexible facilitative arrangement which would enable the US military to deploy quickly, as and when required, into the sort of 'forward operating bases' envisaged in EUCOM's new strategy. The US had already realised that Cold War-style bases were no longer militarily appropriate or politically feasible, especially in Muslim countries, where such bases could become a major source of friction. Indeed, it was precisely for this reason that the US had removed so many of its facilities from Saudi Arabia to Djibouti. The basing of US forces in almost any Muslim country was highly provocative and likely to fuel anti-US sentiments. This was especially true for Algeria, whose Foreign Affairs Minister at that time, Abdelaziz Belkhadem, had been quick to point out that his country's policy had always been to deny a foreign military presence on its territory.

General Jones's new concept of basing rights across Africa was designed to overcome such potential friction with host nations. He envisaged the establishment of a string of long-term military bases across the continent, or what he called a 'family of bases', which would include 'forward-operating bases', or what he called 'lily pads', that could house up to 3,000–5,000 troops with an airfield nearby, and 'forward-operating locations', which would be lightly equipped bases where Special Forces, marines or possibly an infantry rifle platoon or company could land and build up as the mission required.[9]

It was clearly this sort of 'lily pad' arrangement that general Jones envisaged for the Algerian Sahara, with the location being Tamanrasset.

The Tamanrasset Base

Media reports about a US base at Tamanrasset began around May–July 2003 when the US let it be known that it was pushing for permanent military bases in North Africa, notably Algeria.[10] In fact, the construction of this base, alongside Tamanrasset's Aguenar airport, commenced around 2000. At that time the billboard attached to the base's perimeter fence disingenuously proclaimed it to be a NASA project, leading local people to believe that it was part of the US space programme. The billboard was subsequently changed to Kellogg Brown & Root and then to Brown & Root Condor (BRC), both subsidiaries of the Halliburton Company. Although both the US and Algeria have continued to deny the existence of a US military base in southern Algeria, the construction workers in the base were able to tell me about its size and facilities. It is in fact a very large 'lily pad'. Encircled by a high plastered wall with sentry pill-boxes at 100–200-metre intervals, the workers estimated its circumference as around ten kilometres and its runway, the upgrading and extension of one of the two existing runways, as approaching four kilometres. By early 2005, at least five hangar-like buildings had been erected. Since then, further construction by the Canadian subcontractor RSW-SCATT has, according to the construction workers, added lodgings for 2,000 personnel as well as an Olympic-sized swimming pool.

The base's construction has been beset by countless difficulties, not least of which was the political corruption scandal that blew up over BRC in 2006 and led to the company's closure.[11] There have also been several technical difficulties stemming from BRC's failure to undertake a proper site survey. For example, the extension of the runway was delayed by having to blast and remove extensive amounts of harder-than-expected granite, while RSW-SCATT subsequently had to build a number of dams and culverts to protect both the runway and the buildings from flood water. In addition, there was insufficient water to operate the construction plant, a problem that was solved by sinking a deep well into the Oued Otoul, some 10–15 kilometres to the north, and pumping water from there to the base. Not surprisingly, this lowered Otoul's water table and dried up the wells of the local residents whose main livelihood was horticulture. Such 'collateral damage' did nothing to endear local 'hearts and minds', about which US military policy has long made much ado.

The Presence of US Forces

The US had a small number of forces in the Sahel even before the PSI. Since then, there has been a continuous presence of US forces in the region. However, the number has been small, only rising above a few hundred on such occasions as the launch of the PSI and various Operation Flintlock (see below) exercises. In addition to the obvious necessity for secrecy, there have been other reasons why it has been impossible to determine the precise number, nature and location of US forces in the region at any one time during the last decade.

One reason why US troop levels are so difficult to determine is the terminology used to describe them. For instance, there is much obfuscation as to whether US military personnel are members of the regular US armed services, various US Special Forces, private military contractors or merely 'advisors'. The US authorities have been deliberately obtuse throughout this period about the number of US military personnel belonging to any of these categories in Algeria and the Sahel, not only because of the secrecy that has surrounded the US presence in the region, but so that the US authorities can maintain deniability, especially in the many instances when US forces have joined with or backed up local military and security forces in highly questionable and politically sensitive operations. For example, on 18 February 2008, one week after US Special Forces had accompanied Malian troops in ransacking the northern Mali desert town of Tin Zaouatene, General William 'Kip' Ward, Commander of the US Africa Command (AFRICOM), and Theresa Whelan, Deputy Assistant Secretary of Defense for African Affairs, while addressing a conference on US–Africa Security in London, denied the presence of US forces in northern Mali.[12]

A second reason is because US forces in the region have usually been highly mobile, sometimes being flown in directly from EUCOM's headquarters in Stuttgart or elsewhere in Europe on orders from the Pentagon without the US State Department and country ambassadors in the region being notified. For example, both the US State Department and the US Ambassador to Algeria deny having any knowledge of the US Special Forces flown into Tamanrasset from Stuttgart in mid February 2006 and then moved into northern Mali to support the Tuareg rebellion in the Kidal region on 23 May 2006.[13]

However, my own assessment, supported by many journalists and well-informed local people, is that since 2003 the US has up to 1,000 troops of one sort or another in the region at any one time, although with that upper limit having dwindled over the last two to three years. Whether the majority of these have been contractors, as intimated by Pamela Bridgewater, or Special Forces has never been made clear. However, most of the sightings of US military in the area as well as reported actions by US troops, such as the ransacking of Tin Zaouatene mentioned above and the movement of US troops into Mali in May 2006 (see below), seem to have been of Special Forces. My own assessment is that the number of US Special Forces in the region at any one time during this period has probably been around 400, usually operating in small contingents on training exercises, clandestine operations and surveillance activities in the desert border regions. This figure is close to the figure which AFRICOM currently claims to have in the region.

With the exception of the initial 1,000 troops mentioned by Pamela Bridgewater at the launch of the PSI and occasional training exercises, such as the annual Operation Flintlocks, the US troop level in the Sahel countries of Mauritania, Mali and Niger, as far as I am aware, has probably never exceeded a few hundred. The main mystery about the presence of US forces in the region, however, has not concerned the Sahelian countries, but Algeria where a continuous stream of media reports over much of this period has referred to 400 US forces being based somewhere in the extreme south of the country. Senior personnel in both the US State Department and the Ministry of Defense (Pentagon) are adamant that the US has never had troops based at or near Tamanrasset or anywhere else in Algeria,[14] while the Algerian government is equally vehement in its denial for fear of exacerbating its own Islamist problems. On the other hand, numerous local residents are equally adamant that they have seen US forces there.

US Special Forces have been seen around Algeria's extensive southern border regions on numerous occasions since 2002. Substantial numbers of US forces have also been in southern Algeria on various exercises with the Algerian forces, as, for example, during Operation Flintlock (see below) in 2005. US Special Forces have also been stationed at Tamanrasset on various occasions since 2003. For example, multiple sources, including senior members of the airport police, air traffic control and workers within the military base have told me that they saw in the order of 400 US troops at the base at various times in the first few months of 2006. Although both the State Department and the Pentagon denied the presence of these troops at Tamanrasset, so many people could not be wrong. Indeed, Tamanrasset airport's flight records confirm that two US military flights arrived at Tamanrasset on 16 February 2006, with a third on the following day. The flights were logged as having come from EUCOM's main

European base at Stuttgart. The manifest of one plane was for surveillance and other such equipment; those of the other two revealed either 50 or 100 Special Forces in each accompanied by their dogs, the translation being confused over whether there were 50 or 100 troops in each plane. Informants also described seeing these same troops passing through the village of Silet on their way to Mali just before the Tuareg's rebellion on 23 May. The use of the Tamanrasset base for that operation was a perfect example of General Jones's envisaged use of 'lily pads'.

The mystery concerns the number 400. This number of US troops (Special Forces) has been quoted to me frequently by my informants in the region as well as being reported in several press articles that predate the Special Forces flown to Tamanrasset on 16–17 February 2006. I believe the figure stems from Algerian media reports originating in 2004 that have subsequently been re-cited and bandied about the region. It is possible, indeed likely, that the original figure of 400 may have come from a European newspaper (probably French) and then been reproduced in the Algerian media without checking it. It is also possible that it may have been deliberate 'disinformation' from the Algerian security forces, although the purpose of such disinformation is not apparent. Nevertheless, there is some evidence for either deliberate disinformation or complete incompetence by Algerian newspapers in the instance of one newspaper, known to have close links to the DRS, stating that the US was constructing a military surveillance base at Iherir, 500 kilometres as the crow flies to the north-east of Tamanrasset and close to the Libyan frontier. This may have been a deliberate false scent designed to direct attention away from Tamanrasset. Nevertheless, it is one that I followed. I made three detailed reconnaissance trips to Iherir and its surrounds during that period, but found absolutely no trace of any such base or US presence.

In spite of US denials, there is no doubt that US military personnel of one category or another have been in the region throughout this period, from as early as 2002 until the time of this book going to press in May 2012. During this period, small numbers of US Special Forces have been seen by myself and my Tuareg colleagues with whom I was travelling and working on numerous occasions. In addition to the military bases at Tamanrasset and Gao (Mali), we have seen them at several locations, such as: crossing the Algerian border into the Emi Lulu region of north-eastern Niger, presumably from the Algerian military base at In Ezzane in the extreme south-eastern corner of Algeria; at the In Guezzam frontier; at Laouni and several places in northern Niger and Mali, notably at Agades (Niger) and in Mali around Kidal, Tessalit, Aguelhok, Araouane and Tin Zaouatene, as well as several places further south, such as Gao, where they were stationed on longer-term missions.

The Decimation of Tuareg Livelihoods

The PSI was certainly not welcomed with open arms by the region's residents. US rhetoric at the time had been that 'the Pan Sahel Initiative [was] to enhance regional peace and security'.[15] However, an increasing number of regional experts, as well as local people themselves, believed that the initiative would backfire as the US-led crackdown on alleged terrorism would simply create new problems and fuel existing tensions in the region. That is precisely what has happened.

As life in the desert has become more difficult, especially in the wake of the droughts of the 1970s and 1980s and the Tuareg rebellions in both Niger and Mali in the 1990s, the region's nomadic and semi-nomadic pastoralists have become increasingly dependent for their livelihoods on tourism. However, it has been tourism, more than any other component of local livelihoods, that has been decimated by the US's launch of its 'second front' in its 'Global War on Terror' (GWOT) across the Sahara-Sahel. It has impoverished many households and forced many local people to seek their livelihoods through 'semi-criminal' activities, such as various smuggling activities. In times of impoverishment, people resort to desperate means. As Amadou Bocoum, deputy chairman of the Mali government's commission to combat the proliferation of small arms, told the UN's regional news network (IRIN) in 2004: 'cigarette, fuel and weapon smuggling is carried out by the population (especially the desert nomads) and it is difficult to consider them as bandits as it is their only source of income and allows them to survive.'[16]

Furthermore, the view of many senior personages in the region was that the impact of the PSI was more likely to attract terrorists than dispel them. Hervé Ludovic de Lys, for instance, head of the UN's West African Office for the Coordination of Humanitarian Affairs (OCHA), expressed the fear that the local peoples' anger at the crackdown on their livelihoods could be exploited by terrorists hiding in the desert. '[Terrorist] Groups taking refuge in barely-controllable areas could easily take advantage of the frustration of the Toubous and Tuaregs', he said.[17] Similar sentiments were expressed by Aboubacrim ag Hindi, professor of law at the University of Bamako, who told IRIN that 'the biggest danger in this region is not al-Qaeda. It is famine. If the development of these zones is not undertaken, we may see more rebellion.'[18] His fears, as we shall see later, have become horribly true.

Almost all residents in the Sahara-Sahel region seemed to recognise that the region's increased impoverishment was such that if groups associated with al-Qaeda did come into it, they would quite likely find local level support if they were able to provide resources. Local peoples' awareness of this possibility made them additionally resentful of the US 'invasion', which they saw as concentrating on little more than military counterterrorism training, rather than the actual development of the region. As time has moved on, the residents of the Sahara-Sahel have been able to see for themselves that Washington's public statements about the PSI's successor, the Trans-Sahara Counterterrorism Initiative (see below), being a 'broader package, interagency approach', in which 'USAID [US Agency for International Development] would address educational issues; the State Department, airport security; and the Department of Treasury, efforts to tighten up money-handling controls in the region', were nothing more than the propaganda that has come to surround much of the US's contemporary security-development discourse.[19]

Local people were also well aware of world news and thus able to relate the activities of the US forces in their own region to the chaos that US forces were creating in Iraq and elsewhere in the Middle East. They did not want their own part of the world to follow suit. Unfortunately, it has.

It is particularly pertinent that the PSI coincided with the worst locust plagues to blight the Sahel for at least 15 years. With chronic food shortages imminent, West African leaders tried to impress on Washington that the locust invasion should also be treated like a war, as its capacity for the destruction of human life, as one of them told IRIN, 'was far greater than that of the worst conflicts'. And as another Sahelian resident remarked, voicing the views of many: 'If the US had spent the same [money] on locust control as on terrorist control, we would not have this imminent loss of life.'[20]

The Trans-Sahara Counterterrorism Initiative

Eighteen months after the launch of the PSI, Washington expanded its scope to include five more countries, namely Tunisia, Algeria, Morocco, Senegal and, most significantly, Nigeria in what it called the Trans-Sahara Counterterrorism Initiative (TSCTI). Through the TSCTI, Washington succeeded in joining the two oil-rich sides of the Sahara together 'in a complex of security arrangements whose architecture', as Stephen Ellis remarked, 'was American'.[21]

The TSCTI, with a proposed budget of $100 million a year over five years, was officially launched in June 2005 through Operation Flintlock, a two-stage military exercise involving almost 1,000 US troops, mostly Special Operations forces, training about 3,000 African soldiers. The first stage involved twelve-man US Special Forces teams conducting infantry training with African units in Chad, Mauritania, Mali, Niger and Algeria. Training, according to EUCOM's spokesperson Major Holly Silkman,[22] included live-fire rifle marksmanship, first aid, border patrol and airborne operations, human rights and the laws of land warfare. For US forces to be teaching 'human rights' is something of an anachronism, as was soon to become apparent (see Chapter 6, this volume) in the war crimes committed by Niger's forces against the Tuareg civilian population during the Tuareg rebellion of

2007–09. In the second stage, officials from all nine countries participated in a 'command post exercise' in which they had to work together in solving a terrorism scenario.

Operation Flintlock was not welcomed by local people for a number of reasons. The first and most obvious reason was that by 2005, anti-American sentiment was widespread across Muslim countries. Even in the remote corners of the Sahara, local people were not only fully aware of and angered by the chaos, disruptions, torture and other atrocities that accompanied the US invasion and occupation of Iraq, but they had already experienced 18 months of the PSI, during which their own lands had been turned into a new front in the GWOT.

In addition to this broad anti-US sentiment, Operation Flintlock was greeted with widespread suspicion, one might say cynicism, by most of the region's population, as well as some security analysts, because of the coincidence of its timing with an alleged terrorist attack on a military garrison at Lemgheity in the remote north-eastern corner of Mauritania in which 17 Mauritanian soldiers were killed. I shall say more about this attack in the next chapter. For the moment, let me simply give the summary details. These are that Operation Flintlock was launched on 6 June, precisely two days after the attack on Lemgheity. Straight away, the Mauritanian President, Maaouya Ould Sid'Ahmed Taya (who was to be overthrown in a military coup d'état two months later) and US military spokespersons attributed the attack to GSPC terrorists, with US military and government spokespersons immediately citing the attack as justification for both the TSCTI and Operation Flintlock. However, by this time, more than two years after El Para had come on the scene, local people had become cynically aware of the pattern of fabricated terrorist incidents in the region being used to justify further security actions such as the PSI and TSCTI, as well as crackdowns on legitimate elements of local political opposition. It was therefore not surprising that many local people immediately assumed that the Lemgheity attack was merely another false-flag incident to justify Operation Flintlock and the launch of the TSCTI. They became even angrier as the US persisted in asserting that the Lemgheity attack was the work of the Algerian Groupe Salafiste pour le Prédication et le Combat (GSPC), even when all the evidence pointed to the attack being perpetrated by elements of Mauritania's internal opposition. Indeed, as the next chapter reveals, the claims of both the US and Mauritania's dictatorial President were so banal that even Algeria, Washington's ally, had to step in and point out the absurdity of their claims.

The second reason why Operation Flintlock was not well received by the local population was because the Americans' 'hearts and minds' campaign was noticeable by its absence. In Algeria, for instance, a major *ratissage* (combing/rooting out), to use the Algerian army expression, was undertaken in the area between the main north–south road from Tamanrasset to In Salah and the Malian border. Algerian army commanders gave orders that all nomads should move out of the area between the main road and the Mali frontier – an area roughly half the size of France. Whether the nomads, who at that time of the year probably numbered no more than 400 in that area, mostly in an arc between Ti-m-Meskis and Adrar Ahnet, received this absurd order or paid attention to it is not known. My informants at In Amguel said that it was received with a mixture of wry humour and anger, the latter being prompted by the fact that the construction of the Tamanrasset base had already deprived their neighbouring villagers at Otoul of their water supply and livelihoods.

A third reason for alienating the local people was more sinister. It involved an 'incident' that left many local people wondering whether the Algerians and their US allies had deliberately set up a killing spree for propaganda purposes, or so that the Algerian military could impress their ally of their efficiency in combating the alleged transborder arms trafficking. According to Algerian army sources, information was received that arms traffickers, carrying arms from northern Mali into Algeria, had left Kidal in three four-wheel-drive vehicles and were heading towards the Algerian frontier in the region of Bordj Mokhtar. The vehicles were spotted and attacked by Algerian army helicopters before they reached the border. The three vehicles were destroyed and at least 13 alleged terrorists wiped out. One helicopter was reportedly damaged by rocket fire and one army officer reportedly killed. All the dead terrorists were identified by the Algerian security services as belonging to what they referred to as the 'Taoudeni group', reputedly created by El Para, and consisting of GSPC members from Algeria, along with Malians, Nigeriens and Mauritanians. The report stated that the incident took place during Operation Flintlock,[23] but gave no indication whether anyone other than Algerians were in the helicopters.

According to local informants in northern Mali, the occupants of the vehicles were believed to have been cigarette smugglers not arms traffickers. Furthermore, although the attack was conducted by the Algerian military, local sources stated that US personnel were present in the aircraft. Moreover, the reference to El Para's 'Taoudeni group' smacks of the same sort of disinformation that surrounded El Para's alleged escapades in the region 18 months earlier. Indeed, knowing that all of El Para's band were flushed out of Mali in January 2004, we might well ask whether such a group as this existed, or whether it was merely another fiction of US-Algerian disinformation.

3

REPRESSION AND TERRORISM RENTS

Anti-US sentiment, driven by local peoples' resentment and anger at the impact of the US's 'Global War on Terror' (GWOT) and further fuelled by the almost daily news of the US invasion and subsequent occupation of first Iraq and then Afghanistan, has been widespread across the Sahara-Sahel region since 2003. However, what is perhaps surprising, at least to observers unfamiliar with the region, is that peoples' anger has been directed more against their own regimes than Washington. There have been two main reasons for this. The first and most obvious is that there are few US targets in the region which could be attacked, and those that there are, such as oil companies and the US military, have low visibility and are well protected. I should perhaps also add that anti-Americanism has been directed more at the US state and the Bush administration than either individual Americans, who are nearly always treated with the friendliness and hospitality becoming the peoples of the region, sometimes even with a dash of sympathy for having to suffer 'such an idiot as Bush', as more than one Tuareg described the then most powerful man on earth, or American culture per se. The second and more important reason is because all the regimes in the region, without exception – Morocco, Algeria, Tunisia, Libya, Mauritania, Mali, Niger and Chad – used the opportunity of the GWOT in two very specific and related ways: first, as a pretext to crack down on almost all forms of opposition; second, as a form of rent extraction. Let me explain each in turn.

The Repression of Opposition

All regimes in North Africa and the Sahel, at least prior to the Arab Spring, were characterised by their repressive and authoritarian nature. The US would like to argue that its presence in the region, notably through its GWOT, has brought security. Sadly, the opposite is true. Until the Arab Spring of 2011, security in the region has been increased only to the extent that the security establishments – the *mukhabarat*[1] – of all the states in the region have been strengthened, thus prolonging and perhaps even entrenching the power and authoritarianism of fundamentally repressive and undemocratic regimes at the expense of weakening, or delaying, both the development of civil society and the security of individuals. The GWOT has been used by all regimes in the region to repress and silence legitimate political opposition by labelling it or linking it with 'terrorism', 'putative terrorism' (to use an Americanism) or Islamic extremism (a euphemism for 'terrorism'). Even Cold War rhetoric has found its way back into the fray with elements of the US's religious right referring to the present-day Polisario[2] as 'Communists'!

With the possible exception of Algeria, whose 'dirty war' of the 1990s between the state's security forces and alleged Islamic extremists is still continuing,[3] Mauritania is the North African country in which the GWOT has been most extensively used as a pretext to eliminate popular opposition to authoritarian rule. Between the launch of the GWOT in 2003 and his overthrow in a coup d'état in August 2005, Mauritania's dictatorial President Maaouya Ould Sid'Ahmed Taya went to absurd lengths, even to the point of embarrassing Washington, in using the GWOT to suppress legitimate civil opposition. To few peoples' surprise, Taya was overthrown by his own security chief, Colonel Ely Ould Mohamed Vall, in August 2005. Vall returned the country to democratic rule in 2007 under the elected President, Sidi Ould Sheikh Abdallahi. However, it took barely a year for President Abdallahi to be ousted by another military coup. The country's new ruler, General Mohamed Ould Abdel Aziz, first as leader of the August 2008 coup and its subsequent military junta, and then as 'elected' President, has also followed in Taya's footsteps of maximising the supposed threat of Islamic extremism to legitimise the strengthening of his *mukhabarat* and to endear himself to the West. One consequence of Anglo-French support for Abdel Aziz's fight against al-Qaeda in the Islamic Maghreb, especially since July 2010 and as described in subsequent chapters, has been to galvanise jihadist elements in the country.

Mauritania has a long history of political repression. Having himself seized power in a coup in 1984, Ould Taya's subsequent 21-year rule was characterised by the growth of increasingly widespread, legitimate opposition. Three issues had come to underpin much of the opposition to Taya's rule. The first, as noted in a report three months before his overthrow, was that 'Virtually all the main revenue-generating positions in the public administration are held by the President's relatives. Other people and clans, including the security sector, are frustrated and want their share of power and resources.'[4] It was estimated that around 20–25 per cent of the government budget was being misappropriated. Second, successive post-independence governments had perpetuated the country's deep-rooted racial, ethnic and tribal cleavages. Mass violence against Black African Mauritanians especially has been flagrant. By the time of Taya's overthrow, around 100,000 Black Africans had been thrown out of the country, with non-governmental organisations having reported hundreds of extra-judicial executions, assassinations and 'disappearances'. Third, Taya's embrace of the US at the end of the 1990s and his inauguration of diplomatic ties with Israel had made him unpopular both at home and abroad, and especially amongst prospective Islamist movements whose criticisms had been met with increasingly repressive measures.

On top of these long-running issues, opposition to Taya intensified after 2003 as a result of the way in which he used his support from the US and his role as a 'frontline' ally in the GWOT to crack down and imprison both an ever-increasing number of Islamists, whom he tried to demonise as being part of the al-Qaeda network, and a widening and legitimate popular opposition on the basis that they were either members of or linked in some way to the Algerian terrorist Groupe Salafiste pour le Prédication et le Combat (GSPC). In 2007, the GSPC was renamed al-Qaeda in the Islamic Maghreb (AQIM). The fact that recruitment to it since the name-change appears to have been more prolific in Mauritania owes much to Taya's legacy.

Taya's pro-US and anti-Islamist tactics generated a seemingly unusual alliance, albeit perhaps temporary, between reformists in Mauritania's armed services and Islamists who together came to form a Mauritanian opposition group known as Les Cavaliers du Changement (Knights of Change). Indeed, there is good reason to believe that this alliance may have been behind the attack on the Lemgheity garrison in north-eastern Mauritania on 3–4 June 2005 which, as mentioned in the previous chapter, so conveniently preceded the start of Operation Flintlock two days later.

The Attack on Mauritania's Lemgheity Garrison

The Lemgheity garrison is some 500 kilometres to the east-north-east of Zouerate, in the extreme north-east of Mauritania, close to the Algerian and northern Mali borders. On the night of Friday 3 June and Saturday 4 June, it came under attack from what the Mauritanian authorities described as 150 well-armed members of the GSPC. Seventeen Mauritanian soldiers were killed and several more wounded. According to the Mauritanian military authorities, at least five attackers were killed.

Given the known level of opposition to Ould Taya's regime at that time, the attack could just as well have been organised by Les Cavaliers du Changement as the GSPC. Indeed, the evidence, fragmentary though it is, does point in that direction. However, it was far more convenient (and much less embarrassing!) for both Taya and the US, whose intervention in the Sahara-Sahel was being legitimised by the alleged activities of the GSPC, to attribute the attack to the GSPC.

It was therefore perhaps not surprising that the Mauritanian authorities almost immediately confirmed that it was the GSPC who had undertaken the attack. Incriminatory evidence against the GSPC, cited by the authorities, included an alleged admission on the GSPC's website (of extremely dubious authenticity) that they were responsible for the attack; the identification of two of the dead attackers, namely Abdel Aziz, a dentist from Oran, and

Abdel Khadim, the group's alleged explosives expert, as being the 'lieutenants' of the GSPC's chief, Mokhtar ben Mokhtar (MBM),[5] and the 'pillars and *emirs*' of his movement; and vehicle registration papers in the name of MBM found in one of the attackers' vehicles.

According to the Mauritanian army, this evidence left no doubt that the attackers were the GSPC. In fact, it raised a whole host of doubts. The authenticity of the website could not be verified, nor the identity of the dead attackers, while the proposition that one of the Sahara's most successful alleged terrorists would actually leave registration papers in his name in a vehicle was derisory. Moreover, the implication made by the Mauritanians that the attackers were not only GSPC but had come from Algeria also rather stretched the imagination in that Algeria's security in that corner of their country was so tight that it is unlikely that such a large convey could have passed undetected.

Ould Taya's rush to blame the GSPC for the Lemgheity attack on the basis of such feeble evidence was embarrassing even to the Algerians, who felt obliged to release a report in *Le Quotidien d'Oran* through a journalist known to be well-connected with the Algerian military and its Département du Renseignement et de la Sécurité (DRS), which distanced both Algeria and MBM from the Mauritanian claims.[6] 'MBM', said the journalist, 'is currently not in Mauritania [but] at Djelfa, in the region of Boukhil, to the north of Ghardaia, his natal region.' The article also added that, 'according to former, repentant members of MBM's group, Belmokhtar [as he is also known] has no interest in attacking the Mauritanians, as it is the one zone where *salafistes* can still move around freely'. Even more surprisingly, the report directly quoted the Algerian security services as confirming that MBM's group did not exceed 30. As the attack was undertaken by a group five times that size, the Algerian article concluded that it must have been undertaken by 'Mauritanian Islamists'.

There were no hidden meanings in the Algerian article. Its message was very clear: 'We know that MBM is elsewhere, and we have El Para in our hands. Therefore, as the GSPC has no other leaders in the Sahara at the moment, an attack of this size could not be their work.' It went even further, saying that 'an alternative hypothesis of an armed autonomous Mauritanian group, such as the Cavaliers du Changement, is strangely missing from official Mauritanian theses.' It then offered a more plausible thesis as to who might have undertaken the attack by reminding readers that after the previous year's attempted coup against Taya, a few of the coup leaders, mutineers and officers in his own army, had sought refuge in the north of Mauritania and in Burkina Faso. It is quite conceivable, so the article suggested, 'that the Lemgheity garrison could have been taken over by these mutineers who had established an alliance over the course of the previous year or two with Islamists within Mauritania'. The article even went so far as to say that 'all military experts know full well that a successful attack of this calibre could not be accomplished without the active complicity of troops inside the garrison'. This thesis was supported by the fact that the attackers, according to local witnesses, not only spoke Hassania, the local language of north-eastern Mauritania, but showed a familiarity with the layout of the garrison.

Algeria was saying that the attack was an inside affair of disaffected former army officers and mutineers allied with Mauritanian 'Islamists', terms which in Mauritania were synonymous with 'opposition' to the regime.

But was Algeria protesting too much? Perhaps. A short while later, a local Mauritanian reporter in Nouakchott, Mauritania's capital, told me that he had interviewed eyewitnesses from Lemgheity who were adamant that they had seen Algerian helicopters over-flying the attack.

On 3 August, precisely two months after the Lemgheity attack, Ould Taya was overthrown while out of the country attending the funeral of Saudi Arabia's late King Fahd. The coup, led by his chief of police, Ely Ould Mohamed Vall, was peaceful and involved no loss of life. It is widely believed that Vall received the nod from the US administration, which had been increasingly embarrassed and was becoming concerned by Taya's exaggeration of the Islamist threat and his increasingly repressive crackdowns on legitimate opposition to his dictatorial rule.

The Tamanrasset Riots of July 2005

Five weeks after the attack on Lemgheity, Tamanrasset, the capital of Algeria's extreme south, literally 'went up in smoke', as rioters razed many of the town's commercial buildings and government offices. To understand what lay behind these riots and their timing, I must explain briefly the state of affairs that had been developing in Algeria's extreme south since El Para's appearance on the scene in 2003.

Although Algeria's Tuareg population does not number much more than 40,000–50,000, their traditional territory covers some 20 per cent of Algerian national territory. Thus, although the Algerian government has nothing to fear from its Tuareg population in a numerical sense, it has never fully comprehended the nature – socially, politically and ethnically – of its 'Great South', and has always felt slightly queasy about a 'Berber problem' in the form of Tuareg disaffection and possibly even rebellion. The launch of the GWOT through the Algerian Sahara in 2003 consequently generated an increasingly contradictory situation in the south. While Algeria has always feared some sort of Tuareg trouble in its extreme south, its strategy, especially in the wake of the launch of the Saharan front in the GWOT in 2003, was to provoke amongst its Tuareg population the sort of civil unrest and perhaps even open rebellion that it had previously feared. The logic was quite clear: by destabilising and increasing the insecurity of the region, Algeria would not only be helping its new US ally in its promotion of the Sahara-Sahel as a 'Terror Zone', but would also be legitimising its own increased militarisation of the country's extreme south and, in so doing, would also be increasing its terrorism rents from the US.

The profoundly complex political situation that existed in southern Algeria at the time of the launch of the GWOT in the region goes beyond the scope of this book and has been described elsewhere.[7] Suffice it to say that by the time the hostages began disappearing in 2003, Algeria's security services were well established in the region, with the result that societal expressions of and demands for greater democracy were being repressed with impunity. The local population, especially Tuareg, had perceived for some time that the government's increasingly provocative actions against them were part of a deliberate strategy to generate unrest throughout southern Algeria. Indeed, as early as 2001, before the GWOT, the citizens of Tamanrasset had written a most prescient letter to President Bouteflika complaining about the *wali*'s[8] behaviour and warning the President that 'if he did not intervene there was likely to be an explosion of popular anger, the outcome of which could not be predicted'.[9]

Following the launch of the Saharan front in the GWOT and the US's overt support for Algeria's *mukhabarat* state, local people, especially the Tuareg, noticed how the Algerian authorities in the extreme south became more openly confident in their abuse of power. One prominent local citizen expressed the views of many when he said: 'Now that they [the Algerian authorities] have the Americans behind them, they have become even bigger bullies.'[10] For example: corruption, especially through the embezzlement of local authority funds, became more brazen;[11] the repression of the population, especially crackdowns on those elements of civil society that were expressing concern for human rights and democratic organisation, as well as the harassment of individuals who could be seen as potential opposition spokesmen, became more widespread, while the secret police became more pervasive, more visible and open in their actions and less observant of due legal process.

The increase in the repression of civil society that accompanied the US launch of its 'War on Terror' was not limited to the extreme south. Indeed, since 2003, almost every town in the Algerian Sahara had experienced varying outbreaks of unrest and rioting. The civil riots that overwhelmed Tamanrasset in July 2005 were therefore not entirely unprecedented and certainly not unexpected. In fact, the most interesting question is why the town had not erupted earlier. The answer is that the Tuareg had long suspected the government authorities of trying to provoke such a response and had been urging restraint.

So, why did Tamanrasset erupt on 10 July 2005? The date, of course, is not without significance. Coming only five weeks after the Lemgheity attack and an even shorter time after Operation Flintlock, it provided Washington with further proof, if any more was needed, that the Sahara, to quote EUCOM's (US European Command's) military commanders, was 'uncontrolled', 'ungoverned', full of 'bad people' and 'a base for al-Qaeda'. A seemingly peaceful demonstration relating to grievances over the high level of unemployment turned, within a matter of minutes, into a rampaging, rioting mob. The rioting, which continued for two days, was unparalleled amongst other Saharan riots for its violence against state and public property. Numerous government offices, along with other symbols of the state, as well as some 40 premises in the commercial centre, including the main market, were attacked, with many looted and then set on fire. The town really did go up in smoke!

An estimated 150 youths, nearly all Tuareg were immediately gaoled. The townspeople, especially the Tuareg, were furious, demanding that the youths be freed on the grounds that they had been provoked into rioting by the police. The court responded by sitting in closed session under heavy security. The surrounding streets were cleared and no one was allowed to attend the hearings at which 64 youths were given prison sentences and the remainder a range of fines averaging €60.

Evidence was eventually brought before the court proving that the riots, as the Tuareg had claimed all along, had indeed been whipped up and directed by police agents provocateurs. The court had no choice but to free the 64 imprisoned youths immediately.

While that may have been the end of the matter as far as most local people were concerned, there was an even bigger twist to the tail. While the riots provided the Americans with further very timely 'proof' that the Sahara was full of 'putative terrorists', the timing of the riots was impeccable for an even more extraordinary reason. Investigations by local Tuareg had already revealed that it had been the police agents provocateurs who had singled out and targeted the government offices that were burnt. But it was not until later that I and my Tuareg friends made further discoveries. We learnt that the offices that had been singled out for arson were those containing the financial archives which contained the evidence of embezzlement by senior state officials. We also learnt that the riots coincided with the arrival in Tamanrasset of a team from the procurator fiscal's office reportedly sent from Algiers to investigate the *wilaya*'s accounts. Why the procurator fiscal should want to investigate Tamanrasset's accounts at that precise moment in time – in the middle of summer – is explained in the next chapter.

Libya's Crackdown on the Regime's Opponents

Even states that were not as closely allied to the US as Mauritania and Algeria were quick to make use of the GWOT to repress their domestic opposition. Libya is a case in point. A jihadist movement calling itself the Libyan Islamic Fighting Group (LIFG) had emerged in Libya in the 1980s, but was more or less wiped out during the mass arrests of suspected Islamist opponents in 1989. However, it re-emerged again in the 1990s, largely as a result of the experience gained by those Libyans who had fought the Soviets in Afghanistan.[12] On discovering the existence of the LIFG in 1995, Colonel Gaddafi launched a brutal and repressive campaign to liquidate his militant opponents as well as the more moderate strands of underground Islamist opposition that had also developed across the country. By 1998 the regime had succeeded in effectively nullifying the LIFG as well as other Islamist groups.[13] Nevertheless, Libya, like all other North African and Sahelian countries, was not going to miss out on the opportunities presented by the GWOT to strengthen its domestic intelligence and security apparatus – the *mukhabarat* – and to justify crackdowns on internal opposition in the name of fighting international terrorism.[14] The Libyan regime, as the Libyan expert Alison Pargeter noted, was assisted in its attempts to prevent a Libyan Islamist opposition from re-emerging by the willingness of Western governments, notably the US and the UK, to designate the LIFG as a terrorist organisation and to open the way for suspected members of the organisation to be returned to Tripoli.[15]

Extracting Terrorism Rents: The Niger Example

In the Sahelian states of Niger and Mali, where Islamism was marginal and where there was no terrorism in the conventional meaning of the term[16] prior to El Para's arrival, governments have had to be a little more ingenious in extracting their terrorism rents, in the form of US military and financial largesse. The ingenuity to which I refer has taken the form of provoking opposition elements of one sort or another into demonstrations of civil unrest or even taking up arms, so enabling Washington's semanticists to morph 'traffickers', 'rebels', 'bandits' and 'criminals' into 'putative terrorists' and so brand the region as an 'ungoverned area, ... the sort of place where terrorists can hide' – in short, the banana-shaped 'Terror Zone' that is now marked indelibly on Pentagon maps. The victims of these exercises, not surprisingly, have been the already marginalised minority populations, notably the Tuareg.

While there have been incidents of such 'ethnic provocation' in all the Sahelian states, they have been most pronounced in Niger and Mali, two of the world's poorest countries and therefore especially appreciative of American largesse. By the end of 2007, both countries, which had been the least able in the region to excite the Americans with any significant Islamist activity, were engulfed in Tuareg rebellions. But long before then, both governments had earmarked their marginalized Tuareg populations as the means to the acquisition of 'terrorism rents'. If either of these countries is to be singled out as the 'worst offender', it is Niger, at least until President Tandja was deposed in February 2010.

Four weeks after the official launch of the Pan-Sahel Initiative (PSI), the Nigerien government accused a prominent Tuareg, Rhissa ag Boula, of complicity in the killing of Adam Amangué, a young member of the ruling MNSD (Mouvement National pour la Société du Développement)-Nassara Party,[17] at the village of Tchighazérine (40 kilometres north-west of Agades). In the 1990s Tuareg rebellion in Niger, Rhissa had taken over as the leader of the Front de Libération de l'Azawak et de l'Aïr (FLAA) following the death in 1995 of Mano Dayak. Rhissa was accordingly the FLAA's signatory to the 1995 Peace Accord that marked the formal end of the Tuareg rebellion in Niger. As part of the post-rebellion reintegration process, Rhissa was appointed Minister of Tourism and Crafts.

Local people regarded the murder as most uncharacteristic, describing the three bullets in his head and two in his stomach as a 'mafia-style' killing. Rhissa, who denied any involvement in the murder, was dismissed as minister on 12 February 2004. Three days later he was arrested and taken into detention in a move that many people believed was designed to provoke the Tuareg into taking up arms so that the government could secure more military aid from the US.

The move had the desired effect of increasing the political tension amongst the Tuareg, especially in the traditional Tuareg stronghold of the Aïr mountains. During the course of the summer, the region experienced an escalation of banditry, for which Rhissa's brother, Mohamed ag Boula, reportedly claimed responsibility. That was enough for the Niger government to send some 150 troops into Aïr in September in a move that many thought would ignite a new Tuareg rebellion. However, the troops, recently trained by the US as part of its PSI, were ambushed by the Tuareg, with at least one soldier killed, four wounded and four taken hostage. RFI (Radio France Internationale) subsequently carried an interview with Rhissa's brother in which he said that he was leading a 200-strong group which was fighting to defend the rights of the Tuareg, Tubu and Semori nomadic populations of northern Niger, and that he was personally responsible for the ambush.

Northern Aïr remained tense and effectively cordoned off from the outside world throughout the winter months of 2004–05, but without any further serious incidents, due largely to Tuareg restraint and the good offices of Libya's Leader, Mouamar Gaddafi, who secured the release of the Niger soldiers on 8 February. On 4 March, Rhissa was released after 13 months in prison and without any charges being brought against him.

Rhissa immediately sought to negotiate an amnesty for those Tuareg who had taken up arms. Tuareg leaders assumed that this would be readily forthcoming. 'Granting amnesties', a former rebel leader explained to me, 'is something in which the Niger government is experienced!' They were therefore surprised and angry on hearing from their negotiators that the talks had become blocked as a result of the intervention of what the negotiators referred to as 'American advisors' whom, they believed, were angling for a show of force against the rebels to validate the expansion of the PSI into the Trans-Sahara Counterterrorism Initiative (TSCTI). With the Lemgheity attack so conveniently timed for the launch of Operation Flintlock, a conflict with Tuareg rebels-turned-terrorists would have put the icing on the cake in terms of convincing the outside world that the TSCTI region really was a terrorist zone.

The amnesty was finally negotiated in mid summer thanks again to Gaddafi's intervention. What perplexed the Tuareg leadership most about these negotiations was that France, which had hitherto always assisted them in such negotiations, played no part in the proceedings. Their negotiators believed this was because France was becoming increasingly anxious about the labour unrest being generated by the activities in Niger of two of its biggest companies and might soon be more than grateful for the protection afforded by America's military presence. COGEMA (Compagnie Générale des Matières Nucléaires) of the AREVA Group, which is the major shareholder and operator of Niger's uranium mines, was being accused by its workers of causing extensive damage to both the environment and their health and also blocking scientific and medical investigations. Indeed, AREVA, as Chapter 7 explains, became a focal issue in the Tuareg rebellion that began in 2007. Veolia Environnement, formerly known as Vivendi Environnement, is not so well known. Veolia at that time, however, was the world's largest water company, with an extensive track record of questionable environmental practices and accompanying lawsuits. Through the arrangement of World Bank loans, Veolia had become the 51 per cent shareholder in a newly privatised company that controlled 100 per cent of Niger's water sector. Its steep hikes in water prices, in what is one of the world's poorest nations, were threatening widespread unrest.

As we shall see in subsequent chapters, France had very good reasons to be anxious about the anger and resistance that was developing, especially amongst the Tuareg, towards the exploitative practices of its companies in Niger, and was certainly not going to rock Washington's boat.

With the US now directing its 'foreign aid' into the militarisation of Africa,[18] and with Niger provoking sufficient unrest amongst its Tuareg minority to ensure further US backing, it came as no surprise when, in late 2004, the Nigerien government announced a 150 per cent expansion of its army, from 4,000 to 10,000 soldiers, between 2004 and 2008 and a 100 per cent expansion of its paramilitary police force from 2,000 to 4,000. Two years later, on 6 April 2006, the Nigerien government announced the creation of two new army battalions, one to work on ECOWAS (Economic Community of West African States) missions and the other to fight terrorism. As we shall see in Chapters 6 and 7, these troops were soon to excel in terrorising the Tuareg civilian population in the Agades region.

4

FOOTING THE BILL: DID THE WORLD BANK FUND STATE TERRORISM?

The Tamanrasset riots of July 2005, like much of the civil unrest in most of Algeria's other Sahara towns around that time, along with the Lemgheity attack in Mauritania, the provocation of the Niger Tuareg to take up arms and the Tuareg rebellion in Mali in May 2006, which is explained in the next chapter, were all engineered or manipulated in one way or another by the countries' regimes to help justify the maintenance of Washington's Sahara-Sahel front in the 'Global War on Terror' (GWOT).

For all that, it is the twist in the tale of the Tamanrasset riots, namely that Algeria's secret police used them to destroy financial evidence, that provides me with the peg on which to hang this chapter – really as a separate story within a story.

For the reader preferring to stay with the main narrative, skip this chapter. For those who want a cameo insight into the workings of Algeria's regime, read on!

How was El Para Financed?

The narrative of El Para's activities in the Sahara, from the time of his abduction of 32 European tourists in the Algerian Sahara to their eventual release in Mali, followed by his sojourn in Mali and subsequent chase by a combined military operation across Niger into the Tibesti mountains of Chad all of which I described in *The Dark Sahara* – until his reported return to Algeria at the end of October 2004, was a period of some 20 months.

If, as all the evidence presented in *The Dark Sahara* suggests, El Para was a Département du Renseignement et de la Sécurité (DRS) agent, we are faced with the question of how the orchestration and management of such a prolonged and complex operation was financed. Whether the entire operation was planned in advance is another question altogether. I am inclined to think that it would have been impossible to plan for such an intricate and complex series of scenarios from the outset, and that the narrative of *The Dark Sahara* can best be understood through what I think of as 'flip-flop' theory: the way most governments, corporates and other such agencies deal with many, perhaps most, of the situations in which they find themselves. Plans are made to get from A to B, but things don't go quite according to plan and so they finish instead at Bi. At Bi, they reassess the situation and make a plan to move to C, which, like so many things in life, runs into an unknown that takes them to Ci instead; and so on, until, in El Para's case, they find a manageable and plausible exit strategy which allegedly retrieves El Para back to Algeria.

I do not know how much this duplicitous affair would have cost. Nor does the precise sum, which would have been several million euros or dollars, really matter, as the entire El Para operation from start to finish, could easily have been financed from Algeria's murky coffers. Indeed, with the knowledge that I have acquired over the years of the nature and extent of Algeria's corruption (see Chapter 14), especially amongst its higher echelons, and the country's internal mechanisms of money laundering, it is quite evident that the covert disbursement of a few extra millions would have been an almost trivial matter.

Nevertheless, it was essential that such a politically dangerous and sensitive operation be kept absolutely top secret. Few people beyond Mohamed Mediène, the head of the DRS, his second-in-command, Smaïn Lamari (now dead), and perhaps a very small handful of their fellow officers, are likely to have known its details. Over the subsequent years, my research has led me to believe that this 'handful' could have been very small indeed. For example, evidence acquired in 2008, five years after the hostage-takings, has now led me to believe that even the head of the DRS in Tamanrasset (now retired) may not have been 'in the loop'. Those behind the operation would have gone to great lengths to avoid any paper trails or clues that could be picked up by their political enemies, the procurator fiscal's office or other alert state officials, not all of whom are enamoured with the ways of the DRS. In short, to cover their tracks, the DRS would almost certainly have arranged to have a reasonable stash of secret funds available 'on site' and 'off budget', as they are known to do with most of their 'black operations'.

We will, of course, never know precisely how the El Para operation was financed, or to what amount. All I can offer, by way of insight, is the following story, which, bearing in mind that truth is often stranger than fiction, first came to my attention on 10 March 2003. By extraordinary coincidence, that was also the day that I heard the first anxious phone calls from Germany enquiring about missing friends and relatives in the Algerian Sahara. At that moment, neither I nor anyone else, except of course those within the Algerian DRS who had planned the operation, knew that they had been taken hostage, or that the funds that I first heard about on 10 March were possibly being used to finance their capture.

GEF–UNDP Funding

The money I am referring to, some $20 million of World Bank–United Nations Development Programme (UNDP) funding, first came to public attention on 10 March 2003. The announcement of its existence was made in almost complete secrecy at the end of a discrete conference in Djanet.[1] I thought I had misheard the UNDP representative, Paolo Lembo, as he mentioned the figure, almost as a muffled afterthought. Local people to whom I turned for clarification had no idea what the announcement was about, nor were they given the opportunity of questioning or discussing it.

When the conference was over, the local Tuareg said little about the $20 million. Most of those whom I spoke to in Djanet later that day assumed they had misheard or misunderstood. If the UNDP and World Bank really had intended $20 million to be spent on the region's development, surely, so they argued, they would have been consulted, or at least have had some knowledge of it. That was also the view of my small group of Tuareg friends with whom I flew back from Djanet to Tamanrasset later that night. As the weeks went by, a number of things began to reveal themselves. The first was that we were able to check Lembo's statement and confirm that the UNDP and World Bank were indeed making such funds available to the region. The second was that local people soon became increasingly suspicious that the abduction of 32 European tourists was the work of Algeria's DRS. The third was that local people, including local businessmen and other prominent members of civil society, could find absolutely no trace of these funds.

As the year progressed, we began to wonder if there was a connection between our inability to find any public record of some $20 million of development aid funds and the emerging belief that the government was fabricating largely fictitious 'terrorist' actions across the region. Were they related? Was it possible that UNDP and World Bank funds were perhaps being secretly channelled into DRS state terrorism activities?

Some months after the Djanet conference, my Tuareg friends and I made a plan. We decided that they would try and trace where the funds were being held, which persons and/or local organisations were associated with any of the fund's projects and how the money was being spent. I, in turn, would work from the other end, seeing how the UNDP and World Bank became involved in funding some sort of development programme or projects in this part of Algeria. In fact, if I am to be entirely honest, I did very little work compared to my Tuareg colleagues. This was because I soon discovered that a colleague, Dina Giurovich, a consultant with specialist knowledge and experience of the UNDP, had already paved the way for me.[2] Her suspicions had been raised before mine, and while I was able to give her insights into certain Algerian organisations, she had already done much of the groundwork, going back as far as the Earth Summit in Rio de Janeiro in 1992.

Rio will be remembered for turning the philosophy of sustainable development into a global buzzword. Following Rio, the World Bank set up a special fund, the Global Environmental

Facility (GEF) to allocate financial assistance to countries that showed their willingness to comply with the new international charter in matters of biodiversity conservation and environmental policies. In the next few years, most Third World countries created specialised Ministries of the Environment and became signatories to the related protocols and charters. As a parallel process, the 1990s saw the World Bank pursuing its own socio-economic agenda of putting 'poverty alleviation' at the top of its priorities.

Because international organisations cooperate in the design and implementation of development projects, their agendas have tended to coincide, resulting in a number of hybrids. Sustainable development, in particular, came to pervade every aspect of the agendas of national and international development agencies in the context of the fight against poverty. Other international organisations had their own input in their search for activities that were both respectful of the environment and able to generate revenues for impoverished populations: The UN Educational, Scientific and Cultural Organisation (UNESCO) introduced the heritage dimension, while the World Tourism Organisation (WTO) pushed its own agenda, arguing that tourism was the fastest growing industry in the world.

The result was that 'sustainable tourism' – that is, low-impact forms of tourism like 'cultural tourism' and 'ecotourism' – were presented as the panacea for poverty alleviation, while ensuring the preservation of the natural and cultural heritage. It was (and still is) assumed that properly controlled tourism development would create jobs, stimulate private sector investment and donor assistance, build local support for environment and heritage conservation and reinforce cooperation between neighbouring countries.[3] Since the end of the 1990s, almost every international development organisation has set up either framework programmes or action plans for the sustainable development of tourism, a move facilitated by the fact that tourism is not a sectoral activity but one that cuts across a large variety of social, economic and cultural domains.

That was the explicit philosophy that underlay two post-Rio development plans for the Algerian Sahara. However, unlike most less-developed countries (LDCs), Algeria did not rush down the Rio route. It watched and waited, noting that many of the earlier plans were characterised by bureaucratic bottlenecks, corruption and the manipulation of development plans to serve hidden political agendas, with the ultimate outcome frequently being the dispossession of local communities, often by forced displacement, resulting in their economic marginalisation and impoverishment.

Algeria's two plans, namely the UNESCO (2003) pan-Saharan framework plan for tourism development and the related World Bank (GEF)–UNDP (2002) Biodiversity Plan for Algeria's Tassili-n-Ajjer and Ahaggar National Parks, claimed to have learned from these mistakes. However, as the War on Terror has effectively ruined the Sahara's tourism industry, at least for the time being, the UNESCO plan has remained largely academic. The stated aim of the UNDP's Biodiversity Plan was 'to protect the globally significant biological diversity of the region without impairing traditional community needs and lifestyles'. Its underlying assumption was that the biological diversity of the Tassili-n-Ajjer and Ahaggar National Parks and the social and economic livelihoods of their local indigenous communities were under threat from man-related activities: overgrazing, inappropriate agriculture, hunting, pollution, damage to archaeological sites and artefacts, improper development of tourism, inadequate management of the parks, and so on. The plan therefore contained both a biodiversity protection component as well as a strong socio-economic component designed to enhance the income of local peoples through activities that could also be sustained outside the context of tourism, such as handicraft workshops for women, cheese making, the transmission and development of musical traditions, and so on. Some projects were geared more directly towards training for the tourism market, especially as guides.

The main difference between Algeria's two plans for its Saharan regions and many of those devised in the mid 1990s is that they took into account the pressures that civil-society organisations exerted on international development agendas. Unlike the top-down approaches of most previous plans, in which decisions at all stages were taken by national bureaucracies and imposed on local communities with minimal, if any, consultation, both Algerian plans expressed concern for the participation of local communities, recognising the necessity of accommodating local, alternative views of development by fostering consultation with local actors at all levels of the design, planning and implementation of the projects.

While such emphasis on 'good governance' and the participation of civil society was just what the World Bank and the UNDP wanted to hear, it was totally alien to Algeria. The adoption of any international aid-development programme in Algeria would therefore run immediately into two fundamental problems. The first problem, given the country's nationalist and bureaucratic culture, would be how to mediate between the international and local levels. The second would be how to work within a state system that is both very centralised and very corrupt. Algeria's longstanding exclusion and repression of civil society meant that it would be virtually impossible for an organisation such as the UNDP to work with local civil society partners, or for civil society organisations to participate in the programme.

International organisations were familiar with the nature of the Algerian state. Indeed, the World Bank was aware that the Middle East and North Africa had larger 'freedom deficits' than other regions in the world and had even produced a document called 'Better Governance for Development in the Middle East and North Africa'. It outlined a comprehensive programme to enhance both the participation of all sectors of society in the political process as well as the accountability of the decision-makers. Thus, in line with the World Bank's recommendations, the UNDP plan for Algeria's 'Great South' included not only greater decentralisation but a 'governance component' that would ensure the participation of civil society organisations alongside plans for the complete reorganisation of the management of the Tassili-n-Ajjer and Ahaggar National Parks. 'Good governance' meant such things as greater transparency in the management of various decision-making institutions, greater participation by individual citizens and civil society organisations, more equitable rights, an independent judiciary and the greater accountability of elites, especially in the fight against corruption and the removal of government from business.

The Fondation de Deserts du Monde

The Algerian regime was fully aware of these requirements and knew they were the antithesis of its own repressive and fundamentally undemocratic rule. It therefore set out to hoodwink the World Bank and the UNDP by setting up a mechanism that would simply give the appearance of good governance. Its strategy was to create a new civil society partner for the UNDP, the Fondation de Deserts du Monde, to manage the project at all levels of consultation and implementation.

In practice, the Fondation was nothing more than a state-created and managed non-governmental organisation (NGO), a substitute for civil society designed to manage all internal consultation with 'civil society' on behalf of the World Bank, UNESCO and the UNDP. The ingenuity of the *Fondation* was the way in which it was inserted into the overall state structure. The UNDP plan was located at the intersection of tourism, environment, cultural heritage and both social and economic development. It therefore required policy planning and institutional arrangements that bridged several normally unrelated domains of public policy. It also required cooperation at three levels: between national administrations, between national and local administrations, and between the public and private sectors. All three of these levels offered opportunities for bottlenecks, the bypassing of the plans' fundamental requirements and, most pertinently, embezzlement.

The Tassili-n-Ajjer and Ahaggar National Parks are inter-nationally famous for their prehistoric rock-art. Indeed, the Tassili-n-Ajjer National Park is a designated UNESCO World Heritage site. Because of the centrality of this rock-art in the UNDP plan, the implementing partner, to whom the money would be directed from the World Bank (GEF) and UNDP, was the Ministry of Culture which, in terms of the principles of the GEF–UNDP funding, would then reallocate the funds to public, private and civil organisations in the *wilayat* involved, namely Tamanrasset and Illizi.

However, this arrangement presented a problem for both parties. On the World Bank–UNDP side, funds could not be allocated to public institutions, such as ministries, while on the Algerian side the principles of the World Bank–UNDP were quite contrary to the Algerian government's uncompromising practice of retaining strict control over all budgets before allocating funds to local organisations. Algeria's problem was compounded by the fact that several ministries saw the chance of getting their hands on the budget. In addition to the Ministry of Culture, both the Ministry of the Environment and the Ministry of Tourism also wanted a share of the funds on the grounds that the plan was as much to do with the environment and tourism as archaeology (that is, culture). It was at this juncture that the state officials seized their opportunity. The Minister of the Environment quickly outmanoeuvred the tourism ministry in establishing an NGO, the Fondation de Deserts du Monde, with himself as its President and with the Fondation being presented to the World Bank and the UNDP as the representation of civil society. Through this ingenious ruse, the Fondation became the conduit for the receipt and allocation of most of the GEF–UNDP funds.

The Fondation thus established itself as the major civil society partner at all levels of consultation and implementation in the GEF–UNDP plans, presenting itself to the World Bank and the UN as the legitimate expression of civil society. It cloaked itself in the discourse of 'sustainable development', punctuating its public pronouncements with all the right buzzwords such as 'governance', 'participation', 'consultation', and so on, in advocating 'the needs for proximity, delegation and decentralization in any action taken ...' and in 'giving desert peoples ... the possibility of defending their own interests ... with one voice'.

'One voice', of course, was the Fondation. While providing the World Bank and the UNDP with the convenience of having to deal with only one single representative of Algerian civil society, it also served the regime by completely excluding civil society from any aspect of the plan, so much so that the citizens of Tamanrasset and Djanet knew absolutely nothing about the plan or its various projects. Presumably unbeknown to the World Bank and the UNDP, local people, organisations and prospective local partners, the people who should have been at the very centre of the plan, were totally unaware of it.

The World Bank (GEF) and the UNDP had been kept completely in the dark. With one significant exception, they had been seduced by the discourse and impressed by the region's magnificent rock-art and the image of its global heritage. The exception was Paolo Lembo, the UNDP's representative in Algeria at that time. Lembo saw through the 'scam'. He therefore insisted that there should be more civil society participation in the project in order to achieve greater transparency and far greater computerisation of the Ministry of Justice to give the judiciary more autonomy from the executive. However, Lembo's hands were tied. Not only did the UN seemingly pay no attention to his warnings, but he also encountered strong opposition from the regional administrations in Algeria. The result of Lembo's efforts was that the Algerian government declared him persona non grata and asked Kofi Annan, the UN Secretary-General, to remove him from his post. To the shame of the UN, Lembo was duly accused of exceeding his duties and withdrawn from Algeria, with his successor being instructed to 'remain within the limits of diplomatic protocol', a euphemism for being told to turn a blind eye to Algeria's 'dirty tricks' and corruption. Lembo's last function as the UNDP's representative in Algeria was to make his low-key announcement in Djanet on 10 March 2003. By chance, I was there.

Back in Algeria, my Tuareg colleagues in Tamanrasset and Djanet, the respective administrative centres for the Tassili-n-Ajjer and Ahaggar National Parks, could find no trace of the funds. They had searched from March 2003 until the spring of 2005, even accessing the UNDP's website and searching its files online, without finding any evidence of any of its projects for the region being put into practice. Wherever the funds had gone, it was not where the World Bank and the UNDP had intended. Significantly, there was no consultation between either the Fondation or any central or regional government party and the local people and organisations that one might expect to have been associated with the projects. The few traces and rumours of the funds that they did come across pointed either towards local corruption, such as the submission of false invoices to the regional government authorities, or, more disturbingly, to persons or front organisations, such as unknown local NGOs, that were suspected, and in some cases known, to be linked to senior members of the DRS.

Briefing the UNDP

By the end of the summer of 2004, 18 months after Lembo's announcement of the funds, my Tuareg colleagues felt that the coincidence between the fact that some $20 million of World Bank–UNDP development aid funds could not be publicly accounted for and that the Algerian security forces were believed to be fabricating fictitious terrorism across the region warranted a direct approach to the UNDP in New York. In September 2004, a group of local civil organisations consequently asked me to contact the UNDP office in New York. The UNDP official to whom I spoke on the phone appeared shocked by what I said, especially that the UNDP might unwittingly be financing state-sponsored terrorism.

No further action was undertaken by the UNDP at that time, possibly because it did not record my communication, or because it preferred not to investigate such a sensitive case. For their part, the Tuareg undertook more investigations and by the spring of 2005 were convinced that the only acceptable solution was for the project to be frozen and investigated by the UNDP. In April 2005, I contacted, on behalf of the Tuareg, a firm of international consultants in London who agreed to take up the matter with the UNDP. The consultancy firm appointed me as its representative to meet UNDP officials in New York and present them with the evidence underpinning the many allegations of fraud and embezzlement of the UNDP funds, along with details of Algeria's repression of those elements of civil society whom it had excluded from the project. My remit, on behalf of the Tuareg peoples of southern Algeria, was to urge the UNDP as a matter of priority to freeze the project and undertake a thorough investigation.

My meeting with UNDP officials in New York in May 2005 lasted some two hours. The UNDP told me it was aware of these specifically 'Algerian problems', as it called them, but that it did not yet have sufficiently good reason to step in and freeze the account. I therefore offered to provide the UNDP with a detailed report on the allegations of embezzlement, the specific shortcomings of regional governance and the repression of local people and organisations who should have been central to the project. The report, I emphasised, would contain names, locations and dates and provide the UNDP with more than enough 'good reason' to freeze the project and undertake a full-blown investigation.

The UNDP did not contact me again. I was left with the impression that it was not keen to delve into the matter and was frightened of engaging Algeria on these issues, especially now that Algeria was the US's key ally in the region. However, in June, a month after my meeting in New York, I received two pieces of information. The first came from the UNDP, confirming that it had contacted its office in Algeria, presumably to follow up on my allegations. The second came from Tamanrasset, confirming that a team from Algeria's procurator fiscal's office had arrived in Tamanrasset to investigate the *wilaya*'s accounts.

Were these two events related? I do not know, as the evidence is now almost certainly destroyed, but I am inclined to think so. The procurator fiscal's investigation soon led to a number of prominent people being questioned in court. At least one of these was a key figure in the alleged corruption of the UNDP's biodiversity project. By the end of June, my Tuareg informants in Tamanrasset reckoned that many more such cases were soon to come before the court.

That, however, was not to be. Whatever further investigations were in the pipeline could not be undertaken, as only a week or two later Tamanrasset went up in smoke. As I have described (Chapter 3), agents provocateurs incited Tuareg demonstrators to riot on 10–11 July and then directed them to set fire to government offices, including those containing the *wilaya*'s financial archives!

Rather than being able to throw any further light on this story, I can only add to the mystery. The local people of Tamanrasset and Djanet who helped investigate this affair have good reason to believe that World Bank–UNDP funds were embezzled through regional government agencies, including at least one of the National Parks, and almost certainly funnelled into Algeria's secret military intelligence services for use in the fabricated Sahara-Sahel front in the war on terror. If that is true, and it will probably never be proven, it leaves us with the interesting but almost certainly not unprecedented situation of World Bank–UNDP funds being used to finance state terrorism. If that has been the case, then it would also raise the perverse prospect of World Bank–UNDP funds being used to destroy the local livelihoods that they are designed to create.

Exactly one year after I brought these suspicions and allegations to the attention of the UNDP, it was reported in the Algerian media, without any further reference to or consultation with the Tuareg who first brought their concerns to the UNDP's attention, that the UNDP had given Algeria's Tassili-n-Ajjer and Ahaggar National Parks a gift of $10 million and eight all-terrain (four-wheel drive, 4WD) vehicles.[4] The UNDP's website was particularly vague on the subject, providing no matching confirmation of this announcement. It is therefore not clear whether these were new funds, a reaffirmation of the original funds, or an attempt by the Algerians to cover up or make good its embezzlement of the initial funds. If it was the latter, was it the result of pressure from the UNDP to do so? Again, the UNDP has given no satisfactory answers. Vague reference on its website to an Algerian project with a budget of $9,088,287 could be either to the original project or to another project.[5] Either way, it is testimony to the UNDP's 'top-down' approach and complete disregard for its own stated fundamental principles of 'good governance' and consultation with local peoples. Indeed, local people, angry that their complaint to the UNDP has still gone unanswered, see the UNDP's limp website statement that its operations in Algeria 'include the strengthening of NGO and civil society capacities' as nothing more than testimony to its collusion in Algeria's repression of civil society.

*   *   *

On 11 December 2007, a massive bomb destroyed the offices of the UN High Commission for Refugees and the UNDP in Algiers, killing 17 UN staff (14 Algerians and three foreigners). The bombing was attributed to al-Qaeda in the Islamic Maghreb (AQIM). The question of how the suicide bomber was able to drive a pick-up truck containing three-quarters of a ton (1,700 lb) of fertiliser explosive into such a high-security area has led some security analysts not to rule out the involvement of Algeria's secret intelligence services.

5

PUTTING THE GWOT BACK ON TRACK

Between the time of El Para's operation in 2003/04 and 2006, governments in the region, especially Mauritania and Niger (both to be overthrown by military coups in 2005 and 2010 respectively), used the pretext of 'terrorism' to crack down on legitimate political opposition. In Mauritania, the government targeted especially reformist-oriented Islamists; in Niger the target was the minority Tuareg population. Some of these governments, notably those of Niger and Algeria, and as we have seen in Chapter 3, even went so far as to provoke unrest in order to claim further 'terrorism rents' from the US and to justify Washington's Trans-Sahara Counterterrorism Initiative (TSCTI).

Such actions by the governments of the region did much to help Washington justify its 'second' or Saharan-Sahelian front in its 'Global War on Terror' (GWOT). However, there was a problem for the US, as well as its key ally Algeria. This was that by September 2006, when the Groupe Salafiste pour le Prédication et le Combat (GSPC) changed its name to al-Qaeda in the Islamic Maghreb (AQIM) (announced in January 2007), there was still no clear evidence of there having been any GSPC terrorism in the region. The literally thousands of articles that had publicised the terrorist danger in the Sahara-Sahel over the preceding three to four years gave no evidence of terrorist incidents in the south and were thus little more than disinformation and propaganda. Even in the case of the one incident where there could conceivably have been some GSPC involvement, namely the attack on the Lemgheity garrison, the evidence, as explained in Chapter 3, pointed towards internal opposition to the Mauritanian regime from the Cavaliers du Changement. However, as with the entire El

Para operation, the US authorities and Western media, following the Dick Cheney methodology of 'proof by reiteration', insisted that the attack on Lemgheity was the work of the GSPC.

Neither, in spite of what the US and Algerian intelligence services have had to say on the subject, is there any conclusive evidence to substantiate that al-Qaeda was behind or even much involved in the name change of GSPC to AQIM in 2006. Rather, the name change was almost certainly an attempt by the US and Algerian intelligence services to revitalise the dwindling interest in and the waning credibility of their GWOT in the Sahara-Sahel. Indeed, if the GWOT was to gain any further traction in the Sahara-Sahel after the initial El Para operation and the subsequent immense outpouring of disinformation and propaganda, something needed to happen, otherwise the whole GWOT operation in the Sahara-Sahel was in danger of running out of steam.

The name change from GSPC to AQIM aroused about as much interest in the Maghreb at that time as an announcement in a 'births, marriages and deaths' newspaper column. It needed a big push from its promoters, the US and Algerian military intelligence services, in the form of a few high-profile news stories and op-eds, for the name, which hardly tripped off the tongue, to seep into household usage. In northern Algeria, where the GSPC was still active, public consciousness of AQIM was raised by a number of major terrorist 'suicide' bombings, with commensurate loss of life, with 'spectaculars', to use the old IRA (Irish Republican Army) term for them, in Algiers in April and then December 2007.[1] The extent to which these bombings were in fact genuine suicide bombings, as the security services have always maintained, or whether they carried the fingerprints of the Département du Renseignement et de la Sécurité (DRS), has never been subject to full investigation.

In the Sahel, where the GSPC had been little more than a false-flag operation and the subject of 'disinformation' and propaganda, AQIM required a little more 'flesh and bone' if it was to have any credibility worthy of its new 'brand name'. The way in which this was achieved was an extraordinary story in which the truth, once again, might be deemed to have been stranger than fiction.

Algerian and Libyan Rivalry

The story of how AQIM came into being in the Sahel and how the GWOT was put back on track is a convoluted one. It began around the end of 2005 and early 2006, a period when relations between the Tuareg and the Mali government had once again deteriorated. Mali's Tuareg felt that the government was trying to disenfranchise them and was not treating properly the former Tuareg rebels who had been incorporated into the Malian army as part of the peace deal that ended the Tuareg rebellion in the 1990s.

At that time, few, if any, Malian Tuareg realised how their own sentiments towards their own government might feed into the wider, regional hegemonic competition between North Africa's two petro-states, Algeria and Libya. Indeed, one of the indirect consequences of Washington's post-9/11 policy in North Africa was to exacerbate the longstanding rivalry between these two countries. Both of them had been internationally marginalised in the 1990s: Algeria as a result of its 'dirty war' and Libya as a result of post-Lockerbie sanctions. Washington's new post-9/11 alliance with Algeria in its GWOT and the more or less simultaneous readmission of Libya into the world order energised their longstanding regional hegemonic ambitions in the Sahel.

Libya's leader, Mouamar Gaddafi, had dabbled in Sahelian affairs for much of his nearly 42 years in power, with the highlight of his 'Sahelian policy', at least until now, having been the spectacular failure in 1987 of his designs on Chad and the humiliating destruction of his army as the remains of it were driven back into Libya. In 2005–06, nearly two decades later, Gaddafi was aware of how the US alliance with Algeria in its establishment of a new Sahara-Sahelian front in the GWOT might once again thwart his own long-held ambitions towards the Sahel.

In 2004–05, what appeared to have rekindled Gaddafi's interest in the Sahel, if it had ever really waned, was his involvement in the revolt of the Niger Tuareg (see Chapter 3) during the winter of 2004–05. Indeed, no sooner had he seemingly resolved that latest of Tuareg crises than he gave the clearest of possible clues about his new designs on the Sahel. The date was April 2005; the place Oubari, a small town at the western end of the Wadi al Ajal in the Fezzan region of Libya. The occasion was his address to a delegation of Libyan and Malian Tuareg whom he had invited to Oubari. The thrust of his speech was that Libya regarded itself as the protector of the Tuareg; that Libya had been their ancestral home before they spread out into what is now Algeria, Mali, Niger, Mauritania and Burkina Faso and was therefore their 'base and support', and that they therefore constituted what could be construed as 'an extension of Libya'. He even referred to the Tuareg as the original 'Arabs' of the region, when they are, in fact, Berbers.

Gaddafi was aware of how the launch of the Sahara-Sahelian front in the GWOT had caused the loss of many livelihoods amongst the Tuareg, exacerbated their marginalisation and aroused anti-government sentiment across much of the region. Having seen how President Tandja of Niger had tried to provoke the Niger Tuareg to take up arms, the revelation only a few months later that the Tamanrasset riots in July 2005 had been instigated and directed by Algerian state agents provided Gaddafi with a further opportunity to befriend and support his new-found heroes or 'lions of the desert', as he called the Tuareg. And, of course, it was a chance to twist the knife a little into his troublesome neighbour. The Libyan leader therefore sent his condolences to the Tuareg youths and their families for the suffering they had undergone for their unjust imprisonment for their part in the Tamanrasset riots. He also sent them an invitation to visit him in Tripoli. Some 20 of them, partly out of inquisitiveness and with little else to do, took up the offer. They had an enjoyable, interesting and profitable trip. Gaddafi told them that he wanted peace throughout the region and that they were to have all that they wanted. They were to simply let him know what it was they required. Most of them, it seems, plumped for 4WD vehicles, with at least one returning to Tamanrasset with two Toyota Land Cruisers, together worth around €50,000.

The Tuareg reactions to Gaddafi's overtures were broadly threefold. First, there was considerable and genuine gratitude for his intervention on their behalf in negotiating the amnesty from the Nigerien government. Second, and as might be expected, Tuareg were not going to look a gift horse in the mouth. Third, there was wariness about becoming overly reliant and dependent on his largesse.

Gaddafi's concern for the Tuareg, however, was not entirely altruistic. Acting as 'godfather' to the Tuareg, as one local journalist described it, would enable him to further Libyan interests across the region. Indeed, Gaddafi's Oubari speech may have gone unnoticed in the Western world, but it was not lost on Algeria which saw it as a warning shot that Libya was not going to stand by and let its more powerful neighbour establish its hegemony in the Sahel.

The Oubari speech was just the start of Gaddafi's overtures. Further meetings with Tuareg leaders took place in Libya on 15 and 31 July 2005, shortly after the Tamanrasset riots, following which it was strongly rumoured that Gaddafi was planning to expand his armed forces to create employment for some 3,000 Tuareg and other Saharan peoples. There were also reports of numerous offers of Libyan development aid for projects in both Niger and Mali.

By the latter part of 2005, Gaddafi's overtures to the Tuareg were being noted with increasing concern by the governments of the region, especially those of Niger and Algeria, as well as France and the US. The prospect of disaffected ex-rebel Tuareg joining up in some sort of Gaddafi-inspired and financed Libyan foreign legion was not reassuring to them.

It was not until the start of 2006 that a series of seemingly isolated events suddenly began to come together in a way which was to have momentous consequences for the future of this part of the Sahara-Sahel and its peoples. The key players in this extraordinary story were the local Tuareg of Mali, Libya's 'Brother Leader' Gaddafi, the Americans and the Algerians.

As already mentioned, by the end of 2005 relations between Mali's Tuareg and the government had begun to deteriorate.

Gaddafi saw this renewed Tuareg discontent as an opportunity to expand Libya's influence in Mali. Having already befriended the Tuareg of Niger in their time of need and attempted to subvert those of Tamanrasset, Gaddafi accordingly promised massive financial aid to Mali's Tuareg and in January opened a consulate in the politically and strategically sensitive Tuareg stronghold of Kidal in north-eastern Mali.

Tension in the Kidal region heightened further when, in early February 2006, Lieutenant Colonel Hassan Fagaga, a senior Tuareg army officer, deserted, taking many of his men with him to their old rebel base in the Tigharghar mountains some 120 kilometres north of Kidal and about midway between Kidal and the Algerian border.

Libya stated that the consulate's aim was to support economic development and thereby combat insecurity in northern Mali. This was anathema to Algeria, which regarded Kidal as being within its sphere of influence. Algeria was quick to realise that such an entity would provide Libya with a zone of influence that would encircle Algeria's south and enable it to challenge and compete with Algeria's own Sahelian interests. Algeria's immediate reaction was to impose a commercial blockade on Kidal, a desert town of some 20,000 people which received most of its supplies from Algeria. Libya's response was for its Consul at Kidal, Moussa El Kony, to travel around northern Mali's border zone proposing and inaugurating various water, educational and health projects in the villages of the region. Libya was also reported to be financing the construction of mosques, hospitals and schools in the administrative regions of Kidal, Gao and Timbuktu, as well as the airport at Kidal and well-drilling in all three regions. On 22 March, with Algeria's reputation in the region at an all-time low as a result of its commercial blockade and Malian students in Algiers responding by going on a hunger strike, a somewhat provocative ceremony was organised in Kidal to mark the handing over of these Libyan gifts. Four weeks later, a delegation of Libyan and Malian officials met in Kidal with the local administrative authorities, notables and ex-combatants of the Tuareg 1990s rebellion. The Tuareg ex-combatants stated that they wanted a special statute to speed up the region's development. To that end, a designated councillor was appointed to Mali's Ministry of Defence to manage the problems faced by the former rebels. With the Malian government freeing up €1.8 million to fight youth unemployment in the region, Libya stated it would revive two economic projects in the region: a phosphate plant at Bourem, north of Gao, and a plaster-works factory at Tessalit. Algerian concern rose further!

The Algerians and the Americans had both been watching developments in the region very carefully and were fully apprised of both the Tuareg discontent and Gaddafi's designs on the region. They saw the developing situation as a potential opportunity to fulfil at least two objectives. Algeria could discredit Libya and drive it from the region, while Washington could ramp up its GWOT which, in spite of all the propaganda, had gained little traction in the Sahara-Sahel. Since El Para's 2003 operation, there had been no 'real' terrorism in the region in the form of hostage-taking or attacks of any note on Western or other interests.

Washington and Algiers, by now allied in duplicity, began what appears to have been a harmonised plot to regenerate the GWOT in the region. On 15–16 February 2006, three US transporters airlifted some 100 US Special Forces, their dogs and communications equipment direct from what is now AFRICOM's (US Africa Command's) headquarters at Stuttgart to the Tamanrasset base in southern Algeria. Both the US State Department and the US Ambassador to Algeria are adamant that they were not informed by the Pentagon of this covert operation.

Gaddafi's Great Saharan State

The 'final straw' for the Algerians, or what might be better thought of as the 'trigger', came on the night of 10 April 2006, the celebration of *Mawlid* – the anniversary of the Prophet Mohamed, at the symbolic and theatrically chosen venue of Timbuktu. The event, which was initiated and partly financed by Gaddafi, who himself led the prayers, was attended by the Presidents of Mali, Senegal, Niger, Mauritania and Sierra Leone, along with many former Tuareg rebel leaders, traditional chiefs, other dignitaries and some 30,000 Malians.

Since his Oubari speech almost a year earlier, and during his various meetings with Tuareg delegations in the subsequent months, Gaddafi had spoken of some sort of Tuareg or Saharan political entity. His pronouncements – sometimes little more than rants – were bizarre. They ranged from his advocacy of a 'Great Saharan state', stretching from Senegal to the borders of Iraq and incorporating the desert populations of Tuareg, Arabs, Toubous, Songhai and Bambara, as well as the peoples of the Nile Valley, Sinai, Jordan and the Arabian Peninsula, to something far more tangible and potentially threatening to Algeria in the form of a Libyan-backed Tuareg federation that would extend across northern Mali and northern Niger, southern Mauritania, northern Burkina Faso and, of course, southern Algeria.

On the night of the *Mawlid* in Timbuktu, Gaddafi gave a speech in which he launched his idea for a Great Saharan state. He told the assembled multitude that he envisaged a day when the Tuareg of Mali, Niger, Mauritania and Algeria would form a federation with Libya as its base. Taken to its logical conclusion, such a 'state' would necessitate the breakaway of much of northern Mali and northern Niger, part of Mauritania and a large part of southern Algeria.

The question, which most foreign delegates and analysts were asking themselves, was how much of Gaddafi's address should be taken seriously, or could it be written off, as one Algerian journalist put it, as the blustering delusion and crazy dream of empire by 'the muddle-headed colonel'?

Algeria was not prepared to make the call on that question. It had heard enough and let fly on all fronts. In the popular media, Gaddafi received a blast of opprobrious ridicule, while at a more formal level his Great Sahara plan was castigated on TV by Algeria's Prime Minister, Ahmed Ouyahia. On the diplomatic front, there was a flurry of activity between Algiers and Niamey, Bamako and Nouakchott as Algiers rushed to shore up relations with these neighbouring states, while at the same time advising

Libya to 'take a more considered and respectful attitude towards such a strategic neighbour'.

In spite of this, it is now apparent from what was to follow that the Algerian regime had already decided on how it was going to act.

Engineering a Rebellion: Kidal, 23 May 2006

Four days after Gaddafi's speech, Lieutenant Colonel Ibrahim ag Acherif, the most senior Tuareg in the Mali army, was killed in a car incident. The Tuareg were incensed, believing that he had been assassinated by Mali's state security. His death sent even more former rebels to join those already in the Tigharghar mountains. Whether the Tuareg are correct in their belief that Mali's state security instigated the assassination is debatable, for, as I explain a little further on, the beneficiaries of Ag Acherif's death were to be Algeria and the US, not Mali.

The rebellious mood amongst Mali's Tuareg provided the Algerians and the US with their opportunity. Algeria's DRS did a deal with Iyad ag Ghaly (usually referred to simply as 'Iyad'), a former Tuareg rebel leader, to support a Tuareg rebellion in exchange for Tuareg help in the GWOT. The wording of the deal was: 'We [Algeria] are ready to help you achieve what you want, but on the condition that you help us fight the GSPC in the Tuareg Malian Sahara.'[2]

The US Special Forces that had been flown into Tamanrasset, along with their Algerian allies, pulled out from the Tamanrasset base. Local Tuareg told me that they had seen their convoy passing through the village of Silet and then on to the Malian frontier 'just before the Kidal attack'.

At dawn on Tuesday 23 May 2006, several dozen former Tuareg rebels raced into Kidal and Ménaka, a smaller town 237 kilometres to the south-east of Kidal, in 4WD 'pickups' and trucks mounted with machine-guns. They attacked the two army bases in Kidal and the one at Ménaka. The Kidal bases, manned by some 400 Malian troops, put up little resistance. Twenty soldiers were reportedly held hostage, while most of the others, according to eyewitness accounts, fled the scene, in spite of the much-publicised training of the Malian army by US military forces over the previous two years. There was also little resistance at Ménaka. The rebels looted the armouries, helping themselves to a substantial quantity of arms, including heavy machine-guns, munitions, vehicles and other supplies. By afternoon, the whole of Kidal was in rebel hands. Casualties were minimal and the rebels withdrew in the late afternoon before reinforcements sent north from Gao, 340 kilometres to the south, could arrive. The rebels retreated to their well-defended bases in the mountains of Tigharghar. By 24 May, the two towns were back under government control.

Responsibility for the attack was levelled almost immediately at Lieutenant Colonel Hassan Fagaga. A rebel spokesman, quoted by Agence France-Presse (AFP) in Bamako, claimed responsibility on behalf of Fagaga for the attacks. Referring to themselves as the Democratic Alliance for Change, the spokesman said: 'We do not want war. We want to enter into negotiations with the government … Our region is poor and we want to see it developed quickly. We also have problems regarding our integration into the army.'[3]

For its part, the Malian government took two distinct lines. The military clamoured to invade Tigharghar and teach the rebels a lesson. This would almost certainly have led to a blood-bath and with no certainty that the Malian army would have been able to crown itself in glory. Fortunately, the wiser counsel of the President, Amadou Toumani Touré, or ATT as he is known, prevailed and the army was held in check.

The rebellion and this account of it obviously raise a number of questions. One is whether the Malian government received advanced warning about the staged rebellion from either the Americans or Algerians. I believe the answer is almost certainly 'no'. If the Malian government, or perhaps just the President, had been party to the conspiracy, it would hardly have been likely to have expressed its surprise to the media that Iyad had visited the President only a few days before the revolt, but without raising any demands in regard to the rebels' subsequently stated grievances or making any reference to the possibility that the Tuareg felt so aggrieved that they were on the verge of taking up arms. As for

Iyad, it is hardly likely that he was going to brief the President on the Tuareg's plans!

A second question is why other Tuareg, especially in Niger, did not join the rebellion, especially as there were widespread grievances amongst all the Sahelian Tuareg groups at that time. The answer, given to me by some of the key Tuareg leaders in Niger, is that they knew that Iyad had played a key role in the negotiations that led to the release of El Para's hostages in August 2003[4] and had long suspected him of having ties with Algeria's DRS. They therefore suspected that the DRS was in some way involved in engineering the rebellion.[5]

As for the Libyans, Algeria's media pronouncement was such that most people believed that the Kidal revolt had been inspired and incited by Gaddafi's inflammatory Timbuktu speech. Gaddafi was therefore widely blamed in the media and discredited, at least for a while, in both Mali and further afield. The fact that Gaddafi successfully sued the Algerian media for libel in the Algerian courts for this 'smear' was almost incidental. 'Mud sticks', and Gaddafi had little choice but to close his consulate in Kidal and beat a hasty retreat from Algeria's backyard.[6]

The very considerable international media coverage of the incident was out of all proportion to the scale of the incident. That is because it was designed by the Algerians and Americans not merely to discredit Gaddafi, but also to further promote Washington's portrayal of the region as a 'Terror Zone'. The latter did not require much effort: to Washington's spin-doctors, a 'rebel' is an 'insurgent' who is effectively a 'terrorist'. The quirky logic of this reasoning is that as insurgents are fighting the government, then they must be terrorists.

Three further aspects of the Kidal rebellion have subsequently had profound consequences: Algeria's management of the so-called 'peace' process; the continued presence in the region of the Americans, and the not so small matter of the Tuareg's 'payback' deal.

For Algeria to meet its side of the bargain with the Tuareg and to deliver on what they wanted, Algeria used its longstanding influence in the region and hitherto good relations with the Mali government to initiate and take control of the peace process. Algeria also undertook to ensure the provision and cantonment of the Tuareg rebel forces in the Tigharghar. The fact that the Malian Tuareg took up arms again a year later is testimony to the Algerians' lack of sincerity in negotiating a long-term peace agreement with the Mali government on the Tuareg's behalf. It is debatable whether such an agreement would actually have been in Algeria's own underlying interests. However, the Algerians did achieve agreement, established in the peace accords that followed the 1990s rebellion, that no Malian troops would be stationed along the region's borders. While this was initially welcomed by the Tuareg, as it meant that they had some semblance of control or at least freedom of movement in their own region and along the Kidal border area with Algeria and Niger, the practical implications of the arrangement were that it meant that Algeria retained effective control over the Algerian-Malian border region. As we shall see later, this has meant that AQIM has been able not only to establish itself and operate in the region in almost complete impunity, but also to maintain its operational links with Algeria's DRS quite unmolested by Malian border or army patrols.

Many questions still surround the presence of the US Special Forces in the region. Why did they go there, and so clandestinely? Why did they deny their presence? And what did they do after the 23 May rebellion?

The official answer to these questions, as given to me at a Briefing in Washington three months later (August 2006) by senior officials from the US State and Defense Departments and the US Ambassador to Algeria, was that there were no US forces in the region at the time. The Ambassador and officials from both the State and Defense Departments denied emphatically any US presence.[7] Of course, the only rationale for this is that they had to deny any such presence. The movement of US forces into a country to lend support to a rebellion raises a number of legal questions, not to mention that of 'state terrorism'. And yet the evidence is overwhelming. The flight manifests at Tamanrasset airport recorded the arrival of the three planes from Stuttgart carrying US Special Forces, their dogs and their surveillance equipment on

15–16 February. Local people witnessed seeing them crossing into Mali just before the 23 May rebellion. Both senior Malian and US military commanders in Mali confirmed verbally the presence of US Special Forces north of Kidal at that time. They confirmed that the 'Algerians and US were responsible for everything in that region' (that is, north of Kidal).[8]

When I was given this denial by US government officials in Washington, I pointed out to them that I had not only seen the Tamanrasset airport records and the flight manifests but also knew that the Special Forces had brought their dogs with them. Two years later (2008), on another Briefing to the US State Department in Washington, I was invited for a drink by one of the officials who had also been present at what I had called the 'denial meeting' two years earlier. Almost immediately, he brought up the subject of the Kidal rebellion.

'You know, you were quite correct about what you said about our forces being in Mali', he said to me.

'I know. But how did you find out?'

'What you said about the dogs was so bizarre that it had to be true!'

'Yes,' I replied, 'but how do you actually know that it was true?'

'From the veterinary records. I could find no information on troop movements, but then they would have been Special Forces, which fell directly under Rumsfeld at the DoD [Department of Defense], without either State or even the US Ambassador in the country having to be notified. One hundred per cent covert. What you said stuck in my mind. I knew there had to be a clue somewhere. And then I figured that the records on the dogs' veterinary "passports" would show up whether they had flown there or not. And there it was – the smoking gun. They were flown in from Stuttgart just as you said.'

Despite the denials, US Special Forces continued to operate in the region. In May 2007, a new Tuareg faction, for reasons that are explained in the next chapter, took up arms against the Malian government. Two months later (7 July 2007), the Californian KSBW Channel posted the following message on its website:[9]

> KIDAL, Mali – The Department of Defense announced Tuesday the death of a Monterey soldier who was supporting Operation Enduring Freedom.
>
> Sgt. 1st Class Sean K. Mitchell, 35, died on July 7 in Kidal, Mali, of injuries suffered from a non-combat-related incident. His death is under investigation.
>
> Mitchell was assigned to the 1st Battalion, 10th Special Forces Group out of Stuttgart, Germany.

Four other US soldiers were reported as being hurt in the incident and were sent back from Mali to the US EUCOM headquarters in Germany where they were treated in a US military hospital.[10]

In February 2008, seven months after Sergeant Mitchell's death, US Special Forces accompanied Malian Forces in a sweep through Mali's north-eastern region, ransacking and looting the border garrison town of Tin Zaouatene, and driving the entire civilian population into the desert. The action, as mentioned in Chapter 2, was denied by AFRICOM's Commander, General 'Kip' Ward. But, as explained in the next chapter, the action triggered revenge attacks against the Malian army by Tuareg rebels and an escalation of the long-predicted conflagration.

'Payback' Time

The third and most consequential issue resulting from the 23 May Kidal rebellion is that once the dust had settled, it was time for the Tuareg to fulfil their side of the bargain. The deal was that the Tuareg would help the Algerians, and through them the US, inject some credibility into the GWOT and put the Saharan terrorism show back on the road. Iyad's side of the deal was that he would help the Algerians (and the US) by 'fighting the GSPC in the Tuareg Malian Sahara'.[11]

The extraordinary story of how that 'deal' was executed in September 2006, three and a half months after the Kidal rebellion, re-emerged in the local Kidal media[12] exactly four years later, in August 2010. That is because the main actor in the story, Sidi Mohamed ag Acherif, known as 'Merzouk', and the brother of Lieutenant Colonel Ibrahim ag Acherif who was believed to have been assassinated in April 2006, four days after Gaddafi's *Mawlid* address in Timbuktu, was himself murdered by members of AQIM in the Tessalit region of north-eastern Mali on 11 August 2010. The reason for Merzouk's execution is thought to have been his key role in the September 2006 'deal'.

To understand this complicated story, we need to understand the trajectories that finally brought together the lives of Merzouk and Mokhtar ben Mokhtar (MBM), the two main actors in the September 2006 incident.

For both MBM and Merzouk, the story began in 1996: one in Algeria, the other in Mali. In Algeria, 1996 saw the country entering the worst phase of its 'dirty war'. Deep in the Sahara, however, far away from the massacres and killings that were traumatising the north, the enigmatic MBM was taking his first steps towards becoming a 'legend'. Since his name first began to achieve notoriety around 1996, his death has been reported by the Algerian authorities on at least six occasions. Hence his reputation as '*le fantôme du Sahara*'. In 1996, however, MBM was embarking on his own career as a smuggler and 'outlaw'. MBM is a Metlili Chaamba whose family has long been associated with 'commerce'. On his return from a brief period in Afghanistan in the early 1990s (over which there are some doubts), he attempted to move into the space left by Hadj Bettu in northern Niger and Algeria's extreme south (Grand Sud), while Bettu served a ten-year prison sentence in Tamanrasset.[13] Described as a 'warlord', Bettu was effectively little more than the Algerian 'mafia' state's representative in the extreme south, managing the trafficking of arms and other goods on behalf of corrupt elements within the Algerian military into sub-Saharan Africa.

MBM, however, never developed the same cosy relationship with the Algerian military as Hadj Bettu. The killing of his brother by a border patrol in the Deb Deb region led MBM into a revenge war against the Algerian state. Under the slogan '*La Libération du Grand Sud*', he took effective control of most of the desert and trunk routes south of an approximate line from Tuat (Adrar) to Illizi. In 1998, he reportedly hijacked 365 4WDs from within Algeria, belonging mostly to the gendarmerie and oil companies, and is even alleged to have downed a military plane. Only in 1999, when the military went on the offensive, was he pushed into the Sahel of Niger and Mali where he established himself as the Sahara's predominant 'trafficker', especially of cigarettes, which acquired him another of his many sobriquets: '*Le Parrain Marlboro*'.

In Mali, 1996 saw the 'Flame of Peace' ceremony at Timbuktu symbolically mark the demobilisation of some 12,000 combatants and the end of Mali's six-year Tuareg rebellion. Merzouk, however, did not lay down his arms and remained defiant until arrested in Mauritania in 1998. Through the good offices of his elder brother, Ibrahim ag Acherif, who had been integrated into the Mali army as part of the peace deal with the rank of Lieutenant Colonel, Merzouk returned to Mali and was employed by the government as a guide in the Halil–Tessalit Algerian-Mali border region.

Thus, while MBM was trafficking cigarettes across the Sahara and waging his war on Algeria, Merzouk was helping to protect his country's border. It was inevitable that the paths of the two men would cross. And they did. When MBM sought an accomplished local guide, Merzouk agreed to work with him. Their collaboration was to have profound consequences.

When Algeria's DRS, working in hand with the US, called in their favour, Iyad was instructed to organise a specific attack on MBM in northern Mali. He selected Merzouk to lead the attack. Before his untimely death in 2010, Merzouk let it be known that both he and Iyad were paid considerable sums of money by the Algerians. The first attack against MBM on 19 September (Reuters gave two dates: 19 and 27 September) resulted in MBM's right-hand man being killed. Subsequent media reports suggested that three or four of MBM's men were killed. Two Tuareg were wounded and hospitalised in Algeria. A second attack took place on 23 October after the Algerians gave the Tuareg coordinates of a location 60 kilometres from Araouane (north of Timbuktu). This time the Tuareg experienced the worst of the fighting, with five killed, two wounded and two taken hostage.

The international media gave the incidents huge coverage, with the US, along with its governmental allies in the region, saying that Iyad's Democratic Alliance for Change had actively thrown itself into 'the international war on terror' against the GSPC (soon to become AQIM). In words that could have been written by the DRS, the Alliance spokesman told Reuters that 'Our Democratic Alliance handles security in the region and we chase out those who are not from there, that's the position we've taken to control the zone.'[14] This was the language that Washington wanted to hear: its GWOT was now firmly embedded in the Sahara, with the Tuareg tribes, as the US called them, being on the right side!

The two incidents laid the basis for much of the US-Algerian propaganda that has surrounded the post-2006 establishment of GSPC/AQIM in the Sahel. The Tuareg causalities at Araouane also ensured subsequent Tuareg animosity towards the GSPC/AQIM. Indeed, the question of whether the DRS gave MBM, or some other party, forewarning of the Araouane attack in order to ensure Tuareg casualties remains unanswered.

At the time, many Tuareg who did not know about the deal that had been done between the DRS and Iyad told me that the 'reprisal' attack against the Tuareg at Araouane had been undertaken by GSPC *repentis* (repentants). These were GSPC 'terrorists' who had accepted the Algerian government's amnesty.[15] In early 2006, Tuareg in southern Algeria told me that they had come across several such *repentis* in the Malian and Nigerien border regions. They believed that these *repentis*, after turning themselves in, had been sent into Algeria's extreme south by the DRS to 'cause trouble'. We now have good grounds to believe that it is these same *repentis*, sent to the region by the DRS in 2006, who now form the hardcore of AQIM's 'foot soldiers' in the Sahel. With *repentis* in place and the deal between Mali's Tuareg and the DRS accomplished, all that remained was to re-brand the hitherto insignificant GSPC with the al-Qaeda name. That was formerly announced two to three months later.

The GSPC changed its name to AQIM on 11 September 2006, the fifth anniversary of 9/11 and precisely eight days before the first attack on MBM. The timing of the name change with the attack on MBM was not coincidental. The formal announcement of the name change came three months later in January. However, before the implications of the name change for the Sahel could be digested, the region was overwhelmed by Tuareg rebellions, starting in Niger in February 2007 and shortly after in Mali.

6

NEW TUAREG REBELLIONS

Fears of Genocide

Eid ul-Fitr, the festival that marks the end of Ramadan, is an occasion of celebration and religious significance throughout the Islamic world. For the Tuareg of northern Niger, however, the Ramadan that ended on 12 October 2007 brought with it a strong sense of fear and foreboding. Widespread talk in the villages and encampments of Aïr about recent civilian massacres and rumours of an imminent government genocide policy muted any sense of religious and social festivity.

The entire month of Ramadan had been a singularly sombre period for the Tuareg of Niger. In early June, three very old Tuareg men, Sidi Mohamed Imola, known as Kalakoua; Abtchaw Kounfi and Aoussouk Kounfi, two of whom were visually handicapped and one one-legged, were arrested by the Nigerien army (the Forces Armées Nigériennes – FAN) near the Tazerzait well to the north of Tamgak in the north-east of Aïr. The three were murdered by the FAN, with their bodies, one of which was dismembered, being left near the well. Five days later, Tuareg, now operating under the name of the Mouvement des Nigériens pour la Justice (MNJ), launched a devastating and humiliating attack on the FAN troops that had temporarily based themselves at Tazerzait. Fifteen soldiers were killed, 43 wounded and 72 taken hostage.

Tuareg fears of a genocide, or ethnocide as they called it, were therefore not entirely without foundation. Indeed, on 24 August Niger's government declared a State of Alert, effectively placing the region under martial law and sealing it off from the outside world. An Agades resident described the hitherto bustling regional capital as a 'ghost town'. Genocide fears were reinforced on 27

September, during Ramadan itself, when a FAN patrol stopped a small convoy of five vehicles in the extreme north of Aïr that was travelling in the Toussasset area between In Tadera and the Algerian border post of In Azoua. The soldiers forced the passengers out of the vehicles, divided them into light-skinned and dark-skinned and executed the twelve light-skinned ones, presuming them to be Tuareg, in cold blood. The following day, the same troops came across a series of Tuareg encampments near the road between the uranium-mining town of Arlit and the border town of Assamakka. The soldiers rampaged through the tents, killing 22 innocent men, women and children and slaughtering an unknown number of livestock.[1]

In the week after *Eid ul-Fitr*, a government television station twice broadcasted comments from a Nigerien civil society leader who said that ethnic Tuareg rebels could be exterminated in 48 hours.[2] Indeed, a report on the conflict in Niger, commissioned by the UNHCR in August, had already warned that President Tandja was likely to unleash his armed forces on the Tuareg civilian population.[3] That is precisely what he did.

In the week before Christmas 2007, the UK-based Amnesty International and the US-based Human Rights Watch denounced Niger's armed forces for committing war crimes.[4] A local organisation, the Nigerien Association for the Defence of Human Rights, also accused Niger's security forces of summary executions of civilians in the government's fight against what it referred to as a 'Tuareg insurgency'. Niger's government denounced Amnesty International's report that Niger's security forces were arbitrarily arresting and torturing civilians in their attempt to quash what had become a Tuareg rebellion in the north of the country as 'pure tittle-tattle, based on simple rumours that undermine the dignity and honour of Niger'.[5]

At the time of their publication, I suggested that the Amnesty International and Human Rights Watch reports might have come just in time to save the Tuareg from the genocide they feared.[6] But I was wrong. Far worse was to come.

In the third week of March 2008, Niger's recently US-trained soldiers concentrated their firepower on the inhabitants of the

villages along the old road that runs north of the regional capital
of Agades through the SW foothills of the Aïr Mountains. Their
action was triggered by an engagement on 20 March between
the MNJ and the FAN in the Tamazélak valley, 100 kilometres
north of Agades. Four army vehicles were destroyed with their
occupants almost certainly killed or wounded. The army called
for reinforcements from Agades. However, rather than engage
the MNJ, the FAN reinforcements directed their wrath on the
inhabitants of Tamazélak. They set fire to the hamlets in the
valley, destroying at least seven homes completely and the vehicle
of a local trader, and cold-bloodedly assassinated two children:
Liman Houdane and Toukane Assale. From there, the soldiers
headed back south to their base in Agades, stopping first at the
settlements at Sakafat, which they looted before burning down
ten huts, executing two villagers and 'disappearing' another, and
then at Tidene where they proceeded to execute two more villagers
and 'disappear' four others. One gardener had his legs broken as
a form of torture while watching his garden being fired. Before
leaving, the soldiers burnt down seven more huts and scattered
landmines around the village.

Two days later, an MNJ contingent caught up with the FAN
militia south of Tidene, killing at least 15 of them and destroying
two of their vehicles. The FAN survivors, although harassed by
the pursuing MNJ, nevertheless found time to once again exact
vengeance on the civilian population, this time in the village of
Dabaga. The toll was devastating: two villagers[7] were summarily
executed and two more 'disappeared'; 43 houses were looted and
destroyed by fire; one vehicle and twelve motor cycles belonging to
gardeners were burnt; the village produce store was destroyed by
fire, as was the women's cooperative; six gardens were completely
destroyed and at least 60 animals slaughtered.

While these exactions have not been verified,[8] eyewitness
reports from survivors in the area[9] indicate that the atrocities
committed by the FAN on the civilian population may have been
considerably greater. The precise extent of the killings, torture and
other atrocities will probably not be established for some time,
until the military allow external observers and reporters access

to the region. In the meantime, the UN was notified in writing on 29 March that the policy of President Tandja towards the Tuareg and the actions of his US-trained soldiers constituted a genocide as defined in Resolution 260 (III) A of the UN General Assembly on 9 December 1948, namely the Convention on the Prevention and Punishment of the Crime of Genocide.[10] The Tuareg people of northern Niger urged the UN 'to use its powers and considerable influence to intervene as a matter of urgency and to protect them from such genocidal actions'.[11]

The commitment of such atrocities by Washington's proxies was not confined to Niger. On 14 February 2008, the US State Department issued a travel alert, warning US citizens of armed conflict, kidnappings, armed robberies and the presence of landmines in northern Mali, especially the Malian-Nigerian and Malian-Algerian border areas, the Kidal region, areas north of Timbuktu and the city (town) of Tin Zaouatene, and advising them to avoid travel in the area. The warning emphasised that the US-designated terrorist organisation al-Qaeda in the Land of the Islamic Maghreb (AQIM), the recently renamed Algerian Groupe Salafiste pour la Prédication et le Combat (GSPC), and other armed groups presented dangers to travellers and that Americans planning to travel in these regions should register with the Department of State or US Embassy.

Why this sudden urgency to keep US travellers out of northern Mali? Was it because Washington wanted no prying eyes in the region? If so, what was it up to? The answer reached me within hours of my having read the travel alert. It came in the form of several separate communications by satellite phone from inhabitants of the small desert border town of Tin Zaouatene in north-east Mali who had escaped across the border to Algeria. One had even managed to drive the 550 kilometres to Tamanrasset to access email. Their messages were all the same: the Malian army, accompanied by US forces, had ransacked and looted the town, which was now empty and abandoned with the inhabitants having to flee into the desert where they were surviving precariously. Fortunately, good rains in the region enabled them to pasture their goats and trade them across the Algerian border for *semoule* (flour) and other essentials.

The most surprising thing about the incident is that it was given a total media blackout. Not a whisper anywhere. Indeed, the silence was extraordinary, especially as this part of the Sahara had been the focal point of the Bush administration's 'second front' in its GWOT in Africa since 2003. Indeed, the US had continuously asserted that northern Mali had been the locale of al-Qaeda affiliated terrorist training bases that posed a major threat to both neighbouring states as well as Europe. When challenged as to why they had not managed to find a single terrorist base, in spite of US Special Forces on the ground and aerial reconnaissance and satellite observation above, the answer was that the bases, like the chemical weapons factories in Iraq, were mobile. So why can't the world's most powerful army find a mobile terrorist base? And why, when US forces helped clean out a whole town (Tin Zaouatene), was there no great declaration of 'victory'? What happened? What went wrong? Was it simply that there were no terrorist bases in the area? Or was it because the raid was not intended to hunt down 'terrorists', but a 'revenge operation' for recently firing on a US military transport plane? Or was it designed to provoke the Tuareg, as in Niger, to take up arms, thus heightening regional insecurity and political instability in order to justify AFRICOM (US Africa Command), the Pentagon's new military command for Africa?[12]

Four days later, on 18 February, General William 'Kip' Ward, AFRICOM's Commander, and Theresa Whelan, Deputy Assistant Secretary of Defense for African Affairs, both desperate to promote AFRICOM, addressed a packed conference on AFRICOM and US–Africa Security at the Royal United Services Institute (RUSI) for Defence and Security Studies in London. To questions from the floor, the General and Ms Whelan denied the presence of US forces in northern Mali.

The following week, General Ward was in Bamako reassuring the Malian government and the international media that the US was committed to helping Mali maintain the security of its northern regions. Less than a month later, on 20 March, Tuareg rebels led by Ibrahim ag Bahanga undertook a devastating attack on a Mali military convoy eleven miles south of Tin Zaouatene. They seized eight army vehicles, killed at least three Malian soldiers, wounded many others and took a further 33 captive. Representatives of the rebels confirmed that their action was to revenge the Malian-US assault on Tin Zaouatene.

On 25 March, Bahanga's rebels were reported by a Western military source to have moved their 33 captured soldiers across the border into Niger where they were being guarded by members of the MNJ. This action precipitated an Algerian newspaper to pose the question that all the countries in the region feared; namely, was this a sign that the Tuareg rebellions in Niger and Mali had finally linked up?[13]

The Start of New Tuareg Rebellions

How had this appalling state of affairs come about? What had finally led to the creation of a geographically continuous zone of conflict across Africa, from Mauritania in the west, through Mali, Niger, Chad and Sudan to Somalia in the east?

In this and the following chapter, I explain why the Tuareg in the western half of this zone, after so much provocation, not only took up arms, but also linked their struggles on a transnational basis and even aligned themselves with traditional enemies such as the Toubou.[14]

Tuareg rebellions broke out separately, first in Niger in February 2007 and then a few months later in Mali. The incident which precipitated the rebellion in Niger, namely an attack on the village of Iferouane in northern Aïr on 8 February 2007 by three heavily armed Tuareg and a handful of followers, is still shrouded in mystery. I visited and travelled through much of the region shortly after the attack and was able to talk with many of the local people who convinced me that the last thing they wanted was another rebellion. Memories of how the 1990s rebellion had been crushed were still horribly fresh in their minds. I was also able to interview a Tuareg who had seen the attackers the day before the attack. I also knew much about the attackers themselves, notably their ringleader, Aboubacar ag Alembo, who, as I explained in *The Dark Sahara*,[15] had connections with Algeria's Département du Renseignement et de la Sécurité (DRS) and may well have been involved in provisioning El Para during his time in the Sahel.

The course of the Niger rebellion since February 2007 has been substantially chronicled.[16] The emergence of the MNJ within a few weeks of the Iferouane attack, followed by a number of small military engagements, including an attack by the MNJ on a base of the French uranium company, AREVA, led the Nigerien parliament to approve more than $60 million in extra budget funds to confront the attacks. The conflict escalated after the Tazerzait engagement in June. Despite the government's deployment of some 4,000 troops, MNJ attacks continued, with attacks on the coalmine at Tchighozerine,[17] which provides power for the uranium mines at Arlit; strategic installations in and around the regional capital of Agades, including the airport, and on FAN convoys and emplacements.[18] The government was further embarrassed by the MNJ's hostage-taking (and subsequent release) of an executive of the Chinese uranium company, Chino-U,[19] and the defection to the MNJ of a significant number of men from both the FAN and the Force National d'Intervention et de la Sécurité (FNIS).[20]

By the end of July, the rebellion had spread to north-eastern Mali. On 11 May, Bahanga, for reasons which are explained later, attacked and killed two policemen at a police post near Tin Zaouatene. Then, in late August, Tuareg rebels under Bahanga's leadership kidnapped some 50 soldiers in a series of attacks on military convoys and positions, effectively cutting off the Tin Zaouatene garrison from supplies and reinforcements. This was an immensely embarrassing situation for Mali's military command, which, not surprisingly, turned to its military ally and protector, the US.

This was not the sort of situation in which Washington had envisaged becoming involved. In fact, the timing of Mali's request for help was embarrassing for the US for two reasons.

A Sticky Patch in US-Algerian Relations

One reason was that the request came after a year in which US relations with its main regional ally, Algeria, had been going through a sticky patch. This temporary dip in US-Algerian relations was caused by a number of developments, which included Algeria's failure to deliver on certain hydrocarbons expectations, the huge growth in Algeria's FOREX (foreign exchange) reserves, which were making Algeria more financially independent of the US (and everyone else for that matter), Russia's emergence as a major player in the Algerian gas and arms markets and the associated development of tensions between fractions within Algeria's intelligence services. Indeed, it was these tensions within the intelligence services that almost certainly led to the public exposé of the activities of the US Halliburton Company in Algeria and the consequent temporary downturn in US-Algerian relations.

The story of Halliburton in Algeria goes back to 1994, when Algeria's military regime was at the height of its 'dirty war' against the Islamists[21] and the country technically bankrupt. It was at that dire moment for the regime that the Halliburton Company initiated what many now regard as a thoroughly corrupt and illegal arrangement. This was that Halliburton's engineering branch, Kellogg Brown & Root (49 per cent) created a joint venture company with Sonatrach (51 per cent) (Algeria's National Oil Company), called Brown & Root Condor (BRC).[22] On 23 July 2006, an investigative report that President Bouteflika had ordered some months earlier into the activities of BRC was leaked to the media. The leaks revealed that BRC had been given at least 26 major contracts at inflated prices, without tendering, as is required by Algerian law, in the major markets of Sonatrach, National Defence and Security, the Ministry of Energy and Mines and other industrial and real estate projects, including the new military base at Tamanrasset. However, the element of this scandal that most damaged US-Algerian relations was that Russian military information services were reported to have revealed to the leaders of Algeria's military intelligence service that the sophisticated communications system purchased in the US by BRC on behalf of Algeria's General Staff had been tampered with by US intelligence services so that all Algeria's military communications were permanently connected to both US and Israeli electronic intelligence systems.[23] The allegation was damaging to both the US and BRC. BRC was closed down and its Algerian Director gaoled. With money dried up, work on the Tamanrasset base, once General Jim Jones's focal 'lily pad' in EUCOM's (US European Command's) 'War on Terror' across the Sahara, came to a halt. By March 2007, one of Africa's greatest monuments to imperial over-reach stood abandoned, sentry pillboxes empty, gathering sand and dust.

The Relief of Tin Zaouatene

The second reason why Mali's request to the US for assistance to relieve Tin Zaouatene was embarrassing to the US was because the situation was nothing to do with the 'Global War on Terror' (GWOT) or Islamic extremism. Since 2003, Washington had been pinpointing this region, the Nigerien-Malian-Algerian border zones, as an Islamist 'Terror Zone'. Literally thousands of US-inspired media articles had described this specific region as the locale of 'al-Qaeda terrorist bases lurking deep in the Sahara desert'. How, in the light of such propaganda, could the US now explain that the region was immersed in a rebellion which was absolutely nothing to do with Islamism or al-Qaeda, the two bogeymen at the heart of the propaganda which had justified US intervention in the region in the first place? Washington certainly could not admit that the rebellions were an unintended consequence of its ill-thought-out policy of fabricating terrorism in order to justify the launch of its Saharan front in the GWOT.

Moreover, this conflagration was not a good advertisement to the rest of Africa of how US-trained troops perform. The Pentagon had reportedly spent several million dollars since 2004 training Nigerien and Malian forces under Bush's much-heralded Pan Sahel Initiative (PSI) and Trans-Sahara Counterterrorism Initiative (TSCTI). The product of this training was not impressive. Niger's US-trained forces had been severely humiliated in their encounter with Tuareg rebels in 2004–05 and in almost every engagement in the rebellion that had begun in February 2007. At least 80 soldiers had been killed and dozens taken hostage, compared to relatively low rebel casualties. This consistent combat failure of Niger's troops effectively confined them to barracks and fixed bases dotted around the region from where they vented their frustration and anger on the surrounding civilian population. The Tuareg rebellions were very bad for US public relations, especially Washington's promotion of its wider military policy in Africa, which was soon to come to fruition with the creation of AFRICOM.[24] Not only did the rebellions draw attention to the desultory performance of the local troops that the US had spent several million of dollars in training, but they also drew attention to the fact that the US emphasis on its 'hearts and minds' training had been little more than a chimera. The only thing in which the Niger's US-trained troops had excelled was in killing civilians.

The behaviour of US-trained forces in Mali had been little better. In early 2007, there were several reports from local people of Malian troops violating nomadic camps and their womenfolk. Bahanga's attack on the police post at Tin Zaouatene on 11 May was almost certainly an act of revenge by an aggrieved 'former rebel' returning home to find soldiers violating women in his camp, while the major escalation of rebel action in March 2008 was to revenge the US-Malian assault on Tin Zaouatene.

There were other aspects about Mali's request to the US to help it relieve the 'siege of Tin Zaouatene' that irked Washington. First, it coincided with the second anniversary of Operation Flintlock. Although a much more low-key affair than in 2005, the Pentagon and State Department had briefed the media, especially their own, and invited them to attend the planned exercises in southern Mali. As far as I am aware, scarcely any major networks attended. The senior editorial management of major US networks with whom I had discussed the US intervention in the region said that they 'weren't prepared to waste air tickets on it'.

Second, while the media virtually ignored the anniversary of Operation Flintlock, deeming it thoroughly un-newsworthy, the same could not be said of the US 'relief of Tin Zaouatene', which garnered global media coverage for all the wrong reasons. The operation involved a US Lockheed Hercules C-130 undertaking an airdrop of 14,000 pounds of food supplies to the beleaguered Malian garrison at Tin Zaouatene during the night of 11–12 September. The event would almost certainly have gone unrecorded had not rebel Tuareg opened fire on the plane with AK47s and machine-guns. Pam Cook, a spokeswoman for the US command in Stuttgart, confirmed that no one on the plane was wounded, which did not return fire and was able to return to Bamako having sustained only minor damage. 'We would do this for any partner nation that we're working with when their troops are pinned down', said Cook.[25] That is how the US would like its interventions in Africa to be appreciated. However, in this instance, as US spin-doctors had been portraying Tin Zaouatene as an al-Qaeda stronghold, the incident consequently came across as another al-Qaeda victory against the 'Great Satan'. Tin Zaouatene was not good PR in Washington's plans for AFRICOM.

Washington Has No Plan B

The Tuareg rebellions, for all the reasons outlined above, created considerable problems for the US. However, as Washington had no 'Plan B', it continued with what it had been doing since El Para first set foot in the region in 2003, namely dressing up the story to the extent of deception and even lies. In short, it returned to basics, claiming once again that the ungoverned expanses of the Sahara were a potential hornet's nest of al-Qaeda training camps that threatened not only the countries of North and West Africa, but Europe itself, and that the Tuareg rebels were merely bandits, criminals and drug traffickers, categories which, in Washington parlance, equated with terrorists.

Neither of these two strategies was accomplished easily. In the case of trying to present the region as a haven for al-Qaeda and its terrorist training camps, Washington and its local government allies had been claiming the existence of these since 2004. Yet, in the three to four years since El Para's escapade in the region, the US and its allies had failed to come up with any concrete evidence of GSPC/AQIM terrorist activity, let alone 'training camps', in the region. Indeed, even the engagements between the Tuareg and GSPC/AQIM in 2006, described in the last chapter, were spurious. As for the second strategy of trying to portray the Tuareg rebels as criminals, drug traffickers and bandits, that too was equally problematic, although less so – for reasons revealed later – since the end of 2009, by which time the rebellions were in any case effectively over.

In the first of these two strategies the US had an extraordinary stroke of luck. This occurred some 2,500 kilometres east-north-east of the US's local propaganda centre – its Embassy in Bamako – in the little oasis town of Djanet in the far south-eastern corner of Algeria.

The Attack on Djanet Airport

What happened at Djanet on 8 November 2007, a little less than two months after the US relief of Tin Zaouatene, not only saved face for Washington but is pivotal to any understanding and explanation of 'terrorism' and the nature of al-Qaeda in this western half of the Sahel.

The 'official' version of what happened at Djanet, that is the version of events put out in the Algerian media from its intelligence and security services and then quickly adopted and publicised by official US information services, is that al-Qaeda terrorists, based in northern Mali – that is, close to Tin Zaouatene – undertook a daring attack on Djanet's airport some 1,000 kilometres north-east of Tin Zaouatene. However, like so much else in the Sahara-Sahel region at this time, it was not true.

According to reports in the Algerian media, about ten terrorists arrived in three off-road vehicles and fired on Djanet airport with rocket-propelled grenades (RPGs) and machine-guns at about four o'clock in the morning of 8 November. The reports, however, were remarkably contradictory. While *El Watan* said that the attackers damaged an Air Algérie plane, *Le Soir d'Algérie* reported that two helicopters and a military aircraft were hit. *Echorouk Al Yaoumi* embellished a little more, describing how shots were fired from a distance of around 800 metres at a military aircraft and a helicopter in the airport. The military aircraft was reportedly seriously damaged, but did not burn or explode. There were no human causalities and no one was on the aircraft. While most reports said the attackers were able to escape across the border into Niger, *Echorouk Al Yaoumi* said that army forces responded immediately with a helicopter-based operation across the desert that resulted in the terrorists being caught and killed. *El Khabar* added to the confusion two days later by saying that the attack was undertaken by partisans of Lamari Saifi, alias Abderrezak Al Para (El Para), now led by Abdelhamid abou Zaïd, who had been El Para's 'number two' in the 2003 hostage operation, with the intent of undermining Mokhtar ben Mokhtar (MBM), another alleged GSPC/AQIM leader who at that time was reported in the Algerian media to be negotiating his surrender to the Algerian authorities. Five days later, *El Khabar* went into more detail, reporting that the security forces had identified the Djanet terrorists. They were nothing to do with MBM, nor were they either Algerian Tuareg or Tuareg rebels from Niger and Mali, as some reports had suggested, but were, in fact, AQIM terrorists who had travelled from AQIM training camps in northern Mali. The Algerian security forces said that they knew this because they had infiltrated the attackers in their training camps in Mali.

Algeria's security forces further embellished the story to make it sound more plausible by stating that the Djanet attackers had initially been targeting oil facilities in the region. They had learnt this through their infiltration of their training camps. While that might sound convincing, those familiar with the area would know that there were no oil facilities in the Djanet region.

I should also point out, especially for readers not wholly familiar with the geographical and political terrain, that at that particular moment in time it would have been virtually impossible for three vehicles to travel unobserved from Mali to Djanet, whether via Algeria or Niger, because of the massive deployment of Algerian army checkpoints in virtually every passable route and *oued* (river valley) on both the northern and southern sides of Ahaggar, and because the Niger rebellion had turned the mountains of Aïr into a near-impassable barrier stretching from the Algerian border to Agades.

The truth of what happened at Djanet was, in fact, very different. My investigations in the area during the course of the weeks following the incident revealed that the attack had been undertaken by a number of Tuareg youths from the Djanet oasis. According to members of their families, their reasons for attacking the airport were partly to demonstrate their sympathy with the Tuareg rebels in Niger, with whom they were historically and politically closely connected, but primarily to protest their dissatisfaction with the Algerian authorities. The youths and their motives were soon known to the Algerian security authorities who did everything possible to prevent such information leaking into the wider public domain, even going so far as to 'deal' with the problem of the youths by discussing and resolving it with their parents and Djanet's 'elders'. The Algerian authorities were determined to suppress the 'truth' of the incident. This was because Algeria at that time was, as it still is, a tinderbox. Rising unemployment, increasing food prices and a raft of other related grievances threatened to push the country into a state of civil unrest and riots reminiscent of those in 1988.[26] The regime was consequently far more worried about an explosion of civil unrest than the activities of the GSPC/AQIM. Hence all the embellished articles in the Algerian press about al-Qaeda attacks at Djanet.

Nevertheless, the embellishment suited American purposes. It gave them a pretext to claim a terrorist incident and supported the currently favoured discourse that portrayed the northern Malian desert as the home of al-Qaeda bases that threatened both Africa and Europe. The incident was widely published in the international media, with international security analysts explaining how the attack demonstrated the increasing threat being presented in the Sahara-Sahel by AQIM, and that the rebranding of the GSPC with the al-Qaeda franchise earlier that year reflected the terrorist organisation's increasing 'internationalisation' and 'reach'.

Only one security consultancy reported the incident correctly. That was London-based Menas Associates, who, drawing on the author's insight, said that 'there was no terrorist attack on

Djanet airport … and that Algeria had once again fabricated a terrorist incident'.[27]

European intelligence services, which are part of the front line in the dissemination to the media of what can be increasingly regarded as 'myth making',[28] knew that much of the information coming out of the Sahara-Sahel region at this time was, as it still is, nothing more than disinformation. Britain's Foreign and Commonwealth Office (FCO), for example, was briefed on the 'real' events that had taken place at Djanet a few weeks after the incident. I myself gave the details of the incident to an FCO official. His response to me was: 'The Algerians reported that there was a terrorist attack on Djanet airport. Therefore, it is a fact.'[29]

The truth of the Djanet attack was finally revealed, through the oversight of Algeria's own intelligence and security service, the DRS, in October 2010. Faced with the apparent rise in AQIM activity in the Sahara-Sahel during 2010, El Watan's Salima Tlemçani, a journalist who works closely with the DRS, was sent to the region to produce a series of articles designed to highlight the vulnerability of the region to AQIM terrorism.

Ironically, Tlemçani appears not to have been properly briefed by the DRS. She interviewed both the Amenukal ('supreme chief') of the Ahaggar Tuareg and M. Larbi, the President of the Tamanrasset APW (Assemblée Populaire de Wilaya) who explained to her: 'We do not want to repeat the scenario of the youth of Djanet, who took up arms and attacked a military plane [at the airport]. That necessitated the intervention of the notables of the region [ed. mostly their parents] to make them see reason and give up. Very fortunately, they listened to their elders …'[30]

* * *

Many people, especially the Americans, had been calling attention to, and crying 'wolf', over terrorist bases in the 'vast ungoverned areas' of northern Mali during the five or so years since El Para's exploits in the region. During that time, the US had failed, in spite of having Special Forces on the ground and satellite surveillance above, to find any. Its excuse was that the bases (like Iraq's chemical factories) were now mobile.

However, in July 2008, eight months after the Djanet incident, Algeria's DRS came to the rescue. It placed a story in the Algerian newspaper *El Khabar*[31] reporting that Algeria's security services had arrested a man of Sahelian origin who had 'penetrated Algerian territory via the Mali border' in late 2007 and had revealed under interrogation the existence of 183 foreigners in an al-Qaeda training camp in the Malian-Algerian border region. The camp, he revealed, contained fighters from Tuareg tribes in Niger, Chad (where there are no Tuareg tribes!) and Mali, as well as 33 terrorists from Mauritania, 13 from Nigeria, seven from the Western Sahara, and others from Libya, Tunisia and Burkina Faso.

The story was, of course, unverifiable. Nevertheless, such pronouncements, especially when sourced to Algeria's or other regional security forces, were immensely attractive to the Bush administration, which was desperately trying to overcome opposition within Washington to a new African combatant command[32] and was relying increasingly on 'proof' of al-Qaeda's terrorist activity in the vast, 'ungoverned … empty spaces' of the Sahara-Sahel and that this was a threat to both African countries and Europe. By the time this book went to press in May 2012, the Pentagon's 'Terror Zone' across this part of Africa had become a self-fulfilled prophecy. Yet, at this time, the end of 2007, there had still been no terrorist attacks in the Sahara-Sahel region and no verified evidence of their much-talked about training bases in the region.[33]

As one Tuareg who had been intimately associated with El Para's operation in 2003 said to me at the time of the above-mentioned *El Khabar* story (July 2008): 'Europe should indeed be terrified, not because of the alleged existence of so many terrorists in the Sahara, but because the US military, with satellites overhead, high-tech listening equipment on the ground, and thousands of Algerian and Malian troops in the field, as well as its own Special Forces, cannot locate a training camp of at least 183 persons in the middle of the desert!'

Disparaging Tuareg Rebels as Criminals, Drug Traffickers and Bandits

The second strategy the US adopted for coping with the Tuareg rebellions was to insist that the Tuareg were not 'rebels', but merely criminals and drug traffickers. For Washington, drug trafficking and terrorism are two sides of the same coin. The US had little difficulty in promoting this strategy as it was largely done for them, and most vociferously, by the governments of the region. Neither Niger nor Mali wanted to admit, only a decade after having seemingly resolved major Tuareg rebellions, that they were once again facing political rebellions from their Tuareg populations. Both governments, backed by the US, therefore went to great lengths to ensure that the terms 'rebellion' and 'rebel' were never used, as they dignified the 'rebels' with the status, credibility and political recognition that both governments, as well as Western intelligence services, were keen to avoid. Both governments therefore portrayed the rebels as criminals, drug traffickers and bandits who were attempting to take advantage of the insecurity of the desert border areas to seize control of the drugs and other trafficking routes that cross this part of the Sahara.

This strategy, although a grotesque perversion of the truth, has gained increasing traction in the Western media as the rebellions dragged on. This is because drug trafficking across the Sahara, both cocaine from South America and cannabis resin from Morocco, has increased dramatically over the last few years. Moreover, as Chapter 12 explains, the rebel Tuareg movements in both Niger and Mali have, out of necessity, part-financed their rebellions and the subsistence of their civilian communities by levying tolls on the drug traffickers. Also, as the 'War on Terror' has progressively destroyed their livelihoods, especially in tourism, Tuareg have been drawn into the various trafficking businesses as drivers, guides and other such operatives.

It was in this context that a number of French newspapers ran stories in mid April 2008 that the Tuareg rebels in Niger had been cooperating with AQIM. However, unfortunately for France's President Sarkozy, who at that time was busily currying favour with Washington, the French newspapers, when challenged, were unable to produce the evidence.[34] Nevertheless, headlines are remembered and, like the Djanet attack, allegations made are not easily erased.

7
URANIUM GOES CRITICAL: WHY THE TUAREG TOOK UP ARMS

As the rebellions in both Niger and Mali developed through 2007, 2008 and on into 2009, so they took on new dimensions and meanings. Perceptions of the rebellions' causal origins have also changed with time. Indeed, by the time some sort of semblance of a peace had been reached by late 2009, the Sahel was a very different land from what it was when the first shots rang out at Iferouane in February 2007. While the main thrust of the demands and declarations of the Mouvement des Nigériens pour la Justice (MNJ) have consistently given prominence to the way in which Tuareg lands are increasingly being exploited by international uranium mining companies, a more nuanced analysis would reveal that the Tuareg rebellions of 2007–09 in both Niger and Mali were more 'multi-layered'.

However, when we look at the 'causes' of each rebellion in turn, we are left with the disconcerting conclusion that while each one was built on the basis of justifiable grievances and, as at AREVA's uranium mines, even resistance, none of them on their own, as most Tuareg seem inclined to agree, were sufficient to explain why the Tuareg took up arms. Indeed, the question of why the Niger rebellion broke out in the first place and then took on such a horrific course becomes even more vexed when we consider that the vast majority of the local population, with the memories of the 1990s rebellion and the way it was crushed still fresh in their minds, had no desire for another rebellion. Equally problematic is the fact that none of the three Tuareg responsible for the Iferouane attack had any credibility as either a popular or legitimate rebel or political leader. In other words, although the

Tuareg of Niger had many legitimate grievances, we have to face up to the disturbing and sinister possibility that the rebellion, like those of 2004 in Aïr and 2006 in Mali, may have been initiated and orchestrated by external forces. However, before we consider this possibility, we need to understand the grievances that have built up amongst Niger's Tuareg over the last few years.

At least three major issues can be identified: the exploitative practices of foreign mining and oil companies, government's failure to adhere to the 1995 Peace Accord, and the impact of the US 'Global War on Terror' (GWOT).

The Exploitative Practices of Foreign Mining and Oil Companies

The MNJ's most clearly articulated area of grievance and demands related to the expansion of uranium mining in northern Niger. Their concerns related to three main issues: the exploitative nature of these enterprises, the threat of an impending ecological disaster and the abuse by both the government and foreign companies of the Tuareg's indigenous rights. To take each of these in turn:

The Nature of Uranium Mining and Oil Exploration

Niger has long been a major source of uranium and by 2007 was the world's third-ranking exporter. Annual production of some 3,300 metric tonnes accounted for around 72 per cent of Niger's export revenue and approximately 10 per cent of global uranium mine supply.

Uranium was first discovered in 1957 near Arlit in northern Niger. Further discoveries were made at numerous sites in the adjoining Tamesna region during the late 1950s and 1960s. By 2007, the two main mines at Arlit and nearby Akokan were controlled, as they still are, by a consortium led by the giant French corporation, AREVA, with the uranium concentrates, known as yellow-cake, being transported overland to Cotonou and then taken by ship for conversion, mostly to Comurhex in France.

With the world energy crisis giving nuclear energy a new lease of life, the price of uranium rose from scarcely $10 a pound (543 grammes) at the beginning of 2003 to $45 by mid June 2006 and to record $136 in June 2007. Not surprisingly, there was a veritable scramble by foreign companies to acquire exploration rights and for those that already had them to expand uranium production in Niger.

The first company to act on this was AREVA,[1] which signed an agreement with the government in 2004 to expand its exploration, followed in 2006 by a further agreement to develop the large Imouraren deposit about 60 kilometres south of Arlit.

France, however, no longer had a monopoly on Niger's uranium. At the same time as signing the Imouraren deal, Niger awarded licences to a group of Chinese companies led by the China International Uranium Corporation (SinoUranium), a unit of China National Nuclear Corporation, to explore for uranium at a number of sites in the Agades-Tamesna region. With the Niger government targeting a threefold increase of uranium production to 10,500 tonnes of uranium per year (tU/yr) in the next few years, the Nigerien government had granted by the end of 2007 around 90 mining exploration permits for the northern desert region with a further 90 or so under consideration.

This scramble for uranium in northern Niger by international mining companies from France, China, Canada, Australia, South Africa, the UK, India and elsewhere came against a background of increasingly widespread and organised opposition and resistance to the exploitative practices of foreign mining and oil corporations.

Conditions at AREVA's two uranium mines in northern Niger were so bad that in 2003 the workers began organising themselves by setting up a local non-governmental organisation, Aghirin'man,[2] to draw attention to the appalling working conditions to which they were being subjected.

AREVA's shocking track record in corporate irresponsibility[3] underpins the current resistance to foreign corporate exploitation of the region. Not surprisingly, it fuelled local anger towards both AREVA and the French government. Indeed, shortly after the Iferouane attack, the French ambassador visited the region only to be given an exceptionally strong rebuke by a spokesperson for the local community and to be told that France had lost all respect and credibility in the region and that he was to leave.[4]

The Chinese National Petroleum Company (CNPC) also became the object of opprobrium after commencing oil exploration operations in the Ténéré region in 2002–03. The CNPC's lack of respect for local people and their cultural practices caused widespread anger and hostility, with strikes and labour absenteeism becoming commonplace in the year or two prior to the onset of the rebellion. It is consequently not surprising that both the CNPC and SinoUranium received threats from the rebels.

Fear of an Impending Ecological Disaster

At the time of the 2007 rebellion, Aghirin'man saw the expansion of uranium mining as the continuation and acceleration of what it had already referred to as 'Niger's economic, social and environmental tragedy'. The particular environmental tragedy to which it was referring is the impending ecological catastrophe facing much of the country west of the Aïr mountains, notably the regions of Talak, Tamesna and Teguidda.

Local people who understand the issues, and they are rapidly increasing in number, are extremely anxious that the expansion of uranium mining will lead to an extension of the pollution, disease and ill-health that has characterised uranium mining at Arlit.[5] They see the expansion of the present system of unregulated uranium mining around Imouraren, Sekiret, In Gall, the Ighazer valley and elsewhere as a major and extremely serious threat to the region's unique and complex ecosystem, which plays a pivotal and very complex socio-ecological role in the livelihoods of tens of thousands of pastoralists.

The Abuse of Indigenous Rights

The US's intervention in the Sahara-Sahel has done much to raise awareness and politicise local peoples over such issues as their identity, governance, land and indigenous rights. For example, in July 2006, within a matter of days of the United Nations Human Rights Council's adoption of the UN Declaration on the Rights of Indigenous Peoples, the Tuareg of Niger lodged a formal complaint with the UNWGIP (UN Working Group on Indigenous Peoples) about the US presence and its activities in Niger.

Unfortunately for the international mining companies bent on exploiting Niger's uranium resources, Tuareg are acutely aware of their indigenous rights to the Aïr-Talak-Tamesna region. Few places in the Tuareg's extensive domain are perceived as being more indigenous, almost 'sacred', than Tamesna. Reasons for these sentiments are deeply rooted and go beyond the bounds of this book. Suffice it to say that with Niger's Independence in 1960, Tamesna became a sort of no-man's land, a 'Tuareg reserve', legally part of Niger but effectively beyond the reach of either the Nigerien or Algerian administrations. It became a uniquely Tuareg area in which traditional pastoral rights and practices were largely retained. It was the region to which Tuareg went, both from Algeria and Niger, when, to use their terminology, they 'wanted to get away from government'.

International mining companies, the Nigerien government and Tuareg political leaders have all been fully aware of the international attempts to recognise and protect indigenous rights and the long passage of the UN Declaration on the Rights of Indigenous Peoples,[6] which was finally passed by the UN General Assembly on 13 September 2007. The Declaration gives some degree of international legal protection and right to the Tuareg's attempts to protect their lands from the sort of rapacious exploitation by international mining companies that is now being experienced in Niger. Although all the countries in the region, notably Algeria, Mali and Niger, voted in favour of the UN Declaration, they have yet to translate their nominal support for the Declaration into practice. The Tuareg, for their part, are fully aware that they have the indisputable moral weight of the Declaration behind them, but have been reluctant to use it for fear of being accused of separatism.

Government's Failure to Adhere to the 1995 Peace Accord

The extent to which the Niger government has adhered to or fulfilled all the conditions and agreements of the 1995 Peace Accord, which marked the official end of the 1990s rebellion, is debatable. In the government's defence, many of the Tuareg rebels were integrated into the FAN (Forces Armées Nigériennes) and the FNIS (Force National d'Intervention et de la Sécurité). There has also been some devolution of government, especially at the local and regional levels. It can also be said in the government's defence that it has not had the resources to undertake many of the 1995 development proposals as it might have desired. However, the MNJ's claims that the government has not delivered on what the Tuareg regard as the biggest issue, namely participating in the governance and management of the region's resources and an equitable share in their development, are quite true. This latest Nigerien rebellion, which began in 2007, was rooted in this growing resentment at the rapacious exploitation of their lands and their exclusion from its benefits. Indeed, the financial terms and operating practices of these companies, sanctioned by the Nigerien government, are in complete contravention of the 1995 Peace Accord, as well as the many global declarations and conventions on the exploitation of indigenous land rights. In short, the way in which the region's mineral and hydrocarbon resources have been and still are being exploited is seen by local people as bringing no benefit to themselves or to their communities.

The Impact of the US's 'Global War on Terror'

At the most general level, these Tuareg rebellions, in both Niger and Mali, were the product of the increasing destabilisation of the Sahara-Sahel region since 2003 as a result of the Bush administration's fabrication of a Saharan-Sahelian front in its 'Global War on Terror' (GWOT) whose epicentre has been the Tuareg regions of northern Niger, northern Mali and the extreme south of Algeria.

The impact of this 'front' on the livelihoods, lifestyles and identities of the peoples of these regions, especially the indigenous

Tuareg populations, has been catastrophic. The fabrication of the sequence of El Para incidents[7] and the US's subsequent representation of the region as an al-Qaeda 'Terror Zone' have not only done immense damage to the local tourism industry and associated livelihoods, but have angered the Tuareg, who resent their region and by implication their own proud identity, being branded and manipulated to fit the US-authored view of global terrorism.

Prior to El Para's catastrophic entry into the region in 2003–04, tourism was increasingly becoming not only the 'cash' mainstay of local Tuareg economies but the means through which the Tuareg were able to exercise a large measure of control over the way in which they, along with their lifestyles and identities, were being inserted into the increasingly global world economy. Through the use of the internet and accompanying technologies, such as satellite phones, Tuareg were able to retain and develop a large measure of control over both the nature of tourism in their regions and the international tourism market. These technologies enabled them, in their own words, 'to jump over the state'.

The reopening of this large part of the central Sahara to tourism around the turn of the millennium, following the diminution of Algeria's 'civil war',[8] the easing of Western-imposed sanctions on Libya and the cessation of the previous Tuareg rebellions in Niger and Mali, coincided with the arrival of the internet in these regions and the consequent rapid surge in the development of Tuareg-controlled tourism. Sadly, those halcyon days of unbridled optimism were short-lived. El Para's arrival on the scene in 2003 brought tourism in southern Algeria to a sudden halt. While the Tuareg regions of northern Niger and Mali were able to maintain a modicum of business, thanks largely to the tenacity of their French and some other European clients, it was brought to a standstill in 2007 by the start of the new rebellions.

The loss of livelihoods associated with the decimation of the tourism industry has had three main outcomes. First, it has caused widespread hardship; scarcely a household in the entirety of this immense region has not suffered in some degree.

Second, it has obliged an increasing number of men, mostly but not exclusively young, to seek alternative means of supporting their families. With little work available in their own regions, this has meant them migrating to places such as Libya or turning to the many trafficking and smuggling businesses, even direct banditry, that have become increasingly prevalent in the last few years. Many Tuareg have found high-risk 'employment' as drivers, guides, procurers, and so forth, for the big drug and other trans-Saharan trafficking businesses, or as smaller operatives within the smaller-scale, but still high-risk, smuggling businesses providing fuel and other such commodities to the increasingly impoverished local economies. Ironically, the big drug-trafficking networks, about which US counterterrorism agencies make so much ado, are under the control of corrupt elements within the political-military elites of the West and North African states who are Washington's nominal allies in its GWOT.

Third, this loss of livelihoods has become a major contribution to local people's growing level of anger against their governments. As already explained, this anger has been directed more at their own governments than the US because of the way in which the former have used the GWOT as a source of rent and the means for branding legitimate opposition, minorities and other recalcitrant elements of their populations as terrorists.

External and National Interests in the Causation and Escalation of the Rebellion

I suggested earlier that the 2007 rebellions, like those of 2004 in Aïr and 2006 in Mali, may have been initiated and to some extent even orchestrated by external forces. In the early stages of the rebellions, especially in Niger, media elements at one time or another pointed a finger at France and AREVA, Algeria, the US, Libya, China, international oil and mining companies, drug traffickers, Islamists of one sort or another, and, nearer to home, the governments and militaries of both Niger and Mali. However, as the rebellions escalated and dragged on, an extremely complicated picture began to emerge, in which most of the above appeared to have had some sort of involvement.

France and AREVA

France guards jealously its economic and political ties with *la francophonie*, especially Niger, whose substantial uranium deposits supply France, via AREVA, with a secured source of energy and a guarantee of nuclear independence. Not only does France need Niger's uranium to run its own reactors, but AREVA is currently the world's leading constructor of nuclear reactors, a position which is helped in no small measure by being a leading marketer of uranium. It is thus able to deliver turnkey systems: the nuclear reactor package as well as the fuel to run them. This position was assured until Niger decided to place its own self-interest ahead of that of its former colonial master by opening its mineral-rich north to international competition. Suddenly, France was faced with the reality of international companies from China, South Africa, Canada, Australia, India, Nigeria, Algeria, the UK and elsewhere helping themselves to what it had hitherto taken for granted as its own national energy supply.

It is therefore not surprising that there have been rumours and suspicion from the outset that France/AREVA instigated and financed the rebellion in order to frighten off foreign competition. The Nigerien government even went so far as to accuse AREVA of financing the rebels. Although this was denied by AREVA, Niger expelled AREVA's head of operations in July 2007 in a move that provoked the direct intervention of President Sarkozy and high-level Franco-Nigerien talks in Niamey between Jean-Marie Bockel, France's Cooperation Minister, and President Tandja.[9]

France certainly had the means to initiate Tuareg unrest in Niger. Its own security agents, for instance, have long maintained close surveillance of the region, while AREVA's management has close ties to both the MNJ leadership and other parties in the region. The president of the MNJ, for example, Ghaly ag Alembo, was formerly the *sous-préfet*[10] at Arlit where his business was as much to meet the needs of the uranium producer as to administer the mining town and its environs. However, if France/AREVA was behind the rebellion, as many people still suspect,[11] two points should be made. The first is that if France did intend to create a bush fire in the region, it became dangerously out of control. The second is that if this was France's intent, it would have been more likely to operate through the more covert channels of its own foreign intelligence service, the Direction Générale de la Sécurité Extérieure (DGSE), which at that time had especially close ties with Algeria's Département du Renseignement et de la Sécurité (DRS), which, more than anyone, had the means to trigger such a chain of events.

Algeria

Was Algeria involved in triggering such a chain of events? There is evidence to suggest that Algeria's DRS may have been involved in the instigation of the rebellion. The evidence for this is as follows:

First, the three Tuareg who carried out the initial attack on Iferouane, Aboubacar ag Alembo, Kalakoua and Al Charif (Acheriff Mohamed), were known to the DRS. Aboubacar and Kalakoua both had criminal records, while Al Charif was a former rebel who had subsequently deserted the Nigerien army. The leader of the attack, Aboubacar, as I described in *The Dark Sahara*, came on the political scene in 2002 after deserting from the Nigerien army and killing two policemen. Since then he has been responsible for numerous acts of banditry, being described to me by some of his former comrades in the 1990s rebellion as 'psychopathic', enjoying 'violence' and always being entrusted to do the 'dirty work'.[12] More significantly, he was well connected through a complex network of kinship ties to influential members of the regional governments on both sides of the Nigerien-Algerian border. For example, his brother Ghaly ag Alembo, as already mentioned, was formerly the *sous-préfet* at Arlit, while a cousin, at the time of the outbreak of the rebellion, was the Commandant of Niger's FNIS, which, amongst other things, is responsible for the protection of foreign companies, such as AREVA and the Chinese oil and uranium companies, in the region. Another cousin was the director of security for Algeria's Tamanrasset *wilaya*, while other kinsmen are well connected in Djanet. Since 2002 he had been protected and used by the DRS. There is also evidence that the vehicles and arms used in the Iferouane attack came from northern Mali and may have been provided by connections with the DRS, which, as described in Chapter 5, had been instrumental in promoting the short-lived Tuareg rebellion at Kidal on 23 May 2006. However, with Aboubacar being killed at Tazerzait on 22 June and the DRS boss, Smaïn Lamari, dying two months later, it is now unlikely that we will ever get much closer to the truth than this.

Second, Algeria has been the main agent in assisting the US in its policy of creating a 'Terror Zone' across the Sahel since 2003. This, as documented in *The Dark Sahara*, has involved the fabrication of 'terrorist' incidents; the promotion of media disinformation and the provocation of unrest in the region. It also involved arranging the skirmishes described in Chapter 5 (this volume) between Tuareg, DRS-supported rebels and Groupe Salafiste pour le Prédication et le Combat (GSPC) elements in northern Mali in the period September–October 2006.

Third, Algeria has political and economic designs on the Sahel, most notably in north-eastern Mali (the Kidal region) and northern Niger. Precisely how the MNJ rebellion might have furthered these interests is not at all clear. However, some local people believe the destabilisation of the Sahel (Mali and Niger) furthers Algeria's long-term interests, perhaps by making the region less attractive to foreign exploitation, by enabling it to justify the militarisation of its extreme south, or by enabling it to play the role of 'peace-maker', thus strengthening its political influence in the region. This relates especially to the challenge posed to Algeria by similar Libyan interests in the Sahel. For instance, one reason for Algeria's orchestration of the Kidal (Mali) revolt on 23 May 2006 was to discredit Libya's presence in the region. Libya's involvement in northern Niger, especially the Agades region, was at that time far more invasive than in northern Mali, leading some local people to think that the Niger rebellion, at least at its inception, was being engineered by

Algeria in the same way as it had engineered the 23 May 2006 Kidal rebellion. If Algeria did have such designs, I am inclined to think they were short-lived, as the potential for such a rebellion to spill over into southern Algeria could not be discounted. Indeed, Algeria became increasingly anxious that the Nigerien and Malian rebellions might spread into Algeria where the bulk of the country's population, not least the Tuareg, was becoming increasingly discontent with the country's socio-economic and political conditions. As described in the previous chapter, the attack on Djanet airport on 8 November 2007 was the work of discontented local youths and an illustration of the sort of civil unrest which the Algerian government knows is a far greater threat to its survival, should it spread, than any form of terrorism.

Algeria's fear of the rebellions spreading northwards led its DRS to arrange a deal with the Tuareg rebel forces, the main element of which was that Algeria would not intervene south of the borders if the rebels did not allow their rebellion to spread into Algeria. The material basis of this deal was that Algeria allowed local merchants to cross the border and provision the MNJ with fuel and food supplies. It also allowed the MNJ to bring its wounded fighters to its hospitals (notably Tamanrasset and Djanet) for treatment.

The Nigerien government

As the rebellion developed, President Tandja and his government became the major cause of its prolongation and escalation. Since the US launched its GWOT in the Sahara-Sahel in 2003, every country in the region, without exception, has provoked unrest amongst sections of their populations (usually minority, marginal groups) to exact 'rent' from the US in the form of further military and financial largesse. Niger, the world's poorest country, has punched far above its weight in this regard.

Following the initial Iferouane attack, local Tuareg believe that the government used what they called 'The List' to deliberately provoke armed unrest. This was a list of several dozens, perhaps hundreds, of former rebels whom the government was allegedly planning to detain. Irrespective of whether this was an act of retribution or provocation by the Nigerien government, it was enough to persuade many of the former rebels, several of whom had since become responsible local community and political leaders, to take to the mountains with their arms. It is estimated that as many as 200 former rebel fighters, having sent their wives and families to safety (many to Algeria), converged on Tamgak, a near-impregnable massif approximately 150 kilometres in perimeter and over 2,000 metres high, a few miles east-north-east of Iferouane. By 2008, the number of fighters had increased to at least 1,000 and possibly, according to some of those involved, as many as 2,000.[13]

However, having used AREVA's alleged involvement in the rebellion to help break its monopoly on uranium production in Niger and thus gain a greater revenue stream by creating an expanded, internationally diversified and competitive market, there was no obvious strategic benefit to Niger in prolonging the conflict. Indeed, the prolongation of the rebellion has had the effect of deterring rather than attracting foreign investment. Further rents from US counterterrorism were also limited.

Why then, did the Nigerien government spend two years, from the onset of the rebellion in February 2007 until April 2009, refusing to countenance any move towards a peaceful resolution of the conflict? Almost from the outset, the rebels have argued that President Tandja was hellbent on an 'ivoirianisation' policy of exclusion against the Tuareg.[14] They knew that he held longstanding personal grievances against the Tuareg, stemming from the time when, as Minister of the Interior, he was responsible for the Tchin Tabaradene massacres that precipitated the 1990s rebellion. Many Tuareg, rebels and civilians, believe that the successful pursuit of this policy, manifested through what they regarded as genocide (what they called 'ethnocide'), would enable him to avoid recompensing them for the exploitation of their indigenous lands, as agreed in the 1995 Peace Accord.

As the rebellion continued into 2008, it became increasingly clear that President Tandja, through his membership of the US's TSCTI security umbrella, and with the European Union, France, China and Niger's more powerful neighbours having no immediate incentive to see the restoration of regional stability, could rest reasonably assured that his 'low-key' genocide policy was unlikely to invoke external intervention.

With Tandja continuously refusing to either recognise the MNJ as being anything more than what he called 'drug traffickers' and 'bandits', or countenance any attempt to negotiate a peaceful settlement, so the rebels, as well as many other Nigeriens, increasingly came to believe that he was 'progressing' the rebellion in order to place the country on a full state of emergency which he could use, like his neighbour President Déby of Chad, to change the Constitution and mandate himself a third presidential term, which, at the age of 71 at the 2009 elections, would effectively make him 'President for life'. This is precisely what he did in 2009, only for a coup d'état to depose him in February 2010.

The US

When the US 'invaded' the Sahel in January 2004, it had certainly not planned on Tuareg rebellions. Indeed, and as explained in the previous chapter, the rebellions presented Washington with a number of problems. However, the key point is that the USA, with its overarching 'security' interests in the region, was the one party with sufficient influence to point President Tandja in the direction of peace talks and a negotiated settlement. The fact that at no time during the period of the Bush administration did it do so suggests that Washington perceived its national strategic interests in Africa as being better served by instability than stability in the Sahel.

The Bush administration's strategy towards the Sahara-Sahel was to try and persuade the international community, largely through fabricated terrorism and associated disinformation, that its vast 'ungoverned spaces' were havens for terrorists that threatened both the surrounding regions of Africa, especially oil-rich West Africa, as well as Europe.

Other External Interests

China

Although Chinese companies in Niger have been at the geographical centre of the rebellion, they will argue that they have been sucked into the conflagration and had no part, at least wittingly, in what was happening in its early stages.[15] It is certainly true that both CNPC and SinoUranium were remarkably ill-informed of local conditions and sentiments. The MNJ, however, had very good reason to believe that China was giving, or considering giving, military support to President Tandja and consequently warned the Chinese companies that they faced severe repercussions if evidence of such support materialised.

During the course of the rebellion, the general behaviour and labour practices of the Chinese uranium company SinoUranium further severely prejudiced China's interests in the region. Around the beginning of March 2008, SinoUranium, accompanied and protected by Niger's security forces, began denying local pastoralists access to their wells. SinoUranium explained, although it was not correct, to the local pastoralists that as it had paid for the land (through its uranium concession) it also had acquired the priority usage rights to the wells. The pastoralists most affected were those in the Talak region, the rich pastoral zone between Aïr and Tamesna that surrounds China's new $300 million SOMINA uranium mine at Azalik. After several days of armed standoff, the Chinese found a temporary solution by agreeing to build a concrete drinking trough by the wells. However, with the FAN regularly slaughtering Tuareg livestock as part of their 'ethnocide' policy, and with the Chinese accompanying the FAN on some of these missions, it is surprising that there were no serious armed clashes with either the Chinese mining companies or the FAN over the pastoralists' rights of access to their wells.

Serious physical conflict with the Chinese has so far been averted. Nevertheless, both the Chinese companies in the region and Beijing were warned that their labour practices were so bad that labour unrest, especially amongst their Tuareg workers, was almost inevitable. For example, conditions at SOMINA's Azalik mine, which began uranium production in late 2009, were so bad that in February 2010 workers at the mine denounced their working conditions in a written statement, claiming that the mine resembled 'a Chinese colony'. Trouble at the mine has led to Azalik being referred to throughout northern Niger as 'Guantanamo'.

Libya

Libya's recent designs on the Sahel were reflected in Mouamar Gaddafi's many pronouncements on some sort of 'Tuareg political entity' or 'Saharan state' (which were described in Chapter 5). Not surprisingly, there has been widespread speculation about Gaddafi's involvement in the rebellions. However, although there were reports of Libyan observers visiting the MNJ rebels, and presumably briefing the Libyan authorities on the state of the situation, there is no evidence of Libya having played any direct role in instigating the rebellions. Indeed, Gaddafi emerged from the rebellions, albeit perhaps by default, in the role of peace-maker rather than as instigator.

Mali

Although the Tuareg of Mali have not yet experienced the same sort of invasive exploitation of their lands by mining companies as in Niger, the Mali rebellion shared certain key similarities with that in Niger. These were the perceived failure of the Malian government to fulfil the agreements reached at the end of the 1990s rebellion and the abuse and harassment of the Tuareg civilian population by the Malian army. The first act of rebellion by Bahanga, namely his attack on a police post near Tin Zaouatene and the killing of two policemen in May 2007, was almost certainly provoked by the violation of Tuareg women by Malian soldiers. At the same time, there were disturbing indications that the Mali government was moving in the same direction as that of Niger by encouraging the resuscitation of the Ganda Koy, a

Songhai-based militia that was responsible for many of the attacks on Tuareg civilian populations in the 1990s Tuareg rebellion.

After a series of attacks on the Malian army at the end of August and through September 2007, and the mining of many of the routes around Tin Zaouatene, a tenuous peace held through 2007's month of Ramadan. It was broken in March 2008 as a result of the atrocities committed by the Malian and US forces at Tin Zaouatene in February 2008. In other words, the initial act of rebellion and its subsequent escalation, as in Niger, were in response to the commitment of atrocities by the security forces against the Tuareg civilian populations. However, as subsequent chapters show, the later stages of the rebellions in the two countries followed rather different trajectories.

Islamists and Drug Traffickers

At the outset of the rebellions, and notwithstanding the disinformation to the contrary, neither the rebel movements in Niger nor in Mali had any involvement with drug traffickers or Islamists, notably in the form of GSPC/al-Qaeda in the Islamic Maghreb (AQIM). However, as the rebellions wore on, both groups of rebels, in Niger and in Mali, found themselves relying to some extent on the levies they imposed on the drug traffickers crossing their territories to finance their rebellions and their basic subsistence. But, as later chapters show, both the drug trafficking business, which became fully 'internationalised' in 2009, and the almost concurrent re-emergence of AQIM as a major player in the Sahel, have, with the assistance of Algeria's DRS, succeeded in turning the region into the 'Terror Zone' that Washington had envisaged in 2003.

8

THE FIFTH ANNIVERSARY OF 2003: ANOTHER KIDNAP

In early 2008, the name 'al-Qaeda', whether it was al-Qaeda in the Islamic Maghreb (AQIM), al-Qaeda in the Sahel (AQIS), or al-Qaeda anywhere else, was a nonentity amongst the predominantly Tuareg peoples of the western Sahara-Sahel region. After the truth about the September–October 2006 engagements between Iyad ag Ghaly's Malian Tuareg and Mokhtar ben Mokhtar's alleged band of Groupe Salafiste pour le Prédication et le Combat (GSPC) had percolated across the region, followed by the realisation of how the Algerian authorities had falsely reported the Tuareg youth unrest in Djanet as a major al-Qaeda terrorist attack on the town's airport, it was evident to most people in the region, and those who knew what was going on there, that AQIS was nothing more than a construct of the Département du Renseignement et de la Sécurité (DRS) and its propaganda.

Two Austrians Kidnapped in Tunisia

Thus, when I heard news in the last week of February 2008 that two Austrian tourists had gone missing, possibly kidnapped, in Tunisia, I paid it little attention.[1] There was nothing in the initial news reports that their disappearance might have had anything to do with Algeria's DRS, al-Qaeda, the Sahara or the Sahel. It sounded like a 'Tunisian affair' that would probably be resolved in a few days without much further ado.

It was not until I received a telephone call from the Austrian government a week or so later that I gave it any more thought. The official, who knew that I had advised the Austrian government over the 2003 El Para hostage-takings, when ten Austrians had been abducted, asked if I could throw any light on the matter. I explained that I knew absolutely nothing about it; neither had I heard anything on the 'grapevine'. I told the official that if he had any clues, such as names or 'geography', then I could at least check the names against the Algerian police files of all those involved in the El Para kidnappings.[2]

'How does the geography help?' asked the official. I explained that if we had any inkling of the direction in which the abductors were heading, we would at least have a clue as to whether they were genuine terrorists. Real AQIM terrorists, I suggested, would be more likely to make for the relative safety of the forested mountain regions of north-eastern Algeria where they had a modicum of support. If, on the other hand, they went south, into the Sahara, then there was reason to believe that they were being assisted or protected by Algeria's security forces, notably the DRS.

On 10 March, *Al Jazeera* announced that the two Austrians, Wolfgang Eber (51) and his girlfriend Andrea Kloiber (43), had been taken hostage by AQIM. The next day, the Austrian official told me he had received information that the two hostages might be in Mali. He asked whether I might be able to verify the location and sent me a copy of a photograph taken by the abductors that had been posted on Islamist websites.[3] The photograph purportedly showed the two Austrians dressed in robes, kneeling in the shade of a thorn tree and surrounded by their captors who were armed with assault rifles and rocket-propelled grenade launchers.

I looked at the photo for a long time, knowing that somewhere in the picture there was likely to be a clue. It was in the acacia tree under which they knelt. It is known by some as the 'untidy' tree and is much more common in the Sahel than the Maghreb. I contacted the Austrian official and told him that the species of tree in the photograph was found over much of the higher regions of the Sahel and southern Sahara, such as the valleys (*oueds*) draining out of Ahaggar in southern Algeria, the Aïr mountains of northern Niger and the Adrar-n-Iforas of northern Mali.[4] Most of the valleys in which I had found the tree in abundance and growing to the same size as in the photograph had been around elevations of 800–1,500 metres. It indicated that the hostages had therefore probably crossed the Sahara and were most likely being held in one of these three regions, with the most likely being Mali's Adrar-n-Iforas. My reasoning was that it would be far too risky and politically dangerous to hold them in Algeria, while access to Aïr was almost impossible because of the Tuareg rebellion.

The Involvement of the DRS

If the DRS was behind the kidnap, as I was beginning to suspect, what was their motive and who were the kidnappers? A search through Algerian media reports, especially those quoting Algerian security sources, threw up the names of Abou Amar, Hamadou Abid and the Tarik Ibn Zaïd *katibet* (brigade). Abou Amar and Hamadou Abid are both aliases. Abou Amar is Yahia Djouadi. Hamadou Abid is the same Abdelhamid abou Zaïd whose name had been in the media only three months earlier in the context of the Djanet airport attack.[5] Both men were members of the Tarik Ibn Zaïd *katibet*, the terrorist cell from which El Para drew the majority of the 'terrorists' that he used in the 2003 kidnapping operation. Abdelhamid abou Zaïd had been El Para's second-in-command of the 2003 operation. He was also in charge of the Mali end of the operation because of his superior knowledge of the region.[6]

All the signs pointed to this new kidnap, almost five years to the day after El Para's 2003 operation, as being another DRS operation. Indeed, the similarity between the two operations was unnerving. Not only were Abou Amar and Hamadou Abid (that is, Yahia Djouadi and Abou Zaïd) part of El Para's original DRS 'management team', but they had some of their 2003 men[7] with them and had taken the two hostages to the same location in Mali that they had used five years previously.

There were others pointers to the DRS's involvement:

First, how was Algeria's media able to name Yahia Djouadi and Abou Zaïd if Algeria's security services had not had some contact or involvement with the operation?

Second, how had AQIM taken the hostages from Tunisia to Mali? The straightforward route is to drive the 2,000 kilometres, more or less as the crow flies, across Algeria. That, however, as a DRS agent later confirmed to me, would have been virtually impossible, given the high level of Algeria's internal security, without the collaboration of the Algerian security services. The DRS had obviously realised that analysts would pick up on this point. They therefore let it be known to the media that the abductors travelled to Mali via Libya. How they would have known this, begs other questions. But travelling to Mali via Libya would probably have been even more difficult than crossing Algeria, for the simple reason that the Tassili escarpments deny any crossing point into Algeria by vehicle except for an extremely difficult route between Tarat and the Dider basin and a well secured route that loops around the south of the Tassili via the Tin Alkoum border post. Alternatively, if Algeria was entered further south, it would have meant passing close to the Algerian military base at In Ezzane. The only other option would be to travel to the east of the Acacus mountains and enter Niger in the Salvador region. However, that route, over difficult terrain, faced the additional problem of negotiating the Aïr mountains between the Algerian border in the north and Agades in the south undetected by both the MNJ (Mouvement des Nigériens pour la Justice) rebels and the Nigerien army.

In addition to the difficulties that a 'real' terrorist would have in avoiding the security forces of both Algeria and Libya, as well as the MNJ rebels and the army in Niger, there was also the risk in the Sahel of running into French and US Special Forces.

Further evidence of DRS involvement is that Algeria's media quoted official security sources as saying, at the time of the Austrians' kidnap, that Abou Amar (alias Yahia Djouadi) was also responsible for the attack on Djanet airport only three to four months earlier. While this was clearly designed to link the Austrians' kidnappers with another highly publicised al-Qaeda terrorist action, I knew that the story was false as I already knew that the Djanet attack was nothing to do with al-Qaeda.

The fundamental question about this kidnapping was not whether the DRS was involved, as that soon became self-evident, but rather, what was their motive? Related to that was the question of why they took the hostages from Tunisia to Mali.

I will answer the second of these two question first. As I will explain presently, Algeria and its DRS were at the heart of this kidnapping. Algeria, for reasons I shall explain, wanted to absolve itself of involvement and was able to do so by arranging the kidnapping as if it were an 'offshore' operation: kidnapping the hostages in Tunisia and holding them captive in Mali.

The Swiss Connection

There were two very public clues as to what lay behind this kidnap. One was to be found within the various demands made by the hostage-takers, which changed significantly over the eight months of captivity. At the outset, the two main demands were for the release of some ten GSPC/AQIM prisoners held by the Algerian and Tunisian authorities, notably El Para, who was 'officially' imprisoned in Algeria, and an unspecified ransom. The most significant element of this demand was the release of El Para. After the expiry of two ultimatums in March, and a third in April, the focus of the kidnappers' demands changed, with emphasis being placed on Austria's withdrawal of its four military officers from Afghanistan and the release of two recent Muslim converts imprisoned in Austria. Later, as news and publicity of the two hostages dwindled, the demands for El Para's release also fell away.

The second and most pertinent clue lay in a news item published by Swissinfo, a travel website, on 11 February, seven days before the disappearance of the two Austrians. Entitled 'Le mystère subsiste sur le rapt des Suisses au Sahara'[8] (Mystery still surrounds the kidnap of the Swiss in the Sahara), the article referred to a row between the Swiss and Algerian authorities over the four Swiss tourists taken hostage by El Para in 2003.[9]

My investigation into the story revealed that relations between Switzerland and Algeria had grown increasingly fractious after

the coming into force on 16 December of a judicial cooperation
agreement between the two countries, and had come to a head
in early February in the run-up to the imminent expiry of the
five-year statute of limitations that hung over the Swiss federal
government's inquiry into the kidnapping of the four Swiss
tourists taken hostage by El Para in 2003. The presiding judge,
Ernst Roduner, was losing patience with Algeria, which had
continuously failed to cooperate with his inquiry and was refusing
to comply with the international judicial cooperation agreement.
In early February, the judge expressed his frustration publicly,
saying: 'We have tried everything, but Algeria refuses judicial
cooperation with Switzerland, in the same way as it has with the
other countries involved in these kidnappings.'

Roduner highlighted what he called the 'mysterious' case of
Amari Saifi (El Para) who, he emphasised, was in charge of the
hostage-taking, pointing out the strange circumstances of his trial in
absentia – a diplomatic euphemism for saying that he was believed
to be an agent for the DRS. Indeed, to underscore Roduner's
suspicions, Swissinfo quoted Salima Mellah and François Gèze,
who had investigated the El Para case for Algeria-Watch, the
respected human rights organisation, and who had concluded:

> We have undertaken an in depth enquiry into the affair of the European
> hostages in the Sahara. A close study of the facts shows that there is no
> other explanation for this operation than the directing of the hostage-taking
> by the DRS, the Algerian army's secret service.[10]

Roduner's outburst and the Swiss authorities' public declaration of
dissatisfaction with the Algiers regime led to awkward diplomatic
pressure being put on Algiers. Algeria's discomfort was not simply
because the two countries had maintained excellent political and
economic relations since the end of the 1990s, but because the
disclosure of the truth about El Para was, and will continue to
be, a major threat to Algeria's international standing.

However, there was an additional problem for Algeria which
was particularly pertinent at that precise moment of time. This
was that around December–January 2007–08, some 20 or so top
members of Algeria's political and military elite, including both

President Bouteflika and General Mohamed (Toufik) Mediène, head of the DRS, were contemplating 'retirement'.[11] This elite were mostly old men by now, and for several weeks they had discussed in private the possibility of enjoying their own retirements and handing over power to a new and younger generation. Nothing, as we now know, became of this idea. However, while it was being contemplated, the one country they could not afford to anger was Switzerland, for Switzerland's banks were believed to have been the bolt-holes into which many of them had stashed away much of the wealth that they had siphoned out of Algeria.

It was impossible for Algiers to meet Switzerland's request to interview El Para. To have done so would have been the equivalent of writing a national suicide note. The only way out of the extremely awkward situation in which Algeria's rulers found themselves was to somehow absolve themselves of responsibility for El Para's custody, at least until Switzerland's statute of limitations had passed and the matter could once again become buried in history.

El Para's death, if genuine, would have been one solution, but not if it was faked, as it might have invoked awkward demands for habeas corpus and forensic proof. The solution, which I believe the DRS concocted, was to have El Para made the subject of an AQIM hostage-release demand. The logic of this plan was that if AQIM was to make El Para the subject of their demand for the hostages' release, Algeria could hardly make him available to the Swiss authorities when the lives of two innocent European tourists were at stake.

Abou Zaïd and his men were therefore dispatched to Tunisia. Whether they selected Austrian tourists in preference to any other nationality will probably never be known. It is unlikely, in view of the time sequence mentioned earlier, that they had much time in which to select their victims. The key issue, however, from the Algerian perspective was that the abduction and the holding of the hostages were undertaken in countries other than Algeria, thus effectively making Algeria little more than a 'third party', while retaining control of the situation on the ground through their DRS link with Abou Zaïd.

The Swiss investigation had run past its five-year statute of limitation before 6 April, the date which the hostage-takers had set as their third deadline. That raises the question of why the hostages were not released, as by that time they had served their purpose. I do not know the answer to this question, other than that there were a number of other factors involved. One is that the operation had to appear to be a real terrorist kidnapping. If the two Austrians had been freed on the passing of the statute of limitation, perhaps on humanitarian grounds, AQIM's credibility as a serious terrorist threat would have been sorely tested.

A second factor is that Abou Zaïd's foot soldiers, like those of El Para, were genuine Salafists and almost certainly had no idea that their emir (leader), like El Para, was a DRS agent. It was therefore particularly important for Abou Zaïd and the DRS that he be seen by his men to be 'delivering the goods', which, now that the statute of limitations had passed, meant that the demand for El Para's release could be replaced with a ransom demand.

A third and equally important consideration is that Algeria was intent on using this kidnap to establish AQIM once and for all in the Sahel, not only for its own hegemonic designs, but also to assist the US in finally establishing the Sahel as an al-Qaeda 'Terror Zone', as the Pentagon had earlier depicted it, in advance of the official establishment of AFRICOM (US Africa Command) on 1 October 2008 and the US presidential election five weeks later.[12]

What actually happened between 6 April and the hostages' release on 30 October is not altogether clear. What we do know is as follows:

The situation did not run smoothly in Mali for the hostage-takers. Sporadic reports in the Algerian media, almost certainly sourced to or approved by the DRS, kept explaining that the release of the hostages was being complicated by difficulties on the ground, with the implication being that these difficulties were caused by the prevailing Tuareg rebellion. This had the benefit at the propaganda level of enabling the US, the Algerians and their allies to link, albeit quite falsely, the Tuareg rebellions with al-Qaeda.

The real difficulty, however, was that Abdelhamid abou Zaïd and his group, and presumably also the DRS, had miscalculated the local situation. I believe that Abou Zaïd had been planning to use the same local Tuareg negotiators as El Para had used in 2003. However, by now, five years on, most local Tuareg either knew or suspected that the 2003 hostage-taking had been organised by the DRS and, on seeing some of the same kidnappers back in the region, were extremely suspicious of their true identities and real intentions. Local Tuareg were also still very angry about the events of September and October 2006 which had led to five of their number being killed and would have nothing to do with Abou Zaïd or his group. To make matters worse for Abou Zaïd, some of those involved in the 2006 incidents had also been caught up in the 2003 hostage release negotiations and knew that Algeria's DRS was involved in both operations. The situation became even murkier when the bodies of three murdered Tuareg, said to be interlocutors, were found near Kidal on 6 April. Their murderers were never discovered, although it was widely rumoured that their deaths were in some way linked to AQIM's new presence in the region and that the intelligence services, whether Malian or Algerian is not clear, were involved. The result was that Abou Zaïd was obliged to operate through local Berabich (Arab) intermediaries and the Malian security services – a situation, which, given the complexities outlined above, generated even more suspicion and mistrust.

More worrying were rumours in early May that the two hostages had either been killed or that Abou Zaïd was planning to kill them. Since the time of their arrival in Mali, I had known that negotiations for the hostages' release had made little progress and that their execution was becoming an increasingly likely 'exit strategy'. Therefore, to ensure the safety of the hostages, I used my contacts in Algiers to 'leak' information into the DRS channels that the Austrian authorities had been fully briefed on the DRS's role in the hostage-taking, Algeria's motives for the kidnapping and the role of Abou Zaïd as a DRS agent. The DRS was therefore made aware that if the hostages were killed by Abou Zaïd, evidence of the DRS's role in their abduction and killing would be made available to the international media, with potentially disastrous consequences for Algeria.

A few days later, on 21 May, the Malian authorities confirmed that the hostages were still alive.[13] Then, on 14 June, 110 days after their capture, came the first direct contact with the hostages when Wolfgang Ebner was able to telephone his son. In his call, Ebner said that he was suffering from cholera and malaria. On 5 July, a Malian official in Bamako was quoted as saying: 'One of the two hostages [believed to be Ebner] is doing very poorly. He should be placed under medical supervision urgently.'[14]

Negotiating the Release

On 13 October, I received a phone call from a Tuareg whom I had known well for many years. I shall call him 'Aflan'. The essence of his message was that he wanted me to contact the Austrian authorities and to act as an intermediary in negotiating the release of the two hostages. He also wanted me to meet him in Paris as soon as possible so that he could explain the situation to me. I appraised the Austrian authorities of this new development and met Aflan in Paris a few days later.

The situation was that Abou Zaïd, whom we only rarely mentioned by name and referred to as '*le ravisseur*' (the kidnapper), was becoming increasingly irritated with the Malian negotiators. The situation had dragged on for many months because the two Malian negotiators, whom Abou Zaïd referred to as the 'two criminals', were only interested in taking money for themselves. Abou Zaïd was no longer prepared to deal with them and wanted to negotiate directly with the Austrian government. However, as he didn't know how to make contact with them, he sought the services of Aflan, whom he knew to have 'international connections'. Aflan, however, also did not know how to reach the Austrian authorities, but he did remember that I had been involved with them in 2003. Without knowing that I was already in contact with the Austrian government, Aflan asked me if I would act as a 'communications link'. The line of communication was therefore from Abou Zaïd to Aflan, to me and then to Vienna, and then back again.

Abou Zaïd made it very clear that he wanted the whole business finalised without any further delay. I sensed that he was angry with the 'two criminals' and that he was not prepared to spend any more time on further negotiations. I also sensed from what Aflan was telling me that Abou Zaïd did not trust the Malian authorities. He suspected that a release through the Malian authorities might involve a military attack. He feared that the US influence in Bamako might try to engineer a demonstration of the Bush administration's 'get tough/no compromise' policy against 'terrorists' in the final days before the US presidential election.

Aflan made it very clear to me that we had reached what Abou Zaïd called 'the last chance for the hostages', as he was otherwise going to kill them on *Eid al Adha*, the 'Festival of the Sacrifice' or 'Sheep', as it is colloquially known, on 7–8 December. I realised that executing the hostages had finally become a realistic and increasingly likely exit strategy for Abou Zaïd and the DRS. I sensed that this deadline and the planned execution were very real.

We spent a couple of hours in an internet café two blocks from the Gare du Nord where Aflan briefed me on the confidential communications links. Before returning on the Eurostar to London, Aflan gave me the 'bottom line'. It was that '*le ravisseur*' would accept €2 million, a lot less than the €3 million, or perhaps more, that the 'two criminals' had been hassling for. We also discussed how the handover was to be made: I was to carry the money myself to a rendezvous in Mali where the handover would take place. A Red Cross representative would accompany me as a witness.

Communications between Abou Zaïd and Vienna, through the link that Aflan had set up with me, went on for 17 days, from 13 October to 30 October, when the two hostages were released safely – though not by me. The fact that Abou Zaïd had found a means and had been prepared to negotiate directly with the Austrian government had clearly exercised minds in Bamako. The Austrian government never told me whether or not they paid a ransom. But, according to media reports, negotiators working for the Malian government had effected the release for a ransom of €3–4 million, nearly double what I knew Abou Zaïd was prepared to accept.

The names of the 'two criminals', which Aflan gave me on my departure from Paris, and whom I presume to have taken the balance of the ransom above €2 million, were Colonel Mama Coulibaly, head of Malian state security, and Baba Ould Sheikh, the Mayor of Tarkint.

9

THE CREATION OF AFRICOM

Readers, especially those who have also read *The Dark Sahara*, may at this stage be pondering on how US policy towards the region fits into what by 2008, at least on face value, appears to have become nothing more than an unplanned and entirely inchoate series of events.

Washington's policy of fabricating terrorism in the region in 2002–03 in order to justify the launch of its new front in the 'Global War on Terror' (GWOT), followed by the Pan-Sahel Initiative (PSI) and the Trans-Sahara Counterterrorism Initiative (TSCTI) in 2004 and 2005 respectively, were planned and structured events. Although Algeria's Département du Renseignement et de la Sécurité (DRS) and to a slightly lesser extent the autocratic regimes of Mauritania and Niger were the key agents on the ground, Washington was still the puppeteer, with the Bush–Cheney regime pulling the strings and maintaining its high-level 'information war' through an incessant bombardment of what was little more than propaganda. Nevertheless, from about 2006 onwards, it was becoming increasingly apparent that Washington was stumbling, doing little more than reacting to a series of incidents over which it had little or no planning input or control. Mouamar Gaddafi's designs and activities in Mali in early 2006; the subsequent Tuareg unrest in Kidal; the shooting at the Hercules C-130 at Tin Zaouatene in September 2007; the attack on Djanet airport two months later, followed by the murder of a French family in Mauritania;[1] and then Algeria's argument with Switzerland and the kidnapping of two Austrians in Tunisia, were all seemingly unconnected events to which Washington could only react.

They were, indeed, unrelated events, but they became linked, like a conspiracy theory, through Washington's 'information war' into a single narrative that told a story, albeit an entirely false one, of how al-Qaeda in the Islamic Maghreb (AQIM), or, to be more specific, al-Qaeda in the Sahel (AQIS), was posing an increasing threat, not just to the Sahel region but to Europe and other parts of Africa.

The foregoing chapters have shown how these incidents were actually nothing to do with AQIS. Chapter 5 explained how the events in Mali in 2006 were being manipulated and engineered by both Algeria and the US for their own respective interests: in the case of Algeria, to remove Libya from what Algeria regarded as its own backyard; in the case of the US, to show how the Tuareg were on the side of the US in the GWOT. Chapter 6 explained that the shots fired at the US Hercules C-130 at Tin Zaouatene, the Tuareg rebellions in both Mali and Niger and the attack on Djanet airport were also nothing whatsoever to do with al-Qaeda; while the three men convicted in a Nouakchott court in May 2010 for the murder of the French family in 2007 may have been converted to their apparent 'jihadist' beliefs during the course of more than two years in detention during which they claim to have been tortured. And finally, as the previous chapter made clear, the kidnapping of the two Austrians in Tunisia was, as with the El Para kidnappings in 2003, a DRS operation.

Although none of these incidents, with the possible exception of the Tuareg–GSPC (Groupe Salafiste pour le Prédication et le Combat) engagements in September–October 2006, were initiated or contrived by the US, they nevertheless came to Washington's rescue; none more so than the Austrians' kidnapping. In order to understand why this incident was so important to Washington and why Washington was so fixated on what is probably the most unknown, desolate and poverty-ridden tract of Africa, we need to go back to the beginning – to 1997, to be precise.

The Creation of AFRICOM

US Africa Command (AFRICOM) was officially established as a new, fully autonomous combat command on 1 October 2008. However, its creation[2] was much more than a post-Cold War rationalisation of the US's global military command structure. Rather, it reflected the recognition of Africa's new strategic importance to the US. This shift in US interest towards Africa did not come about overnight in 2008, but was, as AFRICOM's website states, 'the culmination of a 10-year thought process within the Department of Defense'.[3]

That 'thought process' began in 1997. Since then, Africa's strategic importance to the US has undergone several reappraisals as a result of the US's increased awareness of its own energy crisis, the post-9/11 GWOT and China's growing economic investment in Africa. 1997 was, in fact, a landmark year in contemporary US history for two related reasons: it saw the founding of the neo-conservatives' (neo-cons) 'Project for the New American Century',[4] and US dependency on foreign oil reaching the psychologically critical 50 per cent level. The threat posed to national security by the latter development was not lost on the neo-cons. They made it an election issue in 2000, with George W. Bush pledging to make energy security a top priority. One of his first executive decisions was to establish a National Energy Policy Development (NEPD) Group under the Chairmanship of his Vice-President, Dick Cheney. The Cheney Report, as it became known, was published in May 2001.[5] Its findings were stark: between 1991 and 2000, Americans had used 17 per cent more energy than in the previous decade, while domestic energy production had risen by only 2.3 per cent. It projected that US energy consumption by 2020 would increase by about 32 per cent, with the oil share remaining at around 40 per cent, more than a quarter of the world's total consumption.

The Cheney Report singled out sub-Saharan Africa as the key source of future US oil supplies. It forecast that by 2015, 25 per cent of US imported oil would come from the Gulf of Guinea. Some subsequent forecasts put this figure at 35 per cent. In 2002, sub-Saharan Africa was already supplying 14 per cent of US oil imports; by 2006, the US imported 22 per cent of its oil from Africa, and by 2007 the country was importing more crude oil from Africa than from the Persian Gulf.[6] The Cheney Report highlighted the strategic importance of Africa, prompting Bush to define African oil as a resource that might require military force to protect.[7]

Taking the GWOT Into Africa

As *The Dark Sahara* and Chapter 1 of this volume explained, the Bush administration decided to create a US military structure for Africa in order to secure consistent access to and control over African oil. However, instead of being transparent and acknowledging that US military intervention in Africa was about resource control, the Bush administration opted to use the GWOT as the justification for its militarisation of the continent. However, launching the GWOT into Africa was a delicate operation, as most of the continent, especially sub-Saharan Africa, had hitherto not suffered the atrocities of terrorism.[8] The main terrorism incidents in Africa had been concentrated in Somalia, East Africa and the Maghreb.

The solution, as *The Dark Sahara* revealed, was to fabricate the terrorism, with the core operation being El Para's abduction in 2003 of 32 European hostages. Once the supposed terrorist threat had been established across the Sahel, the Bush administration launched its PSI and TSCTI.

These operations and 'initiatives' were surrounded by disinformation and hyperbole.[9] For example, President Bush described El Para, a DRS agent, as 'bin Laden's man in the Sahel', while the deputy commander of EUCOM (US European Command), General Charles Wald, described the Sahara as a 'Swamp of Terror', a 'terrorist infestation' which 'we need to drain'. During this period, Washington's 'information war' machine was operating in overdrive. Literally thousands of news articles and 'quasi-governmental' reports of one sort or another gave false testimony to the terrorist threat emanating from the Sahara-Sahel region.

At this point, let me digress briefly to clarify what is meant by Washington's 'information war', as it is not something which either AFRICOM or the US administration has been keen to discuss.

Soon after the 9/11 attacks, the White House began running an 'information war' through a host of shadowy counterpropaganda units and organisations, such as the International Information Centre, the Pentagon's 1,200-strong Psychological Operations group and the White House's Counter Terrorism Information Strategy Policy Coordinating Committee.[10] These covert operations, little known to most Americans until 2005, aimed to 'keep doing every single thing that needs to be done', to quote the former US Defense Secretary, Donald Rumsfeld, and involved contentious means.[11] One such operation involved giving contracts worth millions of dollars to private contractors to plant, fabricate or buy news stories favourable to US interests on an immense scale. In 2005, one such contractor admitted to having planted more than 1,000 articles in the Iraqi and Arab press.

Proof of this came out in June 2008 when the US Senate Select Committee on Intelligence published the final volume of its report into the use, abuse and faulty assessments of intelligence leading to the invasion of Iraq. It confirmed, in the words of its Chairman, Senator John D. Rockefeller IV, that 'In making the case for war, the administration repeatedly presented intelligence as fact when it was unsubstantiated, contradicted or even nonexistent.'[12]

Washington has maintained a similar 'information war' in North Africa's Maghreb and Sahel, with disinformation on the region being second only to Iraq, and perhaps now Afghanistan. The difference between North Africa and both Iraq and Afghanistan is that in the former the US has been able to rely heavily on a key ally in its GWOT, namely Algeria, to produce disingenuous material. Nevertheless, the US Department of Defense, first through EUCOM and now through AFRICOM, has maintained a similar strategy in Africa as in the Iraq theatre by sponsoring its own website, namely Magharebia.com. On the surface, Magharebia.com appears as if it is a regular online news service with numerous links to internationally known and respected news services. It is, however, a creation of the Pentagon. Founded in 2004, at the same time as Bush's PSI, it is one of at least two such websites financed, supervised by and accountable to EUCOM, before being transferred to AFRICOM.[13] Since 2002 the number of deliberately slanted media articles and reports on the Sahara-Sahel front, including their reiteration through wire and online agencies, runs into the thousands.

Thanks largely to the effectiveness of this news generation, this new, fabricated front in the GWOT helped create the ideological conditions for Washington's militarisation of Africa. However, by 2006, just as the idea of AFRICOM was beginning to take concrete shape, and in spite of this barrage of news manipulation, the GWOT in the Sahara-Sahel, as Chapter 5 explained, was running out of steam. Not only had there been no more terrorism after El Para's operation, other than the Lemgheity garrison attack, which was probably nothing to do with GSPC, but my own writings and briefings on the subject were beginning to take root. Questions were beginning to be raised about the veracity of Washington-sourced reports on terrorism in the Sahara-Sahel region.

The two-year period from the time Washington and Algiers connived in 2006 to reinvigorate the flagging profile of the GWOT in the Sahara-Sahel region to the establishment of AFRICOM in 2008, was extraordinary in that there was an almost direct correlation between the amount of energy spent on the promotion of AFRICOM as on the production of false or grossly exaggerated information on supposed terrorism in the Sahara-Sahel region.

Rhetorical Shift from Terrorism to Security and Development

The two-year period 2006–08 also witnessed another development on which I should also digress for a moment. Around the turn of 2005–06, and with the idea of a dedicated US Africa Command beginning to take shape, the Bush administration's justification for its militarisation of the continent began to reflect an apparent transformation in US military thinking, as its rhetoric shifted from the GWOT and counterterrorism to a more humanitarian security-development discourse.[14] This enabled the US military to substitute its overly aggressive and militaristic image that EUCOM commanders had been displaying towards Africa for one that enabled President Bush to announce AFRICOM as a new command that will enhance our efforts to help bring peace and security to the people of Africa and promote our common goals of development, health, education, democracy, and economic growth in Africa.[15]

Such seductive language, emphasising AFRICOM's development-humanitarian aims and stressing its goals of strengthening civilian agencies and civilian capacities, soon characterised all US government references to and descriptions of AFRICOM. For example, AFRICOM's own website, at around the time of its official establishment, stated that

U.S. Africa Command will better enable the Department of Defense and other elements of the U.S. government to work in concert and with partners to achieve a more stable environment in which political and economic growth can take place ... Unlike traditional Unified Commands, Africa Command will focus on war prevention rather than war-fighting. Africa Command intends to work with African nations and African organizations to build regional security and crisis-response capacity in support of U.S. government efforts in Africa.

This shift is seen in the content of the EUCOM and AFRICOM websites and associated publications before and after 2006. Whereas most of their news stories prior to 2005–06 reflected the US military's concerns with the GWOT, counterterrorism and the associated training of African militaries, their post-2006 news stories tended to focus on military involvement in medical training, provision of safe water, care of livestock, civilian capacity building, and so on.

AFRICOM was conceived in the very heart of the duplicity that characterised the Bush administration's GWOT. Therefore, the question of whether the creation of AFRICOM really did reflect a paradigmatic shift in US military thinking, or whether it was nothing more than a new twist in Washington's 'information war', can only be asked and understood within that context. That, however, is not easy as the GWOT, which was used to justify the establishment of AFRICOM, especially its Sahara-Sahel front, was based, as both *The Dark Sahara* and this volume show, on fabricated evidence. The answer can therefore best be found 'on the ground', by looking at what the US military were actually doing in Africa during the two or more years in the run-up to the establishment of AFRICOM. We see that the reality of what the US military were doing in Africa during this period was very different from the gloss and spin on AFRICOM's website.

For example, on 7 January 2007, less than three weeks after AFRICOM's authorisation, US forces killed an unknown number, reportedly hundreds, of Somali fighters and innocent civilians trapped in the 'killing zone' between US-backed Ethiopian forces to the north and west, US-backed Kenyan forces to the south, and the sea. The operation, which was meant to have been secret, was widely publicised, reminding the world that the US presence sought to resolve conflicts in Africa by brute military intervention. The subsequent situation in Somalia, in which the US has played a large part, has not only become a policy nightmare, but has generated a major terrorism security threat.

The gunship that carried out the 7 January bombardment is believed to have been launched from a secret airstrip in eastern Ethiopia. However, the US special operators sent into southernmost Somalia after the aerial attack to search out survivors among the supposed foreign fighters and al-Qaeda operatives were dispatched from the US's new military base at Manda Bay in north-east Kenya, just south of the Somali border. Manda Bay became a strategically important base for AFRICOM operations in both the Horn and East Africa. However, its continued operation was heavily dependent on the pro-US Kenyan President, Mwai Kibaki, retaining office in the December 2007 presidential elections. His challenger, Raila Odinga, was not known to be so supportive of US counterterrorism operations in the country. Odinga was widely expected to win the election, and both pre-election polls and exit poll evidence suggested that he should have won. However, in spite of international observers, the elections were believed by most Kenyans to have been rigged. The result was an explosion of violence that left more than 1,000 Kenyans dead. In January 2009, a couple of months after Barack Obama's presidential election victory, evidence of US involvement in Kenya's vote-rigging was exposed.[16]

The US has been more successful in keeping its military interventions in the Sahara-Sahel secret. As the previous chapters have revealed, both the role of the US Special Forces in support of the May 2006 Kidal rebellion and the subsequent operations in Mali, including their accompaniment of the Malian army in the ransacking of Tin Zaouatene in February 2008, have been kept closely guarded secrets.

Moreover, the US military's presence and actions in the Sahara-Sahel, particularly through the PSI and the TSCTI, have encouraged the regional governments to provoke potentially 'rebellious' local populations, notably the Tuareg, to take up arms. Indeed, Washington's ability to justify its counterterrorism operations and AFRICOM's presence in these countries has been predicated increasingly on the false premise that these Tuareg rebellions, that engulfed much of Niger and Mali after early 2007, were linked to al-Qaeda.

Washington's duplicitous strategy in the Sahara-Sahel region has had little to do with 'security and development'. On the contrary, the post-2003 US presence in the PSI–TSCTI region has been directly responsible for severe economic deprivation, increasing political unrest, rebellion and, in the case of Niger's Tuareg rebellion, war crimes against civilian populations. By 2008, the region had become the 'Terror Zone' that the Pentagon superimposed on its maps of Africa in 2003, but not for the reasons given by the US. The region has become an area of terror for its civilians, not because of al-Qaeda, but because of state-sponsored attacks on civilians, both nomads and villagers.

As for the US's contribution to the training of the PSI–TSCTI countries' troops in counterterrorism and other skills, Niger's US-trained security forces, as Chapter 6 revealed, committed acts of genocide, or what the local Tuareg term 'ethnocide'. In August 2007, a report commissioned by the United Nations High Commission for Refugees (UNHCR)[17] warned that Niger's President, Mamadou Tandja, was likely to unleash the Forces Armées Nigériennes (FAN) on the civilian population. And so he did. In December, both Amnesty International and Human Rights Watch denounced Niger's US-trained armed forces for committing war crimes, including summary executions of the civilian population.[18] By 2008, Niger's US-trained forces had taken to bombing civilian nomadic camps with grenades dropped from light aircraft,[19] a common practice also in Darfur.

AFRICOM's last military operation under the Bush administration was in December 2008, a few weeks after its official establishment, when AFRICOM, which had been training Ugandan troops in counterterrorism for some years, advised, provisioned and part-financed a force of 6,000 Ugandan and Congolese troops to eliminate Joseph Kony and his estimated 700-strong Lord's Resistance Army (LRA).

The operation was an unmitigated disaster. After US satellites and Ugandan field intelligence had located Kony's camp, the plan was for Ugandan helicopters to bomb the camp and for 6,000 Ugandan and Congolese ground troops to cut off LRA fighters. On 13 December, the day before the assault, US military advisors held a final coordination meeting close to the Congolese border. Unanticipated fog delayed the operation. By the time the helicopters bombed his camp, Kony had got wind of the attack and fled. For their part, the 6,000 ground troops failed to cut off the LRA's escape routes and to protect the nearby towns and villages from the slaughter which the fleeing LRA inflicted upon them. Some 1,000 innocent Congolese civilians were slaughtered and hundreds more children abducted to become the latest LRA conscripts. The exercise was a grotesque demonstration of inept military planning and appalling execution.

In those areas where AFRICOM had intervened militarily during this period, either directly or through proxies, as in Somalia, northern Kenya (where refugees fleeing the Somalia violence became a major humanitarian concern), the Democratic Republic of Congo and the western Sahel (Niger and Mali), the outcomes have been disastrous for the civilian populations, and without even any semblance of military 'victories' to be shown for them. In its two main counterterrorism operations in Africa, in Somalia and the Sahel, the US military, first under EUCOM and then as AFRICOM, has, as Catherine Besteman noted, 'orchestrated brutal attacks on civilians, supported unpopular governments, conflated Islamist political groups and terrorism, and enabled rather than reduced the growth of Al Qaeda influence in their arenas of operation'.[20] In short,

> Dressing up AFRICOM in the language of humanitarian and diplomatic engagement fools no one ... AFRICOM will not benefit Africans, it will not enhance African security, and it will not prevent war. Rather, it will benefit the US military, US defense contractors, US oil companies, African governments interested in repressing indigenous, minority, activist, environmentalist and resistance groups and terrorists, who will win new adherents to their causes amongst those attacked by US rhetoric and provoked by the presence of US troops on their soil.[21]

How the Austrian Hostages Saved AFRICOM

Let me now return to the question of why the two Austrian hostages were so important to Washington.

In the months leading up to AFRICOM's establishment in October 2008, it faced three increasing problems, such that its establishment was actually in doubt. The first of AFRICOM's problems, which has not changed, is that nobody wants it. After years of arm-twisting and cajoling by Washington, no African country, with the possible exception of Liberia, has shown any desire to house AFRICOM's HQ. AFRICOM's HQ has therefore remained in Stuttgart, unloved and unwanted. While the US has tended to put this down to the security difficulties that AFRICOM's presence would inflict on the host country, the truth is that the US is seen by African countries as an imperialist power whose rhetoric about 'development and security' lacks credibility. There is widespread belief across the continent that AFRICOM is intended merely to protect US oil interests and 're-assert American power and hegemony globally'.[22]

AFRICOM's second problem is that it does not have the means to accomplish its huge mandate. This was confirmed during the run-up to its official establishment by several authoritative sources. Sean McFate, a pre-eminent advisor on US military affairs in Africa, wrote in 2008 that no dedicated or new military units would be created for AFRICOM. Nor, he argued, would

AFRICOM be able to 'borrow' troops because of the huge demand for troops in Iraq and Afghanistan.[23] Mark Malan, a former military officer, gave testimony in July 2008 to the US House of Representatives Subcommittee on National Security and Foreign Affairs that AFRICOM lacked 'the appropriate policy framework, the depth and balance of professional expertise, or the requisite funding mechanisms to deliver on active security'.[24]

Indeed, there was considerable opposition to AFRICOM at this time from within Washington's own corridors of power. The House of Representatives' Appropriations Committee, for instance, believed that 'traditional U.S. military operations [were] not an appropriate response to most or many of the challenges facing Africa'[25] and accordingly wanted to cut AFRICOM's requested budget. For fiscal year 2009, Congress allocated only $266 million of the $390 million requested by AFRICOM.[26]

The third problem, or perhaps question, for AFRICOM, which became more acute as the November 2008 US presidential election drew nearer, was whether Obama, who looked increasingly likely to be the US's next Commander-in Chief, would countenance a continuation of the Bush administration's policies in Africa. In the run-up to the November elections, there was even talk that Obama might scrap the whole AFRICOM initiative.

It was against this growing state of anxiety within the US military, at least amongst the architects of AFRICOM and those who saw new career paths being carved out for them in Africa, that the kidnap of the two Austrians and their transfer to Mali was more than just a glimmer of salvation. To the architects of AFRICOM, here, at last, was proof that al-Qaeda really was in business in the Sahel. The hostage-taking enabled AFRICOM to show that it had been right all along in portraying the Sahel as a 'Terror Zone'. The US military could now argue that it really was needed, at least in this part of Africa.

It was as if someone had pressed the rewind button on the El Para story: the same kidnappers, the same corner of Mali and the same outcome. Indeed, as we shall see, no sooner had the US's new President become settled in the White House than the word 'Sahel' became synonymous with hostage-taking, al-Qaeda and terrorism.

10

THE FUTURE GROUND ZERO

UN Special Envoy Taken Hostage

Although it was widely publicised that the two Austrians abducted in Tunisia in February 2008 had been taken hostage by al-Qaeda in the Islamic Maghreb (AQIM), I knew that the real story of their kidnapping was rather different. Thus, I had my doubts when I heard, only a few weeks after their release, that the abductions of two Canadians, followed by four more European tourists, were also being attributed to AQIM.

The two Canadians, Robert Fowler and Louis Guay, were diplomats. Robert Fowler had recently been appointed as a Special Envoy to the UN Secretary-General and Louis Guay was travelling with him as his assistant. The two men had arrived in Niger's capital, Niamey, on Thursday 11 December 2008 and had been seized from their vehicle on the main road north of Niamey three days later while returning from a Sunday social visit to the Canadian-run Samira Hill goldmine some two to three hours' drive west of the city. The four tourists were seized close to the Nigerien-Malian border just south of Anderamboukane on 22 January 2009. They comprised an elderly German lady, a Swiss couple and a Briton.

The kidnap of these six Westerners and the subsequent, grotesque execution of the Briton, Edwin Dyer, on 30 May 2009, have been attributed to AQIM, or al-Qaeda in the Sahel (AQIS) as I have called it. That, however, tells only a fragment of the story. This chapter reveals the background of events that led up to these abductions and the circumstances leading up to the release of the Canadians and some of the tourists, while the next throws light on the circumstances surrounding the murder of Edwin Dyer.

The story of the Canadians' kidnap began in February 2008 when I received a request from the UN Secretariat's Department of Political Affairs (DPA) to attend a brainstorming session of DPA staff at the UN headquarters in New York on 'Climate Change and Conflict in the Sahel'. By coincidence, the UN's call came in the same week that Wolfgang Eber and Andrea Kloiber had disappeared in Tunisia. The UN's session had been convened for 6 March to support a mission to the Sahel by Jan Egeland, the UN Secretary-General's Special Advisor on matters relating to the prevention and resolution of conflict.

My address was not welcomed by UN political officers. I said that even if the Sahel was experiencing climate change, and the evidence was still inconclusive, it was quite irrelevant to the causes of the current Tuareg rebellions and the last thing on Tuareg minds, which were preoccupied with far more pressing matters of life and death. I went on to warn that if the UN was not prepared to confront the Malian and Nigerien governments, but was going to allow them to evade their responsibilities by explaining away the Tuareg rebellions in terms of climate change, it would not only discredit the UN but it was also possible that people in the region, especially Tuareg, might even be hostile to the mission.

I heard no more from the UN. Shortly after the New York session, Tuareg representatives in Niger asked me if I could act on their behalf and send a letter to the UN notifying them of the Nigerien government's genocide policy against them. The letter was emailed to the UN on 5 April but has remained unacknowledged. The key section of the letter reads:

> Further to my email of 29th March, notifying you briefly of the situation in Niger and Mali, I have since been in extensive contact, by phone and email, with several of the victims of the latest atrocities being undertaken by Niger's armed forces (FAN) [Forces Armées Nigériennes] in the Aïr region (North of Agades), notably in the period since March 20 of this year.
>
> The people concerned have asked me to notify the UN, through the personage of Jan Egeland, that they regard the actions of the FAN, which are carrying out the orders of President Tandja, to be those of a clear and directed policy of genocide in terms of the definition of genocide as defined

in Resolution 260 (III) A of the United Nations General Assembly on 9 December 1948, namely the Convention on the Prevention and Punishment of the Crime of Genocide. They have also asked me to remind the UN of Article one of the convention, namely that 'The Contracting Parties confirm that genocide, whether committed in time of peace or in time of war, is a crime under international law which they undertake to prevent and to punish.'

The Tuareg people of northern Niger are urging the UN, as a matter of urgency, to use its powers and considerable influence to intervene as a matter of urgency and to protect them from further such genocidal actions.

Jan Egeland duly undertook his trip to the Sahel in the first week of June. However, as I had warned, many key people in the region did not meet with him and he stood down shortly afterwards. It was against this rather dismal background that Robert Fowler was appointed in early July as the UN Secretary-General's Special Envoy to the region with a budget of some $390,000 and the specific task of ascertaining the possibility of a negotiated settlement of the Tuareg rebellions, especially in Niger.

Fowler's last meeting in Niamey before his kidnap was with Albadé Abouba, President Tandja's Interior Minister, on the Friday or Saturday. The minister was not enthusiastic about Fowler's visit or the meeting, regarding his uninvited arrival as something of a breach of protocol. Fowler explained the purpose of his visit and his plans to visit the Agades region and meet rebel leaders, which would have made the minister both angry and more than a little nervous. Not only would Fowler have been familiar with the Human Rights Watch and Amnesty International reports of war crimes committed by Niger's forces against the Tuareg civilian population,[1] but if Fowler were to visit the area he would come across evidence of Abouba and Tandja's latest atrocity: tossing hand grenades into nomad camps from low-flying aircraft (probably microlites) in the same way as President Omar al-Bashir's militias had been doing in Darfur.[2]

Staff at Samira Hill confirmed that Fowler, Guay and their driver left the mine at 3.30 p.m. on Sunday afternoon. Locals at the River Niger Fairie ferry crossing confirmed seeing the vehicle and its three occupants disembark the ferry at 6.30 p.m. Their abandoned UN-marked vehicle was found close to the ferry crossing just off the Niamey–Tillabéri main road, 45 kilometres from Niamey, later in the evening, with the engine running, lights on, doors open and three cell phones, a camera and other personal possessions still in the vehicle. As Fowler confirmed after his release, the abduction took some 20 seconds.

The response of the Nigerien government, not surprisingly, was to point the finger at Tuareg rebels. Very conveniently for the government, a message appeared on the website of one of the rebel groups, the Front des Forces de Redressement (FFR), two days after the disappearance, claiming responsibility for the kidnapping. The message, in the name of the group's so-called 'war commander', Rhissa ag Boula,[3] said that the FFR had led a commando operation in the Tillabéri region on Monday evening in which it seized four people including a Canadian diplomat, Robert Fowler, who was in good health and would soon be transferred to a safe place and handed over to other colleagues who would look after him.

The message was false. FFR spokesperson Mohamed Awtchiki Kriska immediately denied the claim and the message was removed from the website and replaced by a denial some three hours after the sham message was posted. I knew Rhissa well; I was in contact with him at that time and he was adamant that neither the FFR nor any other Tuareg rebel group had anything to do with the kidnap.

The two other suspects were AQIM and the Nigerien government itself. Within a couple of weeks of the kidnap, I picked up strong rumours in southern Algeria that the Canadians were in the hands of AQIM, probably Mokhtar ben Mokhtar (MBM), and had been taken to Mali. The information I was receiving from reliable sources in Niger was that the kidnap had been arranged by President Tandja and Albadé Abouba as an immediate way of putting a stop to Fowler's mission.

Fowler was able to confirm on his release that he had been held captive by MBM. Whether the actual abduction had been undertaken by MBM's men or by some of Abouba and Tandja's lackeys who then handed the Canadians over to MBM is still not clear. Fowler himself is of the view that he was in the hands of MBM's men from the outset, but that the kidnap was undertaken on behalf of the Nigerien government. Although the UN and the Canadian authorities remained silent, it was clear from my own contacts and subsequently confirmed by Wikileaks in May 2011 that the Nigerien authorities were thoroughly uncooperative.[4]

By 7 January 2009, 24 days after their disappearance, neither the Canadian government nor the UN had any indications as to the whereabouts or wellbeing of the two Canadians, other than their belief that they had been kidnapped.

Four European Tourists Kidnapped

The mystery of the Canadians' disappearance took a new turn on 22 January when four European tourists were kidnapped. The four were part of a group of seven tourists returning in three vehicles from a nomad cultural festival at Anderamboukane in Mali, a few miles north of the Nigerien border.[5] The precise location of the abduction remains unclear, as both countries claimed that it took place on the other's territory.

Although no formal claims of responsibility were forthcoming for nearly another month, reliable sources in the region were telling me that both the Canadians and the tourists had been handed up to AQIM. My sources in Niger also believed that the seizure of the four tourists may have been engineered by Niger's Minister of the Interior to divert suspicion from the Nigerien government to AQIM.

By the end of January, it became increasingly clear that the hostages were in the hands of AQIM and that Algeria's Département du Renseignement et de la Sécurité (DRS) was behind it. The first indication of DRS involvement came in an article in the Algerian daily newspaper *El Khabar* on 31 January. *El Khabar* is one of the main sources of deliberate 'leaks' from the Algerian military and its DRS. Having already told its readers that the DRS was well positioned throughout this part of the Sahara-Sahel, *El Khabar* pointed its finger directly at Abdelhamid abou Zaïd, saying that 'well-informed sources', by which it is safe to conclude it meant the DRS, had indicated that evidence showed the al-Qaeda terrorist group 'Hamid Essoufi' was involved in the kidnappings of the four European tourists.

El Khabar also stated that Algerian DRS officers had been on a secret mission in northern Mali since the previous week, at the request of European governments, to help the Nigerien and Malian authorities track down the kidnappers. What *El Khabar* did not say was that Hamid Essoufi is one of Abdelhamid abou Zaïd's many aliases.

The significance of *El Khabar*'s reference to Essoufi is that it was the first time, as far as I am aware, that the name had been associated with a terrorism incident since an attack on a gendarme patrol near El Oued on the night of 7 February 2008, almost exactly one year earlier, in which eight gendarmes were killed. According to an alleged confession made by a *repenti* to Algeria's security services, the leader of the group that carried out the attack was Hamid Essoufi. In other words, the message being sent out by the DRS was that Abdelhamid abou Zaïd was responsible for the kidnapping of Wolfgang Eber and Andrea Kloiber just across the border from El Oued into Tunisia some ten days after the attack on the gendarmes. Thus the DRS was sending a message via *El Khabar* to Western security analysts that Abou Zaïd, who had been responsible for the El Oued attack and the kidnap of the two Austrians, was now behind these kidnappings in the Sahel.

The Future Ground Zero

Around the end of January, both the UN and the Canadian intelligence services received information that the two Canadians (along with their driver) were alive and being held by AQIM. Further confirmation of the Canadians' safety was received on 7 February when Agence France-Presse (AFP) reported the existence of a video-cassette showing both Fowler and Guay alive. AFP gave the video to the Canadian authorities. The Canadian authorities, however, did not comment publicly on the video, nor did Canada's

Department of Foreign Affairs respond to requests asking for confirmation that it had received the video.

There were at least two reasons why the Canadians remained silent. One was because they had received information from a private security consultancy suggesting that the Nigerien government had been behind the kidnap and that the AQIM terrorists now holding them were linked to Algeria's DRS. A second reason was because from 8 February onwards, Algeria's DRS began running a parallel series of news articles on the kidnappings which were written by their own Algerian journalists.

One such 'journalist' is Mounir Boudjemaa, the deputy editor of the Algerian daily newspaper, *Liberté*, who usually signs off under the byline 'Mounir B' or just 'MB'. Boudjemaa is known by those familiar with the operations of the DRS as one of the voices of DRS boss General Mohamed Mediène' (alias Toufik/Tewfik). What Boudjemaa writes on such matters is the message that the DRS wants disseminated into the public domain. The DRS thus manages two channels of information: one is through its own group of 'tame' journalists, or agents, such as Boudjemaa, Salima Tlemçani and Anis Rahmani; the other is through statements attributed directly to AQIM/AQIS itself. In the case of the latter, the DRS's orchestration of AQIM makes it almost impossible to know whether AQIM statements are genuine or from the DRS. The clue is often in the spokesman's identity. In February, both channels of disinformation came into play; first through a Boudjemaa article in *Liberté* on 8 February, then through an AQIM broadcast on 17 February.

Boudjemaa's article[6] stated that the four Europeans that had been seized the previous week (22 January) had been abducted by MBM. This was incorrect. They were in the hands of Abdelhamid abou Zaïd, while the two Canadians were in the hands of MBM. Boudjemaa's article thus served to confuse the roles of Abou Zaïd and MBM.

What was even more extraordinary about Boudjemaa's article was that he was able to foretell, thanks to his association with the DRS, the precise demands that the Groupe Salafiste pour le Prédication et le Combat (GSPC) would make for the release of the hostages nine days before they made them. The claim was made in an audio recording delivered to and broadcast by Al Jazeera, The AQIM spokesman identified himself as Salah Abu Mohammed. His translated words were:

> We are pleased to announce to the Islamic nation the good news of the *mujahideens'* success in carrying out two quality operations in Niger ... *mujahideens* reserve the right to manage the case of six hostages according to Islamic law (shari'a).

AQIM demanded the release of two of MBM's Mauritanian recruits, Sidi Ali Naban and Ould Yahdih, reportedly held in a Malian prison, in exchange for the hostages.   According to the US authorities, Salah Abu Mohammed is an alias for Salah Gasmi. On 17 July 2008, Adam Szubin, Director of the Office of Foreign Assets Control (OFAC) in the US Treasury Department, said:

> Algeria has shown remarkable courage in the face of horrifying terrorist attacks against its people. The four terrorists that we have targeted today are amongst the most culpable for this violence ... We are proud to support the efforts of Algeria and the world community to combat this deadly threat and we will continue to do so.[7]

The four 'terrorists' listed by the US Treasury, all names provided by Algeria's DRS, were: Salah Gasmi (aka Salah Abu Muhamad, Salah Abu Mohammed, Bounouadher); Yahia Djouadi (aka Yahia Abu Amar, Abou Amar, Abu Ala, Abou Alam); Ahmed Deghdegh (aka Abd Al Illah, Aby Abdallah) and Abid Hammadou (aka Abdelhamid abou/abu Zeïd [Zaïd], Abid Hamadu, Hamadou Abid, Youcef Adel, Abu Abdellah). It is particularly significant that all four are associated with the DRS. Both Abou Zaïd and Yahia Djouadi, now managing operations in northern Mali and the Sahel, were with El Para on the 2003 operation, while three of them were involved in the kidnapping of the two Austrians, Wolfgang Eber and Andrea Kloiber, described in Chapter 8. Gasmi was named by Algeria's intelligence services as AQIM's media representative and director of its internet communications. It was Gasmi who claimed responsibility for the Austrians' kidnapping.

THE FUTURE GROUND ZERO 141

According to the same Algerian intelligence source, Degdegh was also involved in the Austrians' hostage negotiations as AQIM's designated negotiator and allegedly issued the ransom demands.

The reason why Gasmi took on a new alias to announce AQIM's claim that it was holding the two Canadians and the four tourists was because members of the Algerian opposition Rachad Movement[8] had acquired reliable information that Gasmi was a DRS agent.

In the immediate wake of Mounir Boudjemaa's revelations, the DRS media outlets ran several media articles of supportive disinformation. For example, on 11 February 2009, three days after Boudjemaa's first epistle, *El Khabar* reported that the region's military and gendarmerie commands had warned oil and gas companies operating in the south of the country to tighten their security against terrorist attacks launched against foreign personnel and infrastructures.[9] However, my checks with Western companies operating in southern Algeria revealed that none of them was aware of having received such a warning. Simultaneously, the Moroccan francophone daily newspaper *Aujourd'hui le Maroc*, drawing on articles published contemporaneously in Mauritania and Algeria, warned of armed AQIM incursions from Algeria targeting French oil interests in Mauritania's Ouadene region, where Total was undertaking exploratory work. The article said that the Mauritanian army and all embassies in Nouakchott had been put on a state of alert following the report that AQIM vehicles had been spotted in the Ouadene region. The grand-sounding but somewhat eccentric and self-styled European Strategic Intelligence and Security Centre (ESISC) was cited as the key source of this unverified information. No attack took place against Total or any other French company in Mauritania at the time.

On 25 February, *El Khabar* reported another equally suspect story. It stated that Mali's customs officials had seized a large stash of weapons at a roadblock. According to a Malian customs official, the weapons, reportedly sent from Guinea, were destined for al-Qaeda's North African wing. The report alleged that the weapons were bought with the ransom money received for the Austrian tourists. The smugglers allegedly told the Malian authorities that this was their third shipment of arms, the other two being handed over to 'light-skinned men in the north of Mali'. The story could conceivably be true, but I was unable to verify it through Malian sources, while the fact that it seems to have originated in an Algerian newspaper known for publishing disinformation provided by the DRS suggests that it was probably fiction.[10]

This spate of local media articles, sourced almost entirely to Algeria's military intelligence services, were treated quite uncritically by most of the world's media, which simply repeated them. On some occasions the hyperbole reached quite outlandish levels. For instance, the Washington-based Moroccan American Community Board described the Sahel as 'The Future Ground Zero'.[11]

Algeria's Intelligence Weakness: Exaggerating the Case

The DRS's major weakness is that it invariably tends to overstate its case, making possibly plausible stories quite implausible, or, as we saw in the case of the Djanet airport attack (Chapter 6), failing to brief one of their own journalists, Selima Tlemçani, of their original story with the result that three years later she inadvertently revealed that the infamous al-Qaeda attack never took place.

Mounir Boudjemaa's two articles in *Liberté* contained similar oversights. The most glaring was his publication of the names of the two prisoners whose release AQIM was going to demand nine days later. On 22 February, Boudjemaa continued with his DRS-prepared script by confirming, as he had 'foreseen' in his earlier article of 8 February, that Salah Abu Mohammed had demanded the release of Sidi Ali Naban and Ould Yahdih from a Sahel prison (known to be in Mali) and a ransom. We will probably never know whether this was the result of a lack of coordination, a 'left hand–right hand' problem, or DRS overconfidence. Indeed, the outcome could perhaps be attributed as much to 'bad luck' as bad judgement. Whatever had been planned between the DRS and Boudjemaa, the end result was that Ould Yahdih either died or was killed before any handover was undertaken.

The reported circumstances of Ould Yahdih's death are highly suspicious and have been covered up, so much so that Biram Ould Dah Ould Abeid, President of the Mauritanian NGO Initiative de résurgence du movement pour l'abolition de l'esclavage (IRA), demanded an independent inquiry into his death, including the exhumation of his body and an autopsy to determine the precise cause of his death while in Malian detention. According to Ould Yahdih's family in Mauritania, they had received no news of him for six months, from the time of a hand grenade incident in Gao, for which he was allegedly detained, until they were told by the Mauritanian police that he had been killed in a road accident while being transferred from one prison in Mali to another. The date of the accident was also fudged, being first reported on 7 March, even though it happened on 27 February. According to Mali's Defence Ministry, four Malian security agents also died in the accident. Although Mali claims that the two prisoners were being transferred to Bamako from an unnamed destination, believed to be either Timbuktu or Gao, no reasons were given for the transfer. Was it so that they could be handed over from Bamako as part of the hostage release, or were they being transferred to Mauritania to fulfil an extradition request? No further information has been given; nor is it known what happened to the other prisoner, Sidi Ali Naban.

Western Intelligence Agencies and the DRS

Mounir Boudjemaa's articles confirmed that even though the DRS may not have been involved in the abduction of these two groups of hostages, it was certainly involved in their captivity. I was particularly worried, however, by reports in *El Khabar*, which could not have been published without the green light from the DRS, that Yahia Djouadi was wanting to execute two of the hostages on the grounds that they were European intelligence agents who had been sent to the Sahara to follow the tracks of the Salafist jihadists in the Sahara-Sahel.[12] This was far-fetched, but nevertheless repeated a few days later in another *El Khabar* article, in the genre of 'the passing nomad', which said that 'well informed sources' had learned from the 'Bedouins of the Sahara' that a disagreement had broken out amongst AQIM's Saharan elements during the last week of January over the question of whether to execute these two (unnamed) hostages.

Such references to execution took me back to the threats made during my negotiation for the release of the two Austrians only a few months earlier, and my assessment that AQIM/DRS would sooner or later have to either execute a hostage or undertake a major attack against Western interests in the region to establish its credibility as a serious 'terrorist' threat.

The Canadian authorities had already asked my views on what might have happened to their two diplomats. They were therefore aware of the information set out in this and earlier chapters, as well as in *The Dark Sahara*. However, in March, I wrote a lengthy report on the hostage situation that heavily incriminated the DRS and which was distributed on 23 March to several Western intelligence agencies. The DRS, which received a copy of the report, would have known that the report would have been distributed through Western intelligence circles.

The DRS's response was electric. It came in the form of a quite incredible article in the 1 April edition of *Liberté*[13] and several other Algerian daily newspapers, notably *Ennahar*[14] and *L'Expression*. Published in another country, it would have been taken for an April Fool's joke! The story, sourced to Algeria's security forces (that is, the DRS), is as follows.

On Monday 30 March, Algeria's security forces, comprising the army and gendarmerie, supported by army assault helicopters, set up an ambush to attack MBM and other AQIM emirs as they travelled back from Libya to meet with a Nigerien arms trafficker by the name of El Hadj of the El M'Hamid tribe in the Oued Righ region. Oued Righ extends to the north and south of Touggourt in the extreme north of Ouargla *wilaya*.

According to the story, Algeria's military intelligence services received the tip-off from an African arms trafficker who operates in the border zone between Algeria, Libya, and Niger.

The ambush reportedly took place in the Ghil region on the Algerian-Libyan border in the south of the Ouargla *wilaya*. According to 'well informed sources', MBM was accompanied by Yahia Djouadi and Abdelhamid abou Zaïd. In short, the three AQIM terrorist leaders whom AQIM has claimed, and the DRS reported, as holding the six hostages were all travelling together on their way back from Libya to Algeria.

The ambush is reported to have begun at nightfall with the army encircling the convoy of 4WDs containing the three emirs and their 40 or so foot soldiers. However, the terrorists realised they were being ambushed and, according to the report, 'began firing back with modern weapons in all directions'. In spite of assault helicopters and an aerial bombardment, the terrorists escaped. One terrorist was reportedly killed, although his body was apparently too badly mutilated to be identified. According to the report, the terrorists were chased as far as Hassi Lefhel (30 kilometres north of Hassi R'Mel) in Ghardaia *wilaya*, where they finally managed to escape.

The main point of the story, from the DRS perspective, was to establish that MBM, Yahia Djouadi and Abou Zaïd were all terrorists and emirs of AQIM, and not DRS agents or associates, as my 23 March report claimed. On 5 April, I sent to those Western intelligence agencies that had received my 23 March analysis of the hostage situation an explicated version of the DRS's story, along with the suggestion that they consider the following questions.

How could Abdelhamid abou Zaïd have travelled from Libya to Algeria on 30 March when *El Khabar,* relying on DRS sources, had reported him being arrested in Mauritania on 23 March? Clearly, at least one of these versions, both of which were sourced to the DRS, was disinformation.

Similarly, how could Yahia Djouadi have also been travelling back from Libya when Reuters, quoting the 28 March edition of *El Khabar*, said that middlemen had just met Djouadi in Mali in an attempt to check that the six hostages were in good health and were in Djouadi's hands?[15]

Moreover, how does this story equate with the AFP report filed from Timbuktu on 25 March, which reported that a security source in Timbuktu had informed AFP that the 'principal suspect' in the abduction of the four tourists had been arrested on 24 March in northern Mali?[16]

In similar vein, if the six hostages were being held by Abou Zaïd, MBM and Yahia Djouadi, either jointly or singly, who was guarding them while all three were some 2,000–3,000 kilometres away in Libya? And, by the same token, if the leaders were away in Libya, who was handling the negotiations for the hostages' release?

Was it realistic to believe that all three would be together in Libya, 2,000–3,000 kilometres away from their alleged stamping grounds, at the same time? Moreover, would they really be buying arms or doing similar business in Libya, whose security forces were thick on the ground and violently opposed to the sort of Islamic extremism that AQIM is alleged to profess?

Furthermore, who was the Nigerien arms trafficker they were allegedly meeting at the Oued Righ? The name given to the newspapers was El Hadj. El Hadj is not a name, but the title given to someone who has made the pilgrimage to Mecca. There are thousands of people known as El Hadj across the Sahara. As for his tribe, I have not come across a tribe called El M'Hamid, and do not believe such a name exists. The nearest I have come to it are the descendents of marriages between noble Tuareg Kel Rela and former slaves in the villages of Ideles and Tazrouk in Ahaggar (Algeria), one of whose ancestors was a certain Chet Mehamed. It is quite conceivable that their descendants travelled to northern Niger, because that is where they kept many of their camels, and some may have subsequently settled there. However, I am not aware of that name being used in that area.

There was also the question of why the three emirs would travel to the extreme north of the Sahara (Oued Righ), especially when that part of the Sahara was a high security region, to do a deal with a Nigerien arms trafficker when the arms were destined for the Sahel. There is no evidence, other than this unlikely story, that there was such a deal or meeting arranged. However, one likely reason why the DRS chose the Oued Righ for its fabricated story is because there actually was an engagement with bandit/terrorist gunmen in or near that region on that same day (30 March). Therefore, if an investigation was to be undertaken, local people might well recall military activity and the sound of gunfire in that region on that same day.

I also questioned whether it was credible that MBM's convoy could have been chased by army helicopters through the night, from the Libyan border to Hassi Lefleh – the best part of 1,000 kilometres. The question becomes even more absurd when we consider that the nature of the intervening terrain – one of the world's largest sand seas – would oblige the terrorists to stick to one of two main routes which are well patrolled by the security forces. The DRS might argue that they escaped under the cover of darkness and by driving without lights. That is conceivable. Traffickers' drivers are chosen partly for their ability to drive at night without lights. I have driven with them under such conditions. However, the speed is necessarily much reduced and it would be impossible to cover that distance in the hours of darkness.

Finally, if the story were true, it would be one of staggering military incompetence, unbecoming of Algeria's armed forces.

Four Hostages Released

On 22 April 2009, Robert Fowler and Louis Guay, along with the two women tourists, Mariane Petzold (German) and Gabriela Greiner (Swiss), were released in northern Mali. Both AQIS groups and their emirs, Abou Zaïd and MBM, were present at the handover of the hostages. The two Canadians had been held by MBM and the four tourists by Abou Zaïd. Robert Fowler noted the tension between the two emirs. As the two leaders conversed, their two groups of heavily armed men remained apart, arms ready, just waiting for the signal to fight.

Salima Tlemçani, writing with inside knowledge of the DRS, stated that the hostages may have been released earlier than planned.[17] One of the parties close to the negotiations for the hostages' release indicated to me that this may have been the result of my 23 March report and the questions listed above, both of which drew Western intelligence agencies' attention to the relationship between the AQIS emirs and the DRS.

It was widely reported by the media that Fowler and Guay were released in exchange for a ransom and the release of several militants. Although the Canadian government has always denied paying a ransom, money almost certainly changed hands. A US diplomatic cable released by Wikileaks in February 2011 suggested that a ransom had been paid. However, the conversation reported in the cable, between a senior Libyan official and a US Ambassador, is not credible. Algeria, which effectively runs AQIM, would never allow a Libyan official to be party to such proceedings.[18]

However, two hostages – Werner Greiner, the husband of Gabriela Greiner, and Edwin Dyer – remained in captivity.

11

PERFIDIOUS ALBION:
THE MURDER OF EDWIN DYER

The British hostage, Edwin Dyer, was executed by Abdelhamid abou Zaïd on 31 May 2009, with unconfirmed reports saying that he had been beheaded. His body has not been recovered.

Many questions still hang over Dyer's death. The first and most obvious is why Dyer and Werner Greiner were not released at the same time as the other hostages. Second, why was Dyer murdered and Greiner released?

The generally accepted answer to the second question is that the British government, in accordance with its policy of not negotiating with terrorists, refused to negotiate the demands of the 'terrorists', while someone, assumed to be the Swiss government, reportedly paid a €3 million ransom for Greiner's release.[1] That is how it was portrayed in the international media. There was, however, much more to it than that: namely, Britain's increasingly compromised relations with Algeria and the Département du Renseignement et de la Sécurité's (DRS's) need to re-establish the credibility of al-Qaeda in the Islamic Maghreb (AQIM) after the events described in the previous chapter.

The distribution to western intelligences agencies of research-based evidence that not only raised direct questions about the DRS's association with AQIM but also demonstrated that the evidence placed in Algeria's newspapers by DRS sources was patently false clearly created problems for the head of the DRS, General Mohamed Mediène. In releasing the two Canadian diplomats and the two women, Mediène had relieved himself of the most high-profile hostages and eased the pressure on him, at least from Canada and the UN. Nevertheless, even though the US and

European intelligence agencies that worked with Algeria's DRS were aware of the DRS's relationship with AQIM, Mediène needed to establish, at least to the international media and in the world that exists beyond the confines of intelligence agencies, that AQIM was a 'real' terrorist organisation and that these kidnappings had been undertaken by 'real terrorists'. The retention of two of the hostages provided him with the means of engineering a situation that would enable him to achieve those ends.

Thus, on 26 April, four days after the release of the two Canadians and the two women, AQIM issued a statement threatening to kill the British hostage if the UK did not release Abu Qatada, the Islamic extremist of Jordanian nationality being held in the Long Lartin high-security jail in Worcestershire, in 20 days; that is, by 15 May. This was a shrewd move, for two reasons. First, it was virtually impossible for the UK to comply, thus raising the likelihood that Edwin Dyer would be killed, so proving that his captors were real, hardline terrorists. Second, the demand for Abu Qatada's release gave the appearance of elevating AQIM from being a local, Algerian-based organisation to being part of the globalised stage of al-Qaeda proper.

The 15 May deadline passed, with media headlines proclaiming: 'Al-Qa'ida Backs Down in Sahara'.[2] Four days later, *El Khabar*, one of the DRS's main mouthpieces, reported that AQIM was now demanding €10 million for both hostages, promising to free the Swiss hostage upon receipt of the ransom, followed by the British hostage a few weeks later. However, quoting an 'anonymous security source', presumably the DRS, *El Khabar* said that Hamid Essoufi (Abdelhamid abou Zaïd) was willing to accept €8 million.

The British government is reported to have responded with a request for assurances that the hostages were alive and healthy. However, as we shall see later, that was certainly not the impression given by the Wikileaks cables released in 2011, which revealed that the Foreign and Commonwealth Office (FCO) refused to speak to Dyer when it had the opportunity to do so.[3] Neither has the British government ever given a satisfactory explanation for refusing to even confirm to the media that a British hostage was being held or to release his name, at least prior to his execution.[4]

UK Support for Algeria's Regime

The impression given by the British government in response to Dyer's murder was that the Sahara-Sahel region was beyond its traditional sphere of influence and that both its knowledge of and involvement and influence in the region were scant. That is only partly true. At the time of Dyer's death, the UK was in the process of getting 'very involved' in the region, especially through its increasingly obsequious post-2006 relationship with Algeria.

That is not to imply that the UK was unfamiliar with the Algerian regime before 2006. On the contrary, the British government and the FCO in particular had established their credentials as supporters of Algeria's repressive regime back in the 1990s. In 1998, three Cabinet ministers – Jack Straw, Geoffrey Hoon and the late Robin Cook – had signed public interest immunity certificates to prevent documents written about Algeria by the FCO and Whitehall's Joint Intelligence Committee from being submitted in court. At the court hearing, the FCO stated that there was 'no credible, substantive evidence to confirm allegations implicating Algerian government forces in atrocities'. However, when the undisclosed documents were produced 18 months later on the orders of a trial judge, they completely contradicted what the FCO had told the court. They revealed that British intelligence believed the Algerian government was involved in atrocities against innocent civilians.[5]

Since 2006, the British government's relationship with Algeria's regime has been driven by two main considerations: one commercial and the other political, or, to be more precise, the UK's desire to play a lead role in north-west African counter-terrorism.

Algeria is not a major trading partner of the UK. It is, however, a significant producer of oil and natural gas and an important supplier to Europe. Although the main source of Europe's gas is Russia, Algeria's contribution is strategically significant, supplying the EU with 20 per cent of its natural gas and more than 30 per cent of its LNG (liquefied natural gas) imports. Most of this gas is exported via pipelines to Spain and Italy. As Europe's energy needs grow and as it tries to reduce its dependence on Russia, so Europe as a whole is likely to become increasingly dependent on Algeria. Algeria's contribution to the UK's energy needs comes in the form of LNG, which can be strategically important at times of high energy demand. For example, in the winter of 2010–11, the coldest in the UK since records began, Algerian LNG imports provided a crucial 'top up'. Figures for November 2010, an unusually cold month, revealed that the UK took around 25 per cent of the total LNG imported into Europe from Algeria.

The Lure of New Arms Contracts

At the time of Dyer's death, however, a very different economic consideration was uppermost in Whitehall minds. In 2006, the UK observed Russia making large-scale arms sales to Algeria and did not herself want to forgo such a lucrative market. It therefore lifted its embargo on arms sales to Algeria that had been in place since the mid 1990s. Then, in 2007, it became known that Algeria was considering the purchase of four new frigates. By the end of the year, media reports were suggesting that it was a certainty that the order would go to France. However, on 27 January 2009, five days after Edwin Dyer's abduction, bloggers in France reported that Gordon Brown, the British Prime Minister, had 'exchanged several letters' with Algeria's President Abdelaziz Bouteflika and that BVT Surface Fleet, a joint venture with BAe Systems, supported by the British government, had opened negotiations with Algeria for the contract to supply four frigates and new dockyard facilities at the Algerian naval base of Mers-el-Kebir (where two of the frigates were to be built) at a reported value of some €5 billion.[6] At the time of Edwin Dyer's murder, the UK bid, according to Algerian sources, was believed to have risen from outsider to front-runner. The seizure of a British hostage at such a delicate moment in UK-Algerian relations was therefore a potentially sensitive issue: any allegation by the British government of DRS involvement in the hostage-takings could threaten the UK's chance of winning the hugely lucrative contract.

The UK'S Priority: Supporting Washington

The UK's political or counterterrorism role in the Sahara-Sahel since 2006 has been even more opaque. At a US State Department Briefing in Washington in August 2006,[7] State Department officials confirmed to me that the US had requested the UK, because of its experience in 'development work', to help clear up the 'mess' that the US had created in the region through its 'War on Terror' there. It was made clear to me that the UK's Department for International Development (DFID) had already been contacted and was 'on board'. Two weeks later, after my return to the UK, I was contacted by an FCO official who explained that the FCO had been asked by the US to help it in its counterterrorism efforts in the Sahara-Sahel, notably southern Algeria, and asked me to advise it.[8]

My initial and immediate advice was that the UK authorities should have nothing to do with the US request, and warned that there could be international legal consequences if they were to become involved. During two long discussions, the first in October and the second in November, I briefed the official on the precise ways in which the US-Algerian military intelligence services had fabricated 'terrorism' across the region, and that the US's request and its counterterrorist strategies should be seen in that context. I also explained that US forces had been involved in the recent orchestration of the Kidal Tuareg rebellion in May and the September and October engagements between Tuareg 'rebels' and alleged Groupe Salafiste pour le Prédication et le Combat (GSPC) terrorists (described in Chapter 5) with the aim of injecting a new lease of life into the 'Global War on Terror' (GWOT) in the Sahel. I also pointed out that I knew, from my meetings in Washington, that the US had effectively lost control of the intelligence situation in the Sahara-Sahel and was looking for an 'exit strategy'.[9]

When we spoke in October, the FCO official confirmed what I had been told in Washington, namely that the 'US had asked the UK for support'. When we met seven weeks later, he undertook a slight semantic shift, explaining that 'the UK's first priority [was] to help [its] allies, in this case the US, in whatever way we think we are able, which in this particular case is to assist in counter-terrorism in the Sahara-Sahel'.

The FCO, so it transpired, had committed itself to assisting its US ally in the Sahara-Sahel a long time before my August 2006 visit to Washington. With the benefit of hindsight, it is quite clear that the FCO never had any intention of accepting, let alone following, my advice on keeping out of the Sahara-Sahel. The first move by the British authorities that I am aware of to assist Washington's policies in the Sahara-Sahel region came in 2005 when the Economic and Social Research Council (ESRC) rejected my application to its New Security Challenges Programme to fund my research on 'The Security Threat to Europe from the US Militarisation of the Sahelian Sahara'.[10] It was not until late in 2006 that I received confirmation that my application had been rejected by the supposedly 'academically independent' ESRC following political intervention from either the FCO or the intelligence services with which it worked.[11]

The FCO and the intelligence services went further than intervening to block a research application on political grounds. In 2006, it co-sponsored with the ESRC and the Arts and Humanities Research Council, to the sum of £1.3 million, a highly duplicitous, irresponsible and ethically untenable research programme, entitled 'Combating Terrorism by Countering Radicalisation'. Designed in large part by MI5's Joint Terrorism Analysis Centre (JTAC), which probably explains its less than scholarly conceptualisation, even to the point of failing to define 'radicalisation', the programme immediately hit resistance from a number of academics. However, notwithstanding the wholly unethical behaviour of the Research Councils and the new low-point to which they had dragged British academe,[12] the response of the guardians of British academic research was simply to double the funding, change the project name to 'New Security Challenges: "Radicalisation" and Violence – A Critical Assessment' and arrogantly relaunch it in 2007, with wholly inadequate peer review, to a small group of academic institutes and individuals more interested in their own financial wellbeing than the maintenance of ethical academic standards.

There are two important reasons for this digression from Edwin Dyer's murder. One is to leave the reader in no doubt that the UK establishment, in its willingness to support Washington's highly contentious policies in this part of Africa, was prepared, through this murky and possibly illegal ESRC–FCO–Special Intelligence Service/MI5 conspiracy, to jeopardise the UK's reputation for high ethical standards of academic integrity. The second is to assure the reader that the FCO and JTAC, having been fully briefed on the nature of the GWOT in the Sahara-Sahel, and having debased British academic standards so disgracefully in the process, cannot plead ignorance, as is its wont, of the situation that had been developing in the Sahara and in which Edwin Dyer found himself hostage.

The unpalatable truth about Edwin Dyer's abduction in January 2009 and his summary execution by Abdelhamid abou Zaïd some four months later is that it provided the British authorities with a fortuitous opportunity to engage in a more direct and 'hands on' manner in north-west African counterterrorism and to develop a much closer relationship with Algeria's DRS, which, as we shall see, was soon to blossom.

One small irritant to whatever plans Britain's intelligence and counterterrorism services may have had in mind were my publications, reports and analyses on terrorism in the Sahara-Sahel that were being distributed increasingly widely in the corporate, journalistic, academic and political worlds. The way the FCO and British intelligence services dealt with my interventions was twofold. On the one hand, they let it be known that I was a 'conspiracy theorist' and a 'loose cannon', whose research was 'trying to construct a conspiracy theory'.[13] The irony of this broadbrush smear was that I was not constructing a conspiracy but 'deconstructing' their own. Second, the Metropolitan Police, who are responsible for 'terrorism' in the UK, set up an office, housed across the road from Scotland Yard in Caxton Street, with the specific purpose of searching for academics and even passing travellers who could advise them on the region and hopefully 'rubbish' my work. The two officers seconded to this bizarre and rather arcane job were DC Paul M. Smith of the

Metropolitan Police's Specialist Operations' north-west Africa desk and 'Mathew'.[14] Their first interview with one of the few academics they could find with knowledge of this part of the Sahara was in March 2009. They were still hard at work twelve months later, having clearly achieved no great understanding of the region but at a considerable cost and wholly irresponsible waste of taxpayers' money.

It was around this time that Patrick Tobin, an Arabist and East African specialist, was appointed as the FCO's regional counter-terrorism security advisor on north-wwest Africa. Tobin was sent to Timbuktu at the beginning of April and then to Algiers, where he has since worked in close association with the DRS, being instrumental in setting up a joint UK-Algerian committee on coun-terterrorism.[15] At my first acquaintance with Tobin in the FCO, just before his departure for Timbuktu, he told me that Timbuktu was of crucial importance to British interests. When I asked him what interests the UK had around Timbuktu, he replied: 'oil'. This struck me as odd, as the nearest British oil interests to Timbuktu were BP's operation at In Salah in Algeria, 1,500 kilometres as the crow flies to the north-east, and Shell's operations in the Niger Delta, just a few hundred kilometres further away to the south-east. Such is the reasoning of our 'intelligence services'. What Tobin probably meant to say was that British oil interests, like the frigate contract, were best served by cooperating with Algeria and not confronting its regime about the relationship between its DRS and AQIM.

From the end of March until the time of Dyer's assassination, copies of all my reports on AQIM and terrorism in the Sahara-Sahel were sent to Paul Smith and Mathew at Scotland Yard, Patrick Tobin in Timbuktu and Algiers, and the Embassies, such as Switzerland, of countries whose citizens were or had been held hostage in the region. This was so that the British authorities could never claim that 'they did not know'.

At the Heart of AQIM is the DRS

On hearing of Dyer's murder, the British Prime Minister, Gordon Brown, said: 'I want those who would use terror against British citizens to know beyond doubt that we and our allies will pursue them relentlessly, and that they will meet the justice they deserve.'[16]

Neither at the time of Dyer's murder nor subsequently have either Abdelhamid abou Zaïd or what I have called al-Qaeda in the Sahara-Sahel (AQIS) been pursued relentlessly. As the remaining chapters will show, the exact opposite has been the case. However, when the Malian security forces detained three members of AQIM/AQIS in the week or so following Dyer's death, AQIM/AQIS believed it had been double-crossed. The man they suspected was Lieutenant Colonel Lemana Ould Bou, who had been playing the dangerous game of double agent between Mali's state security and AQIM/AQIS. The colonel had discovered elements of Algeria's secret services at the core of AQIM/AQIS and was reported by the local press as having said that 'At the heart of AQIM is the DRS.'[17] He was assassinated almost immediately, on the evening of 10 June 2009, in a relative's home in Timbuktu. His brother, Lemana Ould Sheikh, told Agence France-Presse (AFP) that

> two of the gunmen came into their house while two others stayed outside in a getaway vehicle. They came into our house. The lieutenant colonel was sitting in the living room and one of the men pointed at him and said to the other: 'That's him, that's him.' Then they shot him three times.[18]

Lemana Ould Bou's murder was reported in the media in a slightly different context, as being simply another act of al-Qaeda terrorism.

Sacrificed on the Alter of Expediency

Dyer's execution by Abou Zaïd on 31 May 2009 confirmed AQIM as a dangerous terrorist organisation and justified the UK's involvement in north-west African counterterrorism. There remain, though, unanswered questions. Did the UK confront Algeria with the information it had regarding Abou Zaïd's links to the DRS? Did the UK want to help Algeria and the US establish the credibility of AQIM as a 'real' terrorist organisation in the Sahara-Sahel? And why did the FCO reportedly refuse to speak to Dyer on the phone when it had the opportunity to do so?[19] It was not, as the FCO said, because it would have made it appear to be negotiating with terrorists, as the line, according to Wikileaks, was direct between Dyer and the FCO. Indeed, if the FCO had spoken with Dyer, it might have learnt something. Or, was it already wholly in the picture? Further, why were the British authorities so reluctant to name him, when his name was already in the public domain? Why were they trying to create such anonymity, a 'Mr Nobody', as one commentator remarked?[20]

Confronting the Algerians with evidence that AQIM's leaders in the Sahara were DRS agents would have ended the UK's hopes of winning the frigate contract. As for the need to establish the credibility of AQIM, Algeria and the US – and indeed all those Western countries that had bought into the El Para myth – had a serious problem with the GWOT in the Sahara in that there had been no evident act of terror by GSPC/AQIM in the Sahara-Sahel since El Para's false-flag operation in 2003. As previous chapters have explained, both the Tuareg engagements with the GSPC in northern Mali in September–October 2006 and the attack on Djanet airport in November 2007 were not what they were reported to be. Dyer's death set such embarrassing matters aside. His execution finally established AQIM in the Sahara-Sahel as a serious terrorist organisation that had to be reckoned with.

It is inconceivable that the US and UK intelligence services did not know, at the time of Dyer's murder, that AQIM in the Sahara-Sahel was an Algerian DRS construct and that Abou Zaïd was a DRS agent. At the time of Dyer's death, I asked whether the US, in the light of its close alliance with the UK and the latter's commercial predicament over the frigate contract (which it ultimately failed to win), could not have used its close ties with Algeria's DRS and stepped in to save the life of the British hostage.[21] Washington could have intervened on the UK's behalf, but chose not to do so. Indeed, there is no evidence that the UK even made such a request to the US. All three parties, Algeria, the UK and the US, wanted the killing of a Western hostage in order to give credibility to AQIM in the Sahara-Sahel and to justify the militarisation of such a resource-rich region. In the end, Dyer was sacrificed to avoid jeopardising a lucrative arms contract and as part of a sinister and cynical manipulation of the al-Qaeda franchise by wider geopolitical strategic interests.

12

DRUGS AND THE THREAT OF WESTERN INTERVENTION

A Burnt-Out Boeing and Ten Tonnes of Cocaine

Edwin Dyer's execution gave al-Qaeda in the Islamic Maghreb (AQIM), or in the Sahel (AQIS), the international profile and credibility that it had hitherto lacked. Some confirmation of this was given in November 2009 when Richard Barrett, the former British intelligence official, expert on al-Qaeda-related terrorism and, as the Coordinator of the UN al-Qaeda–Taliban Monitoring Team, the UN's highest-ranking official responsible for monitoring the activities of al-Qaeda and the Taliban,[1] said that while attacks by al-Qaeda and its operatives were decreasing in many parts of the world, the situation was worsening in North Africa.[2] Barrett was referring implicitly to the activities of AQIM in Mali, Mauritania and adjoining regions. Indeed, ten Westerners were taken hostage in the Sahel during 2009. As we shall see presently, a further six were taken in 2010 and 14 in 2011, with three of them killed.

Barrett's statement was reinforced during the last few weeks of 2009 by a series of headline-grabbing stories from the Sahel. On 25 November, a Frenchman, Pierre Camatte, was seized from a hotel in Ménaka in north-western Mali. Four days later, three Spanish aid workers, Albert Vilalta, Roque Pascual and Alicia Gámez, were attacked and abducted in Mauritania. Then, on 18 December, an Italian couple were attacked and abducted in southern Mauritania about ten miles north of the border with Mali. All six found themselves in the hands of AQIM. However, in terms of headline-making news, these incidents were no match for the extraordinary story which captured international attention around mid November.

The story that broke in the international media on 16 November was dramatic. Its central actors were the South American drug cartels, their mysterious Tuareg and Arab Saharan intermediaries, Malian state security, Interpol and the US Drug Enforcement Administration (DEA); the stage-set, a burnt-out Boeing 727 in the desert.

Drug trafficking across the Sahara was not a new development. Cocaine from Latin America had certainly surpassed cigarette smuggling as the most lucrative trans-Saharan trafficking business by around 2007. So, although drug trafficking through Mali was certainly not a new development, the discovery of a burnt-out Boeing 727, capable of carrying ten tonnes of cocaine, in the desert wastes of Mali opened up a whole new vista on the scale and operational sophistication of the drug-trafficking business.

On 2 November, local herdsmen in the tiny, isolated desert commune of Tarkint, with an official population in 1998 of 3,554 and some 150 kilometres north of Gao, claim to have heard a loud 'BANG!' The noise came from a rough, one-and-a-half-kilometre airstrip marked out by stones on the sand-blown lateritic ground. A small group of locals are said to have rushed towards the noise, with the alert being raised by a young Arab tradesman who rang the state security (Sécurité d'Etat) regional headquarters at Gao on his Thuraya satellite phone. The security forces were soon on the scene, where the incinerated carcass of a Boeing 727 was apparently still warm. The Director General of State Security, Colonel Mamy Coulibaly, was reportedly notified straight away.

Colonel Coulibaly was one of the many illustrious confidants of the Mayor of Tarkint, Baba Ould Sheikh, a dignitary of the local Arab Berabich tribe and known to almost all involved in the Sahara's kidnapping business as 'The Berabich', the 'Mr Go To' of AQIM's new Sahelian domain. Baba Ould Sheikh had been at the centre of every hostage negotiation in Mali since El Para brought his 14 European hostages into the region in 2003.[3] Since then he had become one of the 'two criminals', the other being Colonel Coulibaly, that Abdelhamid abou Zaïd's intermediary had described to me while I was negotiating the release of the two Austrians in 2008. Not only had Baba Ould Sheikh been involved in the negotiations to release El Para's hostages and the two Austrians, but he had been the key man in the negotiations to release the two Canadians earlier in 2009. In an interview with Geoffrey York of Canada's *Globe and Mail* just three weeks before the discovery of the Boeing, Baba told York that he had received no payment at all from the Canadians, not even for his expenses, nor had he received 'even a piece of paper to thank him'. He had accepted the three-month hostage assignment, so he said, 'because of his sense of duty to the President', but denied receiving any profits from the ransom. York, however, recorded that 'several Malian officials laughed when told of his [Baba's] claim'.[4]

Was it coincidence that the 'crashed' or incinerated Boeing landed on a makeshift airstrip in Baba Ould Sheik's proverbial backyard? The answer, given his close relationship with the head of state security, Colonel Coulibaly, is almost certainly not. At the time of the discovery, Mali's President, Amadou Toumani Touré, or ATT as he is commonly known, was returning from a visit to Qatar with a stopover in Tripoli, Libya. In his temporary absence, Colonel Coulibaly ordered that all the evidence be gathered and sent to Bamako immediately. This evidence, which included the plane's markings, or at least its engine numbers, photographs taken by the gendarmerie at the site, tins of tuna 'made in Vietnam' and bottles of 'Maltin' 'made in Venezuela' and the plane's half-burnt logbook, was sent to Bamako on 3–4 November.

According to the Malian authorities, some of the Embassies, notably those of the US, France, Spain and Algeria, were notified immediately, as their help, so they said, was needed in the inquiry. In the light of what we know now, it seems that the only help that might have been requested from the embassies was to help keep the story under wraps. Thanks to Wikileaks, we now have confirmation that the authorities were not only trying to keep the incident secret but preventing all the responsible national and international agencies, such as the Malian National Civil Aviation Authority (ANAC), the Drug Brigade of the Malian Judiciary Investigation Police, Interpol, and the United Nations

Office on Drugs and Crime (UNODC), from having any access to the investigation, which was restricted solely to Colonel Coulibaly's State security, the DGSE (Direction Générale de la Sécurité Extérieure).[5]

In fact, Colonel Coulibaly kept the investigation so tightly under his control that news of the story did not break in the world media until 16 November when Alexandre Schmidt, head of UNODC for West Africa, told journalists in Dakar that a Boeing used to transport cocaine from Venezuela to West Africa had crashed in northern Mali. Schmidt told the journalists that 'the plane landed on a makeshift landing strip 150 kms from Gao and unloaded cocaine and other illegal substances. The plane tried to take off but crashed on November 5th'. Schmidt stated that the amount of drugs carried on the plane was not known, but he explained that a Boeing could carry ten tonnes of cocaine. He confirmed that the drugs had not been found, but that Interpol was carrying out an investigation. He also said that this was the first time 'as far as we know' that South American drug barons had used a plane of such capacity, rented for the occasion, to smuggle cocaine to Africa.[6]

The Routes and Scale of Drug Trafficking

The first reports of the incident conveyed a sense of shock and the implication that this was a new tactic by the drug traffickers. In a short time, however, there were indications that this may not have been the first such flight. Indeed, one report on Radio France Internationale (RFI) suggested that there had been at least four such flights into neighbouring desert regions in the previous few months. My own enquiries amongst local people suggested that there had been at least a couple of previous flights. However, the most interesting information came from two reports, both written by Algerian journalists associated with the DRS, namely Mounir Boudjemaa (aka 'Mounir B') and Salima Tlemçani.

The first of these reported flights took place in January 2010. Boudjemaa reported that on 25 January an 'air-cargo' flight, crewed by four South Americans, had landed on the road from

Méma, near to the village of Kita, 76 kilometres from Timbuktu. Boudjemaa quoted 'local sources' that the plane was carrying 250 large containers of cocaine, which were unloaded under heavy guard into six 4WDs which made four round trips before disappearing. The plane took off on the morning of 26 January without any Malian official checking the flight.[7]

The second and third flights were reported by Salima Tlemçani, who is even more closely associated with the DRS than Boudjemaa. These flights, described as being from Latin America, offloaded their drug cargoes in Mali. On 6 February, a Bach 300, crewed by four South Americans, landed in the Kita district of the Kayes region carrying four tonnes of cocaine. Then, on 9 February, an identical aircraft put down at I-n-Esséri, close to the Nigerien frontier some 300 kilometres south-east of Tin Zaouatene.[8]

It now appears that these flights may have been just the tip of the iceberg. A Wikileaks file released in 2011 contains a cable sent from the US Ambassador in Bamako to the State Department in Washington on 23 February 2009, which states that

> On February 19 (2009), Tuareg contacts told the Embassy that a group of Tuareg bandits led by Bahanga had held up an Arab Berabiche drug convoy of 15 vehicles between Abeibera and the Algerian border. Twelve of the vehicles were reportedly carrying cocaine. The other three 4x4s served as escorts. The attackers allegedly took all of the vehicles, as well as the drug shipment, and instructed the Arabs to return to Kidal with a message from Bahanga that more incidents of this kind would occur in the future.[9]

The significance of this message is that it reveals that massive quantities of cocaine were being trafficked through Mali at least nine months before the incinerated Boeing was discovered at Tarkint and that it was the Berabich, protected by Mali's 'state security', who were managing it. Moreover, the quantity of cocaine was approximately the same as moved from the incinerated Boeing, about ten tonnes, suggesting that this February load might also have entered Mali in a plane of the same capacity.

North-eastern Mali has for some years been on the South America to Europe drugs route. Small planes or boats have brought the drugs across the Atlantic to West African states, such as Guinea-Bissau, Guinea-Conakry and Sierra Leone, where they are offloaded and taken overland to the various Sahelian jumping-off points to cross the Sahara in small but heavily armed convoys of up to a dozen 4WDs. North-eastern Mali, notably the regions of Kidal, Gao and Timbuktu, has been a key node on this transit network.

By the time the Boeing 727 was discovered in Mali in 2009, the main cocaine route to Europe from Mali was via Egypt, where it joined the huge container traffic to Europe that passed through the Suez Canal. Hashish from Morocco also started taking this route, coming south into Mali and then turning eastwards. From Mali, cocaine and hashish, run by different trafficking networks, follow the same broad route eastwards from Mali into Niger and across Tamesna, the Aïr mountains and Ténéré desert to Chad. In Chad, the traffickers continue eastwards, keeping to the north of Ennedi and then swinging around the eastern side of Tibesti to the Tazerbu region of south-east Libya and then on into Egypt.

This new geographical convergence of the cocaine and cannabis (hashish) routes around the Malian-Algerian border region has heightened the security tensions in the region. For example, on 29 November, almost four weeks after the Boeing was discovered at Tarkint, a convoy of five 4WDs heading south with cannabis resin from Morocco ran into an Algerian border patrol of three gendarmerie vehicles at Hassi Gourdine, on the Algerian side of the Algerian-Malian frontier near Tin Zaouatene. One of the vehicles in the drugs convoy either broke down or was immobilised by the gendarmes' fire. The other four vehicles escaped with all the traffickers. The seized vehicle was full to the brim with 1,175 kilogrammes of cannabis resin carefully wrapped in 47 packages, one automatic rifle, 400 cartridges and two drums of fuel.[10]

The amount and value of drugs crossing the Sahara in both directions is not known. A very rough idea can be obtained from Algeria's Customs Department. In 2009, up to the end of October, it had seized 53 tonnes of drugs, which, if extrapolated to the full year, would give 64 tonnes. Based on the government's estimate that it seizes 10–15 per cent (average, 12.5 per cent) of the drugs crossing the country, we could estimate that 512 tonnes of drugs, mostly cocaine and cannabis resin, crossed Algeria in 2009. If we allocate one-third of trans-Saharan drug trafficking to Algerian territory, then we would have a very approximate figure of 1,500 tonnes crossing the Sahara in 2009. If that is all cocaine (which it is not), that would give a very approximate EU street (retail) value, based on €60 million a tonne, of €90 billion. A UN report in 2012 put the street value of cocaine coming through Mali at between $8 billion and $10 billion.

On the basis of these figures, the ten tonnes of cocaine brought into Mali on the Tarkint 'big jet', as it became known, would have had a street value of some €60 million. The local media at the time put it at 50 billion CFA (Central African francs),[11] which is €75 million.[12]

Who was Involved in these Drugs Shipments and What Happened to Them?

Mounir Boudjemaa, writing about the plane that landed in Kita on 25 January,[13] pointed the finger directly at a local notable whom he initialled as 'B.O.C.', whom we can presume to be Baba Ould Sheikh [Cheikh]. Boudjemaa describes him as a dignitary and an elected official (Mayor of Tarkint) of the Berabich tribe who not only carries a lot of weight within the President's entourage but who is also well connected to AQIM and Mokhtar ben Mokhtar, for whom he acts as a money launderer. Boudjemaa says that B.O.C. was present at and in charge of receiving the cargo. If this is the case, it could not have been arranged without the complicity of the top echelons of the state.

Salima Tlemçani also said that the flights she mentioned were received by persons close to the Presidency and that they all belonged to the Arab community of Gao, amongst whom she singled out and named Baba Ould Sheikh, Sherif Ould Tahar, Hanouni Ould Labiadh and Ould Lagwinate.[14] A question surrounds the drugs' shipment offloaded at Tarkint. How could ten tonnes of cocaine, probably involving a convoy of up to a dozen 4WDs, be driven out of the region undetected? The answer, at least in theory, would be: with great difficulty. I say that for two very specific reasons. The first is that state security had been alerted as soon as the Boeing 727 had been incinerated. The second is that the world had been told incessantly since the murder of Edwin Dyer that security forces were thick on the ground in this part of the Sahara, supposedly tracking down and fighting al-Qaeda.

In addition to Malian and neighbouring Algerian forces, which, one might suppose, would both have been on full alert, the US had had a few hundred forces of one category or another in the region since (and before) the launch of the Pan-Sahel Initiative (PSI) in 2004. Most US forces were based at Gao, with some stationed at the airfield at Tessalit at the northern end of the Tilemsi valley. The US had also trained an elite force of 200 Malian soldiers in desert counterterrorism. In addition, there was an unknown number of French Special Forces reportedly located at Ménaka (Kidal region) and perhaps elsewhere in the country. A small contingent of British counterterrorism and Special Forces were reported to be operating in the country, supporting Mali in its fight against terrorism, as well as small contingents of Dutch troops and police (officially 'trainers') and German military 'trainers', along with military assistance from Spain. In addition, the region is covered by GeoEye's satellite system, enabling detailed situational awareness, especially anti-terrorism surveillance and monitoring, along with more conventional communications and surveillance technologies, to be carried out. Also, two special mission US Hawker Beechcraft 1900Ds,[15] reconfigured by Raytheon with high-tech surveillance equipment (that is, spy planes), were flying out of Tamanrasset daily.

North-eastern Mali and its border regions had been identified by international counterterrorism agencies as the focal operating zone of AQIM in the Sahel. If the information they were issuing was to be believed, then the region was 'swarming' with security and it would be thought unlikely that a drugs shipment of this size could progress very far undetected. However, the information emanating from the counterterrorism agencies, because of their complicity with AQIM, was little more than worthless. Although the international anti-drug agencies clearly had very strong grounds to believe, as the articles already cited have indicated, that Mali's state security was wholly complicit in both drug trafficking and AQIM's presence in the country, they were merely bystanders.

The Tarkint drugs shipment had not left the region, but not for security reasons. On 24 November, about three weeks after the Boeing's discovery, I heard rumours, passed on to me by informants in the region, that the cargo was held up somewhere in the region because of disagreement over the division of the booty. Five weeks later, on 31 December, there was a gun battle near the village of Bouraïssa, close to the Algerian border in the north of the Kidal region.

What happened at Bouraïssa and in the following weeks revealed the complex politics and intrigue of the drugs business and the involvement of the Malian government in it. The battle at Bouraïssa was between two groups involved in trafficking the cocaine. One group, reportedly led by Halid (Khalid) ag Mohamed, consisted exclusively of Kel Iforas (Ifoghas) Tuareg, originally from the Kidal region, who traditionally fell under the supreme religious authority of the Kounta family of Baba Ould Sidi El Moctar. The second group comprised Berabich Arabs from the adjoining Tilemsi valley area, the people of Baba Ould Sheikh, who had been responsible, under the protection of corrupt elements in the highest levels of the Malian state, for the 'importation' of the cocaine on the 2 November flight and were regarded as its 'owners'.

The Tuareg were charging the Berabich a protection levy to pass through the Iforas region, which they controlled. It was a flourishing business that was enriching more and more of Ag Mohamed's people. The problem for the Berabich, however, was that the Tuareg were continually raising the levy. When it came to the ten tonnes of cocaine on the 2 November flight, the Berabich refused to pay the 30 million Algerian dinars (€300,000) demanded by the Tuareg. A gunfight broke out in which two people were killed, at least one other seriously wounded and two vehicles destroyed, with the Tuareg taking possession of the cocaine.

The Berabich were incensed, even more so when they learned that a Kounta, whose identity was not disclosed to me, had negotiated the onward sale of their 'merchandise' to Egyptians in Chad. Whether these were the same Egyptians who would have purchased the drugs from the Berabich was not made clear to me. Neither was I able to establish conclusively whether any of the drugs shipment had yet left the region, although it seems unlikely as the Berabich, to exact revenge and the return of their merchandise, decided to take hostage the patriarchs of both the Kel Iforas and the Kounta, Ag Intallah and Baba Ould Sidi El Moctar respectively. On 22 February, having failed to capture Ag Intallah, the Berabich succeeded in kidnapping the 88-year-old Baba Ould Sidi El Moctar from his home at Anefis, some 80 kilometres further up the Tilemsi valley from Tarkint.

The government's reaction to the kidnapping demonstrates why drug trafficking through Mali has continued to flourish. The President, ATT, sent his Minister of Culture, Mohamed El Moctar, assisted by Colonel Ould Meydou, who had recently been involved in tracking down and negotiating with the Tuareg rebel leader Ibrahim ag Bahanga.[16] The government's two concerns were that the venerated Baba Ould Sidi El Moctar, a frail old man suffering from hypertension and diabetes, should be released unharmed and that the 'merchandise' be returned to its rightful owners, the Berabich. Baba was accordingly released five days later. The small matters of illegal drug importation and trafficking, possession and use of firearms, kidnap and attempted kidnap and a host of lesser offences were not mentioned by the government.

French, Spanish and Italian Hostages

News of the Boeing discovery was still being digested as another European was abducted. Shortly after midnight on the night of 25–26 November 2009, a 61-year-old Frenchman, Pierre Camatte, was kidnapped by three or four men from his hotel in the town of Ménaka in north-eastern Mali. Camatte had been living in Ménaka on and off for the previous couple of years while researching a plant thought to be of possible benefit in the treatment of malaria.[17] He was 'passed up' to AQIM, who claimed responsibility for his capture in an audio-recording to Al Jazeera TV on 8 December, 13 days after his capture.[18]

The audio-tape also gave the message that AQIM was holding Albert Vilalta, Roque Pascual and Alicia Gamez, three Spaniards belonging to the Spanish NGO Barcelona Accio Soldaria who had been abducted on 29 November, four days after Camatte, near the settlement of Chelkhett Legtouta in Mauritania, as their convoy of 13 vehicles travelled south from Nouadhibou to the capital Nouakchott.

Three weeks later, on 19 December, the abandoned shot-up vehicle of two Italians, 65-year-old Sergio Cicala and his 39-year-old wife Philomène Kabouré, was found near the town of Kobenni in southern Mauritania, about ten miles north of the border with Mali. They were travelling from Italy to Burkina Faso and were shot at and kidnapped the previous evening while travelling after dark.

The Threat of Western Intervention

All six hostages were held by AQIM and all six were eventually released, reportedly for ransoms. However, this spate of hostage-takings and the discovery that the region was also a focal point in the global drugs trade raised the stakes to a potentially dangerous level. By the beginning of 2010, the attention of Western powers was fully focused on the Sahel. On 21 January, at an informal meeting of EU Ministers of Justice and Home Affairs and their US counterparts in Toledo, Spain, Home Office ministers and security officials from France, Spain and the US discussed ways of creating a strong security mechanism linking Paris and Washington, with the aim of guaranteeing the security of the Sahel through military intervention if necessary.[19]

When questioned at a press conference in Algiers some seven weeks later, Xavier Driencourt, France's Ambassador to Algeria, admitted that France and the US had taken steps to create special security mechanisms to fight terrorist groups in the Sahel and to zero in on the activities of the Groupe Salafiste pour le Prédication et le Combat (GSPC)/AQIM, especially the kidnapping of

Westerners. Driencourt emphasised France's influence and connections in the region, as the former colonial power, and made clear that France was ready to help and cooperate with Niger, Mali and Mauritania in annihilating terrorist groups and their activities, especially hostage-taking. He went on to say that France and the US were unanimous that the situation in the Sahel was becoming increasingly dangerous and that they were intent on putting an end to it.[20] Indeed, Presidents Obama and Sarkozy reportedly discussed an initiative to intervene in the Sahel during their meeting in Washington on 30 March.[21]

Both the US and France had Special Forces in the region. US figures are usually fairly meaningless as they deliberately confuse regular forces with Special Forces, contractors and other categories of 'US militia'. Officially, AFRICOM (US Africa Command) claims to have had 171 troops (of one category or another) in the region at that time.[22] The strength of French forces stationed in the region is not known. Several informants in the region believed that France had spent much of the previous year, and perhaps longer, looking for a pretext to move Special Forces into the region to provide greater security for its interests there. Although I do not know the precise dates or capacities of all French deployments in the region, within a few months of these events France was operating military facilities from Ouagadougou in Burkina Faso, Niamey in Niger and several bases in Mali, including Ménaka. In addition, on 9 April, a source at Mopti airport confirmed that a French plane carrying French military instructors had arrived quietly at Mopti. An official in the local governor's office confirmed that the French had come to train hundreds of Mali's troops in the fight against terrorism and insecurity in northern Mali.[23]

The threat of Western intervention posed a problem for Algeria. It required a balancing act of testing brinkmanship. This is because Algeria's strategy towards the Sahel required sufficient terrorism and consequent insecurity to enable Algeria to promote itself to the Western powers as the indispensible and only regional power capable of controlling and even defeating terrorism in the region. On the other hand, too much terrorism and insecurity would give the Western powers, especially France, the pretext to intervene militarily in the region.

Algeria's Strategies in the Sahel

The reasons for the Département du Renseignement et de la Sécurité's (DRS's) fabrication of terrorist cells and its clandestine orchestration of terrorism in the Sahara-Sahel have changed over the years. Initially, in 2003, as I explained in *The Dark Sahara*, it was in response to the US's need to launch a new front in the 'Global War on Terror' (GWOT) in Africa. Since then, Algeria has used AQIM in the Sahel in at least three fundamental and related ways.

One has been to try and shift the remains of Algeria's 'dirty war' out of national territory and into the Sahel. However, if the intention of developing AQIM in the Sahel was to draw 'terrorists' to the Sahel, then the continuation of Islamist militancy in northern Algeria would suggest that the strategy has failed. If, on the other hand, the intention was to draw international attention to the expansion of terrorism into the Sahel, then the DRS's strategy has been highly successful.

A second and long-term strategy of Algeria is to establish itself as the regional hegemonic power. This has not only involved presenting itself as the only regional military power capable of eradicating AQIM, but also establishing its influence in the region, as, for example, in its manipulation of the Tuareg Kidal rebellion in 2006 and in trying to diminish, even eliminate, Moroccan and Libyan influence in the region.

Algeria's third and overarching geopolitical strategy is to establish itself on the global stage as an indispensable ally of the US and other Western powers in the GWOT. The core of this strategy, described in *The Dark Sahara*, was honed in the two years after 9/11, as Algeria worked on being embraced by the US as a key ally in the GWOT. This involved Algeria's orchestration of the El Para hostage-taking operation in 2003 that justified the launch of the Saharan-Sahelian front in the GWOT. Since then, Algeria has assisted the US on numerous occasions, not least in engineering the Tuareg Kidal rebellion in 2006[24] that enabled the US to reinvigorate GSPC/AQIM in the Sahel, but also, through the creation and maintenance of the al-Qaeda threat in the Sahel, the continued justification for AFRICOM and Washington's geopolitical strategy in Africa. Moreover, through 2009–10, Algeria very publicly accused Mali, and to a lesser extent Niger and Mauritania, of being 'soft on terrorism', thus ingratiating itself with the West as the one country in the region that was 'tough on terrorism'. The fact that Algeria has been the architect of much of this terrorism is something over which the West has assiduously remained in denial.

Algeria's strategies and actions in regard to al-Qaeda and the Sahel can therefore be understood in terms of its trying to maintain a difficult and precarious balance between, on the one hand, promoting a sufficient amount of al-Qaeda terrorism in the Sahel to fulfil and maintain both its alliance with the US and its own hegemonic interests in the region, while, on the other hand, trying to ensure that the situation does not reach a point at which Western powers, especially France, are tempted to intervene directly.

On several occasions, especially since Richard Barrett's warning in November 2009 and with President Sarkozy adopting a more interventionist approach to hostage-taking, it has appeared that this balancing act might collapse. On each of these occasions, Algeria's fundamental strategy has been to take the initiative by convening highly publicised conferences to give the impression that it is in control of the situation and then creating new impressive-sounding security-type institutions.

The first such sign of Western intervention came in March 2010. Algeria's response was to hastily convene a conference on 16 March on how to combat the terrorist activities of AQIM in the Sahel. The conference, held in the Algiers Sheraton hotel, was attended by the Foreign Ministers of Burkina Faso, Chad, Libya, Mali, Mauritania, Niger, and the host country Algeria. Parallel to this conference, the Algiers-based (and controlled) African Centre for the Study and Research on Terrorism (ACSRT) held a two-day workshop at which 20 or more 'experts' from Egypt, Nigeria,

Sierra Leone, Libya, Tunisia, Mali and Mauritania discussed ways to reinforce the fight against the financing of terrorism in north-west Africa.

A key feature of the conference was the exclusion of Morocco, in spite of its strong expression of commitment to fight terrorism in north-west Africa. Algeria's response was brusque, pointing out that the conference concerned the Sahel and that Morocco was not geographically part of the Sahel. No mention was made of the fact that Egypt, Tunisia, Sierra Leone and Libya are not Sahelian countries.

The conference reached two main outcomes. One was the delegates' confirmation of UN Security Council Resolution 1904 which 'incriminates the payment of ransoms to terrorist individuals, groups, foundations or entities', and their agreement to activate the terrorist extradition treaties between their seven countries and to respect and reactivate the judicial treaties between them. The second and most highly publicised outcome was the assertion, emphasised by Algeria, that the assistance of Western powers in the fight against terrorism must no longer lead to foreign interference in the affairs of these states.

AQIM's response was to issue a statement in the name of Abou Obaida Youssouf[25] accusing the US and France of turning the countries of the Sahel into a new front in the US's crusade against Islam.

The Algiers conference was merely the first act in a fast-moving and well directed piece of theatre. Less than three weeks later, on 4 April, a well publicised but officially 'secret' meeting was held in Algiers between the heads of the seven countries' (Burkina Faso, Chad, Libya, Mali, Mauritania, Niger and Algeria) intelligence services. As the meeting was 'secret', and covered 'security matters', no further information was forthcoming other than the 'official leak' from the Algerian authorities that the main purpose of the meeting was 'to develop a plan of mutual assistance towards those countries facing terrorism threats'. At the time of the meeting, I wrote that, 'given Algeria's duplicitous involvement in the terrorism threat and the lack of trust between the countries concerned, it is unlikely that such a plan will materialise'.[26] That, as we shall see, and as Algeria intended, is precisely how it has turned out.

Next, on 13 April, the seven countries' army chiefs, hosted by Algeria's Army Chief of Staff, General Gaïd Salah, also met in Algiers. The well publicised purpose of their meeting was 'to try and coordinate their actions against AQIM and the drugs traffickers', with their goal being 'to boost cross-border patrols and surveillance so that AQIM and other criminal groups [couldn't] increase their footprint in the Sahel'. Eight days later, on 21 April, the four states of Algeria, Mauritania, Mali and Niger opened a joint command headquarters at Tamanrasset in the extreme south of Algeria. Neither the Committee of the Operational Joint General Staff, or CEMOC as it is known in the region (Comité d'état-major opérationnel conjoint), nor their governments, stated publicly what powers the command centre would have. However, a military source in Niger told Reuters that they planned to 'move towards joint military operations against terrorism, kidnappings and the trafficking of drugs and weapons'.[27]

As we shall see, there have been no 'joint military operations' by the four countries against AQIM, at least involving Algeria. The reason for this is that Algeria never intended that there should be such operations. The purpose of creating CEMOC was to avert the threat of Western intervention and show to the West that the region was quite capable of managing the al-Qaeda threat itself. Indeed, although US and other key Western intelligence services were fully aware of Algeria's strategy, US and Western diplomats publicly welcomed Algeria's initiative, as the largest military power in the region, in playing such a central role in combating al-Qaeda in the region. Indeed, to give the impression that CEMOC meant business, Algeria announced that 75,000 troops would be moved into the region by 2012. That has not happened.

This massive projected troop level raises the question of the strength of al-Qaeda in the Sahel. Estimates of the number of AQIM 'terrorists' in the Sahara-Sahel range from the 100s to 800. The higher figure of 800 can be discounted. It was proffered in 2009 by a spokesman of Ibrahim ag Bahanga's Malian Tuareg rebels at a 'conference' in Algiers at which Bahanga was seeking

Algerian support. In 2008, the Algerian newspaper *El Khabar* put the number at 183,[28] with the Mauritanian authorities putting the number in the 190s. My sources, from AQIM training camps in southern Algeria, put the number in the main training camp at that time at 270. Since then, AQIM in the Sahel has increased, especially in Mauritania, with the result that US intelligence sources put the figure at that time at around 300–400. In July 2011, a French Socialist *Deputé* (MP), François Loncle, who had just returned to Paris from a tour of the Sahel to assess the security situation in the region, put the number of AQIM terrorists at 300, 80 per cent of whom were Algerians.[29] An intriguing question for counterterrorism specialists is why 75,000 troops are required to wipe out 300–400 terrorists, especially when their location and movements are broadly known. But that, like so many other blindingly obvious questions about almost everything else connected with al-Qaeda in the Sahel, is not one that is ever raised by Algeria's Western allies or the media.

CEMOC, as I predicted at the time,[30] would fail, not just because the DRS never intended it to be anything more than 'smoke and mirrors', but because the four countries concerned were prone to conflicts and rivalries, albeit mostly engineered by Algeria, that had derailed previous attempts at such cooperation. Also, the three Sahelian countries, as we shall see, were becoming increasingly suspicious of the role of Algeria's DRS and its army in destabilising the region. Indeed, the West was so busy applauding the CEMOC initiative that its intelligence services ignored the question of whether it might have been anything more than coincidence that another Frenchman, Michel Germaneau, was taken hostage from almost under the metaphorical nose of CEMOC, within 24 hours of its creation.

13

AL-QAEDA IN THE WEST FOR THE WEST

Richard Barrett's statement[1] about the apparent success of al-Qaeda's North African franchise in comparison to that of al-Qaeda 'Central' and its other regional franchises was extraordinary for one particular reason. This was that his statement totally ignored all the evidence that pointed to the linkages between the activities of al-Qaeda in the Sahel and Algeria's Département du Renseignement et de la Sécurité (DRS), and between the DRS and Western, especially US, intelligence services. Indeed, Barrett, as the UN's most senior security expert and spokesperson on al-Qaeda-related terrorism, as well as all major Western intelligence services, most notably the US, British, French and Canadian, would have received information from their own officers, if by nothing more than library research, that all these hostages (now 67)[2] had finished up in the hands of emirs who were all either known to be or were strongly suspected of being associated with the DRS.

Rather in the same way as London's Metropolitan Police, the Foreign Office and its strategic threats and counter-terrorism desk went to so much trouble to discredit my peer reviewed research as that of a 'loose cannon' or 'conspiracy theorist' (which, increasingly no longer means an event explained by a conspiracy, but simply any explanation or 'fact' that is out of step with the government's explanation and that of a subservient media), so this 'evidence' has been systematically excluded from publicly accessible 'official' Western military and intelligence source archives. For example, there is not a trace of it in the US Military policy awareness links (MiPAL) on terrorism that can be accessed through the US's Military Education Research Library

Network (MERLN), compiled and housed at the US's National Defense University in Washington.[3]

The considerable intellectual energy that Western governments and their agencies and media have expended in attempting to erase all the research and evidence put forward in both this volume and *The Dark Sahara*, fits into the long pattern of Western authorities turning a blind eye to the fact that 'terrorism' in the Sahel, from the time of the disappearance of 32 European tourists in 2003, to the latest kidnappings and other events ascribed to AQIM, has, for the most part, been little more than the manufactured appearance of terrorism. The truth of the matter is that al-Qaeda's North African franchise is not just 'in the West', as the word 'Maghreb' means in Arabic,[4] but, and especially as far as al-Qaeda in the Sahel is concerned, 'for the West'.

What makes this 'conspiracy' by Western governments and their intelligence services so short-sighted is that Western intelligence agencies are fully aware of the role of Algeria's DRS in its 'dirty war'[5] of the 1990s: how it infiltrated, and at times even orchestrated, the armed Islamic groups; how it was responsible for many of the worst civilian massacres; and how it managed the 'disinformation' on the whole management and trajectory of the war. Even British intelligence, not always the best informed on Algerian matters, had tried to cover up, as we saw in Chapter 11, its own evidence for believing that the Algerian government was involved in atrocities against its own innocent civilians.

We must therefore ask what reason Western intelligence services would have had for believing that the same DRS, run by the same ruthless generals, might suddenly have desisted from their well-honed and highly successful infiltration practices and false-flag operations? This exoneration by Western governments and their intelligence agencies of the DRS can be explained by their complicity in the 'conspiracy' to fabricate the Saharan Emirate, as AQM in the Sahel is sometimes known, for the benefits of Western (and Algerian) interests.

There were three other events shortly after Richard Barrett's statement in November 2009 which provided clear evidence that the DRS was orchestrating al-Qaeda and its terrorism activities in the Sahara-Sahel region.

How Secure are Algeria's Security Authorities?

The first event involved the journey of three Europeans, two British men, Conrad and Richard, and a German woman Suzanne, by vehicle from Europe to northern Algeria and then across the Sahara to Timbuktu in Mali, where Conrad had a tourism business.[6] The two men left England, each driving a 4WD vehicle. After picking up Suzanne in Paris, they took the ferry to Tunisia and entered Algeria at Nefta on the Tunisian-Algerian border on 28 November 2009, where they were met, as arranged, by one of Conrad's drivers from Mali and their obligatory Algerian guide. The two local men had travelled north together on public transport. On entering Algeria at Nefta, the three Europeans did not present a detailed itinerary of their route, other than to say they were travelling to Tamanrasset.

Conrad had originally been contemplating travelling to Mali via Niger, but as they were behind schedule they decided to drive straight from Tamanrasset to Mali via the border post at Bordj Mokhtar. It was only at Tamanrasset that they gave their itinerary to the Algerian authorities as passing through Bordj Mokhtar. It was also while in Tamanrasset that Conrad telephoned, by satellite phone, two Tuareg business colleagues in Mali requesting that they drive to the Mali border post of In Halil, a few kilometres south of Bordj Mokhtar, where they would meet on 9 December before making the journey south on the next day.

The three Europeans and Conrad's driver from Mali left Tamanrasset and arrived at Bordj Mokhtar at 2.00 p.m. on 8 December. They spent the night in the house of Ahmed, another of Conrad's business friends. On the afternoon of 9 December, they completed their formalities at the Algerian border post and left Bordj Mokhtar for the Malian border post at In Halil. They entered Mali at 4.30 p.m. and met, as arranged, Conrad's two Tuareg colleagues.

The two Tuareg had driven north that day from the village of Aguelhok along the unsurfaced road (*piste*) that passed through the village of Tessalit and then to In Halil, a distance of just over 240 kilometres. To their east were the Tigharghar mountains, where Abdelhamid abou Zaïd's al-Qaeda in the Islamic Maghreb (AQIM) were based. When the two Tuareg met Conrad and his fellow travellers at In Halil, they explained how they had picked up signs on the journey north that made them suspect that they might be seized by Abou Zaïd's men on their return journey south.

They therefore all returned to Bordj Mokhtar for the night to assess the situation and to make alternative arrangements. As it was well after dark by the time they reached Bordj Mokhtar, they were unable to notify the Algerian authorities of their re-entry and instead went directly to Ahmed's house for the night. There they made new plans. They realised that it would be foolhardy for the three Europeans to continue south. They therefore decided that the three Malians would leave at dawn and take all three vehicles back to Aguelhok. The three Europeans would hire a vehicle and driver from Ahmed, return to Tamanrasset and fly to Gao, via Algiers and Bamako, where they would all meet up in a few days' time.

The three Malians left at dawn on 10 December, heading south to Tessalit and Aguelhok. As anticipated, they were seized by AQIM 'terrorists' who demanded to know 'why the three Europeans were not with them'. The 'terrorists' had clearly been forewarned of the number and details of the Europeans. After being held for a few hours and beaten up, they were allowed to leave, a little bruised but at least with their vehicles.

In the meantime, the three Europeans, while waiting in the early morning for the Algerian border office to open, accessed the internet on their laptops in order to notify their friends and relatives in England and Germany of their new plans and to start making the alternative travel arrangements.

To their surprise, Suzanne found an email from her mother in Germany, sent during the night, saying that she had just been visited at her home by the German police who had reported her 'missing'. Richard also found an email awaiting him. It was from his employer in London, warning him that he was in grave danger and should leave the region immediately. On his subsequent return to London, the employer said that he 'was not able to divulge the source of the information'.

The three Europeans met up with their Malian Tuareg drivers in Gao a few days later, as planned, and compared notes. Not trusting either the local or European authorities, Conrad contacted me on his return to England and asked if I could throw any light on what had happened to them. We met three times, during which I spent some twelve hours interrogating him, checking their emails and trying to find any fault or inconsistency in their story. I later met one of the Tuareg drivers in Mali and could find no inconsistency in his story.

The conclusion I reached was that no one knew of the group's detailed itinerary through Bordj Mokhtar except for the Algerian authorities in Tamanrasset, and they only knew less than a day before the travellers left Tamanrasset. This itinerary would have been given to the DRS in Tamanrasset, who would have forewarned the border police at Bordj Mokhtar. AQIM's forewarning of the Europeans' travel itinerary could only have come from the DRS in Tamanrasset or the DRS/border police at Bordj Mokhtar.

The DRS in Tamanrasset would have been notified of the group's departure from Tamanrasset, their arrival in Bordj Mokhtar and their exit from Algeria the following afternoon. They would not, however, have been notified of their return to Algeria until many hours after the emails had been sent from Suzanne's mother and Richard's employer.

The warning given to Suzanne's mother came from the German police. Richard's employer had clearly received a similar warning from British intelligence/counterterrorism services. This begs the question of who informed the German and British services that the group had gone missing. The only possible source is the DRS, who knew that the travellers were going to be taken hostage after leaving Bordj Mokhtar.

On his return to London, Conrad received an email from DC Paul Smith of the Metropolitan Police's Specialist Operations'

north-west Africa desk who said that he would like to meet
with Conrad as, so he told Conrad, 'he didn't know much about
the area and wanted to know about the culture of the people'.[7]
Conrad met with Smith and had what might be described as
a less than informative chat about the 'culture of the people'.
It is particularly strange that Smith expressed no interest in
either Conrad's experience of narrowly escaping being taken
hostage, or in how Suzanne's mother and Richard's employer
had been forewarned.

The Release of Pierre Camatte

The AQIM terrorists who had been lying in wait for Conrad
and his two companions belonged to the same AQIM group that
was holding the Frenchman Pierre Camatte hostage. Camatte
had been seized in Ménaka on 25 November, three days before
Conrad crossed into Algeria, and was being held in the Tigharghar
mountains that border the western side of the road from Tessalit
to Aguelhok.

A week or so after their unnerving experience at Bordj Mokhtar,
Conrad and his two travelling companions met up in Gao with
their Tuareg drivers whom they had bade farewell at Bordj
Mokhtar. From Gao, Conrad and his companions headed north
up the Tilemsi valley to visit a cultural festival in Tessalit on 28–31
December. Not only was the festival well guarded by the Malian
army, but the foothills of the Tigharghar mountains between
Aguelhok and Tessalit were as well. Conrad counted some 30
heavily armed vehicles and 150–200 troops. From Conrad's
description of the troop placements along the Tigharghar foothills,
it struck me as debatable whether they were protecting the road
and the festival-goers from AQIM, or protecting Abou Zaïd from
any attempt that might be made to liberate Camatte.

AQIM had warned that Camatte would be executed on 30
January unless four AQIM members being held in prison in Mali
were not released. There seemed little likelihood of a deal being
done. Not only was France showing little response to Camatte's
capture, saying that it was Mali's problem, but both Algeria and

Mauritania were taking a hardline attitude. Algeria was publicly and vehemently accusing Mali of providing a sanctuary to AQIM and insisting that no ransoms or other such deals should be done with terrorists. Mauritania was adopting a similar line.

30 January came and went without Camatte being killed. However, almost immediately afterwards, AQIM said that it was setting a final deadline for Saturday 20 February: if the four prisoners were not released by that day, Camatte would be executed.

In the second week of February, France appeared to take the matter more seriously and sent its Foreign Minister, Bernard Kouchner, to Bamako to meet Mali's President Amadou Toumani Touré (ATT). Kouchner reportedly asked ATT to do all that it takes to ensure Camatte's release. Again, Mali stated that it was not prepared to shift its stance.

Finally, a week before the deadline, Kouchner made a second visit to Bamako, accompanied by President Sarkozy's personal advisor, Claude Guéant. Kouchner was again reported to have told ATT that 'everything possible must be done to secure Camatte's release'. Mali, however, remained steadfast, insisting that it was an independent, sovereign state, not susceptible to being pushed around by its former colonial ruler and fully supportive of international efforts not to appease the demands of terrorists. Algeria also increased the stakes by reiterating that it was at the forefront in pushing for a UN measure to prohibit the payment of ransoms to hostage-takers.

On the morning of Wednesday 17 February, I spoke with contacts in France and Algeria. All the signs were pointing to Camatte's execution. I remembered the words used by Abou Zaïd when he warned me that he was preparing to kill the two Austrian hostages, Wolfgang Eber and Andrea Kloiber, at *Eid al Adha*, the 'Festival of the Sacrifice'. The appalling murder of Edwin Dyer was also still very fresh on my mind.

I thought for a moment of contacting the UK intelligence services, but as they had consistently rejected my views and seemed determined to have absolutely no contact with me, which was not at all surprising in view of their own close working relations with

Algeria's DRS, I decided to contact General Mohamed Mediène, head of the DRS, directly. My reason for doing so was not political activism. If France had wanted Camatte saved, it had more than enough knowledge of the workings of both Algeria's DRS and the security services of its former colonies in the Sahel to arrange it. My reason was wholly 'academic'. I wanted the nearest thing I could get to certainty (beyond reasonable doubt) of the DRS's involvement in and control of AQIM in the Sahel. I would also like to think that my motive was humanitarian. The thought of another innocent person being murdered in this way was grotesque, and if I had the means to prevent it, I should at least try.

At 11.47 a.m. on Wednesday 17 February, I sent an email to General Mediène. It was sent to him via the senior DRS officer at the Algerian Embassy in London. To ensure that it reached him, copies were sent to the personal offices of both Algeria's President Abdelaziz Bouteflika and Prime Minister Ahmed Ouyahia. A copy was also sent to Bernard Kouchner through a political officer at the French Embassy in London who had already been contacted to ensure that the email would be forwarded to the French Foreign Minister.

The email to General Mediène informed him that copies of it had also been sent to selected global media who were authorised to publish it if Camatte was executed on, before or after 20 February. The email made clear that in the event of Camatte's death, the same selected media contacts would also receive a detailed dossier, which they would be free to publish, containing information covering the DRS's relationship with AQIM and details of the DRS's activities in Mali and other Sahelian countries, thus demonstrating the role and responsibility of the DRS in Camatte's murder.

I have no knowledge of what communications took place between Algiers and Bamako. Yet, at 6.30 a.m. the following morning, Thursday 18 February, 48 hours before Camatte's threatened execution, the four prisoners that AQIM wanted released were brought into an almost empty Bamako court. A judge ruled that the men were guilty of arms offences, for which the sentence was nine months. However, as they had already been in detention for that length of time, the judge ruled that they were now judicially free.

With the four AQIM members duly freed, Camatte was released on 23 February.

Testimony from AQIM'S Training Camp

The third event, which provided me with absolute certainty that elements within Algeria's army and its DRS were, and still are, running al-Qaeda in the Sahara-Sahel, was the testimony of one of AQIM's members who escaped Abou Zaïd's clutches and sought asylum in Europe. Bashir, as I shall call him, had spent the best part of a year in an AQIM training camp in southern Algeria run by Abou Zaïd, between the time that the GSPC was changing its name to AQIM at the beginning of 2007 until Abou Zaïd effectively decamped to northern Mali in 2008. Bashir's testimony has revealed a range of detailed information about the relationship between Algeria's army and its DRS and the Groupe Salafiste pour le Prédication et le Combat (GSPC)/AQIM.

The camp in which Bashir was trained was known to him only by its codename. Most geographical names meant nothing to him. This particular codename was known to me and I was able to identify it as the Oued Tamouret[8] in the Tassili National Park. Bashir's subsequent identification of the Oued through Google Earth enabled him to point out many of the facilities of the camp area, including the graves of those killed in training. Many of the bodies were not buried in graves, but left only partially covered by sand and stones in the natural rock shelters. Wild animals would have carried off many of the remains.

Bashir was able to give details and identities of the camp hierarchy, namely Abou Zaïd in charge, Abdullah al-Furathi as his main trainer and Mokhtar ben Mokhtar, who visited about every two weeks, as being in charge of 'logistics'. Yahia Djouadi was also a frequent visitor. Although the vast majority of the 270 or so in the camp were Algerians, Bashir was able to identify some Egyptians, ten Tunisians, a few youths from Morocco and Libya, a scattering from the sub-Sahara, including Nigeria, Yemen and

Somalia, and even Central Asia. He was able to name many of the trainees and trainers by their *noms de guerre* and to identify and name photographs of many of El Para's original team. He was also able to identify many of the high-ranking army and DRS officers who visited the camp on an almost daily basis. He described how guns and ammunition were delivered directly from Algerian army depots, as well as through arms dealers, two of whom he identified as an elderly French woman, whom he later met again in Paris, and a Swedish man. He was also able to give precise details of training, particularly killing techniques, the most common of which was throat-slitting (*égorgement*), or what he called in Arabic *al-mawt al-baTii'* ('the slow death'). He described how an average of two or three persons were executed in training every three to four days, with those killed including army officers and soldiers, who had presumably stepped out of line or were deemed 'suspect', as well as 'civilians' or 'common criminals', as he called them, from the prisons. These latter, I believe, comprised many of *les disparrus*, the thousands who disappeared at the hands of the regime in its 'dirty war' of the 1990s.

It was this camp that provided the core of Abou Zaïd's group that moved, under the direction of the DRS, to the Tigharghar mountains of northern Mali in 2008.

14

'WASHING THE MOUNTAIN': DESERT BORDERS, CORRUPTION AND THE DRS

Conrad's experience at Bordj Mokhtar and the presence of al-Qaeda in the Islamic Maghreb (AQIM) in the Tigharghar mountains, a metaphorical stone's-throw from the Algerian frontier, raise questions about the nature of Algeria's southern borders, their porosity and the sort of control that Algeria exercises over these borders, both as frontiers and as deliberately created 'zones of instability'. Algeria's borders with Mali and Niger are products of the colonial era, lines on a map that have been resented and mostly ignored by the region's nomadic Tuareg population. Their porosity is notorious and, notwithstanding Algeria's recent burgeoning militarisation of the region and its professed attempts to seal its borders, the chance of smugglers and traffickers being apprehended is small.

For local peoples, barter trade, or *troc*,[1] as it is known, across these regions has been a way of life and means of livelihood since before the colonial period. It was probably not until the 1980s, however, that cross-border trade, whether simple *troc* or more professional smuggling to take advantage of shortages and price differentials in basic foodstuffs, cooking oil, fuel and various other such commodities, gave way to the more sinister and criminal world of arms, people and drug traffickers.

The first of these more criminal elements that I became aware of was Hadj Bettu. When I first heard of Bettu, he was described to me as a 'war lord'. That was too dignified. He was effectively little more than the Algerian 'mafia' state's representative in the extreme south, managing the trafficking of arms and other goods on behalf of corrupt elements in Algeria's army and its Sécurité Militaire

(SM), the Département du Renseignement et de la Sécurité (DRS's) predecessor, into sub-Saharan Africa.

Hadj Bettu's emergence on the scene in the 1980s was intimately linked with the emergence of the trans-Saharan arms trade. Corrupt elements in the Algerian army pilfered army stocks, notably arms, and shipped them clandestinely to Tamanrasset where they were cached in army depots (*casernes*) built near the villages of Otoul and Tit, some 20 kilometres and 40 kilometres north of Tamanrasset respectively. Local Tuareg humorists said the depots were repositories for the army's catering corps!

From there, the arms and equipment were in the hands of Hadj Bettu, the key middleman in a trade network that supplied many rebel movements and militia in sub-Saharan Africa. By the 1990s, hardly a single adult male Tuareg in Ahaggar, Ajjer and northern Niger was not sporting a Kalashnikov, courtesy of Hadj Bettu.

According to my informants, Bettu came from mixed Tuareg-Arab parentage. In recent years, as his family resumed its clandestine relationship with the DRS, his 'Arabism' seems to have come to the fore. On the Niger side of the border, Bettu's main connections were with Tassara, a small Arab enclave within the Tuareg domain of northern Niger, 250 kilometres west of Agades and 200 kilometres north of Tahoua. A key name to be reckoned with at Tassara was, and still is, Mohamed Abta Hamidine (sometimes called Hamaidi), who became the head of the local Tassara militia in the early 1990s and has become, as we shall see,[2] a key player in the DRS's current attempts to strengthen AQIM's presence in Niger.

By 1992, Bettu's operations had attracted the attention of Mohamed Boudiaf, Algeria's President.[3] In a speech in which he promised to clean up Algeria's corruption, Boudiaf pointed a finger at Bettu and the extreme south. Boudiaf had ruffled the Algerian 'mafiosi', as Algerians now call the state's corrupt elites; he had to be stopped. Three weeks later Boudiaf was assassinated by one of his bodyguards.[4] According to the MAOL (Mouvement Algérien des Officiers Libres),[5] the plotters were Generals Khaled Nezzar, Larbi Belkheir, Mohamed Mediène (Toufik), Smaïn Lamari and Mohamed Lamari. Mediène, still the head of Algeria's

DRS, entrusted Smaïn Lamari with the planning and execution of the murder.

By the mid 1990s, with Algeria's 'dirty war' preoccupying the Generals and the DRS, and with Bettu finally languishing in prison in Tamanrasset on a ten-year sentence, it seemed that his clandestine desert empire might have become part of the region's history. Not so. Today, his trucks are rolling again. His family's latest activities are simply one strand in a web of state corruption that makes the 1980s appear mundane by comparison.

This renewed embrace of Algeria's extreme south by its 'mafiosi' began with the onset of the Bouteflika era and the appointment of President Bouteflika's first *wali* in Tamanrasset, Messaoud Jari, in 1999.

For the first few years of his 'reign' (as locals called it), Jari did almost everything conceivably possible to upset the local Tuareg population. His actions were such that senior dignitaries and office bearers of local civil society organisations wrote to the President, imploring him to replace Jari.[6] They finally warned the President in a written letter that they could not be held responsible if Tamanrasset went up in smoke, as it did in July 2005.[7]

Local people could not understand why the President not only failed to respond to their letters, but why Jari remained in office for long beyond the average appointment of a wali. At that time, they did not know that he was married into the family of Interior Minister Noureddine 'Yazid' Zerhouni, and was therefore protected by the Bouteflika 'clan', as well as his own home-town connections in Batna, a town with strong military connections some 400 kilometres south-east of Algiers.

Jari's embezzlement schemes soon became common knowledge in Tamanrasset. One was for his 'contacts' in Tuat (Adrar wilaya) to over-invoice the Tamanrasset *wilaya* for the service of hiring trucks and transporting illegal migrants (*les refoulés*) to Niger. Hundreds, if not thousands, of 'fictitious' migrants entered the *wilaya*'s books as having being expelled from Algeria. Another of his well known 'scams' was the false-invoicing of the *wilaya* for cleaning up litter and refuse around Tamanrasset. Local people referred to it as 'washing the mountains'. However, by the time of his transfer to Adrar, many local people had come to believe that one of Jari's functions was to protect the massive trafficking of cigarettes and drugs through the southern *wilaya*s of Tamanrasset and Adrar on their way from the Sahel to northern Algeria.

At Adrar, where he was transferred in 2006, Jari's main activity was to redirect much of the regime's contraband traffic, notably fuel, to Mali via the Algerian border post of Bordj Mokhtar. Prior to Jari's intervention, the border post on the Mali side of the frontier had been at Tessalit, 160 kilometres south of Bordj Mokhtar. Jari, however, had Mali's border post moved north to In Halil, just a few kilometres south of Bordj Mokhtar, which he established as a 'free trade' zone for the sale and trans-shipment of contraband goods, mostly fuel, into Mali, as well as to Mauritania and other parts of West Africa, and accompanying money laundering.

More important in terms of the region's current security concerns is that it was and still is through this Bordj Mokhtar–In Halil nexus that Algeria is believed to provision AQIM in its northern Mali bases with fuel and other supplies.[8] During Jari's years at Adrar,[9] the Bordj Mokhtar–In Halil frontier crossing became a key locale for both contraband and AQIM operations.

Part of the AQIM presence in and around In Halil centres on the 'installation' there of Taleb Abdoulkrim. Dubbed by Algeria's security forces as 'Le Touareg', Taleb Abdoulkrim is described in the Algerian media as a firebrand, jihadist preacher. His proper name is, in fact, Hamada ag Hama and he is the cousin of Iyad ag Ghaly, the Tuareg Iforas (Ifoghas) leader in Kidal, whose association with the DRS was described in Chapter 5. Iyad and Abdoulkrim were to achieve infamy in the course of the latest Tuareg rebellion which began in January 2012 (See Chapters 19 and 20). Abdoulkrim has become a key component of the DRS's orchestration of AQIM activities in the region since at least early 2010. One of his roles appears to be the link between Iyad and Abdelhamid abou Zaïd's AQIM, thus creating an arrangement whereby AQIM and Abdoulkrim manage the kidnapping of hostages while Iyad then negotiates their release – and, of course, for a substantial percentage of the ransom. For example, when

Frenchman Michel Germaneau was abducted in Niger near In Abangerit and not far from Tassara on 20 April 2010, the Algerian media were quick to report that his kidnap had been undertaken by Abdoulkrim who had then handed him over to Abdelhamid abou Zaïd in Mali.

My own investigations point to a slightly more complex arrangement. This was that Germaneau and his driver, 'Dino', who was abducted with Germaneau but later released, were abducted by two members of Haj Bettu's family, whom I shall refer to as 'the nephews'. It was they, not Abdoulkrim, who actually abducted Germaneau, before handing him over to Abdoulkrim who then passed him up to Abou Zaïd.[10]

Learning that the Bettu family was back in business, and probably had been for some time, I caste my net further afield. I heard from Tuareg in Kidal that another of Hadj Bettu's nephews had been involved in the abduction of Pierre Camatte from his hotel in Ménaka. A local Tuareg militia picked up the nephew's trail and thought they had either killed or wounded him in a shoot-out near the Malian-Nigerien border. It appears, however, that he escaped, but may have been wounded. The same Tuareg militia also began investigating the theft of vehicles from Kidal. They tracked the stolen vehicles over the border into Algeria, only to find that on reaching Silet they melted away, under the protection of Algeria's security forces, into the Bettu family network.

It was through these investigations into the Camatte and Germaneau kidnappings that I became aware of the extent to which the Bettu family had re-established itself alongside key elements of Algeria's 'mafia state', namely the DRS, as key players in huge clandestine 'transborder' businesses. Bettu's trucks now roll across the southern borders: through In Guezzam into Niger and through Bordj Mokhtar into Mali.

Corruption, the DRS and state control

The activities of the Bettu family are merely an example of the normal and expected way of doing business in Algeria, where the interlocking of elite state interests and the clandestine 'smuggling' economy – known as *trabendo*,[11] which, along with other black market activities, is an integral and substantial part of the national economy.

Corruption within the Algerian state is found within almost every interstice of the economy and runs from the highest levels of the state – the Presidency and Army Chief of Staff – through the tiers of the military and administrative hierarchies to the lowest ranks of the police, municipal and other state officials.

At one level, the military and political elites' use of bribery and other forms of improbity to gain influence and ensure their material enrichment is a reflection of the moral turpitude of the Algerian state. At another level, however, the corruption that links the formal economy with all that is encompassed in *trabendo* and the rest of the 'black' and informal economy is regarded by many, perhaps the majority of Algerians, as not just 'normal', but an essential part of the Algerian way of life: it enables the majority of Algerians to make ends meet and survive.

However, at another level, corruption, in the widest sense of the word, is the fundamental system by which an illegitimate regime, and most particularly its secret police, the DRS, maintains control over the state and its individuals, including those within the regime itself. To understand the nature of this control, a short digression to explain the structure of the DRS and the extent of its power is warranted. While formally a department of the army, accountable to the Chief of the General Staff, General Ahmed Gaïd Salah, and above him the President, the DRS has effectively become a state within a state. Its head, General Mediène, has established his own Cabinet within the DRS, comprising 18 DRS Generals under Mediène's 'presidency' who meet at least twice a week.[12] The 18 Generals are allocated specific 'sectors' and 'files'. Each sector 'shadows' a particular ministry, while the files cover such issues as 'AQIM', 'terrorism in the Sahel', and so on. Each General might be responsible for several 'sectors' and 'files'. Mediène's Cabinet has become increasingly powerful in almost direct relation to the decline in power and influence of the 'Le Pouvoir' or 'Conclave' – '*les décideurs*' – as the group of

Generals and their associates behind the 1992 military coup d'état were known, but who, through infirmity, illness and death, have dwindled in number.[13]

The DRS uses corruption as a key tool in exercising control over virtually all elements of Algerian society, including members of the regime itself. Individuals, from the President, Ministers and Generals down to the lowest ranks of state employees are encouraged to enrich themselves and their families by participating in the endemic corruption of the state. Amongst the political and military elites, the acquisition of import licences; shares of business monopolies; under-the-counter, state-backed contracts, and various forms of embezzlement are regarded almost as entitlements: the rewards of service to the state. For those who step out of line, the ultimate sanction is 'disappearance': to be killed in the training exercises of the DRS/AQIM camps, as described by Bashir in the last chapter.[14]

By countenancing such practices, the DRS can keep the elites materially content. But, as these practices are technically 'illegal', the DRS is also in a position to pull the rug out from under almost everyone, from the President and Army Chief of Staff down to the lowest of state functionaries, through the threat of public humiliation and even prosecution.

Algeria's history since Independence has been an ongoing narrative of how the DRS (and its predecessors) have used such practices to exercise control over individual members of the regime and to enhance its own power base within the state. Indeed, the power of Algeria's intelligence service has been a recurrent problem for Algeria's Presidents. No President has succeeded in outmanoeuvring the DRS (or its predecessors). Benjedid Chadli was forced by the army/DRS to step aside in January 1992; Ahmed Boudiaf was assassinated on the orders of the same group six months later, while Liamine Zeroual also had to step aside in 1998 because he crossed the DRS. There have even been rumours that Boumédiène's death may have been at the hands of the intelligence services rather than a 'rare illness'.

The Rise of General Mediène: 'The God of Algeria'

Liamine Zeroual, like Chadli, soon realised that the DRS, and especially its Director, Mohamed Mediène, had become too powerful and a threat to his presidency. He therefore planned in 1996 to appoint General Saidi Fodil as head of the DCSA (Direction Centrale de la Sécurité de l'Armée). Whether Zeroual's intention was to have Fodil watch over Mediène or replace him is not clear. The latter seems to have been his aim. However, as soon as the appointment was announced, Fodil was immediately killed in a 'road accident' arranged by Mediène and his deputy, Smaïn Lamari.[15]

With the death of Fodil, Zeroual planned in 1997 to appoint his 'military advisor', General Betchine, as Minister of Defence in order to get rid of Mediène. As with Fodil, Mediène's retaliation was swift and peremptory. He set the DRS loose on digging up dirt and publishing scandalous information about how Betchine had used his relationship with the Presidency to build up his newspaper business. The result was that Betchine was publicly humiliated, ruined and forced to resign. He was followed a short time later by Zeroual himself.

Mediène made it the DRS's business to know everyone's Achilles' heel. If there wasn't one, he would create one, usually by sexual or business entrapment and blackmail. One of the reasons why Mediène approved the selection of Bouteflika as Zeroual's successor in 1999 was because he had previously embezzled state funds. During his period as Foreign Minister, from 1963 to President Boumédiène's death in 1978, he had stolen 60 million dinars (estimated at $23 million in today's value) of state funds. Bouteflika was the ideal President for the DRS: his embezzlement had established a family fortune, which could always be exposed.

When Bouteflika took over the Presidency in 1999, Mediène was probably the second most powerful man in the country, second only to Lieutenant General Mohamed Lamari who had been Chief of Staff of the Algerian army since 1993. In 2004, with the 'encouragement' of Mediène, Bouteflika dismissed ('retired') Lamari. Mediène approved Lamari's replacement by the ineffectual General Gaïd Salah, described by the US Ambassador 'as perhaps the most corrupt official in the military apparatus'.[16] With an 'embezzler' as President and the equally corrupt Gaïd Salah as head of the army, Mediène was effectively 'unsackable'. He had finally become Algeria's undisputed 'strongman', or 'the God of Algeria', as he once described himself.[17]

The DRS under Mediène has used 'corruption' in two broad ways. One, as we have just seen, is to establish pretexts for allegations against people ('dig up dirt') and establish the 'black files', as they are known, on the 'sexual', embezzlement, business corruption or other such 'illegal' activities, on all those in positions of power.

The second way in which the DRS uses 'corruption' is in its 'recruitment' and 'reward' methods. As more DRS agents defect, seek safe havens in other countries and confess to their activities within the DRS, so we are able to fit together a picture of how the DRS operates on a more day-to-day basis, especially in how it recruits and then rewards its agents.

From detailed discussions with former DRS agents, it would seem that the DRS's key recruiting ground is university campuses, and especially students who show signs of either political ambition, especially in such things as aspiring to office with the Algerian Students League (ASL), or 'criminal' ability. A particular good and currently topical illustration of this is Reda Mehigueni, the recent purchaser of France's Beur TV. As a student at the beginning of the 1990s, Reda aspired to, and, with the help of the DRS, became President of the ASL, thus giving him a foothold within the ruling FLN (Front de Libération Nationale). More significantly, information from former DRS agents has revealed that Reda was running at that time a very successful visa-forging business. What we do not know is whether the DRS recruited him because of his prowess in such criminal activity or whether the visa business was given to him as reward, and as a cover, for spying on other students. In either circumstance, it would have provided the DRS with information on who was acquiring false visas.

New, young recruits into the DRS show two clear routes of progression. One is to act, usually while still students, as spies on the university campuses. The other, especially with young men who are physically tough, is for them to be infiltrated into 'terrorist' organisations, such as the Groupes Islamiques Armées (GIA) and Groupe Salafiste pour le Prédication et le Combat (GSPC) in the early and late 1990s and now AQIM, or into the prison population where they keep surveillance over political and criminal networks within its ranks and, as and when 'freed', amongst the criminal fraternity.

As the campus spies and the terrorist and prison infiltrators grow older and less capable of operating in such milieus, they are promoted. This may be within the interstices of the administration, with the ultimate reward being promotion to Ambassador or Minister (which explains the incompetence of so many of Algeria's ministers, and the prevalence of 'DRS persons' in so many ambassadorial positions), or, more likely, to oversee and manage the higher reaches of Algeria's 'business world'. Indeed, it is unlikely that there are any significant Algerian business or businessmen that are not tied, in one way or another, to the DRS. Or, put another way, it is impossible to succeed as an Algerian businessman without being compromised by the DRS. A good example of this was Reda's purchase of Beur TV in mid 2011.

At some point after leaving university, Reda went to Canada. It is not yet clear what he did there, but when he came back to Algeria he formed two companies: a video production company called VOX and another 'media' company called DZnet. Both made what my informants described as 'rubbish', low grade TV programmes for the national TV service, ENTV. The boss of ENTV at this time was Hamraoui Habib Chawki, Reda's old friend from his visa-forging university days. Reda was rewarded by being paid substantial sums for his 'rubbish' programmes. Some were apparently so bad that they actually had to be pulled, even though he had received substantial payment for them.

Chawki's reward is that he is now Algeria's Ambassador to Romania. In July 2011, Reda acted as the DRS's frontman in purchasing Beur TV. The importance of this move for the DRS is that the current snail's-pace reform process that Algeria is currently undertaking will inevitably result in an opening up of

Algeria's print and broadcast media. That will probably not come about until 2012 or later, by which time the DRS will have bought up a string of private sector channels, such as Beur TV, and will thus be two steps ahead and in control of the opening up of the media to the private sector.

I have undertaken this digression into the workings of the DRS for two very specific and related reasons. The first is so that the reader will not gain the impression that the experiences of Conrad and his friends at Bordj Mokhtar, or activities such as those of Hadj Battu, are somehow peripheral to or beyond the reach of the Algerian state. On the contrary, they are both typical of and central to the workings of Algeria's corrupt 'mafiosi' state and the control exercised within it by the DRS. The second reason is to help the reader understand, especially in the next and remaining chapters, how the DRS, more so than the Presidency or other elements of the government, is the core driver at the very heart of Algeria's policies and actions in the wider region, especially in relation to AQIM in the Sahel.

15

SARKOZY DECLARES WAR ON AL-QAEDA

The events of the morning of Thursday 22 July 2010 are still imprinted firmly in my mind. I was at my home in southern England and the early morning was sunny, ideal summer weather. I had just booked online tickets to fly to Geneva with my wife to spend the coming weekend with my son and daughter-in-law at a chateau in the country of eastern France not far from the Swiss border, and was busy arranging a car hire from Geneva airport when my phone rang. For a second, the sound of a French voice made me think it was the car hire company wanting to speak with me, but I quickly recognised the high-pitched voice of one of my Tuareg informants, Abdulahine.[1] He was calling me on a satellite phone from Tessalit, the village alongside the Tigharghar mountains in north-eastern Mali where a few months earlier Conrad and his friends had narrowly escaped being abducted by al-Qaeda in the Islamic Maghreb (AQIM).

Abdulahine spoke excitedly, telling me that there had been intense air traffic around Tessalit during the night and early morning and that Algerians, supported by French Special Forces (Commandement des Opérations Spéciales – COS), had led a helicopter-borne assault into the adjoining Tigharghar mountains where gunfire had been heard. Tessalit, I should explain, had been a small, French military base in the colonial period. It has a small airport from that era, but with a tarmac runway that is still operational and suitable for large aircraft and which had been used recently by US Special Forces operating in northern Mali. Tigharghar had long been the main base of Abdelhamid abou Zaïd and where the Frenchman, Michel Germaneau, is believed to have been taken after his abduction near In Abangerit in Niger on 20 April.

I tried desperately to conceive what might be happening. It sounded as if the unimaginable had happened and that the French and Algerians had come together in an assault on AQIM's base there. Shortly after Abdulahine's call, I managed to connect to an informant in Kidal, on the other side of the Tigharghar mountains, who confirmed that gunfire had been heard early that morning coming from the Tigharghar. Before long, the phone rang again. It was Reuters in Dakar. They had received similar reports from their stringers in both Mali and Nouakchott as I had heard from Abdulahine.

The first media report came from Reuters (Bamako) at 6.01 p.m. GMT.[2] It quoted Malian officials as saying that planes had circled the Malian-Nigerien border region late on Wednesday where a French national was believed to be held by AQIM and that gunfire had been heard. A senior official in the Kidal region was quoted as saying: 'There were clashes in the area, shots were heard. We don't know whether it was clashes between soldiers and the hostage takers … There were lots of comings and goings of military airplanes at the airport of Tessalit.'

The reports that Reuters and I had received turned out to be a French military assault in Tigharghar. Some days before, France had said it was working to free 78-year-old Michel Germaneau before a 26 July deadline set by AQIM to kill him. However, following the assault on the Tessalit airfield, a spokesman for the French armed forces headquarters in Paris told Reuters: 'For the moment, we have nothing to communicate on the matter. We don't have enough elements.'

At about the same time as the Reuters' report, Spain's *El Pais* newspaper quoted diplomatic sources as saying that French Special Forces (COS) had found no sign of either the hostage or the base where he was believed to be held, which had been located with US help. Subsequent reports over the next 24 hours, although vague in regard to geographical location in that they made no mention of either Tessalit or Tigharghar, said that six 'terrorists' had been killed, four put to flight or wounded (one subsequently died), two vehicles destroyed and a quantity of arms and equipment found. They also said that Germaneau may have been executed by his captors as the assault began.

Whatever France undertook in Tigharghar was clearly an unmitigated disaster. The raid not only failed to find Germaneau, but AQIM leader Musab Abdul Wadoud (Abdelmalek Droukdel)[3] announced two days later that Germaneau had been executed in retaliation for the seven AQIM members killed.

The first reports of the incident in the Algerian media stated that Algerian helicopters and military units were in the operational area. The Algerian daily *Echorouk* also reported that RFI (Radio France Internationale) had confirmed that 'the Algerian government participated in the military operation', while in Nouakchott, the Chinese news agency Xinhua reported that security sources had told it that the operation 'was launched in coordination with the Tamanrasset (southern Algeria) anti-terrorism unit where the Mauritanian, Malian and Algerian armies are represented'.

However, these initial reports were quickly denied by Algerian government sources, which said that Algeria had nothing to do with the operation and had not even been informed of it until two days beforehand. Algeria's denials were not convincing and its assertion that it only received two days' notice of the operation had a hollow ring to it. As the Xinhua report from Nouakchott confirmed, any such attack would have been coordinated, at least officially, through the new joint command HQ at Tamanrasset. Indeed, the air activity seen over Tamanrasset during the two days before the raid could have been associated with the arrival of the French and possibly Mauritanian contingents prior to their being transported to Tessalit and then airlifted into the Tigharghar mountains.[4]

Another reason for believing that Algeria was involved is because it is inconceivable that France would conduct such a politically and militarily high-risk operation within a stone's-throw of Algeria's border without seeking the advice and consent of Algeria's DRS and the 'green light' from the highest levels within the Algerian state.[5]

France and Mauritania remained silent as confusion and speculation in the media continued to mount. Both countries were clearly going to considerable lengths to coordinate their stories before coming out with a 'sanitised' version of what actually happened. It took a whole week, from 22 to 29 July, for France to release its 'official' version of events.[6] When it did so, its story was that Mauritania had received notice from Western intelligence sources at the beginning of July that AQIM was planning to attack Mauritania on 28 July and that Mauritania's President Mohamed Ould Abdel Aziz had warned Paris that he was preparing a large 'cross-border' strike against AQIM. On 13 July, the day after France had purportedly received notice from AQIM that Germaneau would be executed on 26 July if its demands[7] were not met, Abdel Aziz reportedly visited the Elysée.

According to France's version of events, the Mauritanians, helped by the French, claim to have discovered a hitherto unknown camp belonging to an AQIM cell in the Malian desert 150 kilometres from the Mauritanian border. That would locate the camp at approximately 150 kilometres west of Timbuktu and approximately 800 kilometres as the crow flies from Tessalit. Franco-Mauritanian sources claimed that photographs indicated that Germaneau was possibly being held there. France therefore decided that some 20–30 of its Special Forces (COS), including intelligence specialists, would accompany Mauritania's GSI (Groupes Spéciaux d'Intervention) in an assault on the base.

The Franco-Mauritanian force allegedly departed from a base near the Mauritanian-Malian frontier and travelled by night in all-terrain vehicles to a point ten kilometres from the base, from where they proceeded on foot. The attack took place at dawn. Fighting was brief and no trace of Germaneau was found. Six AQIM 'terrorists' were killed (a seventh reportedly died later), four took flight and some military equipment was captured. Mistaken over the hostage, the French claimed to have returned to Mauritania and wrapped up the operation. The Mauritanians claim to have continued tracking AQIM for two more days.

This 'official' account emphasised that there were no aerial operations, which we know to be untrue; that no actions were undertaken in the Tessalit region, which we also know to be untrue; and that contrary to what had been written earlier, 'the Americans did not provide any intelligence enabling the launch of this operation'.

The British Presence

Neither France nor Mauritania has made any reference to one other possible party in this operation, namely the UK. One of the unanswered questions about the 22 July raids is why Major General Robin Searby, the head of UK counterterrorism in North Africa, was in Nouakchott on 20–21 July, just 24 hours before the Mali raid(s). The official reason given by the British Foreign and Commonwealth Office (FCO) was that Searby's visit was to discuss bilateral cooperation in the fight against terrorism.[8] However, it is difficult to believe that the timing of Searby's visit, on the eve of the raid(s), was coincidental, especially as the UK, since the death of Edwin Dyer just over a year earlier, had developed close working relations with Algeria's Département du Renseignement et de la Sécurité (DRS). Was Searby's presence in Nouakchott a symbolic gesture of support for the Franco-Mauritanian initiative, or was the British presence, given London's close relationship with the DRS, simply another case of Perfidious Albion? It is unlikely that we will ever know.

'A Smoke Screen'

So, what really happened?

The raid into Mali to the west of Timbuktu was a diversion. In the week between the Tessalit raid on 22 July and the publication of France's cover-up story on 29 July, more snippets of information came to light. For instance, a 'foreign military source' in Bamako (believed to be French or Mauritanian) was reported by Agence France-Presse (AFP) as saying that the 22 July raid on a suspected al-Qaeda base has just been 'a smoke screen'. 'Somewhere else in the vast desert, another [operation] is underway', the source said, adding that 'forces from other countries in the region were also taking part'.

I also received confirmation from a reliable source in Mauritania that the camp attacked in Mali was not an AQIM base but a traffickers' 'bivouac'. The photos of the dead 'terrorists' displayed on Mauritanian TV and on the web were taken in this camp. The source also doubted whether Mauritanian troops actually participated in the operation.

On 26 July, Mali's *Le Républicain* actually reported that a Franco-Mauritanian raid had taken place in the Tessalit region. It mistakenly gave the date as 24 July rather than 22 July, but that could have been because AQIM announced its claim to have killed Germaneau on 24 July.

On my return from my long weekend in the French countryside, I was able to re-establish communications with my informants in the Kidal region. They were now able to give a little more detail, saying that both planes and helicopters had used the Tessalit runway and that Algerians had led the attack. However, they were unable to clarify whether it was the helicopters and their crews who were Algerian or the ground troops who were fighting alongside the French COS. They also confirmed that they had seen no signs of any Mauritanians.

A number of questions about France's raid still remain unanswered, at least by France. The first and most obvious concerns the fate of Michel Germaneau. Two days after the assault, AQIM stated that it had executed Germaneau in retaliation for the French raid. No body has been found and there is no reliable evidence to support AQIM's claim. In fact, there is reason to believe that Germaneau may have died several weeks earlier. He was nearly 79, frail and dependent on medicinal drugs, which had not been supplied to him, for a heart condition. The last evidence that he was alive was received by the French authorities on 14 May. Shortly after that date, I received information from sources in Niger that indicated that Germaneau might have died. Indeed, after the 22 July raid, there were several reports in the French media saying that 'French officials suspect the elderly aid worker may have died beforehand [before the 22 July raid]'.[9] Moreover, the very vague nature of the demands that accompanied AQIM's threat to execute Germaneau on 26 July, combined with the fact that no negotiators appear to have been mobilised within Mali, as has been the pattern with previous hostage cases, must also have alerted the French authorities to the possibility that Germaneau was no longer alive.

Even stronger evidence that Germaneau had died before 22 July comes from Mohamed Mokeddem (Meguedem), alias Anis Rahmani. Rahmani claims to be a 'security specialist' but is in fact a 'journalist' who works closely with and on behalf of the DRS.[10] In October 2010, Rahmani said that Germaneau had died of a heart attack in early July.[11]

If there were such strong indicators that Germaneau was already dead, why did France undertake such a high-risk raid? France's own rather low-key and belated answer to that question is to the effect that there may have been a small chance that he was still alive and it was worth taking it – just to be sure.

Was France Duped by Algeria?

22 July was an unmitigated disaster for France. Irrespective of what the French and Mauritanian authorities might have tried to tell the world, the evidence points to there having been two operations: a decoy near the Mauritanian border, where six 'traffickers' (supposedly AQIM) were killed, and a more politically sensitive raid into the Tigharghar mountains that failed to find either Germaneau or any AQIM base. Moreover, the evidence, although not conclusive, indicates that Germaneau had already died sometime before the raid.

If there was so little likelihood of Germaneau still being alive, what were France's motives for the raid? President Sarkozy's domestic standing had plummeted as one political misjudgement and scandal after another dogged almost every political step that he took. He desperately needed a piece of 'good luck', something that would divert attention from his domestic political misfortunes and enable him to present himself to the French public as a strong and decisive leader. Sarkozy needed the equivalent of

Mrs Thatcher's bold victory in the Falklands. In the absence of a 'Falklands', the daring and dramatic release of an aged French hostage held by al-Qaeda in the depths of the Sahara, the site of France's past colonial glories, would help in a small way to restore his presidency.

The puzzle is how France could have got its intelligence so badly wrong. My own belief, based on the evidence, is that France was led into a trap by the DRS. If that was the case, how did it come about?

Prior to Sarkozy becoming President of France in May 2007, the relationship between Algeria's DRS and France's main counter-terrorism agency, the Direction de la Surveillance du Territoire (DST), had been particularly good. This had been due to the close personal friendship between General Smaïn Lamari,[12] head of the DRS's counter-espionage directorate and General Mohamed Mediène's deputy, and Raymond Nart, the former Deputy Director (now retired) of the DST. When Lamari died, however, just over three months after Sarkozy assumed office, a chapter closed on Franco-Algerian intelligence relations.

If Smaïn Lamari's death in August 2007 marked the end of a long and trusted intelligence link with Algeria, France's relations with Sahelian and sub-Saharan Africa were already on a downwards trajectory following Sarkozy's highly controversial speech to the 'youth of Africa' at the University of Cheikh Anta Diop, Dakar, in July 2007, in which his allusions to colonialism and the suggestion that Africa had failed to embrace progress outraged public opinion in Senegal and much of the rest of the continent. These two events, along with Sarkozy's deteriorating relations with key elements of France's civil service, were pivotal in what many analysts have come to see as a substantial demise in France's intelligence-gathering facilities in both North and Sahelian Africa. This was epitomised in the most embarrassing of circumstances when Sarkozy's Foreign Minister, Michèle Alliot-Marie, offered Tunisia's President Zine El Abidine Ben Ali the assistance of French riot police to help crush the beginnings of Tunisia's 'Jasmine Revolution'.[13]

The result of these faux pas, both domestic and external, is that the Elysée's foreign policy on North Africa and the Sahel came to rely more on Sarkozy's own personal coterie of hand-picked advisors, such as his Chief of Staff, Claude Guéant, than the experience of France's civil and intelligence services.

There can be little doubt that Mediène was aware of this deteriorating state of affairs. However, the extent to which he saw it as an opportunity to promote the DRS's own agenda remains a central question in any analysis of France's involvement in the Sahel during the Sarkozy era. Similarly, we still have no clear answers as to who within the French establishment actually made the decision to undertake the raid(s) into Mali. Was it Sarkozy's own initiative, that of his Defence Chiefs, or his own personal advisors? Further, and most importantly, what was the input of Algeria's DRS into France's decision-making?

It would be inconceivable in the current era for France's intelligence services not to have consulted Algeria's DRS about a raid that was so close to Algerian territory. US satellite information might have helped France locate AQIM bases, as was implied in the first reports of the raid, but information on their precise location, surrounding approaches, manning levels and the location and condition of Germaneau could only have come from the DRS. The Algerian-Malian border area and the Tigharghar are overflown regularly by Algerian surveillance. Moreover, as I have made clear in previous chapters, there was good reason to believe that Abdelhamid abou Zaïd and the DRS were in close contact. Indeed, this was the relationship to which Mali's intelligence officer Lieutenant Colonel Lemana Ould Bou referred, just before his assassination in Timbuktu 13 months earlier, when he said: 'at the heart of AQIM is the DRS'.[14]

On the morning of Monday 19 July, three days before the raid, Sarkozy was advised by his 'defence council'. In other words, the decision to intervene in the Sahel was not taken lightly and would almost certainly have involved an appreciation of the views of Algeria's DRS. Indeed, we know that Claude Guéant met with General Mohamed (Toufik) Mediène, the DRS Chief, in Algiers on 20 June. It is highly likely that Guéant's 'report back' on his meeting with Mediène would have been discussed and may well have inclined France to its decision.

Although Algeria's first domestic news releases seemed to confirm the information that I had received from Tessalit on the morning of the raid, namely that Algeria was in some way involved in the Tigharghar raid, Algeria obviously has to deny any such involvement. If it became known that French and Algerian forces had been operating together to kill Muslim 'terrorists' in another country, it would be political suicide for the Algerian regime. Nevertheless, the evidence, limited and largely circumstantial though it may be, does point to Algeria being heavily involved in the operation, both in probably giving information about Germaneau's health, false or otherwise, and also providing helicopters and other logistical support.

'Opening the Gates of Hell'

While the failure of France's military intervention gave AQIM an immense propaganda victory, enhancing its hitherto limited appeal in the region, the raid(s) were a personal catastrophe for President Sarkozy. His decision to opt for such a high-risk and ill-conceived strategy was designed to counter his faltering political standing in France. Instead, the French media made comparisons with former US President Jimmy Carter's ill-fated Iranian hostage-rescue mission of 1980 and France's hair-brained bombing and sinking of Greenpeace's *Rainbow Warrior* in 1985.

France's response was multiple: Foreign Minister Bernard Kouchner was fast-tracked on 'damage limitation' visits to Mauritania, Mali and Niger, while the Elysée's spin-doctors worked to minimise the damage by fabricating the 'Mauritani-anised' version of events described earlier.

At a more Presidential level, France's response to AQIM's claim to have executed Germaneau was to issue a declaration, in language reminiscent of George Bush's declaration of 'War on Terror', of 'war against AQIM'.

As for AQIM, its leader, Abdelmalek Droukdel, released an audio recording saying that by approving the operation, French President Nicolas Sarkozy had 'opened the gates of hell on himself, his people and his nation'.

16

OPENING THE GATES OF HELL

Al-Qaeda in the Islamic Maghreb (AQIM) opened the 'gates of hell' some eight weeks after France declared war on it. In the early hours of the morning of Thursday 16 September 2010, seven employees of France's massive nuclear corporation, AREVA, were kidnapped from their residences in the uranium mining town of Arlit in northern Niger. Five were French nationals; the other two were a Malagasy and a Togolese.

The attack was not wholly unanticipated. Shortly after France's raid into Mali, the US State Department had warned that, 'As a result of perceived Western involvement in the raid, it is possible that AQIM will attempt additional retaliatory attacks against Western targets of opportunity.' On 1 September, the Nigerien government, through the office of the Préfet of Arlit, faxed a letter to the Directors of AREVA warning them of the deteriorating and highly dangerous security situation around Arlit and the threat to the company's employees. On 12 September, precisely four days before the kidnap, Bernard Squarcini, head of France's counter-espionage and counterterrorism intelligence agency (Direction Centrale du Renseignement Intérieur – DCRI), warned that 'the risk of a terrorist attack on French soil had never been higher'.

AREVA paid little attention to the security warnings. Indeed, as one local resident of Arlit said to me:

> Given the high level of political insecurity in this region as a result of the recent Tuareg rebellion and its fragmentation into a number of rebel movements; the presence of AQIM; the rapidly escalating level of banditry; the collapse of traditional livelihoods since 2003, notably those associated with the tourism industry; the provocative actions of Algeria's Département

du Renseignement et de la Sécurité and the escalation of drug trafficking;
the kidnappers could be almost anyone!

Eyewitness accounts[1] said that up to 30 persons, speaking Arabic
and Tamashek (the Tuareg language), were involved.[2] They
described how the kidnappers went straight to the homes of the
people taken, 'as if they knew precisely where they were'. The
consensus of speculative opinion amongst most of my informants
in the region was that the operation had been organised by AQIM
but that the kidnappers were probably local Arab and Tuareg
bandits, including, quite possibly young Tuareg Mouvement des
Nigériens pour la Justice (MNJ) fighters who were now being
driven into banditry by the lack of employment and the need for
money.[3] As one Tuareg informant explained to me: 'There are
black sheep in the community. Young Tuareg are mixing with the
many predominantly Arab drug-trafficking and local "war-lord/
AQIM" networks that are now well established in the region to
the immediate south and west of the border town of Assamakka.'

The abductors took their hostages into Mali later on the
next day (Friday 17 September), with the Nigerien army using
microlites[4] to track them across the desert to the Malian border.
I received contemporaneous confirmation by satellite phone from
Tuareg in the Kidal region that the abductors' convoy had been
seen crossing into Mali and that the hostages had been handed
over to Abdelhamid abou Zaïd in the Tigharghar mountains,
about 70 kilometres north-north-west of Kidal and close to the
Algerian border.[5] The same Tuareg sources confirmed that the area
was under more or less permanent surveillance from what they
identified as a French Mirage jet and a long-range French navy
reconnaissance plane. This aerial reconnaissance was confirmed
by the French themselves, who said that the flights were being
operated out of Niamey, 800 kilometres (500 miles) to the south,
although United Press International (UPI) speculated that the
French surveillance was being run out of Tamanrasset. France
also sent an array of Special Forces to Niamey.[6]

On 21 September, five days after the kidnapping, AQIM claimed
responsibility for the abductions, saying that the hostage-taking

was to avenge the 22 July raid by French and Mauritanian forces on an AQIM base in northern Mali.[7] By early November, several reports in the French media were indicating that the hostages had been moved from Tigharghar to the Timétrine hills, some 100–150 kilometres west of Aguelhok.

Towards the end of November, I received extraordinary information from a reliable source in Algeria. The source had run into Tuareg nomads in the Djanet region of south-eastern Algeria who had recounted having seen the hostages, or to be more precise their captors, being supplied with provisions by helicopter. Frustratingly, my source was unable to regain contact with the nomads: they had presumably moved on. They gave neither the markings of the helicopter nor the location where they had seen the provisions being unloaded. They were, however, able to describe the people they saw carrying the supplies off the helicopter as 'bearded, dressed like Salafists' and with 'white skin', a euphemism amongst Tuareg for Algerians from the north. The fact that my source had encountered the nomads in the Djanet region did not mean that the supply helicopter had been seen in the Djanet region. Given the movements of nomads in that region, it could have been almost anywhere in the extreme south of Algeria, or, more likely, in northern Niger, especially the northern Aïr mountains. If there was any truth in this information, it suggested that Abou Zaïd had moved the hostages some 1,000 kilometres, possibly further, to the east. This would have taken them into a region that was probably out of reach of French reconnaissance, closer to Algerian cover and supplies, and too remote for any attempt by the French to launch the sort of military rescue operation that it had undertaken in Mali back in July.

I was in Mali at the end of November and able to organise with local Tuareg a detailed search of the Timétrine hills. There was absolutely no trace of the hostages or their captors. The Tuareg explained to me that the mountainous area between Tigharghar and the Algerian border was also known as Timétrine. That too was searched, but with the same result. With the Mali government insisting that the hostages were 'in another country', I began to think that the information from the nomads in the Djanet region might be pointing in the right direction and that Abou Zaïd had perhaps moved the hostages into Algeria or, more likely, to northern Niger.

These were still speculations, as there was abundant evidence of at least some AQIM still being in Tigharghar. For instance, a few days before 11 December, a group of some ten local Tuareg and Arabs in the Kidal area stole two Malian army trucks and sold them to AQIM. They were caught by the local gendarmerie and handed over on 11 December to US forces who had come into the region and were taken to the US base at Gao for interrogation. Then, on 18 December, five Malian gendarmes from Aguelhok, who were travelling with a Tuareg in the Tuareg's vehicle on the western side of Tigharghar, were hijacked by AQIM 60 kilometres from Aguelhok. The gendarmes were stripped of their arms and equipment before they and the Tuareg were allowed to return to Aguelhok. The following week, on 27 December, local Tuareg spotted five AQIM vehicles entering Tigharghar from the Tilemsi (that is, west) side.

However, in the New Year of 2011, there were two incidents that indicated that Abou Zaïd was operating in the region between Djanet and Aïr and may well have been holding the AREVA hostages there.

An Italian Tourist Taken Hostage in the Tadrart

The first was on 2 February, when an Italian tourist, 53-year-old Maria Sandra Mariani, was abducted in the Tadrart region of south-eastern Algeria, approximately 130 kilometres south of Djanet and 90 kilometres north of the Nigerien border. Ms Mariani, who knew the region well, having returned there for each of the last five years, was travelling in the company of a driver and guide provided by a Djanet-based tourism agency. Her 14 or 15 abductors, driving two 4WDs, were reported as speaking a Mauritanian dialect of Arabic which is used by Mauritanians and some Malian and Nigerien Tuareg in the Sahel. It might therefore be assumed that she was abducted by a mixed Tuareg-

Mauritanian group of bandits to be 'sold on' to AQIM. AQIM subsequently claimed to be holding her.

Four months later, I was able to talk with several people in Djanet who confirmed to me and provided convincing evidence that her abduction had been undertaken by local bandits from northern Niger, but on behalf of Algeria's DRS. I also learnt that the cook and guide who had accompanied her to the Tadrart had been able to get to the nearby Algerian military base at In Ezzane immediately after her abduction to sound the alarm and to ask the military to 'follow the tracks' of the kidnappers. The army, however, refused, saying they had no fuel! In Ezzane is, in fact, a military supply base for Algerian military operations in south-eastern Algeria and northern Niger and is certainly not short of fuel. Further information about the abduction was given to me by another source in Djanet, who, on hearing about the DRS involvement in the abduction, had contacted one of AQIM's more renowned emirs with whom he had been friends since childhood. The emir confirmed to him that the abduction had indeed been arranged by the DRS.

Three AREVA Hostages Released

The second incident was the release of three of the seven AREVA hostages on 24 February. The three released were Frenchwoman Françoise Larribe, Jean-Claude Rakotorilalao of Madagascar and Alex Awando of Togo.[8] Information from sources in Niger indicates that these three hostages were handed over in northern Niger, probably in or close to the Aïr mountains. According to an Agence France-Presse (AFP) report, it appears that an arrangement had been made a month earlier to hand over these hostages. A rendezvous had been arranged between the military and representatives of AQIM at Temet, north of Iferouane. Apparently, the military waited all day but AQIM did not arrive and the military returned to Iferouane. The handover on 24 February appears to have taken place in the same vicinity. The fact that AQIM planned to make the handover at Temet is not without significance, for it was at Temet, precisely seven years earlier in February 2004, that

El Para's group, which included Abou Zaïd, got lost when their Tuareg guide abandoned them while on their way to a rendezvous with El Para at Tabarakatan, some 100 kilometres further north-north-east on the route to Djanet.[9]

The Security Pretext for 'Land Clearance' and 'Dispossession'

Many Tuareg in Algeria's extreme south have a rather different understanding of what is going on in the Algerian-Niger border area. They believe that the Algerian authorities' concerns for 'security' and 'counter-terrorism' are being used as a pretext for 'land clearance' and 'dispossession'.

Tuareg concerns began to be raised in February 2010 when the Algerian government banned tourism access to many regions of the Ahaggar and Tassili-n-Ajjer National Parks, which together cover much of the Tamanrasset and Illizi *wilayat* (provinces).[10] When Tuareg questioned why the authorities were closing down their most lucrative industry and source of livelihood, the answer they were given was 'security'. The region, so the authorities said, was threatened by al-Qaeda terrorists. That, however, was something which most local people knew to be untrue: since El Para's exploits in the region in 2003, it was widely known that 'terrorism' was being orchestrated by the DRS. The fact that the 'closure' of the Tassili-n-Ahaggar put many of the Tamanrasset agencies out of business made local Tuareg even more angry.

As the year progressed Tuareg nomads who had passed through these 'closed' regions confirmed what most local people suspected: that these areas, especially the Tassili-n-Ahaggar, were the locations of extensive mining and 'oil/gas' test drilling operations.

What is going on in this remote corner of Algeria? Why the duplicity? Several Tuareg are concerned that the Algerian government is trying both to circumvent the Tuareg's inter-nationally recognised indigenous land rights and to prevent both local Tuareg and foreigners seeing the damage being done to the environment and cultural heritage by the development of what many believe could become a fairly massive mineral (mostly uranium) exploitation zone. Hence the use of the pretext of 'terrorism' to close these areas and prevent both locals and foreigners from visiting and seeing what is going on.[11]

Around Djanet, the situation has been a bit more difficult for the authorities because most of that region is designated by UNESCO (UN Educational, Scientific and Cultural Organisation) as a World Heritage Site. The authorities therefore said that the Tassili (above Djanet) could mostly remain open, but that the Tadrart, which is the extension of the Tassili from just south of Djanet to the Nigerien border (and which is part of the UNESCO site), would be closed for security reasons. The people of Djanet, however, led by their local tourism agencies, told the authorities that if they were to close the Tadrart, then they would simply set fire to and destroy the municipal offices. The Tadrart therefore remained open, but with an agreed system of 'community guards', comprising local Tuareg who would 'keep an eye' on the region. Many of the same people who had been challenging the Algerian authorities over these issues are now wondering if the abduction of Ms Mariani was the DRS's way of finally closing the Tadrart.[12]

AQIM Demands a €90 Million Ransom

The original demand from AQIM for the release of the hostages, which is both unverified and thought to have been unlikely, was for France to pull its troops out of Afghanistan and to negotiate directly with Osama bin Laden. Paris rejected that demand outright. Then, on Monday 21 March, three and a half weeks after the release of the three hostages in northern Niger, AQIM announced that it wanted a ransom of around €90 million ($128 million) for the release of the remaining four French hostages, as well as the release of AQIM prisoners taken in several countries, including France. The absurdity of this demand suggested that AQIM, or perhaps Algeria's DRS, wanted to hold on to the hostages for a while longer. Not surprisingly, France's new Foreign Minister, Alain Juppé, said that he would not negotiate with AQIM on these terms.

Twenty months after their kidnapping, the four Frenchmen were still in captivity.

The Timing of the Areva Kidnaps: Coincidence or a Poor Joke?

There is one other feature of the AREVA kidnappings that deserves comment. It is that they were undertaken 24 hours after the announcement of the creation of a joint Sahel-Saharan intelligence unit by the Intelligence Chiefs of Algeria, Mauritania, Mali and Niger. That, in itself, may be of little consequence except for the fact that the previous French kidnapping, namely that of Michel Germaneau in April, five months earlier, took place precisely 24 hours after the announcement by the same four countries of their establishment of the CEMOC (Comité d'état-major opérationnel conjoint) joint military command headquarters at Tamanrasset.

The date of the AREVA kidnappings therefore raises the question of whether this timing was coincidence or a manifestation of the DRS's perverse sense of humour.

17

THE PAST CATCHES UP: PRESSURE ON ALGERIA

During 2010, the Algerian regime came under increasing pressure from a combination of both internal and external difficulties. The internal difficulties came from two directions. One, which is discussed in more detail in the next chapter, was the escalation of civil unrest brought about by the increasing failure of the country's sclerotic and corrupt state administration to address the basic needs of its peoples. The second was the emergence of significant ruptures within the regime itself, with the major rift being between the Presidency and the Département du Renseignement et de la Sécurité (DRS) or, to be more precise, between its two key personalities: President Bouteflika and General Mohamed Mediène.

By mid year, around the time of the Franco-Mauritanian raid(s) into Mali, Algeria had been shocked by a succession of scandalous events, beginning with the Sonatrach corruption scandal and Bouteflika's retaliatory commission of inquiry into the assassination dossiers of the 1990s that was designed to put General Mediène himself in the dock, followed shortly thereafter by the assassination of General Ali Tounsi,[1] the head of the National Police, and finally, at the end of May, the long-expected dismissal of oil supremo Chakib Khelil and other key ministers associated with the Bouteflika camp. While these events reduced Bouteflika to an ailing, lame-duck President, the real decision-making of the regime remained firmly in the hands of General Mediène and his DRS.

The 'Terror Zone' Becomes a Self-Fulfilling Prophecy

Algeria's external difficulties, which first emerged within the Sahel and then, as the year wore on, within the EU, were ironically the product of the DRS's own success. By mid 2010, the 'Terror Zone' that the US military[2] had marked on its maps of Africa in 2003 had finally and unequivocally become a self-fulfilled prophecy. Although the structure and organisation of al-Qaeda in the Islamic Maghreb (AQIM) in the Sahel was changing as it subsumed more genuinely Islamist and 'jihadist' components (mostly from Mauritania) and rubbed shoulders increasingly with drug traffickers and Tuareg ex-rebels who had turned to criminal banditry for a livelihood, all the evidence suggests that the DRS was still able to maintain a strong element of control over its leadership. Ironically, it was the DRS's success in inserting and orchestrating AQIM in the Sahel that became the cause of Algeria's first external problem.

The Fingers Point to Algeria

Algeria's difficulties became exposed at two successive security conferences in Bamako: the first on 6–7 August; the second in mid October. The first was called by the countries of the region in the wake of the disastrous 22 July Franco-Mauritanian raid(s) into Mali, for the purpose of discussing the increasing threat of AQIM to the region. The significance of this meeting, and an indicator of Algeria's emerging difficulties, was that only two of the four countries that had set up CEMOC (Comité d'état-major opérationnel conjoint) in April for precisely this purpose, namely Niger and Mali, were present. Algeria and Mauritania, the other two founders of the Tamanrasset joint command and the two countries from which the vast majority of AQIM were drawn, were absent. Mauritania was soon to reverse its decision to attend. However, the absence of Algeria, which had been promoting itself as the region's champion in the fight against terrorism and the only country in the region with the military capability of defeating AQIM, was glaringly apparent.[3]

The question was whether Algeria and Mauritania had been excluded from the gathering, or whether they boycotted it? A reading of Algerian newspapers would have given the impression that there was a major disagreement between Algiers and Bamako, with Nouakchott supporting the Algiers line that Mali was soft on terrorism, encouraging abductions and the payment of ransoms. This diplomatic contretemps, instigated and widely publicised by Algeria, began after Mali's release of four AQIM prisoners in exchange for the liberation of Pierre Camatte.[4]

The real reason for Algeria's absence from both the 6–7 August gathering and the much more internationally high-profile Bamako security conference on 14–15 October was because other countries in the region were becoming increasingly aware that Algeria was not only behind AQIM in the Sahel, but was using it to destabilise the region. Mali's President Amadou Toumani Touré (ATT) had expressed his concerns about Algeria's DRS to the US in the previous year. When AFRICOM (US Africa Command) Commander General 'Kip' Ward visited Bamako on 27 November 2009, ATT told General Ward and US Ambassador Gillian Milovanovic that while he believed Bouteflika and the Algerian leadership genuinely wanted to cooperate, he believed that Algeria's intelligence services (the DRS) and army were holding up cooperation.[5]

Within three weeks of the first Bamako conference, a raft of reports emerged from both Mali and Mauritania saying that the two countries were now cooperating with each other in joint military patrols and other such actions in the fight against AQIM without any Algerian involvement. The sudden rapprochement between the two countries was particularly galling for Algeria. The message that came out of Bamako and Nouakchott was: 'We can manage without Algeria.'[6]

By mid October, matters were getting no better for Algeria. The second and much bigger Bamako conference on 14–15 October – sponsored, much to the irritation of Algeria, by France – was first mooted around 25 September. Mali, seeing an opportunity for the settling of scores with Algeria for all its slights about being soft on terrorism, immediately began suggesting that other countries, namely Morocco, Libya and Chad, should be included within the regional security framework that Algeria had so far managed to limit to the four countries of Algeria, Mauritania, Mali and Niger. Algeria was so angered by these attempts to weaken its grip over the Sahel security situation that it simply boycotted the conference, or the 'Counter-terrorism Action Group' as it became known.

The significance of the conference was not what it discussed, but the fact that it was held at all; that it was attended by many more countries than anticipated,[7] including both France and Morocco, and, most significantly, that it was boycotted by Algeria. Indeed, the fact that it had been initiated by France and attended by so many countries was a direct snub and challenge to Algeria. Not only was it a challenge to Algeria's attempts to keep control over this region to itself, but it also demonstrated the preparedness and ability of the 'weaker' countries of the region, notably Mali, Mauritania and Niger, to stand up to Algeria and the bullying tactics it had been adopting.

The reason Algeria gave for boycotting the conference was because it believed that countries outside the region should not be involved in the battle against AQIM. It maintained that the problem should be dealt with by Algeria, Mauritania, Mali and Niger alone, without any outside intervention.

In reality, the reason for Algeria's peevishness was because Algeria's bluff was finally called. A week before the conference, a senior Mauritanian Minister publicly accused Algeria of being the *porte-parole* (spokesperson) for AQIM.[8] Although such a statement would not have surprised the US, the UK, or Canada, who chaired the conference, or, for that matter, France, all of whom were aware of the AQIM–DRS relationship, it was a very public accusation against Algeria.

To make matters worse for Algeria, both Morocco and Libya were to join in on the accusations. Libya's Colonel Mouamar Gaddafi, always ready to take advantage of a situation, used the occasion to irritate his neighbour by saying that he was not opposed to a 'limited' and 'temporary' French military presence in Niger (following the Arlit hostage-takings). The situation, he said, was an 'emergency' and as long as the French presence was not long term, then he was in favour of it. After his problems with the French in Chad in the 1980s, which saw his army humiliated and left in tatters, such support for France was a major turnaround that further angered Algeria. Gaddafi went on to say that Algeria, by trying to exclude Libya from the Sahel, was damaging the development of the region.

To make Algeria's diplomatic encirclement complete, Morocco also joined in, saying that some of the recent 'drug busts' in Morocco were linked to AQIM. Its message to the international community was very clear: while AQIM was responsible for much of the drug trafficking between the Sahel and Morocco, Algeria was excluding Morocco from all participation in attempts to eliminate al-Qaeda from the Sahel. In short, Morocco was saying that if Algeria was not actually directly aiding and abetting terrorism in the region (with a strong innuendo that it was!), it was certainly making its eradication extremely difficult by excluding countries such as Morocco from the initiatives that were being designed to put an end to it. In early November, there were unconfirmed reports of French Special Forces also operating in the area, suggesting that what Algeria feared most, namely a Franco-Sahelian alliance, was already coming into existence.

These were not the only challenging issues Algeria had to face at this time. Between the August and October Bamako conferences, further evidence of Algeria's involvement in both hostage-taking and drug trafficking emerged from another quarter. That quarter was the release on 22 August of the two remaining Spanish hostages, Albert Vilalta (35) and Roque Pascual (50), who had been seized in Mauritania in November 2009.[9]

The Polisario–Sahraoui Connection

Although the Western media was preoccupied with how much ransom money had been paid and by whom,[10] the real mystery and clue to the kidnapping concerned a certain Omar Sidi'Ahmed Ould Hama, alias Omar Sahraoui. Omar was alleged to have been the original kidnapper. Shortly after the abduction, Mauritanian commandos were reported to have led a raid across the border into Mali, from where the kidnappers were believed to have been operating, and seized Omar, who was taken back to Mauritania and given a life sentence commuted to twelve years' imprisonment. One week before the Spaniards were released, Omar was reportedly 'extradited' back to Mali, a move that the Mauritanians justified by saying that Omar was originally from Mali and of Malian nationality. However, there was no evidence of Mali making a formal extradition request.

According to Western diplomatic sources, Omar was then handed back to AQIM, suggesting that Spain had made a deal with AQIM. According to a number of media reports, Spain pressured Mauritania to release Omar as part of the deal it was trying to put together with AQIM.

In the meantime, Morocco, which was keeping a close eye on the situation, revealed that Omar, as his alias of Omar Sahraoui might suggest, was in fact a member of the Polisario. In addition, Morocco released documents issued by the so-called 'Sahraoui Arab Democratic Republic' (aka Polisario) that revealed that Omar was of Mauritanian (not Malian) origin and born in Farsia, Western Sahara. He was also married to a Sahraoui.

While Morocco, not surprisingly, was quick to claim that Omar's key role in the kidnapping was 'proof' that the Polisario and its Algerian puppeteers were engaged in terrorism, the Moroccan lead opened up a whole new set of possible connections that linked Omar Sahraoui not only to the Polisario and Algeria's DRS, but also to Mokhtar ben Mokhtar (MBM).

MBM, who has longstanding connections with the DRS and whose name had been linked with this particular hostage-taking at various times over the previous ten months, now appeared to have played a key role in the hostages' release. This role was through his association with an even murkier character, a certain Mustapha Ould Limam Chafi. Chafi is allegedly a Mauritanian now living in Burkina Faso as an advisor to President Blaise Compaoré. Behind the involvement of Blaise Compaoré in the hostage release, it is believed that it was Chafi who may have handled the negotiations that led to not only the release of Omar

Sahraoui from Mauritania and his return to AQIM (possibly via Mali), but also the movement of the ransom money which Chafi is believed to have channelled to his longstanding associate, MBM.

Perhaps even more significant in trying to make sense of the so-called 'terrorism' in the Mauritanian sector of the Sahara, Chafi's involvement in this hostage-release has led to suggestions that he may also have been the 'financier' of Mauritania's Cavaliers du Changement, the Mauritanian opposition movement that played a major role in the overthrow of President Ould Taya in August 2005. Indeed, in 2004, Ould Taya had been accusing both Chafi and Compaoré of financing 'criminal' acts in Mauritania.

A remaining question with which we are now left, and on which I can throw no more light for the moment, is whether the complicated release of these two Spanish hostages and the alleged payment of some $8 million of ransom money through the hands of Chafi and MBM was the 'payback' to those involved in the attack on the Lemgheity garrison in northern Mauritania in July 2005,[11] only a few weeks before Ould Taya's overthrow.

Covering the DRS's Tracks in Bamako

Morocco's allegations about the links between AQIM terrorism, drug trafficking, the Polisario and Algeria's DRS, were clearly annoying Algeria, as could be seen from the extraordinary sequence of events on 9 December (2010). During the course of 7–9 December, six members of the Polisario were arrested in Mali in connection with cocaine trafficking. The key drug trafficker arrested was a certain Sultan Ould Badi. Ould Badi was not a bit-part player: he was reportedly the head of Polisario's 'special missions' and believed to have also been involved in AQIM kidnappings.[12] On capture, he was threatening the authorities in Bamako that he would reveal the AQIM–DRS connection.

The situation was clearly extremely delicate for both the DRS and the Malian authorities because of the AQIM–DRS connection with Mali's state security department. As earlier chapters have revealed, some of the highest echelons of Mali's security service were involved in both drug trafficking and hostage-taking.[13]

At the time of Sultan Ould Badi's arrest in Bamako, Algeria's President Bouteflika was on an official visit to Germany, at the invitation of Chancellor Angela Merkel. A key member of his entourage was General Rachid Laalali (Attafi), head of the DRS's Direction de la Documentation et de la Sécurité Extérieure (DDSE). On learning of Sultan Ould Badi's arrest, the DRS General curtailed his mission in Germany, hired a private plane and rushed, on the evening of Thursday 9 December, to Bamako.[14]

What happened in Bamako after Attafi's arrival there has not been revealed; nor is it likely to be. Nothing more was heard of the matter. Sultan Ould Badi was evidently released without any charges brought against him. But the incident was noted within the EU and, as we shall see shortly, it had consequences.

Algeria and the Sahel Come Under the EU Spotlight

The EU, at its External Relations Council meeting in Luxembourg on 27 October 2009, recorded an almost simultaneous expression of concern over the security situation in the Sahel as the UN's Richard Barrett. The Council 'expresse[d] its concern over the security situation in parts of the Sahel region, in particular in Mauritania, Mali and Niger …'[15] One year later, on 25 October 2010, the Sahel was at the top of the agenda at the EU Foreign Council's meeting in Luxembourg. The Council concluded that

> the development of cross-border threats such as terrorism and organised crime, coupled with extreme poverty, unresolved internal conflicts and the weakness and fragility of the States concerned, constitutes a growing challenge for the stability of the region and for the European Union. These threats directly affect the local populations and States of the region, particularly Mauritania, Mali and Niger. They also have an impact on the security of European nationals … In close cooperation with the States of the region, … the European Union intends to … foster security, stability, development and good governance in the Sahel-Saharan strip.[16]

On 27 October, two days after the EU Council meeting in Luxembourg, an audio-tape, claiming to be from Osama bin Laden, but more likely from Algeria's DRS, was broadcast through

Al Jazeera. In the broadcast, bin Laden castigated France for its treatment of Muslims, its role in Afghanistan and its intervention in the affairs of Muslims in North and West Africa.

Bin Laden's supposed intervention in regard to AQIM's abduction of the seven hostages from Arlit on 22 September had ensured that the hitherto little-known Sahel was a place to conjure with. His intervention two days after the EU Foreign Council meeting, coincidental or not, and irrespective of the tape's authenticity, ensured that discussion of the Sahel crisis was no longer restricted to the hallowed and scarcely publicised precincts of the European Council, but placed firmly in the public domain.[17]

The DRS was unlikely to have known that the EU Foreign Council had already instructed the European Commission, the EU's bureaucracy, to commission a 'Study on Political Islam in the Sahel and Neighbouring Countries', which, of course, included Algeria.[18] This was not what Algeria's DRS had wanted: turning the EU's spotlight on to AQIM in the Sahel was likely to reveal, or at least raise questions, about the role of the DRS in AQIM's activities. The immediate response of the DRS was to try and create confusion by using a strategy which it had done on countless occasions in the past, namely to transpose identities. The DRS's emirs of Groupe Salafiste pour le Prédication et le Combat (GSPC)/AQIM, such as El Para and Mokhtar ben Mohktar, have had a string of aliases and have frequently been reported killed, only to be reincarnated under another alias or identity. Abdelhamed abou Zaïd, AQIM's main emir in the Sahel, was now to be given the same makeover treatment.

The DRS has a number of tame media scribes. One of the most imaginative is Mohamed Mokeddem (Meguedem), alias Anis Rahmani, who was introduced in Chapter 15. At some point in 2010, he set to work turning Abdelhamid abou Zaïd into another alias, namely Mohamed Ghadir.

Rahmani's thesis was that the world had been mistaken in the identity of AQIM leader Abdelhamid abou Zaïd. In a tortuous, fascinating and highly incredible story,[19] Rahmani argued that

Abou Zaïd was not, in fact, Abou Zaïd or Abid Hamadou or Hamidou Essoufi, or any other such alias, but Mohamed Ghadir, and that the file allegedly held on him by the FBI, the CIA, Interpol, and so on, was incorrect.

Rahmani's bizarre conclusion was the result of two men, both from smuggling backgrounds, joining the Front Islamique du Salut (FIS) in their respective communes, but with their identities (involving in incomprehensible story about a brother and two cousins) getting muddled up and with one of them, Abou Zaïd, subsequently dying, etc.! The 'real' Abou Zaïd, according to Rahmani, is apparently 'black', while the leader of AQIM in the Sahel, whose real name is allegedly Mohamed Ghadir, is 'white'. The result of Rahmani's 'revelation' was that the Algerian state media immediately began referring to Abou Zaïd as Mohamed Ghadir. If that sounds confusing, that is precisely what the DRS intended.

Rahmani went further. As part of the DRS's attempt to show that the threat of AQIM in the Sahel was diminishing and therefore presumably not warranting 'Western' intervention, Rahmani wrote how AQIM's presence in northern Mali was merely 'a stage' in its strategy of linking up with Boko Haram in northern Nigeria, and that the future of AQIM would be seen in northern Nigeria, not the Sahel. He also described how AQIM in the Sahel was coming under pressure and therefore no longer the security threat that the EU had identified.

UK Support for Algeria and its DRS

Algeria and its DRS had no reason to fear any such intervention from the West. Its Western allies, the US and UK especially, were not going to abandon Algeria's authoritarian and repressive regime: at least, not yet. Indeed, as Algeria's neighbours began pointing accusatory fingers at Algiers, and as the EU began to turn the spotlight on the Sahel, so the UK made it increasingly clear that Algeria's rulers had no cause for alarm. On 11–12 November 2010, the UK MP Alistair Burt, the Parliamentary Under-Secretary of State at the Foreign and Commonwealth Office (FCO) with responsibility for the Middle East and North Africa (MENA) and counterterrorism, went to Algiers to finalise arrangements for a second meeting of the UK-Algerian joint committee on counter-terrorism to be held in London on 29–30 November. The first meeting of the joint committee had been held in Algiers in March. Speaking to the Algerian media, Burt described Algeria as a 'key partner' in counterterrorism and said that 'London is ready to provide Algiers with military equipment required in its war on terror.' The fact that Algeria's neighbours were expressing their concerns about Algeria's role in regional terrorism were ignored by the FCO.

The two-day London meeting was held three days after an EU conference in Brussels on 'Development [a euphemism for security] in the Sahel'.[20] It concluded that Algeria was the main military power in the region and the only one capable of ridding the Sahel of AQIM.

Algeria's delegation to the London meeting was headed by President Bouteflika's counterterrorism advisor and envoy, Kamal Razzak Bara; the UK's by Simon Manley, the Director of Defence and Strategic Threats at the FCO. Major General Robin Searby, the advisor to the British Prime Minister on North African counterterrorism, heaped praise on Algeria's record on terrorism. Searby, who had been present in Nouakchott on the eve of the disastrous 22 July Franco-Mauritanian raid into Mali and who had been previously involved in questionable operations in both Oman and Libya, spoke of Algeria as 'having great experience, being very efficient and a model for the countries of the region'.[21] The UK made it clear that it would not only work increasingly closely with Algeria's DRS, but that it would be providing it with material, intelligence, training and other such cooperative needs.

Kamal Razzak Bara was well pleased by what he had heard in Brussels and London. In an interview on Algeria's state-run radio on his return to Algeria on 1 December, he said that the UK, the US and the EU were fully aware of the correctness of Algeria's position, which was that Algeria strongly opposed any foreign interference in the region's internal affairs and that the countries of the Sahel were fully capable of addressing terror threats themselves. If Kamal Razzak Bara had interpreted Brussels and London correctly, he could reasonably surmise that good friends within the EU would deflect or dilute any serious probes that the EU Commission might make into Algeria's true involvement with AQIM terrorism in the Sahel. He was not to be disappointed.

18

THE ARAB SPRING AND GADDAFI INTERVENE

Through fortuitous circumstances, it so happened that I was the contracted 'expert' and sole author of the EU Commission's *Study on Political Islam in the Sahel and Neighbouring Countries*.[1] I therefore know what information it contained about al-Qaeda in the Islamic Maghreb (AQIM), Algeria's Département du Renseignement et de la Sécurité (DRS) and how much of this information was redacted from the report.

The report was submitted on 18 December 2010. By coincidence, that was the same day as Mohamed Bouazizi, a 26-year-old street vendor in the provincial Tunisian town of Sidi Bouzid, doused himself in petrol and set himself alight in protest at the confiscation of his wares and the harassment and humiliation that he received from a municipal official and her aides. He died 18 days later of his burns, but not until Tunisia had been engulfed in nationwide demonstrations and the start of what became known as the 'Arab Spring'.

In regard to Algeria, the continual question over the last two or more years has been how much longer Algeria's *mukhabarat* (police state) can continue to suppress the simmering anger of the vast bulk of its 36 million peoples against a regime that has abdicated the last vestiges of any responsibility and duty of care for the welfare and wellbeing of its citizens. The country's rulers devote a substantial part of their intellectual activity to the pursuit of the grotesque appropriation of wealth from Algeria's rentier economy,[2] while their political energy is concentrated on prohibiting and suppressing any form of dissent that might lead to the sorts of rebellion that have already swept aside the despots of Tunisia, Egypt and Libya.

Over the last two years, public protests and demonstrations in Algeria have been running at over 10,000 a year, an average of more than one per hour.[3] Despite this, these protests and demonstrations and the violence that the state's repressive apparatus brings to them have not been the stuff of rebellion, although one day, which may not be so far away, they may acquire the momentum and necessary level of political organisation to become so. Nevertheless, these manifestations are 'political' in that they are a form of communication – a new discourse – between the Algerian people and their rulers. It is through this discourse of barricades, burning tyres and rioting that matters of housing shortages, unemployment, the rising cost of living, poor salaries and working conditions, the disintegration of utility infrastructures, refuse collection, road repairs, and a host of other grievances are brought to the attention of the state authorities.

Indeed, the question has been, and still is: when will such protests and demonstrations, which have now become part of Algeria's ritualised daily scene, turn into open and sustained rebellion? For that is the day that both Algeria's rulers and their Western allies in Washington and London fear and endeavour to postpone.

There was a sense, during the initial days of the outrage and demonstrations that swept Tunisia following Bouazizi's self-immolation, that Algeria might follow suit. In the last week of December 2010 there were at least ten outbreaks of rioting in towns and cities around the country. Clashes with police in Algiers on 28 December resulted in at least 53 people injured and 29 arrested. In the same week, there were rumours in Algiers that President Bouteflika's two brothers were moving 'assets', alleged to be in the form of paintings and other valuables, from state palaces to apartments that had been purchased for them in Dubai and Abu Dhabi.[4] Then, between 3 and 10 January, riots triggered by substantial increases in basic food prices broke out in almost every major Algerian town and city. Some commentators talked of an *intifada* on the streets, with the Rachad Movement's spokesman,

Mohamed Larbi Zitout, describing them as 'a revolt, and probably a revolution, of an oppressed people'. The riots, though, died down quickly, with the government claiming that rioting ended as soon as it cut the tax and duties on basic foodstuffs. There is some truth in this claim, although the fundamental reason was because the rioters lacked political organisation and direction as a result of the DRS's sophisticated system of repression and control through which it has atomised and infiltrated almost every vestige of opposition to the regime. Moreover, the DRS is fully aware that the fear of a return to the violence of the 1990s still weighs heavily on many Algerians. It therefore came as no surprise when Rachad's investigations into the rioting revealed that much of it, especially the extensive damage to and looting of shops and other buildings, had been led by police *agents provocateurs*.

As Algeria's 'revolt' stuttered to a halt, the cameras focused first on Tunisia, where growing anti-government demonstrations forced the country's dictator, Zine El Abidine Ben Ali, to flee the country with his family and seek refuge in Saudi Arabia on 14 January, and then on Egypt where sustained protests in Tahrir Square led to the resignation of Hosni Mubarak on 11 February. Four days later, protests and then active resistance to Gaddafi's regime began in Libya.

Western Intelligence Services Caught Flat-Footed

The Arab Spring, or 'Arab Revolt'[5] as it is more appropriately known, caught Western intelligence services flat-footed. There are three reasons for this. One is because the West's intelligence services have been trapped for the last decade in the ideological cul-de-sac of the 'Global War on Terror' (GWOT) and have become obsessed with the Islamist and al-Qaeda 'bogeymen' which they have done so much to help create, but who had little, if anything, to do with the Arab Spring.

A second reason has been the failure of these same intelligence services and their governments to see and understand the fundamental contradiction of the GWOT. This is, quite simply, that the GWOT has done much to exacerbate the fundamental conditions that have given rise to the Arab Spring. Indeed, a fundamental question that hangs over the Arab Spring is the extent to which it is a reaction to the entire GWOT syndrome. The uprisings that began in early 2011 in almost every Arab country were attempts by their peoples to rid their countries of their ruthlessly authoritarian and corrupt regimes, which, without exception, had become increasingly more repressive since 9/11 in the knowledge that they have the backing of the West. Yasmine Ryan, in discussing the relationship between the GWOT and the Arab Spring, said:

> All of North Africa's leaders have been complicit with the West: acting as its torturers, buying its arms and patrolling the Mediterranean Sea to stem the tides of young people desperate to flee their homelands. All were partners in the CIA's controversial 'extraordinary rendition programme' and Libya has been a pro-active partner in a secretive Rome-Tripoli deal, signed in 2009, to intercept boats carrying migrants. In return for the sea patrols, Italy pledged to pay Libya $7bn over 20 years.[6]

Algeria has even gone as far as colluding with the West in the fabrication of false-flag terrorism.[7]

The third reason has simply been the sheer inadequacy of the West's intelligence services. The US and UK intelligence services have little or no reliable human intelligence (HUMINT) on the ground in this region and rely heavily on local intelligence services. In the case of Algeria's DRS, with whom both the US and the UK work closely, this is like using a fox to guard the chickens. The DRS tells them a mixture of what it wants them to hear and what they want to hear.

France's situation is slightly different. Prior to the Sarkozy era, France had good intelligence in the region, but that has deteriorated since 2007, culminating in its debacle over Tunisia in January 2011 when France's then Foreign Minister, Michèle Alliot-Marie, offered the services of French security forces to quell the uprising in Tunisia, just three days before protesters forced Ben Ali to flee. A group of anonymous diplomats condemned French foreign policy as 'amateur' and 'impulsive'.

France's intervention in Libya, under the guise of 'humanitarian intervention', was a last ditch gamble by Sarkozy to gain redemption after demonstrably failing to understand and being slow to react to the uprisings in Tunisia and Egypt.

Thus, for a country like the UK to attempt to play a major counterterrorism role in the region while being almost wholly dependent for intelligence on the US, France and Algeria's DRS is not only a recipe for disaster, but raises serious questions about the competencies, or ideological mindset, of both the UK's counterterrorism services and its Foreign and Commonwealth Office (FCO).

Algeria's Allies Continue their GWOT

Even as the Arab Revolt unfolded across North Africa, neither the US nor the UK were prepared to let it usurp the primacy they had so long given to the GWOT. Nor were they prepared to allow Algeria to become what the media was referring to as 'the next domino to fall'. While British Foreign Secretary William Hague expressed his concerns on a TV political 'chat show' that 'the uprising could provide opportunities for terrorists', Washington returned to beating the GWOT drum in earnest. The US State Department sent David Benjamin, its Counterterrorism Coordinator, to Algiers in what was intended to be a strong reaffirmation of US support for the Algerian regime. Benjamin's task was to set up a new, so-called 'contact group' between the US and Algeria. Its first session, chaired jointly by Benjamin and Bouteflika's security advisor Kamal Rezzag Bara, was held in Algiers on 3 March.[8] Benjamin met with many of Algeria's top security and military officials, with the public message disseminated from these meetings being, in Benjamin's words, that 'The US would not allow terrorist groups to exploit the revolutions of the Arab people.'

Turning to the Sahel, Benjamin said that he was concerned about the security situation in the region, attributing the lacklustre results against AQIM thus far to the vastness of the Sahara and insufficient coordination between the regional states. Benjamin had a point over the lacklustre results against AQIM, but for reasons that neither he nor his Washington overlords were going to admit in public. It was, as this volume has made abundantly clear, because AQIM in the Sahel is a construct of Algeria's DRS.

The EU Sahel Report and its Outcomes

As the Arab Spring took hold of much of North Africa, the EU Commission perused the draft of my report on *Political Islam in the Sahel and Neighbouring Countries*. The most important of the 'neighbouring countries' is Algeria, the home of the Groupe Salafiste pour le Prédication et le Combat (GSPC)/AQIM. But, in a blatantly political decision, the EU Commission insisted that key parts of the report, namely those that provided the EU with an explanation of the origin of AQIM, an analysis of its activities in the Sahel and its relations with Algeria's DRS, be removed.[9] The result is that the EU has two copies of my report: the original copy and its redacted version, neither of which have been made public. The latter, 'official' version, by having removed all reference to the Algerian regime and its DRS, gives a completely false perspective and understanding of what is going on in the Sahel.

There were other outcomes. Although denied by EU officials, it was brought to my attention that the original version of the report, which also highlighted the corruption within the Malian government, was 'leaked' to Mali's President. According to diplomatic sources in Bamako, this led to the resignation and/or removal of almost the entire top layer of Mali's administration. It began around the end of February with the resignation of the head of state security, Colonel Mamy Coulibaly, who, as previous chapters reveal and as my EU report made clear, was involved in both drug trafficking and taking cuts from AQIM's hostage-taking. Coulibaly's departure was followed by the resignation, without explanation, of the Prime Minister, Modibo Sidibe, on 30 March. By the beginning of June, these two had been joined by the heads of the police, gendarmerie and National Guard; the Directors of Finance and Procurement in all government ministries and the heads of most ancillary services such as Customs, Taxation, State Property Management and State Markets. This apparent 'clean-up' of Amadou Toumani Touré's corrupt administration certainly facilitated Mali's receipt of substantial EU funding.

The leak of my report may also explain Algeria's announcement at the end of April to donate $10 million to Mali to fund development in the northern regions of Timbuktu, Kidal and Gao. I believe this was to pre-empt being sidelined by the EU's much larger security-development programme for the region. The danger for Algiers of the EU's Sahel development programme is that it offers France a means of re-establishing its influence in the region, something which Algeria had been successfully undermining through its 'US-backed' AQIM regional destabilisation policy.

Evidence of how France may be turning Algeria's 'meddling' in the Sahel to its advantage was revealed in a government report to the French Parliament on 26 October 2011 that confirmed that the Sahel states of Mauritania, Mali and Niger were enhancing their military strength through arms deals with France. This was a deliberate move by the Sahel states to counterbalance both Algeria's regional military superiority and its failure to act militarily against AQIM.

The Libyan Contradiction

The Libyan rebellion exposed a fundamental contradiction in the West's policy towards North Africa. While the UK and the US, with France, were bent on ridding Libya of Gaddafi, the US and the UK were at the same time also at the forefront of supporting the Algerian regime which, in turn, was covertly doing its best to prop up Gaddafi.

The Algerian regime feared that Gaddafi's fall could precipitate its own overthrow. Elements within the Algerian regime, most notably the DRS, therefore set out to prolong the Gaddafi regime's hold on power. Algeria's initial strategy was to try to persuade the West that Gaddafi's son, Saïf al-Islam, was an acceptable solution. That, however, only lasted a few weeks, until Saïf revealed his true colours. It then tried to convince the West that the only solution for Libya was a partition of sorts between East and West. That too, following the fall of Misrata and then Tripoli, came to naught. It was then left with its final strategy, one in which it is most adept: to create as much confusion and chaos as possible.

Algeria's support for Gaddafi was extensive. It began with energetic lobbying by Algerian diplomats at the UN and with the EU, NATO (North Atlantic Treaty Organisation) and the Arab League to deter any external intervention in Libya. These efforts, first reported by Al Jazeera,[10] were led by Abdelkader Messahel, Algeria's Minister of Maghreb and African affairs.[11] The Rachad Movement[12] also reported that the Algerian government had sent armed detachments to Libya. These were first identified in the western Libyan town of Zawiyah where some of them were captured and identified by anti-Gaddafi forces. Shamsiddin Abdulmolah, a National Transitional Council (NTC) spokesman, later reported the capture of 15 Algerian mercenaries and the deaths of three others in fighting near Ajdabiya. His claims were supported by several independent sources.

According to the same source, Algeria's DRS employed many of the private security forces and Republican Guard of deposed Tunisian President Zine El Abidine Ben Ali and sent them to Libya to shore up Gaddafi.[13] Many of these units were previously used as snipers to assassinate demonstrators in Kasserine, Sidi Bouzid and Thala in Tunisia. Then, following the defection of Libyan pilots to Malta in the early stages of the conflict, and prior to the authorisation of the UN 'No-Fly Zone' on 17 March, Algeria sent 21 of its pilots to the Mitiga airbase in Tripoli. There have also been numerous reports of Algerian military transport planes airlifting mercenaries from sub-Saharan Africa. Data collected from the air traffic control tower at Benghazi's Benina airport ascertained that there had been 22 flights by Algerian aircraft to Libyan destinations between 19 and 26 February. Some were listed as Air Algérie and were possibly evacuating nationals. Most, however, were listed as 'special flights' by aircraft bearing registration codes used by the Algerian military. These records show repeated flights by C-130 Hercules and Ilyushin Il-76, aircraft big enough to carry battle tanks. Destinations included the airports at Sebha and Sirte. By March, in a memorandum to the Arab League, the NTC had put the number of Algerian flights that had landed at Tripoli's Mitiga airport at 51. The memorandum said the shipments included ammunition, weapons and Algerian and mercenary fighters.

On 18 April 2011, Alain Juppé, the French Foreign Minister,[14] confronted Algeria with evidence discovered by French military advisors working with the Libyan rebels that a number of military jeeps and trucks used by Gaddafi's forces, which had been abandoned after a military battle, carried serial numbers which identified them as French military equipment that had been sold to Algeria.

Algeria's actions irritated the UK and US governments so much so that Algeria's Foreign Minister, Mourad Medelci, was 'invited' to meet the US Secretary of State in Washington.[15] Behind the bonhomie of the official press releases, sources reported that Medelci was castigated for Algeria's support for Gaddafi.

Algeria, however, does not take kindly to being rebuked and immediately dispatched one of its rougher political apparatchiks, Sadek Bouguetaya,[16] to address Gaddafi's meeting of Libyan tribes in Tripoli on 8 May. In a rabble-rousing speech, Bouguetaya voiced the FLN's unconditional support for Gaddafi and blasted NATO's Libyan operations, which he likened to the attempts of Paul Bremer, the former US Administrator in Iraq, to control Baghdad. He called Gaddafi's effort to stay in power heroic and criticised the West for its 'bombing of the civilian population'. With specific reference to Algeria's War of Independence, Bouguetaya said that he had confidence that the Libyan people would defeat France, as the Algerian revolutionary forces had done in 1962. At the same time as Bouguetaya was haranguing NATO in Tripoli, the Libyan Ambassador to Algeria publicly announced that his Embassy had purchased 500 'military grade' vehicles from Algerian dealers, with more in the pipeline, to help Gaddafi's forces.

Washington was not pleased by Algeria's belligerence. On 18 May, the Emir of Qatar, Sheikh Hamad bin Khalifa al-Thani, described by Robert Fisk[17] as 'the wisest bird in the Arabian Gulf', paid a one-day visit to Algiers. Sheikh Hamad's message to his Algerian counterpart is believed to have been twofold. One was that Qatar, which was the key Arab state in the NATO alliance, and by implication Algeria's 'other friends' were disappointed at Algeria's lack of meaningful political reform. The other, as Robert Fisk reported a few days later, was to try to 'persuade' the Algerian regime away from resupplying Gaddafi with tanks and armoured vehicles. 'Qatar', said Fisk, 'is committed to the Libyan rebels in Benghazi; its planes are flying over Libya from Crete and – undisclosed until now – it has Qatari officers advising the rebels inside the city of Misrata.' Indeed, one reason suggested by Fisk for the ridiculously slow progress of the NATO campaign against Gaddafi was because Algerian armour of superior quality had been replacing the Libyan material destroyed in air strikes.[18]

AFRICOM'S 'One-Eyed' General

Just as Algeria's intervention in Libya was on the verge of becoming a major embarrassment to NATO, the US stepped forward. On 1 June, the Commander of US AFRICOM (Africa Command), General Carter F. Ham, flew to Algiers and in true Nelsonian spirit, but without the heroism, announced that he 'could see no evidence' of Algerian support for Mouamar Gaddafi's beleaguered regime.

If the US thought that such a declaration from a senior US commander would put an end to the Algerian issue, it was quite mistaken. Saying that one 'cannot see' something is invariably just a disingenuous semanticism for denying the existence of something which, as in the case of Algerian support for Gaddafi, was becoming increasingly evident.

In some respects, it would be surprising if AFRICOM were to actually 'see something'. Unlike other US military commands, AFRICOM is woefully short of boots on the ground. With a force of only 1,500, mostly based in Stuttgart, AFRICOM is very reliant on second-hand and often highly dubious intelligence sources. In fact, its specialties are neither in fighting campaigns nor in intelligence, but in handing out contracts to private military contractors, dabbling in the more intellectually impoverished end of the social sciences and producing false information. General Ham's statement fell within the latter.

AFRICOM's commander may be 'one-eyed', but in this instance his disingenuous statement was not the outcome of AFRICOM's limitations, but part of a 'package deal' believed to have been worked out between top officials in the US and French governments and Algeria's DRS.[19] The talks had two main strands. One was to save the Algerian regime from the same fate as Tunisia's Ben Ali, Egypt's Mubarak and soon, it was presumed, Gaddafi by encouraging it to move more rapidly towards meaningful political reform. The other was to effectively rehabilitate the Algerian regime with NATO and the Pentagon. The deal was both a reaffirmation of the strategic importance of Algeria to the US and a reminder to both sides that they shared too much 'recent history' in regard to their joint activities in the GWOT for them to fall out. In short, neither the US nor Algeria can afford to have their secrets and cooperation aired in public.

The essence of the deal was that Algeria would cease its support for Gaddafi, while the US would save Algeria from international condemnation by reiterating General Carter Ham's 'see no evidence' of Algerian support for Gaddafi. It was agreed that Algeria would also desist from linking Libya's rebels with al-Qaeda and Islamic extremism, which was both irksome and embarrassing to the NATO alliance. In exchange, the US would back Algeria's scaremongering over the threat AQIM presented to Algeria, the wider region and Europe, as well as its grossly exaggerated and largely unverified statements about arms flows from Libya to AQIM.

Algeria uses the threat of AQIM to justify its internal repression and to frighten Algerians. The warning, broadcast almost daily, is along the lines of: 'If you revolt, as in Libya, al-Qaeda will take advantage and spread even further chaos and violence in the country.'

In one respect, at least, nothing has changed since the US and Algeria first conspired to fabricate terrorism in the Sahara in 2002. From the US perspective, the threat of terrorism, real or fabricated, in the Sahel provides AFRICOM with an important justification for its existence. AFRICOM is preoccupied in trying to prove that AQIM, Boko Haram and Al Shabaab[20] are linked together in one continuous belt of terrorism from the Indian to the Atlantic Oceans. In September 2011, for example, General Carter Ham told correspondents that 'the three violent extremist organizations … were trying to forge an alliance to coordinate attacks on the United States and Western interests'. In language reminiscent of Generals Jim Jones and Charles Wald, his predecessors during the time of El Para's escapade, General Ham said that 'They [AQIM, Boko Haram and Al Shabaab] have very explicitly and publicly voiced an intent to target Westerners, and the US specifically.'[21]

General Ham delivered his infamous 'I can see no evidence' speech on 1 June. Ten days later, a high level US delegation led by Mark Adams, senior advisor with the US State Department's Bureau of Political and Military Affairs, and including representatives from the US Departments of Defense and Homeland Security, arrived in Algiers for a four-day visit. The official reason given for Mr Adams' visit was to consult with Algeria on the risks of proliferation of weapons from the Libyan crisis as well as 'an exhaustive assessment of the major risk of seeing such weapons falling into the hands of terrorist groups'.

Gaddafi Incriminated in French Hostage Deal

The Adams delegation's visit was intended to give credibility to General Ham's intervention and give the impression that the US was taking seriously its security and counterterrorism cooperation with Algeria. Any doubt that the Adams delegation might have had as to whether these 'terrorist groups' posed a threat to Algeria's security was possibly answered for them on the second day of their visit,[22] when a sizeable heist of Libyan arms was intercepted by the Nigerien army at Ouraren, a few miles south of the Algerian border. Local and international media, citing Algerian security sources, alleged that it was destined for al-Qaeda in the Sahel.

Added to this, the government controlled newspaper *El Khabar*, sourcing its story to the DRS, reported that on the same day as the Ouraren intercept, 'two Al Qaeda suspects carrying 1.7 million euros and 40,000 US dollars (in cash), light weapons and unspecified documents were captured at a checkpoint

180 kms north of Tamanrasset'.[23] The report, embellished in the international media the following day, said that the two suspects were close associates of Abdelhamid abou Zaïd and that the money was 'believed to be part of a ransom payment for foreign hostages'.[24]

Did either of these two incidents happen, or where they just deceptions? Certainly, their timing could not have been more convenient for the Algerian and US authorities: it was almost as if they had been laid on for the benefit of the Adams delegation.

The basic facts of the arms incident were that on Sunday 12 June, a Nigerien army patrol ran into a three-vehicle convey near Ouraren in northern Niger, roughly midway between the uranium mining town of Arlit and the Algerian border. In the engagement that followed, one of the three vehicles was captured and found to contain 640 kilogrammes of Czech-made Semtex explosive, bearing Libyan markings, 435 detonators and $90,000 (in bank notes). Within the next few days, the two other vehicles were captured. Their contents were not revealed, although the leader of the operation was soon identified, located and taken into custody.

Documents found in the captured vehicle pointed to Mohamed Abta Hamidine (Hamaïdi) and Ibrahim ag Alembo, the younger brother of Ghaly ag Alembo. Ghaly, the former leader of the Tuareg rebel MNJ (Mouvement des Nigériens pour la Justice), had by this time long since abandoned his MNJ colleagues for the high-life of Tripoli where he was serving as both Gaddafi's recruiting agent for Nigerien Tuareg mercenaries and his 'go-between' in fixing certain deals in Niger.

Abta Hamidine, the key figure in the operation, is a Nigerien Arab from Tassara, an Arab enclave in northern Niger. Abta Hamidine had became head of the notorious Tassara militia in the early 1990s and, as described in Chapter 14, was heavily involved with Hadj Bettu and Algeria's DRS in managing the Sahelian end of their trans-Saharan arms trafficking business at that time. The DRS retained close links with this community, some of whom, such as Abta Hamidine, could be regarded as DRS 'agents'. Hamidine had become a powerful personage in this part of the Sahel. Not only was he well connected with the DRS, but he had successfully played both sides of the 2007–09 Tuareg rebellion, aligning his militia first of all with Alembo's MNJ, but being the first to seek peace and deal with the now deposed President Tandja. As locals explained it: 'he has the reputation of being able to get his men out of prison on both sides of the border'.

Hamidine's two associates in this operation, and the drivers of two of the vehicles, were Ghaly's younger brother Ibrahim, known as 'Ouback', and Alhousseini Jaloud who was killed in the engagement. Jaloud, a Malian, was generally known to be 'very close to the AQIM terrorists'. Indeed, my informants in Niger told me they had little doubt that he was an intelligence agent connected to Algeria's DRS.

Hamidine gave himself up to the Nigerien authorities at a prearranged rendezvous 40 kilometres south of Agades three days after the Ouraren engagement, but not until after the authorities had searched his house and discovered $170,000 in cash, a collection of arms, two computers and documents indicating that he was preparing to take over as head of AQIM in Niger. In custody, Hamidine appears to have 'sung like a canary'. According to Ibrahim Manzo Diallo, who recorded and published his 'confession' in *AïrInfo*,[25] he was only too ready to tell his story. His explanation of events is as follows:

The four key players in the operation were Abta Hamidine, who we can possibly regard as the designated head of AQIM in Niger and a longstanding 'associate' of Algeria's DRS; Alhousseini Jaloud, a 'link-man' between the DRS and AQIM in Mali; Ghaly ag Alembo, former head of the MNJ, living at this time in Tripoli at Gaddafi's grace and favour and also well known to the DRS; and Ghaly's lesser-known younger brother, Ibrahim.

Their story, according to Diallo's report, began in late April or early May when Ghaly called Hamidine and asked him to come to Tripoli on a business matter. Hamidine travelled to Libya where he learnt that the Gaddafi family wanted to make contact with AQIM, or, more precisely Abou Zaïd or Mokhtar ben Mokhtar. Gaddafi apparently wanted to get his hands on the four French AREVA hostages being held by AQIM and Ghaly knew that Hamidine was the one person who could arrange this.

Hamidine accepted on the condition that the Gaddafi clan supply him with sufficient arms and wherewithal (presumably cash) to establish a branch of AQIM in Niger. This condition – which, I should add, makes little sense in the light of Gaddafi's animosity to AQIM – was apparently agreed, with the understanding that they all supported the Gaddafi clan's desire to punish Europe and, above all, France for its support of the rebels.

The deal was agreed and Hamidine returned to Niger where he contacted his old comrade Jaloud, who was charged with negotiating the 'sale' of the four French hostages that Gaddafi wanted. AQIM agreed to hand over the hostages for specific equipment, notably explosives, detonators, military uniforms, and so on. Then, at the end of May, Hamidine returned to Libya with Jaloud and Ibrahim ag Alembo, travelling from Arlit to Tripoli where the deal was finalised. The vehicle(s) with the armaments, notably the explosives and detonators, was handed over, along with money for AQIM. According to Diallo, the money was handed to Jaloud, who apparently gave $210,000 to Ghaly as the facilitator of the deal, $90,000 to Hamidine, and kept $100,000 for himself.

This confession raises many questions. How much of it is true? What was the role of the DRS? And what was Gaddafi planning to do with the hostages?

From discussions with my informants, I am fairly certain that the events at Ouraren, the surrender of Hamidine and his confession are all substantially 'true', which would suggest that the timing of the incident in relation to Adams' visit to Algiers was a convenient coincidence. As far as DRS involvement is concerned, both Hamidine and Jaloud were either DRS 'agents' or closely associated with them, while Ghaly has had longstanding connections with them. Moreover, if there is any truth in the AQIM–Gaddafi hostage deal, it certainly could not have been undertaken without the DRS's approval. But, if the DRS was involved in this scheme, why was it handing the hostages over to Gaddafi? Was it a further component of Algeria's support for Gaddafi? Furthermore, what was Gaddafi planning to do with the hostages? Was he planning to use them as human shields, or perhaps to negotiate some sort of deal with France? Or was the DRS involved in some sort of monstrous double-cross, possibly even with the connivance of France, perhaps with the idea of staging their rescue on their transfer to Libya? Even though such questions border on the bizarre, they cannot be dismissed.

Moreover, there is still the question of the €1.7 million reportedly captured on the same day as the Ouraren engagement. The obvious question is whether the money was part of Hamidine's AQIM–Gaddafi hostage deal. A hundred and eighty kilometres north of Tamanrasset is the old French atomic base of In Eker, the location of permanent army, gendarmerie and frequently also police checkpoints. It is consequently a place to which 'real terrorists' would give a wide berth. We must therefore consider, assuming that *El Khabar*'s story is true, whether the seizure of such a large cache of money, possibly linked to Hamidine's operation, was a botched operation by the DRS. It would certainly not be the first instance of a breakdown in communication between the various branches of the security forces.

19

WAR CRIME?

In some respects, the onset of the Arab Spring served as a distraction and therefore eased, at least temporarily, the pressures being placed on Algeria by its neighbours to the south. As described in Chapter 17, other countries in the region, especially those in the Sahel were becoming increasingly aware that Algeria was not only behind al-Qaeda in the Islamic Maghreb (AQIM) in the Sahel, but using it to destabilise the region. Algeria's main defence against this finger-pointing was that it had taken the lead in the establishment of a joint military command, CEMOC (Comité d'état-major opérationnel conjoint), at Tamanrasset in April 2010.

However, the establishment of CEMOC was nothing more than a theatrical gesture to enable Algeria and its Western allies to give the impression that Western intervention in the Sahel was not necessary. The US and its counterterrorism officials, such as David Benjamin, were aware of this, as they were party to the counterterrorism charade being played out in the Sahara-Sahel. However, during those months when the uprisings in Tunisia, Egypt and then Libya were the focus of international attention, the Sahel was reduced to a sideshow. But that was not to last for long. With Carter Ham's intervention and the fall of Gaddafi, the US once again attempted to ramp up the security threat in the Sahel, this time from the alleged trafficking of arms from Libya to AQIM in the Sahel.

The US refocused attention on the Sahel by initiating an international conference on terrorism, crime and security in Algiers in early September 2011, the purpose of which was to highlight the AQIM threat in the Sahara-Sahel and to promote Algeria's standing as the lead country in fighting terrorism in the region.

Whether it was an intelligence failure on Washington's part, or simply the assumption that comes with being the world's only superpower, but not all Washington's client states and Algeria's supposed allies in the Sahel were prepared to follow the US-Algerian conference script. The first to blow the whistle on the CEMOC charade was Niger's Foreign Minister, Mohamed Bazoum, who had the candour to admit to press reporters that cooperation between the four countries – Algeria, Niger, Mali and Mauritania – had been ineffective. 'To date,' said Bazoum, 'the four countries' existing joint military body (CEMOC) based in ... Tamanrasset has been ineffective. So far, we have not seen it execute a single concrete operation.'[1] In Paris, a French intelligence official dismissed the conference as 'diplomatic posturing'.[2]

The same comment came from Mauritania. Mohamed Mahmoud Aboulmaaly, editor of the *Nouakchott Info* newspaper and AQIM specialist, said:

> Nothing has really changed ... The Tamanrasset group [CEMOC] has almost stalled. They have done nothing on the ground, there are meetings, ... Mauritania intervenes in Mali. Mali accepts that there is fighting on its territory. Algeria spends it's time warning against the French presence and not giving any support, same goes for Niger. The interests of these countries are all totally divergent.[3]

Why Algeria has not Fought Terrorism in the Sahara

The obvious question, and the one which has loomed larger as each year has gone by, is why Algeria, the major military power in the region, has done absolutely nothing to put an end to AQIM and its activities in the Sahel. AQIM's camps, albeit mobile, but probably containing no more than 300–400 militants, are only a metaphorical stone's-throw from Algeria's borders. Why has Algeria so singularly refused to send its armed forces – some of the 75,000 that it claims to be mobilising in the region – into north-eastern Mali to eliminate them? Mali, Niger and Mauritania have all urged Algeria to do so. Indeed, it would be a fairly straightforward military operation. The locations of AQIM's main camps are relatively well known. Helicopter gunships could obliterate them within a few hours. Why has that not happened?

Algeria's answer is that its constitution forbids it from sending its armed forces into other countries. While that is true, it has never stood in the way of Algeria using its troops in other countries when it has wanted to do so. For example, in 1973, Algeria sent three aircraft squadrons of fighters and bombers, an armoured brigade and 150 tanks to Egypt to help fight Israel in the Yom Kippur war. Less than three years later, Algerian forces were engaged in direct battles with Moroccan forces around the Western Sahara oasis of Amgala in January and February 1976.

Indeed, as we shall see presently, Algerian armed forces entered Mali in December 2011, although not to fight AQIM. It is therefore abundantly clear that the Constitution does not, in practice, prevent the Algerian army from intervening outside its national territory. The reason why Algeria's forces have not intervened against AQIM in Mali is because AQIM is a predominantly Algerian construct. Its leaders in the region, Abdelhamid abou Zaïd, Yahia Djouadi and Mokhtar ben Mokhtar (MBM) are all associated with the Département du Renseignement et de la Sécurité (DRS), as 'agents' or 'operatives' in the cases of Abou Zaïd and Djouadi, or what I have called a 'freelancer' in the case of MBM.

The Return of Athman Tartag

Although AQIM in the Sahel is a DRS construct, the question that is now becoming increasingly pertinent is the extent to which its emirs are still beholden to the master puppeteer, or whether they are beginning to take on a life and dynamic of their own. Hints that all may not be well within the DRS and that AQIM cells, especially in the Mauritanian sector, may be operating more independently of the DRS began emerging towards the end of 2011. Three highly publicised incidents led to questions being raised in the media and by some analysts as to whether the DRS had taken its eye off the ball. Whether the incidents are related or whether their timing was coincidental is not yet clear.

The first was the arrest by the Swiss authorities on 20 October of General Khaled Nezzar, the former Algerian Defence Minister. Nezzar was responsible for many of the atrocities committed by Algeria's armed forces in the 'dirty war' of the 1990s. A Swiss human rights organisation, Track Impunity Always (TRIAL), aware of Nezzar's pending visit to Geneva for medical treatment, lodged the claims of two Algerians, who alleged they had been tortured by Nezzar in the 1990s, with the Geneva prosecutor's office. The General's arrest and appearance in a Swiss court was immensely embarrassing to the Algerian regime and was seen as a slip-up by the DRS in its normally rigorous protection of its Generals from international prosecution.[4]

The second incident was the kidnap, barely two days later, of three European aid workers from the Hassi Rabuni Sahrawi refugee camp, near Tindouf in the extreme west of Algeria.[5]

The third was the emergence in December of two new jihadist groups in the region. One, called the Jamat Tawhid Wal Jihad Fi Garbi Afriqqiya (Unity Movement for Jihad in West Africa/ Mouvement pour l'Unicité du Jihad en Afrique de l'Ouest – MUJAO), came to public attention on 10 December when it sent a message to the Agence France-Presse (AFP) correspondent in Bamako claiming responsibility for the Tindouf kidnappings. The claim came two days after AQIM had delivered a statement, the authenticity of which also cannot be confirmed, to the Nouakchott Information Agency saying that it denied all responsibility for the Tindouf kidnappings. The other new jihadist group, calling itself Ansar al-Din ('the Supporters of the Faith'), announced its existence on the Mauritanian *Tawassoul* website on 15 December.[6]

Some analysts saw the first two incidents as a failure of the DRS's internal security and counterterrorism directorate, headed by General Ahmed Kherfi. Some of these analysts also saw the emergence of the two new jihadist groups as a sign of the growing assertiveness of Mauritanian and other West African and Sahelian jihadists who had been growing increasingly resentful of the Algerian domination of AQIM, especially at its leadership level. A few, who were aware of the DRS's links to AQIM's leaders, wondered if this was a sign of a weakening of DRS control or influence over AQIM in the Sahel.

These suspicions appeared to be confirmed with the announcement on 26 December that Kherfi was being replaced by General Athman Tartag.[7] The decision by General Mediène, the DRS's overall boss, to recall Tartag, known as General Bachir, one of the most ruthless hardliners of the 1990s and with the blood of many Algerians on his hands, to take over as his second in command and in charge of the DRS's internal security and counterterrorism directorate, was seen as an indication that Mediène was prepared to resort to ruthless means to stop any further haemorrhaging of DRS control.

Although Mediène's replacement of Kherfi may be related to slip-ups over Nezzar's trip to Switzerland and the security situation in the Polisario camps, I believe it had much more to do with a combination of Mediène wanting to secure his own succession, and, with Tartag beside him, to ensure that President Bouteflika's political reforms would not lead to any revival of Islamism. Mediène and Tartag were both hardline '*eradicateurs*' (of Islamists). Having tried to destroy them in the 1990s, they were not prepared to let Bouteflika allow them in through the back door. Neither do I think that there is much evidence to suggest that the DRS was losing its control over AQIM in the Sahel. On the contrary, I believe the evidence points in the exact opposite direction. That evidence comes from the way in which the DRS retained its links with and influence over the leadership of the new AQIM offshoots.

The first question to be asked of both these new jihadi groups, as well as a third led by Taleb Abdoulkrim (aka Abu Abd al-Karim al-Tariqi, Taleb Abdoulkrim le Tuareg), is whether they are genuine jihadist organisations or simply further creations of the DRS.

The least known of these groups at the moment, in terms of its leadership and composition, is MUJAO. Most journalists and bloggers who have passed comment on it have given the impression that it is an offshoot or break-away from AQIM, possibly as a result of the tension that several commentators have noted between the Algerian leadership of AQIM and its recruitment and membership in Mauritania, West Africa and other Sahelian regions. Some have even suggested a 'racial' dimension, describing MUJAO as comprising mostly Black West African/ Sahelian jihadists.

An article by Mohamed Mokeddem in *Al Ahram*/AFP just after MUJAO declared itself in December, said that MUJAO is a new offshoot of AQIM.[8] Mokeddem was described as an 'Algerian analyst'. He is, in fact, none other than Anis Rahmani, one of the DRS's most prominent media operatives. Mokeddem's words are therefore those of the DRS. The fact that he describes MUJAO in this way therefore immediately raises the question of how, not if, it is linked to the DRS.

The answer would seem to be through the personage of Sultan Ould Badi (and perhaps others). This is the same Sultan Ould Badi (also known as Abu Ali) who, as described in Chapter 17, was saved from a long prison sentence, perhaps worse, by the intervention of the DRS's General Rachid Laalali. No one person has yet been publicly associated with MUJAO's leadership, although Sultan Ould Badi, formerly of AQIM, is widely believed to have created the group, along with the Mauritanian Mohamed Ould Lamine Ould Kheirou, after his proposals for reorganising AQIM's Saharan branches were thought to have been rejected by AQIM's leadership. This fits with the general belief that it was established to overcome the tension in AQIM between the Algerian leadership and its growing Mauritanian and Sahelian membership. Although Ould Badi is known to have associations with the Polisario, probably through his DRS-linked drug trafficking business, he is a Malian, said to be half-Tuareg and half-Arab from north of Gao. The name of Baba Ould Sheikh, Mayor of Tarkint, and another prominent drug trafficker and hostage negotiator, has also been associated with MUJAO.

Ansar al-Din and Iyad ag Ghaly

The links between Ansar al-Din and Algeria's DRS are more clear-cut, for the simple reason that the leader of Ansar al-Din is none other than Iyad ag Ghaly, who, as explained in Chapter 5, has longstanding ties with Algeria's DRS.

Iyad's sudden emergence as a jihadist leader in the region raises questions about his religiosity and politics as well as his ties to both the DRS and AQIM. The fundamental question is whether his creation of Ansar al-Din is an expression of his own agency and religious beliefs, independent of the DRS, or whether he is once again being manipulated by Algeria's secret service.

The DRS's awareness of Iyad's activities stretches back over 20 years, to the time when he was the most prominent of Mali's Tuareg leaders of the 1990s rebellion. In 1988, Iyad had founded the Mouvement Populaire pour la Libération de l'Azawad (MPLA) that led the initial uprising that began at Ménaka in June 1990. When the MPLA split into three groups in 1991, Iyad led the Mouvement Populaire de l'Azawad (MPA), which was drawn predominantly from the politically dominant Ifoghas (Iforas) *taoussit* (tribe). By the time that the MPA was dissolved at the Flame of Peace ceremony at Timbuktu in 1996, Algeria's Département des Renseignements et de la Sécurité (DRS) had already identified Iyad as a key player in the region's future and possibly one that they could use to their own advantage.

However, by the end of the decade, Iyad was recognised by his own family, friends and followers as having changed. They described him, albeit jokingly, as having been 'touched by religion'. He had succumbed to the preaching of Tablighi Jama'at (Jama'at al-Tabligh) missionaries who came to Kidal in 1999.[9] When people asked his whereabouts, they would often be told jokingly that he was busy saying his prayers!

It is quite possible that the DRS recognised that Iyad's newfound religiosity would make him an ideal facilitator of the negotiations for the release of the 14 hostages taken to Mali in 2003 in that it would have given him a certain entrée with El Para and Abou Zaïd's Groupe Salafiste pour le Prédication et le Combat (GSPC) foot soldiers, who had no knowledge that their leaders were DRS agents.

Between the time of the release of El Para's hostages in 2003 and the 23 May 2006 Kidal rebellion,[10] there was widespread suspicion and rumour amongst Tuareg in Mali, Niger and Algeria that Iyad was in some way involved with Algeria's DRS and that the DRS satisfied his increasingly noticeable 'love for money', as many Tuareg described it to me. Indeed, one reason why the 23 May rebellion received little support outside Iyad's immediate group was because other Tuareg leaders were already suspicious of his dealings with the DRS. And they were right. As described in Chapter 5, the Algerians used the rebellion to oust Gaddafi from the region, while the US availed itself of Iyad's fighters to conduct the September–October 2006 raids that were used to ramp up the propaganda on terrorism in the Sahara-Sahel region and which effectively underpinned the GSPC name change to AQIM.[11]

With the start of a new rebellion amongst Mali's Tuareg population in 2007,[12] Mali's President, Amadou Toumani Touré (ATT), realised that the region might be more manageable if Iyad was not in it. On 21 November 2007, ATT accordingly appointed him as Consul General to Saudi Arabia and dispatched him to Jeddah. Although we know little of what Iyad got up to in the Kingdom of Saud, it appears that he furthered his religious interests, this time gravitating from the pacificism of the Tablighi Jama'at to the jihadist Salafism of more radical sects. Indeed, it is strongly rumoured that his premature return to Mali was the result of a deportation order from Saudi Arabia for alleged subversive activities.

Iyad's return from Saudi Arabia has been marked by his increasing involvement and association with AQIM. However, the basis of this association is still largely conjectural. Is it attributable to his earlier links with the DRS or his religious radicalisation in Saudi Arabia, or a combination of both? Similarly, what is the precise nature of the apparent AQIM–DRS– Iyad triangulation? Indeed, is Iyad aware of the relationship between AQIM's leaders and the DRS and their involvement in the Oued Tamouret training camp? Or, does he believe that AQIM in the Sahel is a genuine jihadist-Salafist organisation, quite independent of Algeria's DRS? What we know of the relationship between Iyad and AQIM, especially with Abdelhamid abou Zaïd's brigade, makes it very difficult to believe how Iyad could not be aware of the fact that

Abou Zaïd is a DRS operative. Indeed, since Iyad's return from Jeddah, his relationship with AQIM has formed a distinct pattern.

This pattern has two dimensions. One is that Iyad is part of what appears to be a network of negotiators, appointed by the Malian President, ATT, to negotiate the release of western hostages held by AQIM. Other known negotiators are Baba Ould Sheikh, now linked with MUJAO, and Mustapha Ould Limam Chafi,[13] who is closely involved with Burkina Faso's President Blaise Campaoré. Chafi is believed to be closely linked to MBM. These three, Iyad, Baba and Chafi, have been involved in negotiating the release of almost all the Western hostages held by AQIM since 2008 and are believed to have enriched themselves substantially by taking a share of the ransom.

Cousin Abdoulkrim (Hamada ag Hama)

Iyad, however, appears to have become more than just a 'negotiator'. Through his relationship with Taleb Abdoulkrim, who, as I explained in Chapter 14, was involved in the kidnap and death of Michel Germaneau, Iyad seems to have got more closely involved with both kidnapping and AQIM.

The name of Taleb ('preacher') Abdoulkrim[14] first appeared in the media in April 2010 when the French authorities received information from an unidentified security source in Niger, via the Quai d'Orsay, that a certain Taleb Abdoulkrim was responsible for the kidnap of the Frenchman Michel Germaneau on 20 April.[15] The gist of this report was that Germaneau had been taken by Taleb Abdoulkrim's men; that Abdoulkrim was the name of the chief of a group that claimed to be inspired by AQIM, but that it had never before taken a hostage; that Taleb Abdoulkrim led the mosque at In Halil and that his sermons preached violence in the name of the supremacy of Islam. These reports did not specify whether Abdoulkrim would handle the negotiations for Germaneau's release or whether he would be passed on to AQIM's Abou Zaïd, as appears to have been the case. The most detailed report on Abdoulkrim was written by the DRS-linked journalist Salima Tlemçani. Her report provided details of Abdoulkrim's route, as well as sightings of his group, which could only have come from inside knowledge or agents on the ground.[16]

Abdoulkrim, or 'Le Tuareg', as the Algerians had now named him, next came to prominence in August 2010 when Algerian sources, clearly the DRS, alleged that on 24–25 August he had executed an Algerian customs official who had been taken hostage following an AQIM attack on Algerian border forces near Tin Zaouatene in June.[17]

The reference to In Halil led me on a blind chase. As I was unable to find any trace of anyone called Taleb Abdoulkrim in the In Halil region, I began to think that he might be just another of the DRS's many phantom identities. Indeed, an article in *Le Monde*, which queried whether his name was in fact real, was clearly thinking on the same lines.[18] However, by late 2011, I was receiving confirmation from a number of sources that Abdoulkrim was not only real, but none other than Iyad's first cousin, his proper name being Hamada ag Hama.[19]

The picture being established was that Abdoulkrim was operating as some sort of 'field officer' for Iyad, his key link with AQIM and Abou Zaïd, and perhaps also with Yahia Djouadi and MBM. Indeed, by 2012, I was picking up references to the Abu Abd al-Karim al-Tariqi group as a separate AQIM unit in the region. I was also soon to learn that Iyad himself had also been given the *nom de guerre* of Abou El Fadl (Abu Fadhil) by AQIM. It was becoming evident that Iyad was moving closer to AQIM. If Iyad was not associated with AQIM's activities directly, then his association with AQIM was through his cousin Hamada ag Hama (Abdoulkrim).

This new information and perspective on the relationship between AQIM, Iyad and the DRS raises a number of crucially important questions, the most serious of which was, and still is: what is the nature of the relationships between Iyad ag Ghaly, Taleb Abdoulkrim, AQIM and the DRS? There is also the question of whether the Americans, who have a contingent of AFRICOM (US Africa Command) forces at Gao and information-gathering facilities at Aguelhok (at least until the beginning of 2012), are not only aware of how much Iyad helped their cause in 2006 but also how his links with both AQIM and the DRS have become, since late 2011 and the start of a new Tuareg rebellion in January 2012, integral to our understanding of all that is currently (mid 2012) taking place in northern Mali, or Azawad as it was to become known in 2012.

The Hombori and Timbuktu Hostage-Takings

In the space of less than 24 hours, on 24 November 2011, six Europeans were seized and taken hostage in Mali, with one of them shot dead. At 1.00 a.m., two Frenchmen, allegedly geologists but with connections to the security sector, were kidnapped by heavily armed gunmen from their hotel at Hombori, a small town on the main road from Mopti to Gao in eastern Mali, some 60 kilometres north of the Burkina Faso border. Later in the day, gunmen drove into the main square of Timbuktu and, in the first ever attack on Westerners in the city, seized four tourists at gunpoint – a German, a Swede, a Dutchman and a South African – from a restaurant in the centre of Timbuktu. The elderly German, who resisted, was shot dead. The remaining three were bundled into the kidnappers' vehicles and rushed out of town.[20]

The two attacks bore the signs of a new phase in terrorism in the region. Both local and Western intelligence services, along with their media, jumped immediately to the conclusion, without any evidence, that the attacks had been undertaken by AQIM, even though the initial indications suggested that the Hombori attackers, who were heard to speak Tamashek, were almost certainly Tuareg. Some of the earlier reports from Timbuktu also indicated that those kidnappers were also Tuareg, although local informants later insisted to me that they were Berabich. Other sources in the region suggested that the Tuareg kidnappers might have been returnees from Libya whose motive was revenge against France and NATO (North Atlantic Treaty Organisation) for the toppling of Gaddafi. Others suggested that the kidnappings marked a new phase of Tuareg unrest in Mali and was intended to damage the government.

On 8 December, the Nouakchott News Agency (ANI) and the AFP office in Rabat received communiqués in which AQIM claimed responsibility for the kidnappings. These reports were misleading: although the hostages may have been in the hands of AQIM, local sources indicated that it was not AQIM that had undertaken the kidnappings. Before AQIM claimed responsibility, I had already received information from sources in the region suggesting strongly that the Hombori kidnappers were Tuareg and that Iyad ag Ghaly had visited the hostages 'in the camp of the Salafistes' to ensure their safety. Similar information indicated that the Timbuktu hostages had been passed up to AQIM's Yahia Djouadi by their Berabich kidnappers. On the same day as AQIM made its claim, the Malian authorities arrested four suspects accused of kidnapping the two Frenchmen. According to the authorities, the kidnappers had apparently discarded a 'pay-as-you-go' cell phone card at the hotel where the Frenchmen were staying, which led to their identification. However, their arrest was not announced until 12 December, four days after their capture, with their identities not being revealed until 13 December.

According to the Mali authorities, three of them were local Tuareg, well known in Kidal. According to local sources, two of them, Hamad Ali ag Wadossène and Heiba ag Acherif, and possibly the third, were well known in Kidal. The same sources thought that Heiba ag Acherif was related to the late Sidi Mohamed ag Acherif (d. August 2010) and Lieutenant Colonel Ibrahim ag Acherif (d. April 2006),[21] both of whom were very close to Iyad. Indeed, it was 'Merzouk' who was central to the September 2006 'deal' between Iyad and the Algerians and the US described in Chapter 5. If this is true, then it suggests that Iyad might be closer to the kidnappings than merely ensuring the safety of the hostages. Indeed, this was given some degree of confirmation on 7 December when *Ennahar*, an Algerian newspaper closely linked to the DRS, reported Malian security sources as saying that the Hombori kidnapping had been undertaken by 'the men of Abdelkrim, head of a branch of AQIM'.[22]

The fact that Iyad announced his creation of Ansar al-Din just two days after the Malian authorities had revealed the identities of the suspected kidnappers, suggests that Ansar al-Din was Iyad's response to being linked, either directly or through Abdoulkrim, to the Hombori kidnappings. While that may have been the case, Iyad's involvement in the kidnappings had been suspected some three weeks earlier: on 27 November, the French newspaper *Le Journal du Dimanche*, citing unnamed security experts in Niamey, blamed the kidnappings on 'the terrorist group being led by former diplomat and President[ial] negotiator Iyad Ag Ghali'.[23] There were suspicions earlier in that same week that Iyad may have been planning to move against the government when he was seen leaving Kidal with his men on 23 November to join up with an estimated 2,000 fighting men, most of whom had recently returned from Libya, who were gathered in the Abeïbara region, east-north-east of Kidal.

Rebellion and the Aguelhok Executions

The precise number of Tuareg fighters who returned from Libya to Mali is not known. Estimates range between 1,000 and 4,000, with the likely number being towards the lower end of the range. The majority of these veteran fighters were under the leadership of Mohamed ag Najim (Nagim), a former Colonel in Gaddafi's army. A smaller contingent, who had recently fought at Bani Walid, one of the last redoubts of Gaddafi loyalists, were led by another of Gaddafi's Tuareg Colonels, Awanz ag Amakadaye.

Most of these returning, battle-ready fighters stopped short of Kidal in the mountainous region around Ti-n-Asselak in the Abeïbara district, some 130 kilometres from Kidal, where they linked up with many of the former rebel fighters of Ibrahim ag Bahanga's Mouvement Touareg du Nord Mali (MTNM).[24] On 16 October, these and various other groups merged to form the Mouvement National de Libération de l'Azawad (MNLA). The MNLA's first press statement said that 'This new organisation aims to free the people of Azawad from the illegal occupation of its territory by Mali.'[25]

By early December, many people, including the diplomatic corps in Bamako, were anticipating imminent skirmishes. The first shots, which marked the beginning of this new Tuareg rebellion, were fired on 17 January when a group of Tuareg rebels attacked the town of Ménaka. On the following day, MNLA forces attacked both Aguelhok and Tessalit. The outcome of these three engagements is still not entirely clear as the reports from the Mali government and the MNLA were totally contradictory. Within the next three weeks, the MNLA undertook further attacks on the towns of Anderamboukane and Léré (26 January), Niafounké (4 February) and Tin Zaouatene (8 February). At Tin Zaouatene, a substantial contingent of Mali forces were driven out of the town and forced to take refuge in Algeria.

By mid March, the UN's Office for the Coordination of Humanitarian Affairs (OCHA) had reported that 195,000 people had fled their homes in Mali since mid January, with about half of them fleeing to neighbouring countries. The number had risen by 50,000 since 24 February. This human catastrophe was to get much worse.

However, notwithstanding what may still happen before this rebellion is over, there are fundamental questions that have to be addressed and answered before there can be any serious attempts at resolution. One relates to what happened at the village of Aguelhok on 24 January.

The outcome of the MNLA's first assault on the army bases at the two Tilemsi valley towns of Aguelhok and Tessalit that began at dawn on 18 January was unclear, with both sides giving wildly divergent accounts. The army claimed to have lost two soldiers while killing 45 rebels. The MNLA denied such losses and claimed to have killed many more government soldiers.

After a lull of three or four days, the MNLA launched a second assault on Aguelhok on Tuesday January 24. What happened on that day must be the focus of an international inquiry. Reports from both civilian and military sources stated that the army forces at Aguelhok ran out of ammunition and were overwhelmed. A Malian security source in Bamako told Reuters that dozens of Malian troops were killed. 'It was real carnage', he said. 'Dozens of dead and several vehicles were burnt … This is a turning point in the conflict', he continued, adding that after being pushed back the previous week, the rebels returned with reinforcements, with the army, which ran out of ammunition, being forced to abandon its positions in Aguelhok. An MNLA spokesman confirmed that at least 50 soldiers were killed in the fighting.[26]

What happened during the course of the next few days, especially in the capital, Bamako, some 1,000 miles from Aguelhok, can be best described as a state of confusion and anger. News of the Aguelhok slaughter sent angry demonstrators into the streets of the capital demanding to know why their menfolk had been sent into battle so unprepared. Their anger was directed at the government and army.

News of the army's debacle at Aguelhok was almost immediately punctuated with rumours that dozens of the soldiers, perhaps as many as a hundred, had been taken captive by the Tuareg rebels and then executed in cold blood, either with a bullet to the head or by slitting their throats. With demonstrators in the streets, the government sought to turn people's anger against the Tuareg by directing a black propaganda campaign against the MNLA. The core of the campaign was the posting of explicit photographs of dead soldiers, the authenticity of which could not be established, on Facebook and the internet. Hostility towards the Tuareg was whipped up further when an announcement from the Defence Ministry on Thursday 26 January stated that the Aguelhok assault had been carried out by 'AQIM jihadis, MNLA forces and others'. The next day, the government publicly reiterated the statement, accusing the Tuareg rebels of joining forces with AQIM and attacking Aguelhok.[27] This was the first time an official connection had been made between AQIM and the Tuareg rebels. It was denied adamantly by MNLA spokesmen.

On 2 February, after a week of government propaganda, mob violence, directed at Tuareg and anyone who appeared 'light-skinned' or was suspected of being from the north, took hold of Bamako. The violence started in the small military town of Kati, just north of Bamako, where people spilled out of the barracks and began attacking and looting Tuareg homes. Within a matter of hours, almost all Tuareg, Arabs and other northerners had left the capital, its environs and other main towns in the south and were fleeing from Mali.

Whether the Mali government's motive in linking the alleged executions at Aguelhok to AQIM was to divert attention from its own military incompetence or to get more support from the US, France and other Western countries, or both, is largely immaterial. By mid February, the Malian government had succeeded in revamping its inept defence against MNLA rebels into a campaign against what it called 'Al Qaeda-linked Tuareg terrorists', for which Western countries, and not least the US, were prepared to provide logistical military support.

On 13 February, Colonel Idrissa Traoré, head of the Malian army's information service, re-confirmed that both soldiers and civilians had been executed at Aguelhok on 24 January, some with their throats cut, and that these acts could only have been done by AQIM.[28] Speaking earlier the same day, French Development Minister Henri de Raincourt, who had visited Bamako on 9 February, told RFI (Radio France Internationale) that 'there was absolutely atrocious and unacceptable violence in Aguelhok. There were summary executions of soldiers and civilians ...' 'There's talk of around 100 who were captured and killed in cold blood', he added, saying the tactic 'resembled that used by Al-Qaeda'.[29]

Whereas Traoré said he did not know the exact number of soldiers killed, putting the number of dead at 'about 60', a source close to the matter and citing Malian official sources told AFP that 'In total there were exactly 82 deaths, no civilians.' An officer involved in burying those killed told AFP that he had counted 97 dead soldiers and seen a military camp 'completely destroyed'.[30]

In spite of the assertions by the Malian government, its military and its allies, the proffered evidence for such executions consisted of little more than statements from Malian government and army officials and photographs whose authenticity remains in doubt. Photographs placed on Facebook and the internet by Malian government 'supporters' in the last week of January were quickly removed. However, five of them remained accessible. One was soon indentified by the MNLA as being of a massacre undertaken by Boko Haram in Nigeria on 2 March 2010. This photograph was included in a widely circulated pro-Malian government video posted on YouTube on 16 February under the title 'Les Meurtres du Mouvement national de liberation de l'azawad MNLA: les meurtres et assassinats commisent par le MNLA le 24 janvier 2012 à Aguel'hoc, avec des Salafistes de Iyad ag Ghali' ('The murders of the National Liberation Movement of Azawad, MNLA: the murders and assassinations committed by the MNLA on 24 January 2012 at Aguel'hoc [Aguelhok], with the Salafists of Iyad ag Ghaly').[31] The authenticity of the other four photographs has not yet been established: they may be from Aguelhok or, like the identified photo, from some other time or location. The MNLA's communications officer confirmed that the four photographs were not of Aguelhok, while international news agencies, for their part, remained suspicious of their authenticity.[32]

If soldiers were captured at Aguelhok and then executed, as the Malian government claims, then we are talking about a war crime, which must be investigated. Such an investigation requires the exhumation and forensic examination of the bodies by a credible international agency to determine their cause of death. Until that investigation has been undertaken, the executions must remain unproven allegations.

However, if we accept, for the time being, that a war crime was perpetrated at Aguelhok, the question is: who was responsible for it?

The MNLA's emphatic denial that it conducted any such executions is supported by statements acquired from villagers themselves. According to these Aguelhok residents, the MNLA attacked Aguelhok on 24 January and killed only soldiers in the fighting. The next day, people whom the villagers identified as AQIM came and carried out the massacre. The MNLA returned three days later and raised their flag over Aguelhok.

In spite of these statements, which are known to the Malian authorities, the Malian government, as well as Mauritania's President Abdel Aziz, have continued to accuse the MNLA of being in an alliance with AQIM and insist that the executions are proof of this alliance. This accusation seems to have gained some support amongst French, US and other Western agencies. However, as Tuareg are not known to slit throats as a form of killing humans or to kill their captives in cold blood, the accusation is directed more at the AQIM part of the supposed MNLA–AQIM alliance, with Iyad ag Ghaly's name increasingly being mentioned. Indeed, the video mentioned above, along with Mauritania's President Abdel Aziz[33] and a number of reports attributed to Malian official sources, have all pointed the finger at Iyad.

If Iyad and his new jihadist group, the Ansar al-Din, were involved in the alleged executions, then a number of other rather serious questions are raised. The first, of course, is whether Iyad was operating on his own initiative or whether he was tied up in some way with either or both Algeria's DRS and Abdelhamid abou Zaïd's group of AQIM, which is known to be based in the Tigharghar mountains close to Aguelhok.

If Abou Zaïd and AQIM, either independently or in association with Iyad, were responsible for the alleged executions, as the villagers' statements suggest, then Algeria's DRS immediately becomes implicated. This is because Abou Zaïd is a senior DRS operative. Abou Zaïd is not only AQIM's top emir in the Sahel, but he was in charge of AQIM's main training camp at Oued Tamouret in southern Algeria. That camp, described in Chapter 13, was under the direct control of the Algerian army and the DRS. It was there that AQIM's foot soldiers were trained in throat-slitting, or, as they call it in Arabic, *al-mawt al batii'* ('the slow death').

These connections pose a problem for Iyad. No matter how hard he and his followers may insist that he is not involved with the DRS, he has, in fact, been associated with them for a long time. He was 'used' by the DRS in its 2003 hostage-takings. As described in Chapter 5, he was central to the Algerian-US scheming that lay behind both the 23 May 2006 rebellion and two false-flag 'terrorist' incidents contrived in northern Mali by the US and the DRS in September–October 2006. He has also been close to Abou Zaïd since the latter's return to northern Mali around 2008, both through negotiating the release of hostages held by AQIM and through the activities of his cousin Abdoulkrim (Hamada ag Hama).

The linkage of the alleged Aguelhok executions to AQIM and the DRS raises two further questions. The first is: what was the Algerian army doing in Aguelhok? Algerian armed forces crossed into Mali on 20 December. While the Algerian government eventually admitted that 15 military instructors had been sent to Mali, local observers reported an Algerian army convoy of five army trucks with trailers and 24 heavily armed 4WDs heading south on the Bordj Mokhtar–Tessalit–Aguelhok road. The number of troops was not given, but can be assumed at around 200. The same sources confirmed that Algerian troops were garrisoned at the army bases in both Tessalit and Aguelhok. In addition, an army transporter was seen flying into Kidal. It contained an unspecified number of Algerian army officers and was reportedly 'heavily armed'.

What were these troops doing in Aguelhok and had they been withdrawn to Algeria by the time of the alleged executions? A high-ranking Algerian military officer confirmed that 'Algerian troops are currently stationed in northern Mali to assist the Malian army in the fight against terrorism.'[34] That, however, was untrue, as no attacks have been launched at any time against AQIM in Mali by either Malian or Algerian forces. All the signs are that the Algerian army's presence at Tessalit, Aguelhok and Kidal was not to help Mali fight AQIM, but rather to protect AQIM from any assault on it by the MNLA, which has threatened to rid Mali of AQIM.

Indeed, it is clear that while Mali's government has been prepared to contract Russian and/or Ukrainian pilots to fly its helicopter gunships to strafe and bomb both the MNLA and Tuareg civilians, to sacrifice its soldiers and to use the logistical support of the US, France and Algeria to fight its own Tuareg peoples, it has been noticeably reluctant to undertake any meaningful attacks on the AQIM bases that are a metaphorical stone's-throw from Tessalit and Aguelhok. The explanation for this, according to the MNLA is simple: AQIM is protected by both Algeria and Mali, and their Western allies, because AQIM is a cover for the massive, billion-dollar, cocaine-trafficking business which is controlled by elements of the political-military elites and their security services in both Mali and Algeria. Indeed, if Mali was not such a close client state of Washington, it is likely that it would already have been labelled a 'narco-state'.

The MNLA threat to AQIM was evidenced on the night of Saturday 4 February when an MNLA patrol came across an AQIM camp of Abdelhamid abou Zaïd in the Tigharghar mountains and opened fire on it. Under the cover of darkness and the chaos of a three-hour skirmish, two of the French AREVA hostages being held in the camp escaped. However, they were recaptured the next day. Local sources in Aguelhok told me that AQIM came to the village at first light and offered large sums of money for their recapture. [35] News of this story broke in the media on 1 March.[36] A week later, a brief news item in the Algerian state-controlled daily newspaper *Echorouk* stated that AQIM had moved its base camp from Mali to 90 kilometres north of Timaiouine in southern Algeria.[37] If this report was true, and it would not have been published without the green light from the DRS, it is evidence of the protection afforded AQIM by Algeria's DRS: the area immediately surrounding Timaiouine is effectively a 'military zone'.

The second question raised by the linkage of the alleged Aguelhok executions to AQIM concerns the matter of complicity. The line of reasoning is as follows. If Abou Zaïd and AQIM were involved in executions at Aguelhok, then the DRS is also implicated. That raises the question of whether the DRS's allies and backers, namely the US and the UK, may also be deemed complicit. Although that may seem far-fetched, especially to those not aware of the closeness of the relationship between the DRS and both the US and the UK authorities, the reality of the situation is not very hard to grasp. It is that the US has colluded with the DRS in false-flag and fabricated terrorism in the Sahara-Sahel region since 2002, while the UK became an active party in that relationship in 2009, if not earlier, following Abou Zaïd's execution of the British hostage Edwin Dyer. Not only are US and British intelligence services aware of the DRS's AQIM training camp at Tamouret, but the UK, in a policy decision that it is likely to regret, now provides training to the DRS.

Thus, if AQIM did execute Malian soldiers at Aguelhok as the Malian government claims, then it is likely that the persons who undertook the executions were under or closely associated with Abou Zaïd's command and almost certainly trained in such black arts at the DRS-managed Tamouret training camp. If an international inquiry into the alleged Aguelhok executions were to establish such a chain, then the question becomes one of how far the DRS's Western allies, notably the UK and the US, might also be held accountable. That question inevitably leads into all that has been raised, explained and exposed in this book, and possibly a lot more. That is why calls for a full investigation into what took place at Aguelhok are likely to fall on stony ground.

20

PREPARING FOR THE 'LONG WAR'

Mali's Coup D'état and the Independence of Azawad

The start of this latest Tuareg rebellion is a fitting end to this book and a fitting epitaph to a decade of US policy, which, aided and abetted – at least in part – by Washington's European allies and regional client states, has reduced this vast tract of Africa to a human catastrophe.

This chapter was completed in mid March, 2012. I wrote then that although it was the end of the book, it was by no means the end of the story. The region, I remarked, was about to 'change gear'. Now, in mid June, and with the typescript already in the hands of the copy-editor, that gear-change has taken place. The publisher, Pluto Press, has therefore kindly allowed me to withdraw this last chapter and rewrite it, or at least add in a brief summary of events, by way of an epilogue, in an attempt to update and question what has happened in Mali in these last three extraordinary months (March–June) and with an eye on what the future may behold. Such questions will, at least, pave the way for what I suspect may well become a third volume on the disastrous outcome of Washington's post-9/11 foreign policy in North and West Africa in what the Obama administration now prefers to call the 'Long War'.

By mid March, there were clear signs that the MNLA (Mouvement National de Libération de l'Azawad) was more than a match for Mali's army. For several weeks, there had been heavy fighting around the town of Tessalit, whose Amachach army base and airport, less than 100 miles from the Algerian border, are important strategic locations. On 6 March, Reuters confirmed that three army units, after many days of fighting, had failed to relieve the Amachach base and had been forced to retreat to Anefis, 300 kilometres to the south.[1] Their casualties, in terms of men killed, wounded and deserted, and equipment destroyed or captured, was not revealed. Then, on 11 March, the army confirmed that its troops besieged at Tessalit had fled to Bordj Mokhtar in Algeria, leaving the base and the airport in MNLA hands.

Even before this humiliating defeat, the Malian army had lost control of about half of the Azawad region. Algerian media sources estimated that at least 500 Malian troops had been killed, taken captive or had deserted. By the time Tessalit fell, that number was thought to have risen to well over 1,000. For the civilian population, the rebellion had become an even greater nightmare. Relief agencies in Niger, Burkina Faso, Mauritania and Algeria struggled to cope with the increasing number of refugees, which by mid June reportedly numbered around 350,000.

With Tessalit's base and airport in MNLA hands and the Malian army in clear disarray, there were fears that the government might switch to attacking the highly vulnerable civilian population. There had already been reports of Mali's Russian- or Ukrainian-piloted[2] helicopter gunships firing on encampments near Kidal, while rumours spread that the government would let loose the Ganda Koy and Gandaïzo militia,[3] as it had done in previous Tuareg rebellions.

By early March, there were rumours of fissions within Malian government circles. The casual attitude of the government towards the Libyan returnees, the slowness of its response to the rebellion, the lack of any clear military or political strategy and the subsequent military set-backs were drawing increasing criticism. Anxiety in government and civilian circles was being heightened by the ease with which the MNLA had launched attacks as far south as the Mopti and Ségou regions, little more than 200 kilometres from the capital. There were even rumours that the military based in Gao, whose commander was allegedly involved in cocaine trafficking, might attempt a coup d'état.

As it was, the coup came not from Gao, but from an army mutiny in Bamako on 22 March led by Captain Amadou Sanogo. The army's humiliation at the hands of the rebels, which was the result of its ill-preparedness and incompetent leadership, along with the complete lack of political will by the Bamako government to face up to the problems caused by the return of Tuareg fighters from Libya, led to an army mutiny and an effective coup d'état by junior army officers led by Sanogo.

Sanogo's overthrow of the government in Bamako coincided with the MNLA's takeover of the strategic Anefis garrison north of Gao and the encirclement of the regional capital of Kidal. The military situation at Kidal was shrouded in uncertainty for several days, partly because Iyad ag Ghaly claimed to have occupied the town before it actually fell, but also because negotiations between the MNLA and the military commander at Kidal, Alhadji (El Hadj) ag Gamou, went on for several days. Ag Gamou (himself a Tuareg) eventually defected to the MNLA on 28 March, only to abandon the rebels two days later and take his 500 or so men across the border into the relative safety of Niger.

On 29 March, the rebels headed south to Gao. The nearby towns of Ansongo and Bourem fell to them with little or no fighting, and on 30 March they entered Gao. Mali's troops undertook a 'strategic withdrawal', while local militias put up little resistance. Timbuktu fell to the rebels the next day, with the army, after reports of some heavy incoming fire, making another 'strategic withdrawal'.

On 1 April, the MNLA took over Timbuktu, thus placing the whole of Azawad, including the three regional capitals of Kidal, Gao and Timbuktu, in rebel hands. None of these towns had ever been captured in previous Tuareg rebellions. Mali, was now a divided country.

On 3 April, the AQIM's three emirs, Abdelhamid abou Zaïd, Yahia Djouadi (Abou Al-Hammam) and Mokhtar ben Mokhtar (MBM), met with Iyad ag Ghaly in Timbuktu. Confused reports suggested that the MNLA had effectively been driven out of Timbuktu by AQIM and Ansar al-Din, who had ensconced themselves in the vacated army base. By evening, there were reports of Iyad already imposing shari'a law on the town.

In Paris, Foreign Minister Alain Juppé confirmed that Ansar al-Din was closely linked to AQIM and that France was encouraging the UN to mobilise against AQIM's threat to turn the whole of Mali into an Islamist state. Juppé called for a joint regional response from Algeria, Mauritania and the West African states, helped by France and the EU, to block the Islamist threat.

Three days later, on 6 April, the MNLA proclaimed the Independence of Azawad.[4] The statement stressed the MNLA's 'firm commitment to create the conditions for lasting peace [and] to initiate the institutional foundations for a state based on a democratic constitution for an independent Azawad'.

The MNLA's move was immediately questioned by Ansar al-Din, which claimed to be against Independence but in favour of 'a holy war ... a legal war in the name of Islam'.[5] While some lawyers and academics claimed that the lack of a constitutional government in Bamako gave the Tuareg some legal basis for the Independence of their state, their declaration of Independence was wholly condemned on the international front.

An 'Islamist Terror'

The international media paid little attention to the legalities or merits of the Independence declaration. Rather, it focused its reports on the looting, violence and atrocities of the emerging 'Islamist terror' that seemed to be accompanying Ansar al-Din's imposition of shari'a law. It was not the MNLA's flag that appeared over the towns of Kidal, Gao and Timbuktu, but the black Salafist flag of Ansar al-Din.

Throughout April and May, reports of chaos, anarchy and human suffering flooded the international media. Each day brought new reports of seemingly more horrific examples of Iyad's imposition of supposed shari'a law and the seeming inability of the MNLA to do anything about it. Indeed, the relationship between the MNLA and Ansar al-Din was becoming increasingly perplexing.[6] While the MNLA made lame statements about being opposed to the excesses of Iyad's Ansar al-Din, all the signs pointed to the fact that political and military power had effectively shifted from the MNLA to Ansar al-Din and the Islamists. The picture was one of Iyad and his Ansar al-Din literally laying down the law in Timbuktu, Gao and Kidal as the MNLA stood impotently aside. Iyad, who proclaimed himself, at least for a short while, as the President of Azawad, even went so far as to appoint AQIM's Yahia Djouadi, now calling himself Jemel Okacha (Oukacha), as *wali* (governor) of Timbuktu.

However, while the international media and countless self-proclaimed 'experts' warned of northern Mali and much of the Sahel being turned into the 'next Afghanistan' or 'a Somalia', and a launch-pad for Islamist terrorism, they singularly failed to address a number of key questions.

Throughout this period, two issues have been studiously avoided by the media. One is that almost all parties involved in Azawad have interests in the cocaine trafficking that has turned the region into the main hub in the trafficking of cocaine from Latin America to Europe. The second is that leaders of all the Islamist groups in Azawad are agents, operatives or associates of Algeria's DRS.

The disinclination of the media to raise these two facts is not borne from ignorance. On the contrary, in the two months since the declaration of Azawad's Independence, I have given interviews to approximately four dozen media organisations in which I have given detailed information about these two issues. While there have been occasional, largely superficial references to drug trafficking, there has been absolutely no mention, even in the form of a question, of the relationship between the Islamist groups in Azawad and Algeria's Département du Renseignement et de la Sécurité (DRS). It is as if the subject, as it was in the case of my commissioned report to the EU, is taboo.

The precise amount of cocaine passing through Mali and the Azawad region is not known. Neither do we know the details of all those involved in its trafficking. Current estimates reckon that the street value of cocaine passing through the region is between $8 billion and $10 billion a year.[7] We also know that many of the more prominent dignitaries in Azawad, as well as the main groups involved in the current struggle for the region's control, all have vested interests in the trafficking. So too do senior elements of Algeria's DRS and, at least until the coup d'état of 22 March, the head of Malian state security and many of the army's Generals and senior officers.[8]

Algeria's Involvement in Azawad

As for Algeria's involvement in Azawad, all the Islamist groups in the region, namely al-Qaeda in the Islamic Maghreb (AQIM), the Mouvement pour l'Unicité du Jihad en Afrique de l'Ouest (MUJAO) and Ansar al-Din, as well as Taleb Abdoulkrim's group, as this volume has revealed, are associated in one way or another with the DRS. This, of course, raises enormously serious questions. For instance, on 6 April, the same day as MNLA's declaration of Azawad Independence, the Algerian Consul in Gao, Boualem Sias, and six of his staff were kidnapped from their Consulate. Local people said the kidnappers were members of MUJAO. Indeed, it was MUJAO who subsequently claimed responsibility for the kidnap and demanded a €15 million ransom for their release. Reliable sources in Algiers have confirmed to me that Sias is a DRS Colonel.[9] We also know that Sultan Ould Badi, a renowned drug-trafficker protected by the head of the DRS's external security service, has been reported to be a MUJAO leader. Does this mean that the DRS has staged the kidnapping of its own people and, if so, for what purpose? To further damage the reputation of the MNLA? To legitimise an Algerian military intervention, should it be deemed necessary? To further promote the reputation of MUJAO as a 'terrorist' group?

Fabricating false-flag terrorism incidents, such as staged hostage-takings, are a DRS specialty, as both this volume and *The Dark Sahara* have revealed. Indeed, to add to these suspicions, local witnesses have said that they heard the kidnappers speaking 'Algerian Arabic'. This claim would support many other local witness statements which have said that both AQIM's and Ansar al-Din's men are mainly Algerians. We already know that most of AQIM's members are Algerians. Ansar al-Din's 70 or so members at the time of its creation in December were not Algerians, but Tuareg from the Kidal region who speak Tamashek and not Arabic. Since then, however, Ansar al-Din's number are said to have risen to about 500 and his vehicles from about 10 to 200. Where have the additional 400 or more men come from? There have been media reports that he has recruited child soldiers; there are also reports that he is 'buying' recruits at €5,000 a time. It is also apparent that some MNLA have swapped sides and joined him, as have members of other groups, no doubt. But it is difficult to see how he could have increased the size of Ansar al-Din this much in such a short time by these means. Reliable evidence from France's military intelligence[10] and local Tuareg informants[11] points to his receiving support from Algeria, either directly from the DRS or by 'secondment' from AQIM.

It is almost certainly this infusion of Algerians into Ansar al-Din's ranks that explains why there have been so many reports of local people hearing Arabic rather than the Tuareg language, Tamashek, being spoken by Ansar al-Din's fighters. For instance, on the evening of 26 May, MNLA and Ansar al-Din signed an agreement in Gao to fuse their movements and work together to create an independent Islamic state in the region of Azawad. Alghabass ag Intallah, one of the leaders of Ansar al-Din, was widely reported in the media as saying: 'I have just signed an accord that will see an independent and Islamic state where we have Islamic law.'[12] Two days later, both sides confirmed that the deal had collapsed, at least for the time being. Some local sources present at the negotiations suggested that one reason for the collapse was because some of Ansar al-Din only spoke Arabic and could not understand the Tamashek spoken by MNLA members.

There is also widespread evidence from local people who claim to have seen logistical support from Algeria, notably in the form of fuel, crossing the Algerian-Malian border, in spite of claims by Algeria that the border is closed. Such evidence challenges the veracity of the information being disseminated by Algeria regarding the Islamist groups on both sides of the border. For instance, a suicide car-bomb detonated in the headquarters of the gendarmerie in Tamanrasset on 3 March, wounding at least 23 people, is officially attributed to MUJAO. Almost immediately after the bombing, the Agence France-Presse (AFP) office in Bamako (Mali) received a message from MUJAO claiming responsibility for the bombing. Algeria's security services also stated that MUJAO was responsible. The truth may be rather different: local sources[13] in Tamanrasset believe the bombing was not a 'terrorist' attack but a settling of scores between the DRS and the gendarmerie. Rogue elements in the DRS are involved in the cocaine trafficking from Mali and the gendarmerie is believed to have overstepped the mark in fulfilling its proper duties.

Similarly, on 30 April, the Algerian daily newspaper *El Khabar*, which is close to the security services, reported that Algerian security forces had the previous day killed 20 members of MUJAO who were allegedly about to attack two fuel tankers near the Malian border. The tankers were carrying fuel from Tamanrasset to Tin Zaouatene. The report said that the militants were attacked just before they were allegedly about to attack the fuel tankers. The incident may conceivably have occurred, although there is no verification from local sources, as might be expected in a case of 20 deaths. As it is, the only 'proof' we have of this incident is *El Khabar*'s citation of Algeria's security services, which, as the evidence of this book makes abundantly clear, are not known for their veracity.[14]

What are Algeria's motives in Mali? Clues to the answer(s) are found throughout the preceding chapters. In addition to those, however, there is no doubt that Algeria was genuinely concerned about the possibility, indeed likelihood, of a major upsurge of Tuareg nationalism in the Sahel, especially Mali, in the wake of Gaddafi's overthrow. Algeria could not have easily foreseen the impact of the Libyan revolution on the Sahel. Similarly, while it had played no small part in undermining the Mali regime and contributing to its rottenness, it could not have foreseen the speed and ease with which it would be overthrown. For reasons which have rarely made much sense, Algeria has been concerned, ever since its Independence from France in 1962, about what it has frequently referred to as the 'Tuareg problem', although without ever defining what the 'problem' was. Aside from all its own propaganda, pumped up by the US, about the flood of weaponry being trafficked from Libya to al-Qaeda in the Sahel, the Algerian regime was genuinely alarmed by the very real prospect of a strong Tuareg nationalist movement suddenly emerging on its southern borders and possibly spreading into Algeria itself. The Algerian regime may have friends in Washington, London, Paris and Brussels, but it has few in its own country and probably even fewer on the other side of its southern borders.

Whatever Algeria has done in northern Mali since it sent its own special forces into the region in December, whether through the unleashing of Tamouret-trained killers at Aguelhok on 24 January, or creating and supporting Islamist groups in the region to invoke a reign of 'Islamist terror', it has succeeded in effectively turning the MNLA into a dismembered and discredited organisation. The threat of Tuareg nationalism, at least for the moment, has been destroyed. Whether the DRS played a part, as many people believe, in the death in August 2011 of Ibrahim ag Bahanga, the one Tuareg who could have provided Tuareg nationalism with a very sharp cutting edge, remains unresolved.

The extent to which Algeria's strategy in Mali since December 2011 is also a continuation of its policy, in support of broad US interests, of furthering the destabilisation of this already fragile region and enhancing its perception by the world as the 'Terror Zone' that the Pentagon daubed across its maps of Africa as long ago as 2003, will be the subject of a future volume. Mali's 'crisis' does, after all, keep the threat of al-Qaeda and the 'Global War on Terror' (GWOT) in the world's headlines and, by so doing, provides major justification for the continuation and expansion of AFRICOM's (US Africa Command's) presence and operations in Africa.

The West's, especially Washington's, complicit relationship with Algeria's DRS is a very dangerous game. The parallel with the US's ultimately disastrous relationship with Pakistan's ISI (Inter-Services Intelligence) is now exposed for all to see. The situation in North Africa and the Sahel threatens to go the same way. The US may feel that the Sahel can be safely managed, as it has been since 2002–03, as part of its global geo-political strategy of the Long War to US global domination. But the Sahel is not a simple matter of 'geopolitics'. There is, as the US has so often ignored, the small matter of agency. In the Sahel, all the signs are that local agency is likely to play an increasingly greater and more uncontrollable role in the future of the region. If that happens, and there are many 'nightmare scenarios' that can be envisaged, it would leave the West with little alternative but to intervene military.

At the moment, however, Western military intervention looks highly unlikely, not simply because the US is preoccupied with an upcoming presidential election and the EU is in the midst of a financial crisis, but because three alternative and conceivable scenarios, which may well become entwined, are already beginning to make themselves felt and look likely to pre-empt it.

One such scenario is that growing resistance amongst the peoples of Azawad to Ansar al-Din, the Islamists in general and Iyad ag Ghaly's attempts to impose shari'a law could lead to Azawadians taking up arms against Iyad and Ansar al-Din and persuading Iyad that his best path to achieving what many people believe to be his personal political goal, namely political supremacy in the Azawad region, might be to engage in the Economic Community of West African States (ECOWAS)-mediated peace talks. Indeed, a delegation of Ansar al-Din, believed to have been led by Ansar al-Din's 'number two', Alghabass ag Intallah, was reported travelling to Burkina Faso on 15 June amidst speculation that it intended to meet the Burkinabe President and ECOWAS mediator Blaise Compaoré.

Popular resistance to Ansar al-Din and the imposition of shari'a law has been simmering in Timbuktu, Gao and Kidal since Iyad's initial declaration of shari'a, but especially since the Islamists destroyed one of Timbuktu's historic shrines and began intervening heavily in the daily lives and customs of local people. This growing anger at Ansar al-Din became overtly manifest on 8 June when youths and women demonstrated in Kidal, Iyad's home town, against Ansar al-Din and its imposition of shari'a. Ansar al-Din retaliated by attacking the women and beating them up in public, an action which sparked fury throughout what is a predominantly matrilineal society. Five days later there were reports of fighting between MNLA and Ansar al-Din in Timbuktu.

A second scenario is that the above-mentioned peace talks accomplish what they are intended to achieve. A MNLA delegation, led by Ibrahim ag Mohamed Assaleh, met Blaise Compaoré for the first time on 9 June in Ouagadougou, while Alghabass ag Intallah's Ansar al-Din delegation, as mentioned above, was on its way to meet Compaoré on 15 June.[15]

ECOWAS Seeks UN Mandate for Military Intervention

A third scenario, which attracted increasing media attention and credibility during the first two weeks of June, was that ECOWAS, backed by the African Union (AU), would seek a UN Security Council mandate for military intervention in Mali on the grounds that rising Islamist militancy had made the country an international security threat.

President Hollande of France said that Paris would be ready to support military action as 'there is a threat of terrorist groups taking root in northern Mali.' He emphasised, however, that it was up to African nations, through the AU and ECOWAS, to take the initiative in leading any military operation. In other words, France said it would be ready to help restore stability in Mali if there was a Security Council resolution. The US, which had helped resupply the besieged Tessalit Amachach military base before it fell to the rebels in March, and which has also been covering the region with 'spy planes',[16] let it be known that it was prepared to lend 'logistical support' as long as ECOWAS 'had a plan'.

In early June, Niger's President Mahamadou Issoufou, who described Mali as 'turning into an African Afghanistan'[17] and is a leading regional hawk in advocating military intervention, visited both Paris and London to drum up support for a UN Security Council resolution. On 11 June, he said in Paris that ECOWAS wanted a 'Chapter 7' mandate if talks with armed groups fail to resolve the escalating crisis. This allows the Security Council to authorise actions ranging from sanctions to military interventions. Issoufou also said ECOWAS would seek logistical support from the US and France for any military intervention.

On the same day as Issoufou was drumming up support in Paris, I received emails from Tuareg in Niger saying that US and French forces were being seen in the streets of Agades and Arlit and around Mano Dayek (Agades) airport. A small contingent had arrived in Agades a month earlier, but had grown in number. The 11 June email described them as numbering some dozens and positioned along the Teguidda and Tourrayet scarps to the north-west of Agades. The official reason given to my informant for their presence was that they were helping to train the Niger army. The more likely reason is that they were there to help with intelligence and logistical support in the event of a military intervention into Mali.

Two days earlier, a Reuters report confirmed that 'An advance party of European military and civilian security advisors has arrived in northern Niger in a mission brought forward due to deepening fears over the threat of terrorism from neighbouring Mali.'[18] A senior Nigerien military officer was quoted as saying: 'We have more than 30 European military and civilian experts who are looking at the security situation in the north.' The official said the experts had deployed to Niger's Agades region as part of the EU's plans to provide counterterrorism training and advice to Nigerien forces.

Karidio Mahamadou, Niger's Defence Minister, was reported as saying that the instructors were in the country as part of bilateral agreements with the US, France and Algeria, but any presence was temporary.[19] Another Defence military official was quoted as saying that the EU mission would be in place by the end of July, several months ahead of schedule. 'Initially, the mission had been planned for September but because of the deteriorating security situation in the region, preparations', he said, 'were accelerated.'[20]

During his warmongering talks in Europe, Issoufou had told his audiences in Paris and London that Afghan and Pakistani jihadists were training recruits for Islamist groups in northern Mali.[21] This information could conceivably be correct. However, I am more inclined to believe that Issoufou was unwittingly referring to members of the Oued Tamouret camp who moved from southern Algeria into northern Mali during and after 2008. Many of the Oued Tamouret trainees, according to my informants from the camp, were from Central Asian countries including Afghanistan and Pakistan.[22]

A military intervention into Mali has been on ECOWAS' agenda since shortly after the 22 March coup. Some 3,000 ECOWAS troops have reportedly been on standby since March, although it was only at the ECOWAS meeting in Abidjan on 15 June that the precise number of 3,270 was specified, with the majority to come from Nigeria, Senegal and Niger, but with all ECOWAS members contributing. However, an ECOWAS force still has no mandate. There is also uncertainty as to both how quickly it could be mobilised and how adept it would be at fighting seasoned fighters in desert terrain. There is also the small matter of how such a mission, estimated to cost more than $200 million, would be financed.

In addition to the ECOWAS force, there were reports in early June of Mali being able to mobilise some 2,000 of its own troops, although their fighting ability, like ECOWAS troops, is questionable.

Mauritania, another of Mali's neighbours, whose President, Mohamed Ould Abdel Aziz, is known for his 'pro-Western', 'anti-terrorist' stance, is also keen to support a military intervention. It would provide basing facilities, if required, and possibly manpower, to either or both the US and France, as it did in the disastrous 22 July 2010 raids into Mali. On 29 May, Mauritania's Army Chief, General Mohamed Cheikh Ould Ghazwani, made a four-day visit to France with a delegation of senior army officers at the invitation of Admiral Edouard Guillaud, the head of France's armed forces. It was speculated that the visit was designed to secure Mauritanian cooperation in any military intervention in Mali. On 2 June, the UN's regional representative, M. Said Djinnit, visited Mauritania to discuss ways to support efforts by ECOWAS to find a solution to the Malian crisis.

Azawad's other neighbour, Algeria, although in many eyes the architect of the crisis, has kept a low public profile on this issue and has made it position of non-intervention quite clear. Nevertheless, it has reportedly given assurances, agreed by General Mohamed Mediène, head of the DRS, that it would provide intelligence information, transport and supplies to whatever future African force might intervene in northern Mali, including an air bridge into the region from Tamanrasset and Reggane airports.

The most significant force awaiting the signal to intervene in northern Mali might yet prove to be the 500 or so Tuareg troops under the command of Alhadji ag Gamou encamped just over the border in Niger.[23] There is speculation that this unit may serve as a 'front line' in any attempt to retake Azawad. In mid May, Ag Gamou set up a new organisation called the Mouvement républicain pour la restauration de l'Azawad (MRRA). Its two goals are to maintain Azawad as part of Mali and to drive the Islamists out of the region. Ag Gamou is well-placed to re-enter Azawad as a third force, especially as there is little love lost between him and both Iyad ag Ghaly and Ag Najim. Enmity between Ag Gamou and Ghaly goes back to the rebellion of the early 1990s, while the dispute between Ag Gamou and Ag Najim is more personal.

In spite of the enthusiasm of the AU and ECOWAS for military intervention, the UN Security Council (UNSC) has, at least for the moment, held back support for an African intervention force. The UNSC held three meetings with the AU's Peace and Security Council (AUPSC) during the second full week of June. The 15-member UNSC failed, however, to give ECOWAS a green light to intervene in Mali. While France, Morocco and Togo expressed enthusiasm, most UNSC diplomats were more cautious, saying they wanted to know more about how an ECOWAS military operation would be mounted. Quite aside from the questions of logistics and funding, most UNSC members were sceptical about whether ECOWAS actually had the 3,000 troops it claimed to have on standby, whether they had credible objectives and a sound strategy for conducting such an operation and whether they are actually up to fighting the rebels.

Although ECOWAS's first push to get a UNSC mandate has faltered, most of its members seem determined to continue pressuring the UNSC for a mandate. An African military intervention therefore remains a very real possibility. However, there are two extremely important aspects of the UNSC's position that have not really been raised in the media.

One is the UN's own fears that such an intervention could have catastrophic implications. An ECOWAS force, unless well supported by the West, has little chance of militarily defeating the rebels, who are likely to put aside their differences and unite in common cause against an invading force. They would also get a modicum of support from other Malians, whose interim government has let it be known that it is opposed to foreign troops intervening. There is also the very high likelihood of Niger's Tuareg coming to the 'defence of Azawad' rather than supporting their own hawkish government. A wider Tuareg rebellion would also threaten southern Algeria, not to mention Libya where most of the south of the country is in the hands of local militia, as well as northern Nigeria and other fragile West African states such as Senegal and Mauritania. In Mauritania, mounting political opposition to the regime of President Abdel Aziz could easily tip into open rebellion.

Such a regional conflagration, which I have long predicted as a likely outcome of US policy in the region, would have catastrophic humanitarian consequences. The Azawad issue has already led to the displacement of some 350,000 people across a region in which some 18 million people are reportedly desperate for food and where a locust plague is imminent.

The second reason for the UNSC's position, and the one which has been completely ignored by the entire international media, not through lack of knowledge, is that at least three of the permanent members of the Security Council, namely the US, the UK and France, are aware of Algeria's role in the current Azawad situation. These three countries have also been briefed by their military intelligence services about the Oued Tamouret training camp, Algeria's construction of al-Qaeda in the Sahel and the DRS's relationship with its leaders, including those of both MUJAO and Ansar al-Din. They therefore know that the current threat of Mali becoming 'Africa's Afghanistan', a 'new Somalia' and a 'launch-pad for Islamist terror' is less dangerous, at least operationally, than such media headlines suggest.

The more the West and the UNSC prevaricate on the military option and push both ECOWAS and Mali towards negotiating a peaceful solution, the more likely Algeria, the West's ally in the GWOT and the traditional mediator in Malian-Tuareg disputes, is to be invited in as the ultimate mediator and peace-broker.[24]

The outcome of such a scenario is likely to be one that sees Azawad gaining greater regional autonomy within the Malian state, possibly with the creation of two more provinces – Taoudeni and Ménaka – within it, in order to safeguard the Arab population from Tuareg domination. Iyad ag Ghaly, if he is still alive and if his people have not totally rejected him, is likely to trade his religious mantle for one which fulfils his political leadership ambitions.[25] The future of AQIM is difficult to predict. Algeria certainly does not want it eliminated, at least in the Sahara-Sahel regions. Under this scenario we could therefore see a number of its 'foot soldiers', the genuine jihadists, being 'eliminated' in orchestrated skirmishes, but with its 'leadership' preserved and withdrawn to the shelter of the DRS. The new Azawad region would then revert to being Algeria's 49th *wilaya*, as it was often considered, in pre-Gaddafi days, but with drug trafficking more secured under the protection of elements within Algeria's security establishment.

In the meantime, the current threat of 'Africa's Afghanistan' will have done much to justify the US's current expansion of AFRICOM (mostly through contractors) across the continent,[26] while Algeria, for its part, will receive the accolades and gratitude of the West for being the region's saviour, once again, from 'Islamist terror'.

* * *

Until now, the world's media has paid little attention to the Sahel. When it did, it was usually about drought, starvation and famine, which were usually explained in terms of climatic change. Even now, when the international media does talk about terrorism in the region, it is never in the context that is explained in this book,[27] but increasingly in terms of Washington's desperate attempts to substantiate links, in spite of little hard evidence, between AQIM,

Boko Haram and Al Shabaab and thus establish a conjoined 'Terror Zone' from the Atlantic to the Indian Oceans.

Now that the Azawad situation and the 'crises of the Sahel' have become internationalised, blame is likely to be allocated in roughly equal amounts on the Tuareg, al-Qaeda and climatic change. Little is likely to be said about US policy and its GWOT, the drivers, as this book has explained, of the disaster that has been in the making since the Pentagon and Algeria first decided to fabricate terrorism in the region.

FARC, al-Qaeda and the US System of Justice

Finally, there is the overriding question, namely: where do the US and the Sahel go from here? In the days of the first Operation Flintlock in 2005,[28] the US said much about 'hearts and minds'. That appears to have been merely PR. There are few in Washington who know much about the Sahel and probably even fewer who care. The region has served the US as an instrument in its imperial grand design. In 2003, Washington used the pretext of the El Para operation to launch the GWOT across the Sahara-Sahel region. The Azawad crisis and the threat of 'Africa's Afghanistan', which could not have been easily foreseen or engineered before the overthrow of the Gaddafi regime, is now being used to justify the current expansion of US militarisation of Africa.

In addition to that, however, the US is today planning to reuse the Sahel not simply to further justify the continuation and expansion of AFRICOM, but to help launch the Long War. This is being assisted through another operation entirely, which many might regard as even more duplicitous and shocking than that of Rumsfeld's P20G (Proactive, Preemptive Operations Group) operation. This new operation is proof, if any were needed, that neither Washington nor its military have ever given more than lip service to the 'hearts and minds' stuff, nor envisaged the Sahel as being anything more than one of the world's impoverished regions that could be callously exploited in the cause of world domination and its peoples as nothing more than metaphorical cannon fodder.

This latest revelation of how the US is using the region and its peoples for its own interests and purposes began in December 2009, when US government agents from the Drug Enforcement Administration (DEA) kidnapped three Malian citizens of Songhai ethnicity in Ghana in a US government-planned and financed 'sting'. The operation was designed to prove, through the medium of a US Federal law court, that the Fuerzas Armadas Revolucionarias de Colombia (FARC) and al-Qaeda are linked. The three entrapped Malians, who at that stage had committed no crime, were seized, handcuffed, bundled into a US government-chartered jet and flown to New York. During the flight, the three captives gave statements, allegedly without being read their Miranda rights, or at least not in any language that they understood. On arrival in New York, they were arrested on charges of (1) 'smuggling narcotics in connection with two terrorist organisations', (FARC and al-Qaeda), and (2) 'providing material support to those organisations'. Since then, they have languished in a Manhattan prison to await trial in the US Federal Court of the Southern District of New York, close to Ground Zero.

Washington has not yet stated its true motives for this operation and probably never will. Nevertheless, it is clear from the documents and testimonies that the US agents set out to acquire evidence by any means possible through which they could establish that the FARC and al-Qaeda worked together. This would enable the US authorities to claim that FARC and al-Qaeda are a single, global narco-terrorist organisation, thus providing Washington with further justification to advance its Long War of global domination.

The thousands of pages of pre-trial documentation, including the transcripts of hours of conversation from bugged hotel rooms in Accra, make it abundantly clear that the US agents knew little about either AQIM or trans-Saharan cocaine-trafficking, while the three Malians, who lived in Gao, clearly had no knowledge of FARC and only minimal, probably only hearsay, knowledge of both al-Qaeda and Saharan drug-trafficking. But, the purpose of the operation was not to actually entrap the three innocents into actually handling any drugs or even to have any dealings with

AQIM, but merely to establish, through weeks of garbled and often little-understood conversations, that they were prepared to assist the two FARC impostors in their supposed plan to smuggle cocaine from South America across the Sahara to Spain.

Both before and during the battle for Tessalit, the MNLA had been claiming that the US had been providing the Malian army with logistical support, mainly in the form of airlifts. The US Embassy in Bamako insisted, however, that it only dropped one plane-load of food supplies to the civilian population trapped at Tessalit. Evidence gathered by the MNLA suggests that the US provided much more assistance to the Malian army than one food-drop to civilians. The result is that the US has become intensely unpopular in northern Mali, at least among those who were and still are fighting for their independence. Such anti-US sentiment is likely to spread much further afield when news of the New York trial and the perceived injustice of the US action reaches the streets of Gao and the rest of Mali, as it is likely to do after sentencing is announced in November. One Gao citizen who is already aware of the trial and its history explained to me, in the context of AQIM's hostage-taking, that since 'the Americans pick people up like that, why can't we?'

If the New York court passes heavy sentences on the Malians, a storm of anti-Americanism is likely to overwhelm the region. Given the US's familiarity with such sentiments, that is unlikely to make the US position in the Sahel, or anywhere else in Africa, untenable. Rather, Washington will no doubt explain it away as evidence of the supposed AQIM–Boko Haram–Al Shabaab grip on the region and simply use it as one more prop in its Long War.

NOTES

Acknowledgements

1. John R. Schindler, 'The Ugly Truth about Algeria', *The National Interest*, 10 July 2012, http://nationalinterest.org/commentary/the-ugly-truth-about-algeria-7146.

Chapter 1

1. Stewart M. Powell, 'Swamp of Terror in the Sahara', *Air Force Magazine*, Vol. 87, No. 11, 2004.
2. Colonel Victor Nelson cited by Jim Fisher-Thompson, 'US-African Partnership Helps Counter Terrorists in Sahel Region: New Maghreb Co-operation Central to Pan-Sahel Initiative', Washington File, US Department of State Information Service, 23 March 2004; General Charles Wald cited by Donna Miles, 'US Must Confront Terrorism in Africa, General Says', US American Forces Press Service, US Department of Defense, Washington, DC, 16 June 2004.
3. Jeremy Keenan, *The Dark Sahara: America's War on Terror in Africa*, London: Pluto Press, 2009.
4. François Gèze and Salima Mellah, '"Al-Qaida au Maghreb", ou la très étrange histoire du GSPC', *Algeria-Watch*, 22 September 2007, www.algeria-watch.org/fr/aw/gspc_etrange_histoire.htm.
5. James Bamford, *Body of Secrets: Anatomy of the Ultra-Secret National Security Agency from the Cold War through the Dawn of a New Century*, New York: Doubleday; first edition, 24 April 2001.
6. US Joint Chiefs of Staff, 'Justification for US Military Intervention in Cuba (Top Secret)', US Department of Defense, 13 March 1962. The Northwoods document was published online in a more complete form by the National Security Archive on 30 April 2001: 'Pentagon Proposed Pretexts for Cuba Invasion in 1962', National Security Archive, 30 April 2001.
7. Bamford, *Body of Secrets*, chapter 4: 'Fists'.
8. Bamford, *Body of Secrets*.
9. Defense Science Board, 'DSB Summer Study on Special Operations and Joint Forces in Support of Countering Terrorism', US Department of Defense, Final Outbrief, 16 August 2002, 78 pages (in PowerPoint format), www.fas.org/irp/agency/dod/dsbbrief.ppt.

10. Ibid.

11. Pamela Hess, 'Panel Wants $7bn Elite Counter-terror Unit', United Press International, 26 September 2002, http://bailey83221. livejournal.com/107138.html.

12. William M. Arkin, 'The Secret War: Frustrated by Intelligence Failures, the Defense Department is Dramatically Expanding its "Black World" of Covert Operations', *Los Angeles Times*, 27 October 2002, http:// web.archive.org/web/20021031092436/http://www.latimes.com/ la-op-arkin27oct27001451,0,7355676.story.

13. David Isenberg, '"P2OG" Allows Pentagon to Fight Dirty', *Asia Times Online*, 5 November 2002, www.atimes.com/atimes/Middle_ East/DK05Ak02.html.

14. Chris Floyd, 'Into the Dark: The Pentagon Plan to Promote Terrorist Attacks', *Counterpunch*, 1 November 2002, www.counterpunch.org/ floyd1101.html; Nafeez Mosaddeq Ahmed, 'Our Terrorists', *New Internationalist*, October 2009, pp. 17–20.

15. Andrew Cockburn, 'Secret Bush "Finding" Widens War on Iran', *Counterpunch*, 2 May 2002, www.counterpunch.org/ andrew05022008.html.

16. Ahmed, 'Our Terrorists'.

17. Cockburn, 'Secret Bush "Finding" Widens War on Iran'.

18. Nafeez Mosaddeq Ahmed, *The War on Freedom: How and Why America was Attacked, September 11th, 2001*, Tree of Life Publication, Joshua Tree, Calif.: Institute for Policy Research and Development and Progressive Press, 2002.

19. Nafeez Mosaddeq Ahmed, *Behind the War on Terror: Western Secret Strategy and the Struggle for Iraq*, London: Clairview, 2003.

20. Nafeez Mosaddeq Ahmed, *The War on Truth: 9/11, Disinformation and the Anatomy of Terrorism*, London: Arris Books, 2005.

21. Nafeez Mosaddeq Ahmed, *The London Bombings: An Independent Inquiry*, London: Duckworth, 2006; New York: Overlook Press, 2007.

22. Ahmed, 'Our Terrorists'.

23. Seymour Hersh, 'The Coming Wars: What the Pentagon can Now Do in Secret', *New Yorker*, 24 January 2005, www.newyorker.com/ archive/2005/01/24/050124fa_fact#ixzz0gr8isUqf.

24. Marion E. (Spike) Bowman, statement to Senate Select Committee on Intelligence, 31 July 2002, www.fas.org/irp/congress/2002_ hr/073102bowman.html.

25. Keenan, *Dark Sahara*, pp. 172–4.

26. Details of AF DAS Robert Perry and S/CT Deputy Coordinator Stephanie Kinney's mission were confirmed publicly by the Office

of Counterterrorism, US Department of State, Washington, DC, on 7 November 2002.

27. See Keenan, *Dark Sahara*, chapters 8 and 9.
28. See ibid., chapter 7.
29. National Intelligence Council, 'External Relations and Africa', discussion paper, 16 March 2004, www.dni.gov/nic/PDF_GIF_2020_Support/2004_03_16_papers/external_relations.pdf (10 May 2007).
30. Daniel Volman, 'The Bush Administration and African Oil: The Security Implications of US Energy Policy', *Review of African Political Economy (ROAPE)*, Vol. 30, No. 98, December 2003, pp. 573–84.
31. See Keenan, *Dark Sahara*, chapter 10.

Chapter 2

1. Associated Press (AP) (Nouakchott), 12 January 2004.
2. Office of Counterterrorism, US Department of State, Washington, DC, 7 November 2002. See S. Ellis, 'Briefing: The Pan-Sahel Initiative', *African Affairs*, Vol. 103, No. 412, 2004, pp. 459–64.
3. 'Airmen support Pan-Sahel Initiative', EUCOM press release, 17 March 2004, cited by Ellis, 'Briefing', p. 460.
4. R. Khatchadourian, 'Pursuing Terrorists in the Great Desert', *New York Village Voice*, 24 January 2006.
5. *Le Quotidien d'Oran*, 20 July 2003; *Middle East Newsline* and *World Tribune*, 22 July 2003.
6. *World Tribune*, 6 May 2003.
7. Ibid., 6 May 2003; *New York Times*, 4 July 2003. EUCOM's second-in-command, air force General Charles Wald described these groups as 'similar to al-Qaeda, but not as sophisticated or with the same reach, but the same objectives. They're bad people, and we need to keep an eye on that' (ibid.).
8. *World Tribune*, 12 January 2004.
9. Eric Schmitt, quoting General Jones, *New York Times*, 4 July 2003.
10. See, for example, World Tribune.com, 6 May 2003, 22 July 2003 and 24 July 2003; *New York Times*, 4 July 2003; *Le Quotidien d'Oran*, 20 July 2003.
11. See Chapter 6, this volume.
12. Ibid.
13. See Chapter 5, this volume.
14. Personal communications with both US State Department and Ministry of Defense personnel.
15. Senior official, US Central Command, Washington, quoted in IRIN (the UN's Integrated Regional Information Networks), 14 October

2004. A particularly good example of EUCOM's view of its role in the Sahara-Sahel can be gleaned from reading the evidence given to the US House of Representatives: 'Eliminating Terrorist Sanctuaries: The Role of Security Assistance', Hearing before the Subcommittee on International Terrorism and Non-proliferation of the Committee on International Relations, House of Representatives, 109th Congress, First Session, 10 March 2005, http://commdocs.house. gov/committees/intlrel/hfa99825.000/hfa99825_0f.htm (accessed 14 July 2008).
16. Ibid.
17. Ibid.
18. Ibid.
19. See Chapter 9, this volume, for details of the development-security discourse.
20. IRIN, 14 October 2004.
21. Ellis, 'Briefing', p. 461.
22. Todd Pitman, 'US Begins Military Training in Africa', *Guardian*, 8 June 2005.
23. Flintlock was reported as having ended on 26 June, whereas this incident was reported as having taken place on 30 June.

Chapter 3

1. *Mukhabarat* is the Arabic term for 'intelligence', as in 'intelligence agency'. In this context, the term '*mukhabarat* state' is used to describe a 'security-led state', or the state's 'security apparatus'.
2. Frente Polisario: from the Spanish abbreviation of Frente Popular de Liberación de Saguía el Hamra y Río de Oro (Popular Front for the Liberation of Saguia el-Hamra and Río de Oro). Polisario is a Sahrawi national liberation movement working for the independence of Western Sahara from Morocco. Since 1979, the Polisario Front has been recognised by the United Nations as the representative of the people of Western Sahara.
3. See chapter 9, 'Islamists and Eradicators: Algeria's "Dirty War"', in Jeremy Keenan, *The Dark Sahara: America's War on Terror in Africa*, London: Pluto Press, 2009.
4. 'Islamism in North Africa IV: The Islamist Challenge in Mauritania: Threat of Scapegoat', International Crisis Group (ICG), Middle East/ North Africa Report No. 41, 11 May 2005.
5. Mokhtar ben Mokhtar is described in some detail in Keenan, *The Dark Sahara*.

6. B. Mounir, 'Le GSPC et les "preuves" de Nouakchott. L'énigme Belmokhtar et le jeu de la Mauritanie', *Le Quotidien d'Oran*, 13 June 2005.

7. Jeremy Keenan, *The Lesser Gods of the Sahara*, London: Frank Cass/Routledge, 2004: see chapters 'Contested Terrain: Tourism, Environment and Security in Algeria's Extreme South' (pp. 226–65); 'Ethnicity, Regionalism and Political Stability in Algeria's *Grand Sud*' (pp. 67–96); 'Indigenous Rights and a Future Politic amongst Algeria's Tuareg after Forty Years of Independence' (pp. 1–26).

8. The *wali* is the government's chief administrator in a *wilaya* (province). He is appointed by the President.

9. Letter published in Keenan, *The Lesser Gods*, pp. 255–6.

10. Meetings and interviews with prominent representatives of civil society.

11. The opinion of employees associated with the handling of these funds, who effectively acted as 'whistle-blowers'. (Personal communications.)

12. Alison Pargeter, 'Libya: Reforming the Impossible?', *Review of African Political Economy*, Vol. 33, No. 103, 2006, pp. 219–35.

13. Ibid.

14. 'In April 2005, for example, Qadhafi gave the police military powers in order to better tackle terrorist infiltrators.' Pargeter, 'Libya: Reforming the Impossible?', note 41.

15. Ibid.

16. There are many definitions of terrorism. By 'conventional', I mean that terrorism is the threatened or employed use of violence against civilian targets for political objectives. 'Terrorism' does not include such fairly normal Saharan pursuits as smuggling, acts of political rebellion or the many forms of resistance of civil society towards the corrupt and authoritarian regimes which hold sway over most of this part of Africa.

17. National Movement for a Developing Society – Nassara.

18. See Chapter 9, this volume.

Chapter 4

1. This was the conference referred to in Jeremy Keenan, *The Dark Sahara: America's War on Terror in Africa*, London: Pluto Press, 2009, pp. 10–12.

2. D. Giurovich and J. Keenan, 'The UNDP, the World Bank and Biodiversity in the Algerian Sahara', *Journal of North African Studies*, Vol. 10, Nos 3–4, 2005, pp. 585–96; Jeremy Keenan, 'Who Thought Rock-Art was about Archaeology? The Role of Prehistory

in Algeria's Terror', *Journal of Contemporary Africa Studies*, Vol. 25, No 1,2007, pp. 119–40.
3. In this context, tourism is often presented as a 'peace industry'.
4. *El Watan*, 14 May 2006.
5. www.undp.org (accessed August 2006).

Chapter 5

1. On 11 April 2007, two suicide bombings targeted the Prime Minister's office and a police station near the airport. At least 23 people were killed. On 11 December, two massive car bombs were detonated almost simultaneously, one outside the constitutional court in Ben Aknoun, the other outside the UN offices. At least 31 people were killed.
2. The obituary to Sidi Mohamed ag Acherif, aka 'Merzouk', published on www.kidal.info a day or two after his death on 11 August 2010.
3. 'Desert City Back in Control after Rebel Attack,' IRIN, Bamako, 24 May 2006, www.irinnews.org/printreport.aspx?reportid=59107.
4. Jeremy Keenan, *The Dark Sahara: America's War on Terror in Africa*, London: Pluto Press, 2009, p. 72.
5. This explains why Algeria denied visas to prominent Tuareg leaders from Niger who wanted to attend the Algiers-brokered peace talks. Algeria's DRS knew that Niger's Tuareg leaders suspected their involvement and consequently was unlikely to want them questioning the agenda of the peace talks or making any such 'exposés'.
6. On 31 October 2006, an Algerian court sentenced the editor of the Arab-language *Echorouk* newspaper, Ali Fadil, and journalist Naila Berrahal to six months in prison and a fine equivalent to €220 after the Libyan President had sued them for libel. The court suspended the newspaper for two months and ordered it to pay Gaddafi €5,500 in damages. The paper had carried two articles on 3 and 12 August reflecting the Algerian government's line that the Libyan leader had played a part in negotiations with Tuareg tribal leaders to create an independent state.
7. Personal meetings at US State Department Briefing, Washington, DC, August 2006.
8. These sources must inevitably remain anonymous.
9. KSBW is the NBC affiliate for the Monterey-Salinas-Santa Cruz California market. Its studios are in Salinas. The call letters KSBW stand for 'Salad Bowl of the World.'
10. This was confirmed by Major John Dorrian, a spokesman for US EUCOM.
11. Personal communication from Tuareg involved in the deal.

12. www.kidal.info.
13. For details of Bettu, see Chapter 11, this volume.
14. 'Mali Tuaregs say Algerian Militant Killed in Clash', Reuters, Dakar, 1 October 2006, www.algeria-watch.de/en/articles/2006/mali_tuaregs.htm.
15. A peace and reconciliation accord, proposed by President Bouteflika and granting an amnesty to GSPC members who laid down their arms (and impunity to the security forces), was approved in a September 2005 referendum.

Chapter 6

1. Eyewitness reports were collected and published less than two weeks later by the Society for Threatened Peoples (GfbV), Göttingen, 09 October 2007.
2. *Voice of America*, 20 October 2007.
3. Jeremy Keenan, 'Niger: Tuareg Unrest, its Recent Background and Potential Regional Implications', a Writenet Report commissioned by the United Nations High Commissioner for Refugees, Emergency and Technical Support Service, August 2007.
4. Amnesty International, 'Niger: Extrajudicial Executions and Population Displacement in the North of the Country', 19 December 2007; Human Rights News, 'Niger: Warring Sides Must End Abuses of Civilians: Combatants Engaged in Executions, Rape, and Theft', Human Rights Watch, Dakar, 19 December 2007, http://hrw.org/english/docs/2007/12/19/niger17623.htm.
5. Statement by Communications Minister Mohamed Ben Omar. Abdoulaye Massalatchi, 'Niger Government Denies Army Abuses in Sahara', Reuters (Niamey), 21 December 2007.
6. Menas Associates (London), *Sahara Focus*, 2007:4, pp. 9–10.
7. Ikizaba Attoulel and Mouhmoud Alain.
8. Although this information is available on the MNJ's website (http://m-n-j.blogspot.com/), it has been verified through several eyewitness reports from the locations where the exactions were inflicted.
9. Given to me directly by satellite phone links.
10. Article 1 of the Convention states that 'The Contracting Parties confirm that genocide, whether committed in time of peace or in time of war, is a crime under international law which they undertake to prevent and to punish.'
11. Letter sent by Jeremy Keenan, at the request of residents of the villages attacked by the FAN, to Jan Egeland, Special Advisor on Conflict to the UN Secretary-General, 29 March 2008. Jan

Egeland was formerly (2003–06) the UN Undersecretary-General for Humanitarian Affairs and Emergency Relief Coordinator.

12. See Chapter 9, this volume.

13. K. Abdelkamel, 'La rébellion touareg malienne soutenue par des groupes de pays voisins', 26 March 2008, www.liberte-algerie.com/send_jour.php?idjournaliste=66&journaliste=K.

14. The Toubou-led Revolutionary Armed Forces of the Sahara (FARS) announced in the first week of April 2008 that it was joining forces with the Tuareg-led MNJ.

15. See Jeremy Keenan, *The Dark Sahara: America's War on Terror in Africa*, London: Pluto Press, 2009, chapter 5, for details.

16. My own documentation is found in: Keenan, 'Niger: Tuareg Unrest'; 'Resisting Imperialism: Tuareg Threaten US, Chinese and other Foreign Interests', in I. Kohl and A. Fischer (eds), *'Tuareg' Moving Global*, London: I.B. Tauris, 2010; Menas, *Sahara Focus*, 2007:3, 2007:4 and 2008:1; 'Uranium goes Critical in the Niger: Tuareg Rebellions Threaten Sahelian Conflagration', *Review of African Political Economy* (*ROAPE*), Vol. 35, No. 117, 2008, pp. 449-466.

17. Forty kilometres north-west of Agades. The coalmine is run by the national coal company, SONICHAR.

18. Notably at Abardokh and Gougaram, in southern and north-western Aïr, respectively.

19. The Chinese National Petroleum Company (CNPC), which is also operating in the region, also received threats.

20. The FNIS, comprised almost exclusively of local Tuareg, falls under the command of the Ministry of the Interior.

21. Algeria's 'Dirty War' is explained in chapter 9 of Keenan, *The Dark Sahara*.

22. Jeremy Keenan, 'Military Bases, Construction Contracts and Hydrocarbons in North Africa', *ROAPE*, Vol. 33, No. 109, 2006, pp. 601–8.

23. Madjid Laribi, 'Que cache le dossier Brown & Root Condor', *Le Maghrébin*, 9 October 2006; 'Brown & Root Condor: une holding "militaro-énergétique"', *Le Maghrébin*, 13 November 2006.

24. See Chapter 9, this volume.

25. Numerous press reports, such as AP, Reuters, AFP, 13 September 2007.

26. See Keenan, *The Dark Sahara*, chapter 8, for details.

27. Menas, *Sahara Focus*, 2007:4, p. 19.

28. See, for example, David Sharrock, 'Out of Africa: A Growing Threat to Europe from Al-Qaeda's New Allies', *The Times* (London), 6 May 2008.

29. Personal communication, December 2007.

30. Salima Tlemçani, 'La région de Tamanrasset sous haute pression', *El Watan*, 12 October 2010.
31. 'Terrorists from Tuareg and Western Sahara Join Al-Qaeda Fiefs." *El Khabar*, 15 July 2008.
32. See Chapter 9, this volume.
33. Recent research has revealed that such a training camp existed, run by Algeria's army and DRS, not al-Qaeda, and almost certainly known to the US. See Chapter 13, this volume, for details.
34. See, for example, 'MNJ Denies Contacts with Al Qaeda', *El Khabar*, 21 April 2008.

Chapter 7

1. Then called COGEMA Niger.
2. aghirin_man@yahoo.fr.
3. See, for example, Greenpeace, *Left in the Dust: Areva's Radioactive Legacy in the Desert Towns of Niger*, April 2010, www.greenpeace. org. See also www.dissident-media.org/infonucleaire/niger2.html, www.sortirdunucleaire.org/acctualites/presse/affiche.php?aff=1660, and the film *Arlit, deuxième Paris*, www.newsreel.org/nav/title. asp?tc=CN0180.
4. Personal communication with the spokesperson.
5. See Greenpeace, *Left in the Dust*.
6. UN General Assembly Resolution 61/295, 13 September 2007. There are several other international conventions and declarations which recognise and give some measure of protection to indigenous land rights, utilisation and practices.
7. For details, see Jeremy Keenan, *The Dark Sahara: America's War on Terror in Africa*, London: Pluto Press, 2009.
8. For details, see ibid., chapter 9.
9. 'Bisbilles entre Niamey et Areva', *L'Humanité* [Paris], 3 August 2007, www.humanite.fr/2007-08-03_International_Bisbilles-entre-Niamey-et-Areva (accessed August 2007).
10. A *préfet* in France (and its former colonies) is the state's representative in a department or region. *Sous-préfets* are responsible for the subdivisions of departments, *arrondissements*.
11. Ele B. Smith, 'France's Destabilisation of Africa Continues: The Case of the Republic of Niger', *African Path*, 5 November 2007, www. africanpath.com/p_blogEntry.cfm?blogEntryID=2586.
12. As mentioned in Keenan, *The Dark Sahara*, chapter 5, it was because of his dastardly and shameful behaviour that senior Tuareg had unsuccessfully arranged his 'elimination' four years earlier.
13. MNJ, personal communications.

14. The term '*ivoirité*' ('Ivoirian-ness') was coined in 1994 by President Henri Konan Bédié of Côte d'Ivoire in his campaign to exclude and disenfranchise politicians and potential voters from the north of the country. The term – and the policy of exclusion – was continued under President Laurent Gbagbo.
15. Personal communications and interviews with Chinese operatives in region.

Chapter 8

1. Most reports say that the kidnap occurred on 22 February, although friends of the couple told me that they had lost contact with them on 18 February and feared that they had had an accident.
2. In 2006, I received a copy of the 41-page dossier, dated 12 April 2004 (that is, following the El Para kidnappings of 2003), compiled by the head of the Algerian Bureau des Affairs Judiciaires de la Division de la Sécurité Publique/C.GN for the Général-Major Commandant of Algeria's Gendarmerie Nationale. The dossier contains details, compiled from police and gendarmerie interviews, and files of the approximately 75 'terrorists' involved with El Para in the 2003 hostage-takings.
3. The photograph was downloaded by the Search for International Terrorist Entities (SITE) Intelligence Group.
4. I believe the species is *acacia ehrenbergiana*, although it may well be *acacia seyal* with which it is often confused.
5. *El Khabar*, quoting 'security sources', had said that El Para's terrorist group, which had been behind the Djanet attack, was now led by Abdelhamid abou Zaïd.
6. In addition to Yahia Djouadi and Abou Zaïd, Harald Ickler, one of the 2003 hostages, was able to identify two of the Austrians' kidnappers from their web-photos as being amongst his kidnappers in 2003. *New York Times* (Algeria Time Line), 1 July 2008, www.nytimes.com/interactive/2008/07/01/world/africa/20080701_ALGERIA_TIMELINE.html (accessed 3 July 2008).
7. Identified by the 2003 hostages.
8. www.swissinfo.ch/fre/a_la_une/detail/Le_mystere_subsiste_sur_le_rapt_des_ Suisses_au_Sahara.html?siteSect=105&sid=8715236&cKey=1202671171000&ty=st.
9. For details, see Jeremy Keenan, *The Dark Sahara: America's War on Terror in Africa*, London: Pluto Press, 2009.
10. François Gèze and Salima Mellah, '"Al-Qaida au Maghreb", ou la très étrange histoire du GSPC', Algeria-Watch, 22 September 2007,

www.algeria-watch.org/fr/aw/gspc_etrange_histoire.htm. Quoted by Swissinfo.

11. This information was received from an informant involved in the deliberations.

12. There was some anxiety in US military circles that if Obama should win the election he might scrap AFRICOM. It was therefore important for the Pentagon that AQIM was seen as being a real terrorist threat in the Sahel and to the wider region.

13. Reuters, 'Al Qaeda Austrian Hostages are Alive', 21 May 2008.

14. AFP (Bamako), 'Austrian Al-Qaeda Hostage is "Doing Very Poorly"', 5 July 2008.

Chapter 9

1. On Christmas Eve 2007, four French tourists were shot and killed while picnicking near Aleg, 250 kilometres east of Nouakchott.

2. President Bush authorised AFRICOM in December 2006. It was officially established on 1 October 2008.

3. www.africom.mil/AboutAFRICOM.asp.

4. Project for the New American Century (1997) 'Statement of Principles', www.newamercancentury.org.

5. National Energy Policy, report of the NEPD Group, May 2001, http://whitehouse.gov.

6. US Department of Energy, Energy Information Administration (2007) 'US Imports by Country of Origin', http://tonto.eia.doe.gov/dnav/pet/pet_move_impetus_a2_nus_ep00_im0_mbblpd_m.htm.

7. D. Volman, 'The Bush Administration & African Oil: The Security Implications of US Energy Policy', *Review of African Political Economy*, Vol. 30, No. 98, 2003, pp. 573–84.

8. I am referring primary to 'international' terrorism, associated with organisations such as al-Qaeda, whose 'terror' tends to target civilians indiscriminately, as distinct from 'state terrorism', as practised by many states in Africa, as well the 'terror' practised by many of Africa's counterinsurgency movements.

9. For details, see Jeremy Keenan, *The Dark Sahara: America's War on Terror in Africa*, London: Pluto Press, 2009.

10. J. Gerth, 'Military's Information War is Vast and Often Secretive', *New York Times*, 11 December 2005.

11. Ibid.

12. US Senate Select Committee on Intelligence, *Report on Whether Public Statements Regarding Iraq by US Government Officials were Substantiated by Intelligence Information*, http://intelligence.senate.gov/080605/phase2a.pdf, and *Report on Intelligence Activities*

Relating to Iraq Conducted by the Policy Counterterrorism Evaluation Group and the Office of Special Plans Within the Office of the Under Secretary of Defense for Policy, Washington, DC, 5 June 2008, http://intelligence.senate.gov/080605/phase2b. pdf. See also Press Release of Intelligence Committee, 'Senate Intelligence Committee Unveils Final Phase II Reports on Prewar Iraq Intelligence', 5 June 2008, http://intelligence.senate.gov/press/ record.cfm?id=298775.

13. Al-khiyal, 'US Department of Defense behind www.magharebia. com', *The Algeria Channel*, 16 June, www.algeria.com/forums/ computer-internet/20556-u-s-department-defense-behind-www-magharebia-com.html.

14. The political and intellectual origins of this discourse are discussed in Jeremy Keenan, 'Africa Unsecured: The Role of the Global War on Terror (GWOT) in Securing US Imperial Interests in Africa', *Critical Studies on Terrorism*, Vol. 3, No. 1, April 2010, pp. 26–46.

15. The White House Office of the Press Secretary, 'President Bush Creates a Department of Defense Unified Combatant Command for Africa', 6 February 2007.

16. M. McIntire and J. Gettleman, 'A Chaotic Kenya Vote and a Secret US Exit Poll', *New York Times*, 3 January 2009.

17. Jeremy Keenan, 'Niger: Tuareg Unrest, its Recent Background and Potential Regional Implications', a Writenet Report commissioned by the United Nations High Commissioner for Refugees, Emergency and Technical Support Service, August, 2007.

18. Amnesty International, 'Niger: Extrajudicial Executions and Population Displacement in the North of the Country', 19 December 2007; Human Rights News, 'Niger: Warring Sides Must End Abuses of Civilians: Combatants Engaged in Executions, Rape, and Theft', Human Rights Watch, Dakar, 19 December 2007, http://hrw.org/ english/docs/2007/12/19/niger17623.htm.

19. These may have been microlites, possibly the same ones used by the Nigerien army to track the hostages abducted by AQIS from Arlit on 16 September 2010 (see Chapter 16, this volume).

20. Catherine Besteman, 'Counter AFRICOM', in Network of Concerned Anthropologists, *The Counter-Counterinsurgency Manual*, Chicago: Prickly Paradigm Press, 2009, pp. 115–32 (p. 124).

21. Ibid., p. 117.

22. M. Malan, 'US Civil Military Imbalance for Global Engagement: Lessons from the Operational Level in Africa', Refugees International, Washington, DC, July 2008.

23. S. McFate, 'Outsourcing the Making of Militaries: DynCorp International as Sovereign Agent', *Review of African Political Economy*, Vol. 35, No. 118, 2008, pp. 645–55.
24. M. Malan, 'Africom: Joined-up Geographical Command or Federal Business Opportunity?', testimony given before the House Subcommittee on National Security and Foreign Affairs, Committee on Oversight and Government Reform., Washington, DC, 23 July 2008.
25. McFate, 'Outsourcing the Making of Militaries'.
26. 2009 Defence Appropriations. Washington, DC: House of Representatives, Committee on Appropriations, 22 September 2008. For details of Obama's 2010 budget increase, see D. Volman, 'Africom to Continue under Obama', *Pambazuka*, Issue 437, 11 June 2009, http://pambazuka.org/en/category/features/56855.

Chapter 10

1. Amnesty International, 'Niger: Extrajudicial Executions and Population Displacement in the North of the Country', 19 December 2007; Human Rights News, 'Niger: Warring Sides Must End Abuses of Civilians: Combatants Engaged in Executions, Rape, and Theft', Human Rights Watch, Dakar, 19 December 2007, http://hrw.org/english/docs/2007/12/19/niger17623.htm.
2. These may have been microlites, possibly the same ones used by the Nigerien army to track the hostages abducted by AQIS from Arlit on 16 September 2010 (see Chapter 16, this volume).
3. See Chapter 3, this volume, for details of Rhissa.
4. Jorge Barrera, 'Canada Frustrated by Niger during Search for Kidnapped Diplomats Fowler and Guay', APTN National News, Ottawa, 5 May 2011, http://aptn.ca/pages/news/2011/05/05/canada-frustrated-by-niger-during-search-for-kidnapped-diplomats-fowler-and-guay/.
5. The other three were able to or allowed to escape.
6. Mounir Boudjemaa, 'Les prises d'otages dans le sahel se multiplient. Révélations sur les liaisons GSPC-Mali', *Liberté* (Algeria), 8 February 2009.
7. US Department of the Treasury, 'Treasury Targets Al Qaida-Affiliated Terror Group in Algeria', Press Center, US Treasury Department, Washington, DC, 17 July 2008, www.treasury.gov/press-center/press-releases/Pages/hp1085.aspx.
8. www.rachad.org/.

9. Mounir Boudjemaa, 'La sécurité met en garde: Al Qaida planifie des attaques contre des intérêts étrangers au Sud', *El Khabar*, 11 February 2009.

10. The story, published by Reuters on 25 February 2009 under the heading 'Mali Customs Seize Weapons Bound for Qaeda' (http://af.reuters.com/article/maliNews/idAFLP13390620090225), was sourced to *El Khabar*'s web edition of the same date.

11. Hassan Masiky, 'The Sahel Region; the Future Ground Zero', MoroccoBoard News Service, Washington, DC, 13 February 2009, www.moroccoboard.com/viewpoint/68-hassan-massiki/407-the-sahel-region-the-future-ground-zero-.

12. *El Khabar*, 23 February 2009.

13. Lynda Nacer, 'BELMOKHTAR accroché alors qu¹il venait de LIBYE Une vente d'armes avortée dans le Grand-sud', *Liberté* (Algeria), 1 April 2009.

14. *Ennahar* was established by the DRS in 2007.

15. Tiemoko Diallo, 'N. Africa Qaeda Demands Hostages-for-Militants Swap', Reuters (Bamako), 28 March 2009, citing *El Khabar*, 28 March 2009.

16. AFP, 'Mali: arrestation du "principal suspect" dans l'enlèvement de 4 européens', 25 March 2009. The security source indicated that the interrogation of 'two suspects' caught in northern Mali the previous week had led to the arrest of the 'principal suspect'. It transpired that this story was false and part of the 'disinformation' being put out by the Mali government in apparent complicity with the DRS. It later transpired that the chief negotiator in the release of the hostages was the same Baba Ould Sheikh whom Abdelhamid abou Zaïd had accused of being a 'criminal' (for wanting too big a share of the ransom money) during my negotiations for the release of the two Austrians in September 2008.

17. Salima Tlemçani, 'Libération de quatre otages au nord du Mali – Quelle contrepartie a-t-on encore promise au GSPC?', *El Watan*, 25 April 2009.

18. See Barrera, 'Canada Frustrated by Niger'.

Chapter 11

1. Released on 11 July.

2. The Media Line, 'Al-Qa'ida Backs Down in Sahara', 17 May 2009, www.themedialine.org/news/news_detail.asp?NewsID=25152, also at www.algeria.com/forums/current-events-actualit%E9s/24480-203.htm.

3. Matthew Moore, 'WikiLeaks Cables: FCO "Refused to Speak with Doomed British Hostage"', *Telegraph*, 4 February 2011, www.telegraph.co.uk/news/worldnews/wikileaks/8303489/WikiLeaks-cables-FCO-refused-to-speak-with-doomed-British-hostage.html.

4. Information provided in a personal communication from the head of the appropriate Reuters desk.

5. Richard Norton-Taylor, 'Terrorist Case Collapses after Three Years', *Guardian*, 21 March 2000, cited by Nafeez Mosaddeq Ahmed, *The War on Truth: 9/11, Disinformation, and the Anatomy of Terrorism*, Moreton-in-Marsh: Arris Books, 2005, p. 73.

6. DefenceWeb, 'French see British, German Muzzle in on Algerian Deal', 27 January 2009.

7. Described in Chapter 5, this volume.

8. Between August and November we exchanged five emails and had two full discussions: one by phone in October, and a second at a meeting in November.

9. I also told the official that I knew that Washington had been asking the FCO for counterterrorism assistance in the Sahara-Sahel for almost twelve months.

10. A key concern of ESRC funding is 'value for bucks', with 'value' being measured largely in terms of publications output. This research project, which went unfunded, nevertheless resulted in approximately 100 publications, which is fairly conclusive evidence that the ESRC's rejection was not based on academic criteria.

11. Information provided by a highly reliable party associated with the relevant ESRC committee.

12. P. Baty, 'Life-risking "Spy" Plan Pulled', *Times Higher Education Supplement* (*THES*), 20 October 2006; A. Frean and M. Evans, 'Universities "Asked to Act as Spies for Intelligence Services"', *THES*, 19 October 2006; G. Houtman, 'Double or Quits', *Anthropology Today*, Vol. 22, No. 6, 2006, pp. 1–3; P. Sooben, 'Double or Quits: A Response from the ESRC', *Anthropology Today*, Vol. 22, No. 6, 2006, p. 3; Jeremy Keenan, 'My Country Right or Wrong', *Anthropology Today*, Vol. 23, No. 1, 2007, pp. 26–8; Jeremy Keenan, 'Conspiracy Theories and "Terrorists": How the "War on Terror" is Placing New Responsibilities on Anthropology', *Anthropology Today*, Vol. 22, No. 6, 2006, pp. 4–9; Mandy Garner, 'Are Academics being Put at Risk by Anti-terrorist Measures?', *Independent*, 14 June 2007, http://education.independent.co.uk/higher/article2653206.ece.

13. Information provided by interviewees.

14. Mathew presumably had another name, but never provided it when asked by those being interviewed.

15. Its first meeting was held in March 2010.

16. 'British Hostage Edwin Dyer "Killed by Al-Qaida"': Gordon Brown condemns "barbaric" killing of Briton, who was reportedly beheaded in North Africa', *Guardian*, 3 June 2009, www.guardian.co.uk/uk/2009/jun/03/edwin-dyer-hostage-killed-al-qaida.
17. M. Ag Khelfa, 'Assassinat, affrontements meurtriers, prises d'otages, trafics d'armes et de drogues dans l'espace Sahel-saharien: Comment l'Algérie a exporté sa "sale guerre" au Mali', *L'Indépendant*, 7 December 2009. In a report on Radio France International (RFI) on 9 April 2010, Frederic Couteau described Algeria as 'a wolf which cries wolf' (*un loup qui crie au loup*), when, quoting the Malian paper *Le Challenger*, he reported that 'it now turns out that Algeria's generals are supporting the narcotraffickers'.
18. BBC News, 'Malian Al-Qaeda Hunter Shot Dead', 11 June 2009, http://news.bbc.co.uk/1/hi/8095040.stm.
19. Moore, 'WikiLeaks Cables'.
20. One possible explanation for Dyer's execution, attributed to an FCO official through a personal communication (but without any supporting evidence), was that Britain had arranged with AQIM for the SAS to undertake a 'rescue' at which money would be handed over, but had to cancel the operation at the last minute because of the unavailability of helicopters. Abou Zaïd was apparently so angry that he murdered Dyer. This story may relate to an article published in the *Sun* eleven days after Dyer's murder, which quoted a senior SAS (Special Air Service) source as saying that a British SAS mission to rescue Dyer, comprising '100 troops [who] had been kept on standby for a month, [was] blocked by senior military officials' shortly before he was killed. T. Newton Dunn and V. Wheeler, 'Top Brass Bottled SAS Hostage Rescue', *Sun*, 11 June 2009, www.thesun.co.uk/sol/homepage/news/campaigns/our_boys/2475658/Whitehall-bottled-mission-to-rescue-a-British-hostage.html#ixzz0grkUgWlP.
21. Jeremy Keenan, 'Al Qaeda Terrorism in the Sahara?', *Anthropology Today*, Vol. 25, No. 4, 2009, pp. 14–18; Jeremy Keenan, 'Africa Unsecured: The Role of the Global War on Terror (GWOT) in Securing US Imperial Interests in Africa', *Critical Studies on Terrorism*, Vol. 3, No. 1, April 2010, pp. 26–46.

Chapter 12

1. Before taking up this role in 2004, Richard Barrett worked for the British government's Security Service and the Foreign Office. He also served as Director of Global Counter Terrorism Operations for the Secret Intelligence Service (SIS).

2. Barrett's first such comment was made in a lecture, 'Al-Qaida and Taliban Status Check: A Resurgent Threat?', delivered to the Washington Institute for Near East Policy, 29 September 2009, www.teachingterror.net/resources/AQ%20Status%20check.pdf. His comment, as quoted here, was widely publicised in the international media in November. See Menas Associates (London), *Sahara Focus*, 2009:4, www.menas.co.uk.

3. For details, see Jeremy Keenan, *The Dark Sahara: America's War on Terror in Africa*, London: Pluto Press, 2009.

4. Geoffrey York, 'The Shadowy Negotiator Who Freed Fowler and Guay', *Globe and Mail*, 12 October 2009, http://m.theglobeandmail. com/news/politics/the-shadowy-negotiator-who-freed-fowler-and-guay/article1320522/?service=mobile.

5. This information, with other details of the plane and its lack of airworthiness certificate, was confirmed in a Wikileaks report made available through the *Guardian* on 14 December 2010. The US Embassy cable, entitled 'Three-week Delay for Mali "Drug Plane" Crash Investigation', was dated 1 February 2010, classified by Political Counselor Peter Newman of the US Embassy in Bamako under the subject title 'New Information on Crashed Drug Plane', www.guardian.co.uk/world/us-embassy-cables-documents/246478.

6. Agence France-Presse, 'Venezuelan Drugs Boeing Crashed in Mali: UN', 16 November 2009.

7. Mounir Boudjemaa, 'Le Sahel devenu une poudrière – Al-Qaïda Maghreb entre otages et cocaïne', *Liberté*, 7 February 2010.

8. Salima Tlemçani, 'Cinq algériens arrêtés à Kidal, QG d'Al Qaïda et barons de la cocaïne au nord du Mali', *El Watan*, 21 February 2010.

9. Wikileaks file: from US Embassy, Bamako; subject: 'Rebel Disarmament and Bahanga's Complaint', 23 February 2009.

10. *Ennahar* and *Liberté*, 'Weapons and a Ton of Marijuana Seized Near the Algerian-Malian Border', 1 December 2009, www.liberte-algerie.com/edit.php?id=125991&titre=Saisie%20de%2012%20 quintaux%20de%20drogue%20%C3%A0%20Tamanrasset.

11. One euro = 650 CFA.

12. The UNODC put the value of drugs passing through West Africa in 2009 at $800 million. David Lewis, 'West Africa Drugs Trade Going the Way of Mexico – UN', Reuters, 20 June 2011.

13. Boudjemaa, 'Le Sahel devenu une poudrière'.

14. Tlemçani, 'Cinq algériens arrêtés à Kidal'.

15. Decked out in Algerian military livery.

16. See Chapter 6, this volume.

17. The plant is *Artemisia annua*, also known as Sweet Wormwood, Sweet Annie, Sweet Sagewort or Annual Wormwood.

18. The spokesman identified himself as Salah Abu Mohammed. This is the same Salah Abu Mohammed, aka Salah Gasmi, discussed in Chapter 10 of this volume and associated with the DRS.
19. CL10-020EN, EU Presidency, 21 January 2010, www.europa-eu-un. org/articles/en/article_9427_en.htm.
20. Xavier Driencourt, interview in *Le Matin* (Algeria), 13 March 2010, www.lematindz.net/news/3024-paris-et-washington-vont-ils-intervenir-au-sahel-.html.
21. Information provided by confidential source.
22. Personal communication with Press Officer at AFRICOM HQ at Stuttgart. Observers in the region believe this figure to be on the low side.
23. Notably the 62nd Motorized Infantry Regiment, based in Sévaré (15 kilometres from Mopti).
24. See Chapter 5, this volume.
25. Probably a DRS pseudonym.
26. Menas, *Sahara Focus*, 2010:1.
27. Reuters (Algiers), 'Saharan States to Open Joint Anti-Qaeda Command HQ', 21 April 2010, http://af.reuters.com/article/topNews/idAFJOE63K05W20100421
28. *El Khabar*, 'Terrorists from Tuareg and Western Sahara Join Al-Qaeda Fiefs', 15 July 2008.
29. 'France: Un député évalue le nombre des membres de l'AQMI à 300 terroristes', *Pana*, 8 July 2011. Loncle was accompanied by the former Secretary of State, Henri Pagnol.
30. Menas, *Sahara Focus*, 2010.

Chapter 13

1. Richard Barrett, 'Al-Qaida and Taliban Status Check: A Resurgent Threat?', lecture delivered to the Washington Institute for Near East Policy, 29 September 2009, www.teachingterror.net/resources/AQ%20Status%20check.pdf. See also Menas Associates (London), *Sahara Focus*, 2009:4, www.menas.co.uk; and Chapter 12, this volume.
2. At the end of 2011 and excluding Nigeria and Chad.
3. http://merln.ndu.edu/index.cfm?type=section&secid=149&pageid=3.
4. 'Maghreb' is an Arabic word for 'West' and refers specifically to the western region of North Africa.
5. See Jeremy Keenan, *The Dark Sahara: America's War on Terror in Africa*, London: Pluto Press, 2009, chapter 9: 'Islamists and Eradicators: Algeria's Dirty War'.

6. These are pseudonyms.
7. See Chapter 11, this volume.
8. This is a pseudonym.

Chapter 14

1. *Troc* is the French word for 'barter'; that is, exchange without money.
2. See Chapter 18, this volume.
3. Chairman of the High Council of State.
4. Lembarek Boumaarafi.
5 Algeria-Watch MAOL file, www.algeria-watch.org/infomap/ infom08/i8maol.htm.
6. For details of these incidents and letters, see chapter 8, 'Contested Terrain: Tourism, Environment and Security in Algeria's Extreme South', in Jeremy Keenan, *The Lesser Gods of the Sahara*, London: Frank Cass/Routledge, 2004.
7. See Chapter 3, this volume, for details.
8. Information from local informants.
9. He was moved in October 2010.
10. See Chapter 18, this volume.
11. Derived from the French word *contrebandier* ('contraband', 'smuggling', to smuggle).
12. My main informants are former DRS agents. For more details of Mediène, see Jeremy Keenan, 'General Toufik: "God of Algeria"', Aljazeera.net (English), 27 September 2010, http://english.aljazeera. net/indepth/briefings/2010/09/201092582648347537.html.
13. For example, Smaïn Lamari died in August 2007, Larbi Belkheir in January 2010. Mohamed Lamari is in exile, while Khaled Nezzar is also retired and fighting possible extradition proceedings to Switzerland.
14. Lower down the hierarchy, it may be little more than the graft and backhanders that enable the lower ranks of state bureaucrats to supplement their meagre salaries and keep their families from destitution.
15. Evidence given in President Bouteflika's commission to investigate the assassination of prominent Algerians in the 1990s. The commission was closed suddenly in February 2010.
16. As described by US Ambassador Robert Ford in a cable to the US State Department entitled 'An Ailing and Fragile Algerian Regime Drifts into 2008', Wikileaks, ID 135031, 19 December 2007; Origin: 07ALGIERS1806; Source: Embassy Algiers.
17. Keenan, 'General Toufik: "God of Algeria"'.

Chapter 15

1. A pseudonym.
2. Reuters (Bamako), 'Shots Heard, Planes Circled by Niger Border: Mali', 22 July 2010, http://af.reuters.com/article/topNews/idAFJOE66L0UP20100722.
3. Droukdel is the overall leader of AQIM.
4. Information from informants in Tamanrasset.
5. Such as the President, the Army Chief of Staff and possibly the Foreign Minister.
6. Attributed to Wikileaks and published by 'Secret Defense' sources (a blog of Libération.fr, http://secretdefense.blogs.liberation.fr/) and then published in *Le Républicain* (Mali), www.maliweb.net/category.php?NID=63538, and other media sources.
7. These were never clearly specified.
8. The FCO confirmed to me that General Searby was the most senior member, along with the UK Ambassador to Morocco, Tim Morris, of a British delegation visiting Mauritania on that date to discuss bilateral cooperation in the fight against terrorism.
9. AFP, 26 September 2010.
10. Rahmani writes for *Ennahar Al Jadid* ('The New Day'), a newspaper created for him by the DRS in November 2007.
11. Mohamed Mokeddem, *Al-Qaïda au Maghreb Islamique: contrebande au nom de l'Islam* (*Al-Qaeda in the Islamic Maghreb … Smuggling on in the Name of Islam*), Paris: Harmattan, December 2010. See also a review article in *Algérie-focus*, 28 October 2010, www.algerie-focus.com/2010/10/28/aqmi-abou-zeid-ne-serait-pas-celui-quon-croit-selon-mokeddem/.
12. For details of Smaïn Lamari, see Jeremy Keenan, *The Dark Sahara: America's War on Terror in Africa*, London: Pluto Press, 2009, chapter 9.
13. Alliot-Marie resigned at the end of February 2011.
14. See Chapter 11, this volume.

Chapter 16

1. Cited by Nigerien government spokesman Laouali Dan Dahdit.
2. An AREVA Tuareg guard, who was accosted in the raid and later interviewed by security officials, said that the languages he heard being spoken were Arabic and Hausa (*Journal du Dimanche*, 19 September 2010).
3. Regarding Tuareg involvement, see Jeremy Keenan, 'The tribulations of the Tuareg', Aljazeera.net (English), 20 November 2010, http://

english.aljazeera.net/indepth/briefings/2010/11/201011112161535
322.html.
4. French: *ultra léger motorisé* (ULM).
5. Approximately 100 kilometres.
6. French official sources gave the number of the French contingent as 80.
7. There is no certainty as to whether the claim, posted on the internet, was authentic.
8. Few details of the release or whether a ransom was paid have been made available, although a source close to the negotiations subsequently said that a ransom had been paid.
9. This incident is described in Jeremy Keenan, *The Dark Sahara: America's War on Terror in Africa*, London: Pluto Press, 2009, pp. 83–7.
10. Nothing has ever been put in writing. The local population was given only verbal instructions, which were often contradictory and unintelligible.
11. Local Tuareg who have raised concerns with the authorities about 'environmental damage' and the 'protection of cultural heritage' have been subject to heavy harassment, including threats to demolish all or part of their homes on the basis of so-called 'planning irregularities'.
12. A month later, in March, the authorities used the excuse of the Libyan conflict to finally close the Tadrart region, irrespective of its status as a UNESCO World Heritage Site.

Chapter 17

1. On 25 February 2010. Tounsi was head of the Direction Générale de la Sûreté Nationale (DGSN).
2. At that time, US EUCOM (European Command).
3. The other countries of the region that attended were Chad, Senegal, Burkina Faso and Nigeria. None of these were involved in the establishment of the Tamanrasset joint command.
4. See Chapter 13, this volume.
5. The meeting between Mali's President, General Ward and US Ambassador Gillian Milovanovic in Bamako on 27 November 2009 was the subject of a US Embassy cable (Wikileaks): 'President of Mali Links Drug Trafficking to Terrorism', Subject: Ambassador and General Ward Meet with Malian President Amadou Toumani Touré. REF: A. A. BAMAKO 754 B. B. 2008 BAMAKO 217. Tuesday 1 December 2009. (See guardian.co.uk, Tuesday 14 December 2010.)
6. Mauritania's *La Tribune* carried a full-page story: 'War Against AQIM: Mali and Mauritania Team Up'. On the visit of General

Gabriel Poudiougou, Chief of Staff of the Malian army, to Nouakchott on 4 November, *Nouakchott-Info*'s front-page headline read: 'Visit of the Head of the Malian Army: Nouakchott and Bamako Unite Against AQIM'; while *Le Rénovateur* described the alliance between Nouakchott and Bamako as 'a new bulwark against terrorism'.

7. The conference was attended by counterterrorism experts from all G8 countries (the UK, Canada, France, Germany, Italy, Japan, Russia and the US); their counterparts from Burkina Faso, Mali, Morocco, Niger, Nigeria and Senegal; and representatives from Spain, Switzerland, Australia, the EU, the African Union (AU) and the Economic Community of West African States (ECOWAS).

8. Mauritania's Health Minister, Cheikh El Moctar Ould Horma. The Minister's remark was first reported in *Al Hassa,* (Nouakchott), 2 October 2010. It was then reported, with strong criticism, in Algeria's Arab-language newspapers *Al Fajr* and *Echorouk* (amongst others). See 'Tirs de barrage de la presse algérienne contre le Ministre de la Santé ... Cheikh Ould Horma Ould Babana', CRIDEM, www.cridem.org/C_Info.php?article=47961

9. Alicia Gamez, who was captured at the same time, had been released in March.

10. Most reports reckoned it was around $8 million, although the Spanish government has always denied that a ransom was paid.

11. See Chapter 3, this volume.

12. See, for example, Radio Netherlands Worldwide, 9 December 2010, www.rnw.nl/africa/bulletin/six-major-drug-traffickers-arrested-mali; *Sahara News*, www.sahara-news.org/index.php?option=com_content&view=article&id=162:the-polisario-involved-in-the-drug-traffic-in-favour-of-aqmi&catid=1.

13. See Chapters 12 and 8, respectively, this volume.

14. 'Le général Attafi au Mali pour sauver le Polisario', Bamanet, 21 December 2010, www.bamanet.net/index.php/actualite/les-echos/12478-le-general-attafi-au-mali-pour-sauver-le-polisario.html; 'L'adjoint du général Tewfic au Mali pour sauver le Polisario', Maghreb Intelligence, 10 December 2010, www.maghreb-intelligence.com/algerie/101-ladjoint-du-general-tewfic-pour-sauver-le-polisario.html.

15. Council of the European Union's 2971st External Relations Council meeting in Luxembourg, 27 October 2009.

16. Council of the European Union's 3041st Foreign Affairs Council meeting, Luxembourg, 25 October 2010. See www.eu-un.europa.eu/articles/en/article_10261_en.htm.

17. http://wn.com/France_threatened_in_alleged_Bin_Laden_tape__27_October_2010.

18. European Commission, *Study on Political Islam in the Sahel and Neighbouring Countries*, HTSPE Project No. 2010/245936, December 2010.
19. The story was written in book format, entitled *Al-Qaïda au Maghreb Islamique, contrebande au nom de l'Islam* (*Al-Qaeda in the Islamic Maghreb ... Smuggling the name of Islam*), Algeria: Editions Casbah; Paris: Harmattan. It is believed to have been funded by the DRS. See www.algerie-focus.com/2010/10/28/aqmi-abou-zeid-ne-serait-pas-celui-quon-croit-selon-mokeddem.
20. The conference was attended by a number of key counterterrorism officials, including the UK's Patrick Tobin, rather than 'development' specialists. Algeria is reported to have sent seven officials from several of its embassies in the EU to act as observers.
21. Searby was reported as saying: 'For the UK, Algeria has already great experience [in counterterrorism] and we will offer full assistance to the Algerian Government in its fight against Al Qaida in the Maghreb. The Algerian government is very strong in combating terrorism and the United Kingdom is confident and optimistic about this approach' (http://menasassociates.blogspot.com/2010/12/uk-working-closely-with-algeria-on.html).

Chapter 18

1. European Commission, *Study on Political Islam in the Sahel and Neighbouring Countries*, HTSPE Project No. 2010/245936, December, 2010.
2. Almost 98 per cent of Algeria's foreign earnings come from hydrocarbons.
3. Official government statistics revealed that in March 2011, the Direction Générale de la Sûreté Nationale (DGSN) (police) registered 11,710 *services d'ordre* (police call-outs) to maintain order in public places. *El Watan*, 12 May 2011.
4. See also Wikileaks cables: from US Ambassador Robert Ford, 25 January 2008 (source: US Embassy, Algiers; E.O. 12958. ID 138656).
5. The revolt is as much Berber as Arab.
6. Yasmine Ryan, 'Anti-terrorism and Uprisings', *Al Jazeera*, 25 February 2011, http://english.aljazeera.net/indepth/features/20 11/02/2011213101698283350.html.
7. This is detailed in Jeremy Keenan, *The Dark Sahara: America's War on Terror in Africa*, London: Pluto Press, 2009. Washington was the main party to this collusion. An FCO source confirmed to me later that it [the FCO] 'knew that the El Para story was a myth'. French intelligence would almost certainly have been aware of the collusion

as a result of its own close links at the time with the DRS, while there are strong indications that Germany's Bundesnachrichtendienst (Federal Intelligence Service, BND) and Bundeskriminalamt (Federal Police, BKA) were both aware of El Para's identity and the role of the DRS.

8. W. Ramziand N. Fethi, 'Algeria, US Launch Joint Anti-terror Body', Magharebia, 7 March 2011, http://magharebia.com/cocoon/awi/xhtml1/en_GB/features/awi/features/2011/03/07/feature-05.

9. Over 16,000 words were removed.

10. Al Jazeera, *Inside Story*, 25 February 2010. Sourced to a memorandum from the Rachad Movement.

11. Amar Bendjama, Algeria's ambassador to Belgium and Luxembourg, and Belkacem Belkaid, Algeria's representative to the EU and NATO, playing key roles.

12. The Rachad source is: www.rachad.org/index.php?option=com_content&view=article&id=672:le-pouvoir-algerien-use-de-tous-les-moyens-pour-faire-avorter-les-revoltions-tunisienne-et-libyenne&catid=65:communiquesfr&Itemid=87. This was cited on the Algeria-Watch website, accessed in cached form at: http://webcache.googleusercontent.com/search?q=cache:Vnfo_5oH8d4J:www.algeria-watch.org/fr/article/pol/ligue_arabe/drs_mercenaires_libye.htm+Le+DRS+alg%C3%A9rien+use+de+tous+les+moyens+pour+fa ire+avorter+les+r%C3%A9volutions+tunisienne+et+libyenne+...+N ous+avons+appris&cd=1&hl=en&ct=clnk&gl=uk&client=firefox-a&source=www.google.co.uk .

13. According to the Rachad Movement (see note 12 above), this operation was directed by Colonel Djamel Bouzghaia, who works directly under Major General Rachid Laalali (alias Attafi), the head of the DRS's external relations directorate.

14. Alain Juppé took over as Foreign Minister following Michèle Alliot-Marie's resignation on 28 February 2011.

15. On 2–3 May 2011.

16. Bouguetaya is a member of the central committee of the Front de Libération Nationale (FLN) and right-hand man of Abdelaziz Belkhadem, the Secretary-General of the FLN and Special Representative of President Bouteflika.

17. The *Independent*'s acclaimed Middle East correspondent.

18. Robert Fisk, 'Who Cares in the Middle East what Obama Says?', *Independent*, 30 May 2011, www.independent.co.uk/opinion/commentators/fisk/who-cares-in-the-middle-east-what-obama-says-2290761.html.

19. In the third week of May, DRS Generals Rachid Laalali and Ahmed Kherfi travelled secretly to France to meet first with French government and then US military officials.

20. Boko Haram is a social movement in northern Nigeria, often described as a jihadist militant organisation (the term 'Boko Haram' is Hausa and means literally 'Western education is sinful/forbidden'); Al Shabaab (Harakat al-Shabaab al-Mujahideen) is a Somalia-based militant Islamist group generally regarded as being linked to al-Qaeda.

21. Thom Shanker and Eric Schmitt, 'Three Terrorist Groups in Africa Pose Threat to US, American Commander Says', *New York Times*, 14 September 2011, www.nytimes.com/2011/09/15/world/africa/three-terrorist-groups-in-africa-pose-threat-to-us-general-ham-says.html.

22. On 12 June 2011.

23. *El Khabar*, 12 June 2011.

24. 'Al-Qaeda Suspects Caught with 1.7m Euros', Magharebia, 13 February 2011, www.magharebia.com/cocoon/awi/xhtml1/en_GB/features/awi/newsbriefs/general/2011/06/13/newsbrief-02.

25. 'Abta Hamadine a'apprêtait à livrer les quatre otages français au clan Khadafi', *AïrInfo* (Agades), 29 June 2011.

Chapter 19

1. Aomar Ouali and Paul Schemm, 'Niger Official Doubts Anti-terror Efforts,' Associated Press, 8 September 2011, www.news24.com/Africa/News/Niger-official-doubts-anti-terror-efforts-20110908.

2. Ibid.

3. 'Mauritania: Fighting the invisible Enemy', France24, 28 October 2011, www.france24.com/en/20111028-reporters-mauritania-aqim-terrorism-france24.

4. Nezzar was released pending further legal procedures against him by the Swiss authorities.

5. The Spaniards, Ainhoa Fernandez de Rincon and Enric Gonyalons, worked for the Spanish NGO Mundobat, while the Italian, Rossella Urru, worked for the Italian Committee for the Development of Peoples (CISP). They were abducted during the night of 22–23 October.

6. The announcement was made on the news website Tawassoul.net. See www.thememriblog.org/blog_personal/en/41395.htm.

7. The decision, which was known in Paris on 23 December, had clearly been taken some time earlier.

8. AFP, 'New Qaeda Spin-off Threatens West Africa', 22 December 2011, http://english.ahram.org.eg/~/NewsContent/2/9/29968/World/International/New-Qaeda-spinoff-threatens-West-Africa.aspx.

9. Known also as '*foi et pratique*' in France and the Da'wa al-Tabligh, or more often, simply Da'wa in the Sahel, Tablighi Jama'at was founded by Muhammad Ilyas in 1926 in Mewat Province, India. It subsequently moved its headquarters to Pakistan. Present in more than 150 countries with over 3 million adherents, it is the biggest Muslim missionary society in the world.

10. Described in Chapter 5, this volume.

11. Ibid.

12. See Chapter 6, this volume.

13. See Chapter 17, this volume.

14. Sometimes spelt Abdelkrim.

15. See numerous reports in the French media on 23 April 2010, notably RFI, *Figaro, Libération* and *Le Monde*.

16. Salima Tlemçani, 'Enlèvement d'un algérien et d'un français au Niger: Les otages transférés au nord du Mali', *El Watan*, 25 April 2010.

17. 'Droukdal Claims to have Executed an Algerian Customs', *Ennahar*, 26 August 2010.

18. Isabelle Mandraud, 'Al-Qaida, une tentation pour de jeunes Touareg, *Le Monde*, 14 October 2010.

19. This was confirmed by *Jeune Afrique*, 'Mali: Aqmi et la Touareg Connection', 13 December 2011, and by Robert Fowler (personal communication), who had been held hostage by AQIM in the region between late 2008 and April 2009.

20. This brought the number of hostages being held in the Sahara-Sahel to 13.

21. For their details, see Chapter 5, this volume.

22. 'French Nationals Kidnapped in Mali would be in the Hands of AQIM', *Ennahar*, 7 December 2011.

23. Nathalie Prévost, Niamey correspondent (Niger), 'Mali: des otages et des barbouzes,' *Le Journal du Dimanche*, 27 November 2011, www.lejdd.fr/International/Afrique/Actualite/Mali-des-otages-et-des-barbouzes-430035/

24. Bahanga himself died in August (2011) near Ti-n-Essako, while allegedly returning from Algeria. The cause of his death remains uncertain. It was widely reported as being either a car accident or a fight with other arms traffickers, although there is evidence to suggest DRS involvement.

25. Azawad is the Tuareg name for their traditional territory north of Timbuktu, but can also be used to designate Tuareg lands in both Niger and southern Algeria.

26. Tiemoko Diallo and Adama Diarra, 'Mali Rebels Push South to Open Third Front', Reuters, 26 January 2012, www.reuters.com/article/2012/01/26/mali-fighting-idUSL5E8CQ3JY20120126.

27. Bakari Guèye, 'Touareg Refugees Pour into Mauritania', Magharebia (Nouakchott), 3 February 2012, http://magharebia.com/cocoon/awi/xhtml1/en_GB/features/awi/features/2012/02/03/feature-03.

28. AFP, 13 February 2012.

29. Ibid.

30. Ibid.

31. The suspicious photograph was originally published in an online news article on Tuesday 2 March 2010, according to the date in the original photograph at http://hespress.com/international/19160.html. The photo was taken in a different country (Nigeria) and concerns a Boko Haram massacre in northern Nigeria. Right-click on the image in this website to see the title: _img_bukuharam1500.jpg. Right-click on the image to check the 'Associated Text' (in Arabic), which says: 'Nigeria arrests involved in the massacre of Boko Haram.' The URL of the original photo is: http://t1.hespress.com/cache/thumbnail/article_medium/_img_bukuharam1500.jpg

32. Personal communications.

33. President Mohamed Ould Abdel Aziz, interview with *Le Monde*, 10 February 2012, cited by Raby Ould Idoumou, Magharebia (Nouakchott), 17 February 2012.

34. 'Algerian Troops in Mali to Fight Al-Qaeda', Sapa-AFP, 20 December 2011, www.timeslive.co.za/africa/2011/12/20/algerian-troops-in-mali-to-fight-al-qaeda.

35. Boris Thiolay, 'AQMI: 2 otages s'enfuient et sont repris', *L'Express*, 1 March 2012, www.lexpress.fr/actualite/monde/aqmi-2-otages-s-enfuient-et-sont-repris_1088231.html. Confirmed through personal communications with AREVA's insurance company.

36. Ibid.

37. *Echorouk*, 7 March 2012. See report at www.adnkronos.com/IGN/Aki/English/Security/Algeria-AQIM-moves-base-from-northern-Mali_313059440363.html.

Chapter 20

1. Reuters, 'Mali Government Forces Fail to Lift Garrison Town Siege', 6 March 2012, http://af.reuters.com/article/topNews/idAFJOE82501720120306?sp=true.

2. The MNLA claims the pilots are Ukrainian. Mali has signed a contract for Ukrainian pilots to fly its helicopter gunships. However,

as the contract had not yet started, it is believed that the pilots, in the meantime, may have been Russians.

3. The Ganda Koy is a Songhai-based militia used by the Malian government to commit civilian killings. It killed hundreds of Tuareg in the 1990s. The Gandaïzo is similar. Both militia have recently been remobilised. On 8 March, the Gourma Gandaïzo attacked camps in the Tessit commune of the Ansongo district. Two Tuareg men were killed, several women and children tortured, and three men taken hostage.

4. www.mnlamov.net/component/content/article/169-declaration-dindependance-de-lazawad.html.

5. *Al Jazeera*, 6 April 2012, www.aljazeera.com/news/africa/2012/04/20124644412359539.html.

6. One reason for this is that there are many close kinship ties between members of MNLA and Ansar al-Din, with individuals consequently switching their loyalties from one group to the other.

7. 'Nearly 60 per cent of all the cocaine consumed in Western Europe, with a street value of $18-billion, is believed to be transported through Guinea-Bissau and other West African states – including Mali.' Geoffrey York, 'Coup in Guinea-Bissau Shines a Light on Powerful West African Drug Trade', *Globe and Mail*, 13 April 2012, http://m.theglobeandmail.com/news/world/world-view/coup-in-guinea-bissau-shines-a-light-on-powerful-west-african-drug-trade/article4100045/?service=mobile).

8. Information provided from confidential and anonymous sources.

9. The source's name is protected. Algerian 'diplomatic' posts in the Sahel are nearly always DRS appointments.

10. Personal communication from senior French military intelligence officer.

11. Source identities withheld for safety.

12. Baba Ahmed and Martin Vogl, 'Rebel Groups Merge in Mali, Agree on Islamic State', Associated Press, 26 May 2012. Accessed on multiple sites. See, for example, www.thejakartapost.com/news/2012/05/27/rebel-groups-merge-mali-agree-islamic-state.html.

13. The sources must obviously remain anonymous for their safety.

14. Aomar Ouali, 'Algerian Forces Kill 20 Alleged Militants', Associated Press, 30 April 2012, http://news.yahoo.com/report-algerian-forces-kill-20-alleged-militants-092200909.html.

15. Writing of this chapter ended on 15 June.

16. I have received at least five communications from local sources detailing sightings of US 'spy flights' in the region. For details of US spy-flight operations, see Craig Whitlock, 'US Expands Secret Intelligence Operations in Africa', *Washington Post*, 14

June 2012, www.washingtonpost.com/world/national-security/
us-expands-secret-intelligence-operations-in-africa/2012/06/13/
gJQAHyvAbV_story.html.

17. Interview in *Le Journal du Dimanche*, 17 June 2012, Accessed at:
http://english.ruvr.ru/2012_06_17/78414947/

18. Abdoulaye Massalatchi, 'EU security experts in Niger amid Sahel
fears', Reuters, Niamey, June 9, 2012. Accessed at: http://uk.reuters.
com/article/2012/06/09/uk-niger-eu-idUKBRE8580FS20120609

19. Ibid.

20. Ibid.

21. Ibid.

22. Chapter 13: see information from Bachir in section on 'Testimony
from AQIM's training camp'.

23. Some reports say Ag Gamou's forces now number as many
as 1,000 men and over 200 vehicles. See, for example, http://
libya360.wordpress.com/2012/05/22/northern-mali-new-tuareg-
independence-movement-emerges/.

24. Ahmed Ouyahia, Algeria's current Prime Minister, was the main peace
negotiator between the Tuareg and the Malian government in the
1990s. Algeria also mediated the 2007 peace agreements. Algeria's
official position today is that it opposes military intervention in Mali
and has called for intensifying international mediation efforts to deal
with the situation. On 8 June, Algeria's Foreign Ministry confirmed
that Algeria's position on Mali was to secure stability, constitutional
legitimacy and Malian territorial integrity. A ministry spokesman
said that 'Algeria backs a peaceful solution between the Malian
government and rebels in the north. That,' said the spokesman, 'can
only be achieved through dialogue, which must focus on combating
terrorism and organised crime for the safety of region.'

25. Iyad ag Ghaly has always sought political leadership. His latest
pronouncement, in Kidal on 15 June, will please Mali, Algeria and
most other ECOWAS members. He said: 'We [Ansar al-Din] are not
asking for much: just the application of shari'a law in the northern
and southern regions. We are Malians and we are against the division
of Mali.'

26. Craig Whitlock, 'Contractors Run US Spying Missions in Africa',
Washington Post, 15 June 2012, www.washingtonpost.com/
world/national-security/contractors-run-us-spying-missions-in-
africa/2012/06/14/gJQAvC4RdV_story.html. Since March there have
been a number of unverified reports of US and/or French drones being
used in the region. See, for example, *El Khabar*, 19 March 2012,
http://fr.elkhabar.com/?Un-drone-occidental-s-ecrase-pres; 'Sahel: un
drone occidental abattu aux frontières algéro-maliennes', *Le Matin*,

14 June 2012, www.lematindz.net/news/8088-espionnage-au-sahel-un-drone-occidental-abattu-aux-frontieres-algero-maliennes.html. On 17 June there was an unverified emailed report from a Tuareg that a drone had attacked 'Salafis' near Taoudeni, killing seven and wounding ten.

27. Exceptions are *Al Jazeera* and *Democracy Now*.

28. See Chapter 2, this volume.

INDEX

Direction de la Surveillance du Territoire (DST) xiv, 204
Direction Générale de la Sécurité Extérieure (DGSE) xiv, 101, 162
Direction Générale de la Sûreté Nationale (DGSN) xiv, 303, 305
Directorate for Documentation and External Security (DDSE) xiii, 222
Dirty War (in Algeria) 9, 29, 58, 70, 81, 98, 177, 185, 188, 246, 286, 290, 300
Djanet xvii, xix, 44–5, 51, 54, 85–9, 91, 102–3, 109, 111–12, 121–2, 142, 158, 209–13, 292
Djelfa 32
Djibouti 15–16
Djinnit, Said 276
Djouadi, Yahia (alias Abou Amar, Yahia Abu Amar, Abu Ala, Abou Alam, Jemal Okacha) 111–12, 140, 143, 145–6, 184, 245, 252, 254, 266, 268, 292
Dorrian, John (Maj.) 288
Driencourt, Xavier 169–70, 300
Droukdel (see Abdelmalek) 199, 206, 302
DRS (see Département du Renseignement et de la Sécurité)
Drug Enforcement Administration (DEA) xiii, 160, 281
Dubai 228
Dunn, T. Newton 298
Dyer, Edwin xx, 133, 148–53, 155–9, 166, 182, 201, 262, 298

Earth Summit (see Rio de Janeiro) 45
East African Counter-terrorism Initiative (EACTI) xiv, 15
Ebner, Wolfgang xx, 118
Echorouk 85–6, 199, 262, 309
Economic and Social Research Council (ESRC) ix, xiv, 154–5, 297
Economic Community of West African States (ECOWAS) xiv, 41, 273–8, 304, 311
Egeland, Jan 134–5, 289–90
égorgement 185
Egypt xxii, 164, 168, 172–3, 184, 228–9, 231, 237, 243, 245
Eid al-Adha 119, 182
Eid ul-Fitr 74–5
El Hadj 144, 146
El Khabar 86, 89, 137–8, 141, 143–5, 150, 175, 238, 242, 271, 291–2, 296, 300, 307, 311
El Kony, Moussa 61
El M'Hamid 144, 146

El Moctar, Mohamed 168
El Oued 138
El Pais 198
El Para xviii, 1–5, 7–8, 11–13, 15–16, 25, 27, 32, 34, 38, 42–4, 56–7, 62, 66, 80, 84, 86, 88–9, 98, 110–11, 113–17, 122, 124, 126, 132, 140, 158, 160–1, 171, 185, 212, 223, 238, 249, 280, 292, 301
El Watan 85, 88, 288, 291, 296, 299, 305, 308
elections (in US) 10, 116, 119, 123, 132, 273, 293
elites (Algerian, Malian and corruption) 49, 99, 114–15, 187, 190–2, 262
Ellis, Stephen 24, 285–6
Elysée 200, 204, 206
Emi Lulu 22
emir (Ar.) 32, 116, 144–8, 176, 211, 223, 235, 240, 260, 266
Energy Information Administration (EIA) 293
Ennahar 144, 254, 296, 302, 308
Ennedi 164
Entreprise Nationale de Télévision (Algeria) (ENTV) xiv, 195
environment (see also conservation, cultural heritage) 40, 45–6, 49–50, 95, 131, 212, 287, 301, 303
éradicateurs (les) 247
Essoufi, Hamid (see Abou Zaïd) 138, 150, 224
ESRC (see Economic and Social Research Council)
Ethiopia 128
EU External Relations Council xx, 222, 304
Europe (EU) x, xiv, 3, 11, 13, 19, 21, 78, 84, 87–9, 98, 105, 122, 138, 150–1, 154, 163–4, 178, 180, 184, 222, 237, 241, 264, 268, 275, 290, 310
European Commission xxi, 223, 305
European Council 223, 304–5
European Strategic Intelligence & Security Centre (ECISC) xiv, 141
Evans, M. 297

Fadil, Ali 288
Fagaga, Hassan (Lt. Col.) 61, 65
Fahd, King 33
Fairie (ferry) 135
Falkland Isles 204
FARC 280–2
Farsia 220

UNHCR (UN High Commission for Refugees) xvi, 75, 129
United Nations Development Programme (UNDP) xvi–xvii, 44–5, 287–8
United Press International (UPI) xvi, 208
uranium 40, 75, 80, 92–6, 100–1, 104, 106–7, 207, 213, 239, 290
Urru, Rosella 307
US (United States) *passim*: (*see* Washington, White House and George W. Bush)
US Africa Command (*see* AFRICOM) xi–xiii, xix–xx, xxii, 12–13, 19–20, 62, 69, 78, 83–4, 116, 121–32, 170, 172, 217, 236–7, 252, 272, 279–80, 293–5, 300
US Agency for International development (USAID) xvi, 23
US Congress 7, 132, 284, 286
US Department of Defense xi, xiv, 6, 8, 68–9, 123, 125, 127, 283, 294
US Department of Energy 293
US Drug Enforcement Administration (EDA) 160, 281
US energy crisis 10, 123
US European Command (USEUCOM) xiv, 2, 14, 16, 19–20, 24, 36, 38, 69, 82, 124–7, 130, 285–6, 288, 303
US foreign policy 13
US House of Representatives 132, 286
US intelligence xi, 8, 82, 175–6, 236
US Naval War College xi
US Office of Counterterrorism 14, 285
US Rangers 14
US Senate Select Committee on Intelligence 125, 284, 293
US Special Forces xviii–xix, 9, 18–21, 24, 62, 64, 67–9, 78, 112, 129, 197
US State Department 8, 14–15, 19–20, 23, 62, 69, 77, 83, 153, 163, 207, 231, 238, 285, 288, 301

Venezuela 161–2, 299
Veolia Environnement 40
Vienna 118–19
Vilalta, Albert xx, 159, 169, 219
Village Voice 285
Vivendi Environnement 40
Vogl, Martin 310
Voice of America (VOA) xvi, 289
Volman, Daniel xii, 285, 293, 295

Wald Charles (General) 3, 15, 124, 238, 283, 285
wali (Ar.) 35, 188, 268, 287
Ward, 'Kip' (General) xi, xx, 19, 69, 78, 217, 303
Washington D.C. (*see* US) xi, xii, 2, 5–13, 23–4, 26, 28–9, 36, 38, 41–2, 56, 58, 62, 66–8, 72, 77, 80, 82–5, 89–91, 99, 105, 108, 121–2, 124–7, 129, 131–2, 142, 153–5, 158, 163, 169–70, 172, 177, 228, 231–2, 235, 244, 262, 264, 272, 279–83, 285, 288, 294, 295–7, 299–300, 306, 311
Washington Post 311
weapon systems 9
weapon(s) (arms), (*see* trafficking)
Weiss, Robert ix
West Africa (*see* Africa, West)
Western Sahara 89, 220, 245, 286, 291, 300
Wheeler, V. 298
Whelan, Theresa xix, 19, 78
White House (*see* US, Washington) 3, 124–5, 132, 294
Whitehall 151–2, 298
Whitlock, Craig 311
Whyte, David x
Wikileaks 137, 148, 150, 158, 161, 163, 297–9, 301–3, 305
wilaya (pl. *wilayat*) (Ar.) 37, 50, 53, 88, 102, 144–5, 188–9, 212, 279, 287
Worcestershire 150
World Bank xvii, 40, 42–55, 287
World Tourism Organisation (WTO) xvi, 46
World Trade Center (NY) xvii, 9
World Tribune 285
Wour 5

Xinhua news agency 199

Yemen 184
Yom Kippur (war) 245
York, Geoffrey 161, 299, 310
Youssouf, Abou Obaida 173

Zawiyah 234
Zerhouni, Noureddine 'Yazid' 188
Zeroual, Liamine 192–3
Zitout, Mohamed Larbi ix, 229
Zouerate 31